Marriage and the Law
in the Age of Khubilai Khan

Marriage and the Law in the Age of Khubilai Khan

Cases from the *Yuan dianzhang*

BETTINE BIRGE

▋▌ Harvard University Press

Cambridge, Massachusetts, and London, England   2017

First printing

Library of Congress Cataloging-in-Publication Data

Names: Birge, Bettine, translator. | Container of (work): Birge, Bettine. Age
    of Khubilai Khan and the Yuan dianzhang.
Title: Marriage and the law in the age of Khubilai Khan : cases from the Yuan
    dianzhang / Bettine Birge.
Other titles: Container of (expression): Yuan dian zhang. 18. English.
Description: Cambridge, Massachusetts : Harvard University Press, 2017. |
    Includes Part I "The Age of Khubilai Khan and the Yuan dianzhang"—a text
    by Bettine Birge, and Part II "Chapter 18 'Marriage' from the Yuan
    dianzhang"—an annotated translation of a medieval Chinese legal text. |
    Includes bibliographical references and index.
Identifiers: LCCN 2016046674 | ISBN 9780674975514 (alk. paper)
Subjects: LCSH: Marriage law—China—History—To 1500—Sources. | Marriage
    law—China—Cases—Early works to 1800. | Yuan dian zhang. |
    China—History—Yuan dynasty, 1260–1368. | LCGFT: Court decisions and
    opinions.
Classification: LCC KNN542 .A49 2017 | DDC 346.5101/609023—dc23
LC record available at https://lccn.loc.gov/2016046674

For Peter and Henry

Contents

Maps, Figures, and Charts

Abbreviations

Art.	Article
CSJC	Congshu jicheng 叢書集成
QMJ	*Qingmingji* 清明集
SBBY	Sibu beiyao 四部備要
SBCK	Sibu congkan 四部叢刊
SKQS	Siku quanshu 四庫全書
SXT	*Song Xingtong* 宋刑統
TLSY	*Tanglü shuyi* 唐律疏議
TZTG	*Tongzhi tiaoge jiaozhu* 通制條格校注
YDZ	*Yuan dianzhang* 元典章
YDZXJ	*Yuan dianzhang xinji* 元典章新集
YS	*Yuanshi* 元史

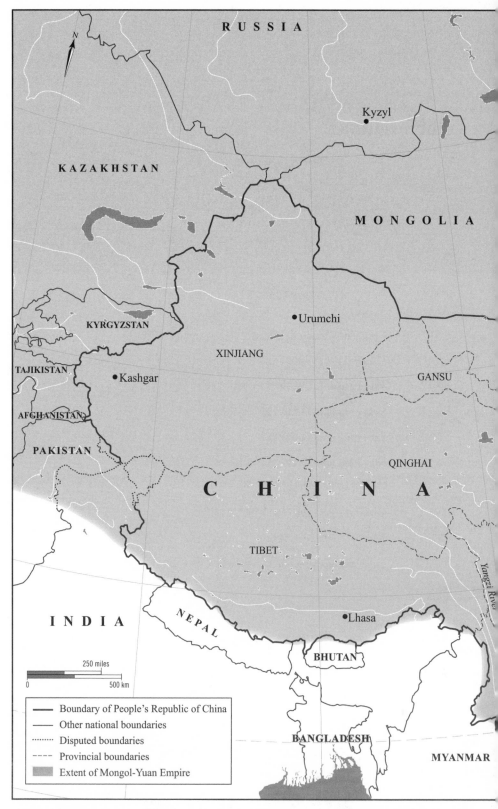

Map 0.1 The eastern portion of the Mongol-Yuan empire superimposed on the provinces and major cities of modern China.

Map 0.2 Location of marriage cases in the *Yuan dianzhang*, including names of circuits (*lu*) and branch secretariats (*xingsheng*). The numbers in parentheses indicate how many trials take place in that circuit, if more than one. Names in parentheses indicate that the name of the circuit changed during the dynasty.

Introduction

In the summer of 1317, a young widow named A-Duan, who had been living in northeast China with her natal father and caring for her four children, filed a lawsuit accusing her late husband's younger brother of raping her and forcing her to marry him in a levirate union (in which a widow marries a younger male relative of her deceased husband). As recorded in case 55 of chapter 18 of the great legal compilation *Yuan dianzhang,* in her plaint A-Duan testified:

> My mother-in-law, A-Ma, summoned me to her house to cook a meal. In the afternoon, I wanted to go back home. But suddenly my brother-in-law Tian Changyi took me, A-Duan, and dragged me into the main room of the house where he lived. He closed the door and ordered his brother Tian Lu'er to watch it. Then [his other brother] Tian Wu'er grabbed my two hands, while Tian Changyi took a cudgel and hit me twice on the left shoulder until I couldn't move. Then they tied my hair to the window lattice and stripped off my clothes. My brother-in-law Tian Wu'er held my hands down so that his older brother Tian Changyi could consummate the levirate marriage.

Chapter 18, titled "Marriage" (*hunyin* 婚姻), of the 1322 legal compendium *Yuan dianzhang,* or *Statutes and Precedents of the Yuan Dynasty* (full title *Dayuan shengzheng guochao dianzhang* 大元聖政國朝典章 [Statutes and precedents of the sacred administration of the great Yuan dynastic state]) provides a vivid portrayal of life in medieval China under the Mongol empire. The text is a remarkable collection of local case records, judicial verdicts, imperial edicts, and administrative decisions, which reveal the social tensions and political changes that accompanied the imposition of Mongol rule and China's transition into the early modern era.

This book presents a complete translation of chapter 18, "Marriage," of the *Yuan dianzhang*. The chapter contains seventy-five documents varying in length from a few lines to several pages. These span the years from 1268 to 1319, but the majority take place during the reign of Khubilai Khan (1260–1294), the grandson of Chinggis Khan, who established Mongol rule over China and presided over a vast world empire. They bring alive the poignancy and drama of everyday life as well as the dilemmas faced by local magistrates and high officials in governing thirteenth- and fourteenth-century China. They record conflict and contention in local communities over issues such as marital infidelity, divorce, wife-selling, runaway slaves, widow remarriage, absconding husbands, and maintenance of hereditary military households.

The denouement of the case of A-Duan illustrates the multiple significances of the *Yuan dianzhang* text. The verdict reflects the particular time during the Yuan dynasty that her case came to court. Years earlier, in 1271, Khubilai Khan had legalized forced levirate marriages for all people under his rule, in accordance with Mongol customary law (case 18.49). Under the law, the actions of A-Duan's brother-in-law would have been perfectly legal. Indeed, in a nearly identical case, a widow in 1273 lost her suit and was forced to marry her brother-in-law who had violated her (case 18.51). By contrast, A-Duan in 1317 won her suit. She was allowed to return to her father's household with her children, and her brother-in-law received the harsh punishment of 97 blows of the heavy stick for "Rape of a Woman without a Husband." In the years between 1271 and 1317, the legal climate had radically shifted, and new laws allowed a widow to resist levirate marriage by staying chaste. Such shifts and reversals of marriage law were common during the century of Mongol rule in China (1260–1368), as the Mongol khans and their Chinese and Inner Asian advisors wrestled with the contradictions between different legal traditions, different local practices, and different value systems in their attempts to keep order among an ethnically and socially diverse population. Chapter 18 of the *Yuan dianzhang* draws us into the tangled world of Yuan administration and the judicial system.

The extraordinary value of the *Yuan dianzhang* has been widely recognized. Faculty study groups in Tokyo, Kyoto, Taipei, and Beijing have focused on it for decades, and their members have produced numerous studies of the text. In recent years there have been lively discussions in print and online over the meanings of terms and interpretation of passages. These discussions reflect the linguistic challenges the text presents. The text contains Yuan-era specialized terms and lacunae and corruptions that have made parts hard to decipher. It is written in a combination of classical bureaucratic Chinese, Yuan colloquial Chinese, and Sino-Mongolian, the last a form of direct translation from Mongolian that preserves the Mongolian syntax and uses Chinese characters to represent Mongolian words. This hybrid language is one of the most important features of the *Yuan dianzhang,* for it purports to record the actual pronouncements in Mongolian of the Mongol rulers and their close advisors. It gives us a sense of "listening in" on the speech of Khubilai Khan and other Yuan emperors.

The translation in this volume is based on the original 1322 Yuan edition of the *Yuan dianzhang* published in photoreproduction by the National Palace Museum in Taipei in 1972 and 1976. It is the first translation into any language of this section of the text, and it is intended to make available to a wide audience one of the most important sources we have for understanding Yuan law and social history. Part I of this work provides background to the translation. It contains chapters on the historical and social context of the *Yuan dianzhang;* Yuan administration and the legal system; the origins, contents, and transmission of the *Yuan dianzhang* text; and notes to explain the conventions I use in the translation. Part II consists of the translation itself.[1] The translation includes annotations with short introductions to each case explaining its context and historical significance. The translation and annotation are meant to convey the meaning and significance of the text both in its own historical context and as interpreted for a Western audience eight centuries and a world away from the age of Khubilai Khan.

Mongols, Marriage, and the Law

The Mongol conquest of most of Asia, the Middle East, and parts of Europe in the thirteenth century was an event of world historic proportions. The occupation

1. The cases in chapter 18 of the *Yuan dianzhang* are not ordered chronologically overall; they are in chronological order only within each of twelve sections of the chapter. For readers who are interested, a list of all the cases in chronological order appears in Appendix B.

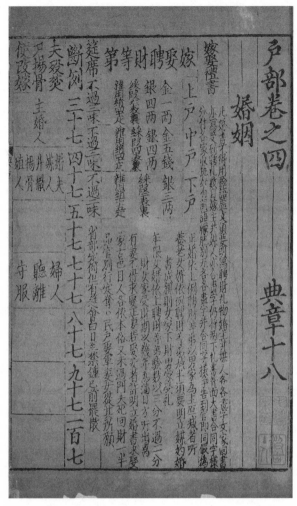

Figure I.1 First page of chapter 18, "Marriage" (*Hunyin*), of the *Yuan dianzhang*. The chapter begins with a chart summarizing the final decisions described in the seventy-five cases. (From the collection of the National Palace Museum.)

of China and the establishment of the Yuan dynasty, completed by Khubilai Khan (r. 1260–1294), brought together under one government people of different languages, religions, legal traditions, and social practices.

Mongol marriage practices were traditionally very different from those of the Chinese. The Mongols were a nomadic people from the northern steppe who practiced little or no fixed agriculture. A Mongol man could have multiple wives. Most often a prospective husband obtained a wife through the payment of brideprice. If he could not afford the cost all at once, the groom might labor in the home of his father-in-law for a period of time to pay off the debt before leaving with his wife to rejoin his family's camp. By steppe custom, a man could also obtain a woman to be his wife by capturing her in battle or abducting her in a raid. Chinggis Khan's mother, Hö'elun, was captured from her first husband in this way.[2] Mongols and other steppe peoples practiced the levirate, whereby a widow could be "inherited" by a younger male relative of her late husband. This could be a younger brother, cousin, nephew, or even the son of one of her husband's other wives. Elite Mongol widows might resist a forced levirate marriage but only by staying chaste and not remarrying at all.[3]

In traditional Chinese law, a man could have concubines but only one legal wife. A Chinese bride typically moved into the home of her husband and his parents. Much less common was uxorilocal marriage, where the husband moved into the wife's home. Yuan law recognized temporary uxorilocal marriage, whereby a husband labored in the home of his wife's parents for a limited number of years before leaving with his wife, a practice reminiscent of Mongol customs. Sexual relations between a widow and her husband's relatives were considered incest, and levirate marriage was harshly punished in codified Chinese law. Instead, a Chinese widow of marriageable age usually returned to her natal family and from there could contract a remarriage. Commentators in the Yuan period and before identified the practice of the levirate as a feature that distinguished the Chinese from their northern steppe neighbors. In particular, they contrasted steppe customs, whereby a widow stayed in the husband's family to marry in a levirate union, with Chinese practices, whereby a widow returned to her natal family. One Chinese author, writing in 1138 about the Jurchen people of the north, stated:

> If the husband dies, the wife is not allowed to return to her family. Instead, brothers or nephews [of the deceased] are all allowed to become engaged to her. There are even those who have made their stepmother their wife, just

2. Ratchnevsky 1991, 15, 34–37; Holmgren 1986, 144–145.
3. Holmgren 1986, 129–135, 143–167; Birge 2002, 201–208.

like dogs or pigs. With the Chinese it is not like this, and they know it would be against the law.[4]

The Mongol-Yuan government had to address these different practices, among many other issues, in its adjudication of marriage law.

The marriage cases of the *Yuan dianzhang* reveal how the government responded to these challenges. The collection contains legal decisions by offices of the central government or its regional representatives issued in response to appeals from local judges or proposals from lower officials. The documents include quotations of the initial plaints in lawsuits, witness testimony, and provisional verdicts issued by lower-level judges in a case. Each document ends with a final ruling and is prefaced by a statement of which office is issuing the ruling and, in most cases, to whom it was sent. Such communiqués from the central government were sent out to local offices around the country to serve as precedents and sources of law in adjudicating future cases. The Yuan court never adopted a formal legal code, so these records of legal decisions became the paramount source of law for Yuan jurists. They were filed in local government archives for reference, and the *Yuan dianzhang* would seem to be based on such an archive, perhaps one maintained at the level of a circuit or the Yuan equivalent of a province, called a branch secretariat. It was probably compiled as a ready reference book for magistrates and for the growing numbers of private legal specialists who, like modern-day lawyers, helped people file lawsuits, draw up contracts, and in general use the law to their advantage.

The *Yuan dianzhang* is of particular value for historians because it lacks any systematic editing of the documents or official agenda. Later decisions contradict earlier ones, and verdicts by judges at one level of government or branch of the bureaucracy disagree with those of another. This is in contrast to other extant legal texts from the Yuan, which were imperially approved and heavily edited. The central government periodically issued collections of decisions to use as a source of law, similar to the *Yuan dianzhang,* and the documents in these resemble in many respects those of the *Yuan dianzhang.* But the compilers of these more official works eliminated conflicting verdicts within a case and contradictory decisions between cases, thereby promoting a coherent legal agenda.

---

4. *Luting shishi* 8:48a; Franke 1981, 228. Not all Chinese shared this attitude. For an example from a thirteenth-century legal case of a Chinese widow marrying a brother of her late husband, see QMJ 10:389-390; de Pee 2007, 197.

The general lack of editing in the *Yuan dianzhang* allows us to see the complex workings of the Yuan legal system and hear the competing discourses within it.

The documents of the *Yuan dianzhang* most fundamentally are communications between offices, created in the process of governance, from the lowest local courts up to the emperor himself. The texts illustrate the workings of the Yuan bureaucracy in actual practice, with its peculiar characteristics. The path of the documents, often through numerous offices both up and back down the levels of bureaucracy, and across different branches of government, reveals the communication system and protocols within the administration. We find separate and sometimes conflicting lines of authority between the executive, censorial, and military branches of government, and overlapping legal jurisdictions. One can also discern the expansion and evolution of the Yuan administration, as offices and units of government were added or sometimes taken away. The language and visual design of each document reinforced the administrative hierarchy and a system of power relations. Specialized terms announced the relative rank and status of offices, and the visual layout of the page manifested the authority of the emperor and the highest offices of government.

The final decisions recorded in the *Yuan dianzhang* marriage cases, including the pronouncements of the emperor himself, reveal how the government and legal system struggled to reconcile competing legal traditions and cultural values. The Mongol regime vacillated in its response to these challenges, revealing the lack of a consistent vision within the Yuan government over the basic role of the state and the nature of governance. The emperor and those around him grappled with the question of what laws should apply to what people and whether to allow legal pluralism with separate laws for different ethnic groups or to apply the same law to everyone within the jurisdiction of the Yuan state. During some periods they allowed different laws to apply to different groups, but when this proved unworkable, they tried to unify marriage law and issued rulings that applied to all peoples within Yuan territory. These in turn generated new problems and conflicts, leading to further revisions in the law. Khubilai's order in 1271 declaring levirate marriage legal for all people caused a flood of lawsuits. In response, the government issued various restrictions on the operation of the levirate, including a ruling in 1276 that a widow could escape levirate marriage by staying chaste and not remarrying. Conflict and lawsuits continued, however, until finally, in 1330, the Yuan emperor outlawed the levirate "among those for whom it is not their original custom."[5] The government thereby returned to separate laws for different ethnic groups, even as intermarriage and cultural borrowing made the boundaries between these groups highly permeable.

Similarly, there was a lack of consensus at court over what constituted fundamental values and the role of government in enforcing those values. Yuan authorities wavered between a laissez-faire approach to government that tolerated a variety of local practices and a more consistent but harsh imposition of universal values onto the realm of marriage and family. The latter policy reflects the influence both at court and in local offices of followers of a new fundamentalist Confucianism called Neo-Confucianism. Neo-Confucians regarded the institution of marriage as the foundation of social and moral order, and they advocated for marriage laws that would institutionalize timeless moral principles as they understood them. The multiple discourses of the *Yuan dianzhang* allow one to trace the spread of Neo-Confucian ideas as applied to law and local society.

Communiqués issued by the central government, as recorded in the *Yuan dianzhang*, include earlier verdicts by judges at all levels of the Yuan bureaucracy, and these shed light on the dilemmas arising from the application of law at the local level. Notable is the lack of consensus among judges. Conflicting verdicts reveal disagreements over such issues as how to define a legal marriage, when a woman could be forced to marry, what defined rape, when divorce could be allowed and whose choice it was, whether slaves could marry free commoners and what would become of their children, and legal rights of widows over their property or their own person, among others. Ethnic mixing exposed people to new ideas and customs, and plaintiffs and defendants might appeal to the laws of other ethnic groups. The judicial establishment endeavored to sort out these many conflicts. In the absence of a legal code, judges often appealed to higher courts for a precedent-setting decision, and judgments were frequently overturned upon review. The same suit might be judged by five or six offices, each differing from the others. The judicial writings on marriage

---

5. YS 34:767. See also ZZTG *Duanli*: 103–104; YS 103:2644.

can be seen as part of a broader discourse on government, morality, ethnicity, gender, and social order during the thirteenth and fourteenth centuries.

Illuminating Everyday Life

The documents of the *Yuan dianzhang* provide some of the best evidence we have of social life and local practices in medieval China. The pages are filled with accounts of people trying to make the best of their lives in the face of life's inevitable trials. Men and women in both north and south China brought all kinds of grievances to court. Some of the conflicts are not unlike those found in marriages across the ages, while others reflect the particular world of China under Mongol rule. We find stories that pull at our heartstrings as we read them even today. A girl married as a child to a boy raised as her brother runs away at age fifteen and finds a new husband. An adulterous wife is sold by her husband into slavery, and her son goes to court years later to gain her freedom. A widow successfully resists a forced marriage to her late husband's young brother, whom she helped raise from childhood. A wife files suit to get a unilateral divorce after her husband runs off with another woman. The resolution of a particular case might depend on when it came to court, for, as the records show, the laws around many of these issues changed over time. The narratives of the *Yuan dianzhang* also provide traces of more quotidian aspects of life. We see in its pages how people made their living, the uses of paper money, the mobility of commoners, and how animals and products were used for marriage exchanges, among many other things.

The quotations of plaints in lawsuits and witness testimony are the closest we come in any Yuan source to hearing the voices of the common people, including the poor, the illiterate, and the enslaved. Aggrieved parties filed written plaints, which they could prepare with the help of professional scriveners. The authorities would then summon the plaintiff, the accused, and any witnesses to appear in court for questioning. Local constables also arrested offenders directly and delivered them to the court. As in other dynasties, a judge would investigate a case through a process of interrogation, perhaps supplemented by beatings or other coercion. Court scribes transcribed the testimony of plaintiffs, witnesses, and the accused, as elicited by questions from the judge. The case summaries in the *Yuan dianzhang* include snatches of quotations from these records. The Chinese legal system placed great emphasis on a confession from the accused. Passages in the *Yuan dianzhang* often include lines like "I should not have done such-and-such." Judges constructed case narratives for particular ends as a function of their position within the bureaucratic system. They selected excerpts from court testimony to support their decisions and to reaffirm the efficacy of the judicial process and their own part in it.[6] In this way, some protagonists are given a voice and others are silenced in the historical record. In the case of A-Duan, both the local and the central courts repeated her account of the assault, which helped support their verdicts in her favor. In the earlier case, which went against the widowed plaintiff, the legal record included no such details.

Particularly noteworthy about the marriage cases in the *Yuan dianzhang* are the narratives they tell of women's lives. Daughters, wives, mothers, and mothers-in-law appear throughout the documents as plaintiffs, witnesses, and defendants. Women are depicted getting out and about. One verdict describes how a woman accidentally met her first husband "on the road" (case 18.16). Remarriage of widows appears routinely in the texts. Some women remarried two or three times, as recorded in the documents. Blended families of step-children and half siblings were commonplace. Widow suicide, which is well documented in legal writing of later centuries, is completely absent from these records. We find women and their natal families using the law to assert agency and maximize their advantages within the judicial system. These lawsuits tested the legal parameters of gender privilege. The verdicts were inconsistent, but at times they favored the wife and her family against traditional Confucian ideas of patriarchal male authority. More than a third of the lawsuits in the marriage section of the *Yuan dianzhang* were filed by women. Moreover, my survey of the cases shows that women plaintiffs were slightly more likely to win their suits than were male plaintiffs.[7]

At the same time, the cases translated in Part II document changing discourses around gender and marital relations. Judges weighed the legal rights

6. On criminal procedure and legal writing in the Yuan and other dynasties, see Chen Gaohua (2000) 2005; Johnson and Twitchett 1993; Miyazaki (1954) 1975, 1980; Sommer 2000, 26–29; Barbieri-Low and Yates 2015, 1:147–171; and essays in Hegel and Carlitz 2007.

7. Birge 2011. In 1313 the Yuan government issued a law that placed restrictions on women filing lawsuits and appearing in court, but these were later relaxed and may never have been enforced. See YDZ 53:19a; Birge 1995, 140.

of a wife and her natal family versus a husband and his. New laws during the Yuan tended to support the rights of the husband's family over the wife's, and they tied women legally and financially more closely to their marital family. Some judges wrote of the importance of wifely fidelity and the problems generated by widow remarriage, mirroring concerns found in other writing that survives from this time. Along these lines, a series of decisions in the early fourteenth century established new laws that discouraged remarriage and supported widows who vowed to remain chaste. These laws in some instances deprived women of legal rights they had previously enjoyed, but they also opened up new avenues for women to pursue their interests. Widow A-Duan successfully appealed to the laws supporting widow chastity to resist a levirate marriage to her brother-in-law and as a result was able to take her children and leave the household of her mother-in-law, contrary to the original intention of the widow chastity laws. These and other issues come to light in the documents translated in this volume.

This book is intended for students, specialists, and general readers alike interested in the social, legal, intellectual, and gender history of China and the Mongol world empire. It is also meant to provide a global, historical perspective on the history of marriage and the family worldwide and resonate with issues of current relevance, such as the fluidity and instability of marriage law across time and place, the intrusion of government into private life, and the challenges of applying universal laws in a multi-ethnic society. In the end, I hope that those who pick up this book will enjoy reading these cases as much as I have enjoyed translating them.

PART I

The Age of Khubilai Khan
and the *Yuan dianzhang*

CHAPTER ONE

The Historical and Social Context of the *Yuan dianzhang*

When the Mongols completed the extended process of their conquest of China, first the north by 1234 and then the south by 1276, they brought all of China under foreign domination for the first time in its history. Nevertheless, by this time parts of north China had been ruled by non-Chinese people for more than three hundred years. Administrative policies of these northern regimes provided important precedents for Mongol rule and the legal system, as seen in the *Yuan dianzhang*. These regimes also faced the same challenges that would later plague the Mongols.

The Pre-Mongol Period

As early as 936, sixteen prefectures around the area of modern Beijing were ceded to the non-Chinese Khitan rulers of the Liao dynasty (907–1125). The Khitans were originally horse-riding people from the northeastern steppe who lived by hunting and herding. With the fall of the Tang dynasty in China in 906, they expanded their rule into the vacuum left by the Tang, and with their formidable cavalry they established an empire that at its height included Manchuria, Mongolia, and parts of north China, Korea, and eastern Russia. (See Map 1.1.) This area, called Khitai, gave its name to north China, which Marco Polo and others called "Cathay" on the basis of this word. The Russian name for China, Kitai, also comes from "Khitai."

As they brought more sedentary peoples under their control, the Liao developed a dual system of administration: the Southern Administration for the

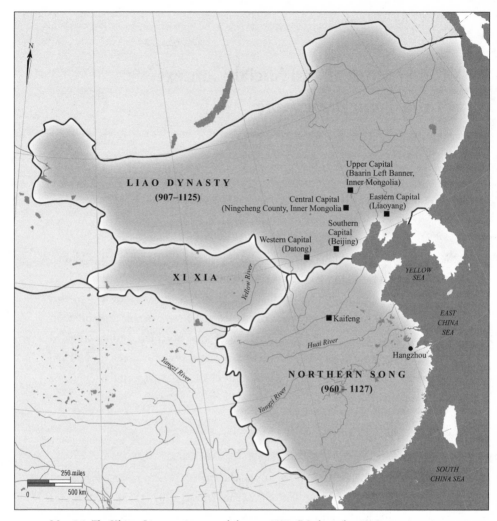

Map 1.1 The Khitan Liao empire around the year 1100. (Modern place names are in parentheses.)

sedentary peoples and the Northern Administration for the Khitan nomads and other steppe peoples. The sedentary people comprised mostly Han Chinese and Bohai (in Korean, Balhae or Parhae), a people in the northern Korean peninsula and eastern Manchuria. Having defeated the Tang in battle, the Bohai founded an independent state at the end of the seventh century on formerly Chinese lands in the northeast, which lasted until the Khitan annexed them in 926.

They originally lived by hunting and fishing, but by the tenth century they were largely sedentary agriculturalists who had adopted many institutions and customs from the Chinese. Documents in the *Yuan dianzhang* make reference to the Bohai, who were grouped together with Han Chinese in the application of the law.[1]

The Liao Southern Administration employed the Chinese language in addition to Khitan and adopted Chinese institutions, taxation systems, bureaucratic titles, and even Chinese dress. The Northern Administration employed only the Khitan language and maintained traditional Khitan methods of rulership. Officials of the Northern Administration had exclusive control of the military, and they traveled with the emperor, who maintained a semi-nomadic existence, moving between seasonal hunting camps and the five Liao capitals. As part of this mobile palace entourage close to the emperor, the Northern Administration had greater authority than the Southern.

In addition to their dual administration, the Liao emperors themselves adopted some Chinese imperial institutions, such as reign titles and succession practices, to bolster their position and consolidate their rule over both steppe and sown areas. Rather than being seen as a process of "sinicization" or "assimilation," these adoptions are better understood as a process of improving dynastic governance, to prevent fratricidal wars and strengthen the position of the emperor vis-à-vis other claimants to the throne. The Khitans developed their own written scripts, but Chinese writing and bureaucratic practices also helped them to govern the sedentary populations effectively.

The Liao used the language of geography—"Northern" versus "Southern"— to identify the diversity of its subjects. Nevertheless, the population of each area was mixed. The Liao rulers applied separate policies and laws to different peoples, no matter where they lived, according to labels such as "Khitan" (*qidan* 契丹) or "Chinese" (*hanren* 漢人 literally "Han people").[2] Chinese law based on the Tang code applied to the Chinese and Bohai, whereas various forms of Khitan customary law applied to the Khitans and other steppe peoples. The Liao dynasty

---

1. On the persistence of the Bohai as a distinct ethnic group and its eventual disappearance in the late thirteenth century, see Sloane 2014.

2. See, for instance, *Liaoshi* 61:937. These terms elude simple definition or translation. On the different meanings and complex evolution of the term *hanren*, see Liu 1999; Elliott 2012.

made attempts to unify its laws, but these attempts failed, and separate laws prevailed for the duration of the dynasty.[3]

Although the Khitans made distinctions based on notions of difference, such as Northern and Southern, or Khitans and Chinese, the Liao example demonstrates the difficulty of categorizing people in essentialized terms. The Khitan rulers strove initially to maintain a separate cultural identity, and they outlawed intermarriage between Khitans and Chinese, but this was soon relaxed. In 941 the emperor decreed that Khitans who held offices governing Chinese were allowed to marry Chinese and were to "follow Chinese manners and customs" (從漢儀).[4] Chinese officials in the Liao administration were sometimes given honorary membership in the ruling clan and thus status as "Khitans." The ranks of the "Khitan" were also filled with diverse tribal groups who came over to the Khitan side at various times during the latter's conquests.[5] This blurring of ethnic lines and the unstable, fluid nature of identity suggests the difficulties of applying different laws to different peoples. This may help explain why the Liao rulers tried to unify their laws, however unsuccessfully. The Mongols faced similar challenges.

Many of the Khitans became highly literate, multilingual, and experienced in the administration of Chinese and other sedentary populations. When the Mongols conquered the former territories of the Liao, many Khitans entered the Mongol administration and became trusted advisors to the rulers. The Mongol emperors relied on Khitan advisors, officials, and scribes, and the Liao experience provided models and lessons for their administration of China. Other occupants of the steppe who were highly literate and lived in large numbers under Khitan control, such as the Uighurs, also filled the ranks of high officialdom in the Mongol-Yuan government.

The Northern Song dynasty (960–1127), which ruled north and south China at this time, was under constant threat from the Liao. In 1004 the Song concluded a humiliating peace with the Liao and agreed to make large indemnity

3. See discussion in Birge 2008, 451–456.

4. *Liaoshi* 4:49. See *Liaoshi* 16:186 for other modifications of the intermarriage prohibition. See also Wittfogel and Feng 1949, 228.

5. On the changing loyalties and fluid identity of local rulers in the border areas (often multilingual and from mixed marriages) and the people under their dominion, see Standen 2003, 2007. For illuminating studies of these same issues of sovereignty and identity under the conquest dynasty of the Manchu-Qing (1644–1911), see Elliott 2001; Crossley 1999.

payments of silk and silver. To the west, another group called the Tanguts founded the Buddhist state of Xia (or Xi Xia, "Western Xia").[6] Unable to subdue them in warfare, the Song concluded a treaty with them in 1006 that also included indemnity payments. With both the Khitans and the Tanguts, the Song dynasty had to accept terms of equality or even subordination in its diplomatic exchanges and treaty arrangements, learning to coexist in a multistate world of equals.[7] Beginning in the early eleventh century, a third non-Chinese group was gaining strength to the east of the Khitans, in the area of modern Manchuria. These were the Jurchens, who also provided important models for the Mongols in their rule over China.

The Jurchens were forest dwellers who engaged in hunting, fishing, cattle raising, and some farming. Nevertheless, they were horse-riding warriors who shared various customs with steppe peoples such as the Khitans and later the Mongols. In 1115, their leader Aguda (r. 1113–1123) united the disparate tribes in Manchuria and proclaimed himself the ruler of a new dynasty, the Jin ("gold" 金). The Jin waged a series of successful campaigns against the Khitans and in 1116 captured the Liao heartland. In 1120 the Jin formed an alliance with the Northern Song against the Liao, and by 1125 the Liao dynasty had come to an end. In the face of the Jurchen advances, many Khitan commanders joined the Jin forces, bringing along their troops. Chinese officials were also retained as administrators of territory conquered by the Jin. A smaller group of Liao elites fled westward and founded the Western Liao state in modern Xinjiang and Uzbekistan. These people, called Black Khitans, provided many of the advisors on whom the Mongols relied in their rule over China.

The Jurchens continued their conquests south, and in 1127 they seized the Northern Song capital of Kaifeng, capturing the emperor, his family, and the members of his court. After years of continuing warfare and more Jurchen successes, the Song finally managed to conclude a peace treaty with the Jurchens in 1141, fixing the border at the Huai River and agreeing to pay a huge indemnity of silk and silver. The Song established their new capital at Hangzhou, ushering in what we call the Southern Song dynasty (1127–1276). (See Map 1.2.)

6. See Dunnell 1996. On Tangut influences on Mongol rule, see Dunnell 1992.
7. Tao 1988; Wang 1983; Rossabi 1983.

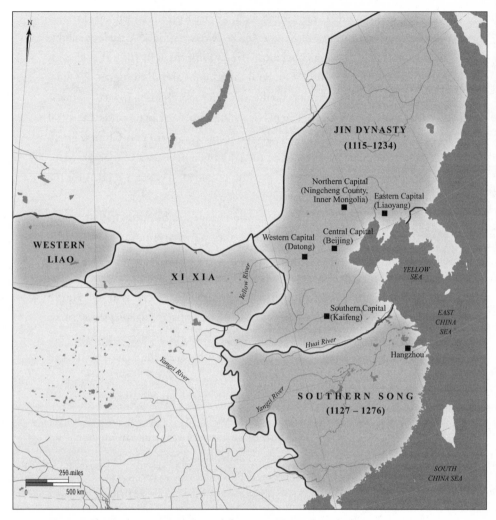

Map 1.2 The Jurchen Jin empire around the year 1170. (Modern place names are in parentheses.)

In the north, the Jurchens proceeded to set up a Chinese-style administration. They adopted many Chinese bureaucratic institutions such as the Secretariat and the Six Ministries. Jurchens occupied the highest posts, often appointed on the basis of heredity. But the Jin administration also included Khitans, Chinese, and other peoples, and it used Chinese and Khitan writing systems.[8] Jurchen

8. Franke 1987, 1994, 2004.

emperors continued the civil service examinations for the Chinese and over the course of the twelfth century greatly expanded them, recruiting Chinese officials into the bureaucracy through the examination system in numbers comparable to those of the Southern Song. Chinese literati in the north accepted Jurchen rule as legitimate and freely served in the government. Confucian learning flourished under the Jin, promoted by both Chinese and non-Chinese scholarly elites.[9] In the mid-twelfth century, as many Jurchens adopted Chinese customs and language, Emperor Shizong (r. 1161–1189) launched a campaign to revive a distinct Jurchen identity. He developed a writing system for the Jurchen language, for the first time, and ordered that Jurchen language and dress be used exclusively at court. But these efforts failed. Even though Confucian classics and other books were translated into Jurchen, the Jurchen written language never caught on, and it gradually died out in China. Many Jurchens embraced Chinese literature and Confucian learning, and they freely adopted Chinese ways. There is evidence that intermarriage between Chinese and Jurchens was also common.[10]

Under Jin rule in north China, a new kind of literature and entertainment appeared, a form of musical play called "all-keys-and-modes" (*zhugongdiao* 諸宮調). This was the precursor to the popular drama of the Yuan. By this time, footbinding for Chinese women was also taking hold, first among the Chinese elites. Tombs in both the north and the south from this era contain small shoes and binding cloths.[11] In the Jin all-keys-and-modes play *Romance of the Western Chamber,* the female protagonist Oriole has bound feet.[12]

Legal developments under the Jin mirrored other aspects of administration, reflecting the tension between preserving Jurchen ways and adopting traditions from the conquered peoples such as the Chinese or Khitan. Like the Liao, the Jin also contended with the problem of applying different laws to different peoples or unifying their laws for everyone within their territory. Early Jurchen penal law, like that of the Khitans and other steppe peoples, was based on a system of compensation or vendetta. If one stole an ox or a horse, one had to pay back 10

9. On these developments, see Bol 1987; Tillman 1995; Iiyama 2011.

10. Franke 1994, 281. On the Jurchen language, see Kane 1989.

11. See Ebrey 1993, 37–43. On the cultural context of footbinding, see Ko 2005.

12. This play, written between 1190 and 1208 is available in English; see Dong 1994. The Yuan version of the play is one of the most famous in Chinese literature; see West and Idema 1995.

head: 6 to the victim and 4 to the government.[13] After conquering north China, the Jin emperors moved to systematize and codify their laws, combining elements of Khitan, Jurchen, and Chinese legal traditions.[14] Punishments in general were more severe than in Chinese law, and amnesties were fewer.[15]

The culmination of Jin efforts to codify laws was the comprehensive Taihe code (*Taihe lü* 泰和律), promulgated in 1202 under Emperor Zhangzong 章宗 (r. 1189–1208). This was a Chinese-style law code modeled on the Tang code. It had 12 sections, with titles identical to the Tang code, and a total of 563 articles (compared to 502 in the Tang code) with commentary added.[16] The Taihe code no longer survives, but about 130 of its statutes can be found in other sources, mostly in the *Yuan dianzhang.* Of these, about half differ from the Tang code, usually with harsher punishments. The Taihe code combined traditional Chinese law with aspects of customary law practiced by the Jurchens and Khitans. For instance, it allowed redemption payments in lieu of punishments such as exile or beatings and required compensation for theft and other crimes.[17] Following traditional Chinese law, it required observation of a mourning period after the death of a parent, spouse, or other relative.[18]

The Taihe code operated in north China under the Jin; and after the Mongol invasion, according to the Yuan dynastic history, local magistrates continued to apply it in the absence of any new Yuan code, until Khubilai in 1271 abrogated it. Judges under the Yuan regularly cited the Taihe code as a source of law or for reference both before and after 1271. They referred to it as the "Old Regulations" (*jiuli* 舊例), never citing the code by name.[19] But they almost never applied the punishment prescribed in the Taihe code, instead choosing a lighter sentence. This conforms to the many complaints at the time that the Taihe code

13. *Sanchao beimeng huibian* 3:6a–b; Franke 1981, 221. See also Niida (1959) 1991, especially 463–472, on compensation.

14. On early Jin statutes, see Franke 1975; Franke 1981, 224–225; *Jinshi* 45:1015.

15. *Jinshi* 26:1013; Birge 2008, 458–459; Franke 1981, 225.

16. *Jinshi* 45:1024; Franke 1989. The commentary was also modeled on the Tang code. See Ye 1972; Zeng 1995.

17. *Jinshi* 45:1024.

18. *Jinshi* 45:1024.

19. Ye 1972, 17–18; Franke 1981, 216; Ratchnevsky and Aubin 1972–1985, 1:x; Kobayashi 1977. There is some disagreement over whether the term "Old Regulations" always refers to the Taihe code, especially after Khubilai abrogated it in 1271. I argue that it usually did, and that one can discern the exceptions (Birge 2010, 392–394).

was too harsh.[20] The Taihe code then was used more as a foil to justify a verdict, making it seem more reasonable.

The Taihe code was an attempt to unify the law for all people under Jin rule, but in some areas of the law the Jurchens found it necessary to retain separate laws for different cultural groups, in particular in the areas of inheritance and marriage. Chinese inheritance practices differed from those of the Jurchens in significant ways, and the Taihe code specified different inheritance practices for Jurchens and Chinese. For instance, for the Jurchens the Taihe code allowed separate registration and division of property during the life of the parents. For Han Chinese, it forbade separate registration but let them divide movable property with the parents' permission.[21]

Marriage law presented the area of greatest conflict between traditions of the Jurchens and the Chinese. Both the Khitans and Jurchens allowed elopement, where young people could choose their own spouses, and they allowed "wife stealing" around the New Year season, a form of ritualized elopement, where the girl was willing and often urged her future groom to go ahead and "steal" her.[22] In traditional Chinese law, only one's parents or other senior family members could contract a legal marriage as long as they were living.

Most significant of all was the issue of levirate marriage, the practice whereby a widow could be forced to marry a relative of her late husband, including a brother, cousin, nephew, or even a son by another wife. This was articulated in terms of a man "inheriting" his relative's wife (e.g., *shouji* 收繼 or *jiexu* 接續). Both the Khitans and the Jurchens practiced levirate marriage, as did the Mongols and other steppe peoples. Among the Khitans it may have been compulsory.[23] In sharp contrast, levirate marriage was considered incest by Chinese

---

20. YS 102:2603. See discussion in Yao 1986, 118ff.

21. YDZ 17:12a–b. See also Ye 1972, 83–84, 230. The Tang code and earlier Chinese codes forbade division of family property and separate registration before the death of both parents (TLSY 12:236 [Art. 155]), though early law of the Chin and Han did not prohibit this (Dull 1978). For a summary of the evolution of these laws, see MacCormack 2008, 411–416; for Song developments and beyond, see Lau 1994, 2015.

22. On Liao and Jin marriage practices, see Johnson 2011, 80–105. For a contemporary description, see *Sanchao beimeng huibian* 3:4b–5a, translated in Franke 1975, 136–137; *Luting shishi* 8:48b, quoted in Franke 1981, 231; Franke 1975, 182. See also comments in Franke 1981, 227; Franke 1989; Zeng 1995, 138–145.

23. Wittfogel and Feng 1949, 201, 211; Franke 1992, 124.

law, punishable by penal servitude and even by death.[24] In 1169, the Jin emperor Shizong (r. 1161–1189) decreed that the levirate be forbidden for Chinese and Bohai. His order stated that Chinese and Bohai widows should be allowed to return to their natal families after the mourning period and contract a remarriage.[25] The Taihe code of 1202 included the same prohibition for these two groups.[26] But the levirate was legal for all others under Jin rule for the duration of the dynasty. The Jurchen rulers were never able to reconcile differences in marriage law. The Mongols faced a similar situation, as will be seen in the translations.

The Coming of Mongol Rule

In the late twelfth century, a charismatic leader named Temüjin, of the Borjigin clan on the Mongolian steppe, rose from circumstances of extreme deprivation to build a world empire. When Temüjin was as young as nine years old, his father was murdered, and he was forced, together with his mother and siblings, to hunt and forage on his own to survive.[27] Gaining followers little by little, he began to conquer the warring and disparate tribes on the Mongolian steppe, uniting them into what would become the Mongol nation.[28] By 1206 the conquest of the Mongolian steppe was complete, and he took the new title Chinggis Khan, which came into English through Persian and Turkish sources as Genghis Khan.[29]

The Mongols were nomadic horse-riders who raised livestock on the Inner Asian grasslands. The men participated in group hunts, which also served as

24. Relevant articles in the Tang code are: TLSY, Articles 6, 183, 411, 413. In Ming law levirate marriage was punishable by strangulation; see *Da Ming lü,* 6:20b. On the contradictions between the operation of the levirate and Chinese marriage laws, see Holmgren 1986.

25. *Jinshi* 6:144. See also Ye 1972, 91, 230; Zeng 1995, 145; Franke 1981, 228.

26. See case 18.57 (YDZ 18:26a), translated in Part II.

27. The birth date of Chinggis Khan is not known with complete certainty. Possible dates range from 1155 to 1167 (see Ratchnevsky 1991, 17–19).

28. The peoples who came to be called Mongols were originally a diverse group. The nomads on the Mongolian steppe spoke various dialects of Mongolian and Turkic, and non-Mongols also joined them in their conquests. See discussions in Allsen 1994, 321–333; Sugiyama 1997, especially 25ff.; Sugiyama 1998, especially 68.

29. Atwood 2004, 99. The meaning of this title is not known with certainty. Some think it means "Oceanic" thus "Universal Ruler," but a more likely meaning of Chinggis is "severe" or "hard" (see de Rachewiltz 1989). For good accounts of Chinggis Khan's life and conquests, see Ratchnevsky 1991; Dunnell 2010.

training for warfare.[30] A Mongol soldier might have as many as three to five horses that he could switch to, which allowed the later Mongol conquerors to cover great distances without stopping. Leaders who were successful in warfare gained more followers, to whom they distributed captured booty, including horses and women in addition to livestock and valuables. Men were taken captive in large numbers as well and forced to serve in the military as infantry soldiers. Artisans and literati who were seen as useful might be transported back to the Mongol capital of Khara Khorum to serve the Mongol rulers directly. Mongol women were left in charge of the camp in the men's absence, and they took on all aspects of herding and providing food and shelter for the family. Mongol women rode horses like the men and did not bind their feet. Elite women from the khan's family could also be included in a grand council (Mongolian: *khuriltai*) called to elect the next khan or decide a major campaign. In this way, Mongol women wielded considerable authority within the family and within the political realm.[31]

Having united the Mongolian tribes located in what is now the Republic of Mongolia and Inner Mongolia in China, Chinggis Khan turned his attention to the sedentary peoples on the edges of the steppe. He attacked the Jin state of the Jurchens, and in 1215 his forces took the Jin capital of Beijing, forcing the Jurchens into a narrow area of land between the Yellow and Huai Rivers. Chinggis Khan himself died in 1227, but fighting continued, led by his sons and generals. In 1234 the Mongols conquered the Jurchen capital at Kaifeng, and the Jin state came to an end. North China suffered much destruction during the Mongol invasions. During the same decades, the forces of Chinggis Khan conquered nearly all of the Middle East, southern Russia, eastern Europe, and northern India, founding the largest empire ever known.[32]

After taking north China, the Mongols began preparing an attack on south China. The Southern Song were cut off from their supply of horses, so could not field an effective cavalry. At the same time the Mongols built a navy, manned largely by north Chinese and other non-Mongols. The final conquest took forty years, but by 1276, the south had been defeated and the Mongols ruled all of China. In 1279, the last emperor of the Southern Song and his mother perished

30. On these hunts and their wide significance, see Allsen 2006.
31. Rossabi 1979, 1988; Franke 1980; Birge and Broadbridge, forthcoming.
32. For a classic account, see Morgan 1986.

at sea off the south coast, having fled the Mongol takeover of the capital. For the first time in Chinese history, non-Chinese controlled all of China. Moreover, in the eyes of the Mongols, China was just one part of a larger empire.

A unified Mongol world empire did not last for long. After the death of Chinggis, the empire was divided into four khanates, each controlled by the descendants of one of his four sons by his principal wife, Börte. His grandson Khubilai, the son of Chinggis's youngest son, Tolui (d. 1232), inherited East Asia and the Mongolian heartland and took responsibility for the conquest of south China. In 1260, Khubilai Khan was elected to be Great Khan in a contested *khuriltai* council. From this time on, Khubilai (r. 1260–1294) reigned as Great Khan of the world empire, but his direct power was limited to China and eastern Inner Asia. His cousins who ruled at the other end of the empire in Persia and the Middle East stayed loyal to him as great khan and maintained close ties, but his other relatives who controlled Central Asia and southern Russia mostly had antagonistic relations. Khubilai's long reign stretched from 1260 until he died in 1294.[33] The majority of cases in the *Yuan dianzhang* are from this period.

In 1256 Khubilai moved the seat of his khanate away from Khara Khorum, on the steppe, to East Asia to pursue the conquest of China, and he founded a new city about two hundred miles north of Beijing, called Shangdu ("Supreme Capital"). This was the "Xanadu" of Marco Polo and, later, the poet Samuel Taylor Coleridge, and it became the Mongols' summer capital during their rule of China. In addition to urban sectors, it had large hunting parks and open areas for the khan and his entourage to set up their tents when in residence.[34] Then, in 1264, Khubilai established his main capital at Beijing, called Dadu 大都 (or Daidu, "Great Capital"), which became the formal seat of government for the Mongol world empire and the Yuan dynasty. It was known to Marco Polo and Western Asians as Khanbalikh ("City of the Khan"). The city had been the Southern Capital of the Liao, the seat of their Southern Administration, and the Central Capital of the Jin. Like Shangdu, it had open areas for tents in the palace quarters. It also had a thriving urban population that included many non-Chinese from as far away as Persia and Europe, and it became not

33. For the definitive biography of Khubilai, see Rossabi 1988.
34. Rossabi 1988, 31–34.

just a great administrative center but also a center of commerce and entertainment.[35] From there, Khubilai reigned over an empire of unprecedented size and grandeur.[36]

Like his immediate predecessors, Khubilai had to figure out how to administer the sedentary population of China, a task in which the Mongols had no direct previous experience. Khubilai did not trust the Chinese and Jurchens enough simply to continue with the bureaucratic structure in place in north China, as the Jurchens had done when they conquered the Northern Song. Instead, he adopted elements from Jin, Liao, and Song administration and even some agencies found in earlier Chinese dynasties. Like his predecessors, he employed Central Asians as his advisors, notably Khitans and Uighurs, but also many Western Asians, who introduced administrative practices found in Persia and other sedentary societies newly under Mongol rule.[37] Khubilai built his administration through an unsystematic, ad hoc process, adding organs of the central government and countless agencies and bureaus as, in his estimation, the need arose.[38] The result was a confusing mixture of overlapping and sometimes redundant bureaucracies, with names of bureaus changing over time or new ones being added and others disappearing. But they managed to carry out the basic functions of government and to enforce changing policies over the course of the Yuan dynasty. The cases of the *Yuan dianzhang*, translated in Part II of this volume, well demonstrate this complex and fluid structure of government.

Society and Law under Yuan Rule

If one were to walk down the street of the Yuan capital, Dadu, one might hear people talking in Chinese, Mongolian, Jurchen, Khitan, Turkish, Persian, Arabic, Korean, Tibetan, and countless other languages, including European ones such as Italian or French. Although Chinese speakers still constituted the majority, the

---

35. On Dadu and its many aspects, see Chen Gaohua and Shi Weimin 2010; Chen Gaohua 2015; Steinhardt 1983; Sugiyama 2004, 128–167.

36. For a global, historical perspective, see Abu-Lughod 1989.

37. On these groups, see Rossabi 1981; Brose 2002, 2005, 2007, 2008.

38. This is well described in Farquhar 1990, who characterizes the Yuan administration as "the most complex imperial government in Chinese history" (4). See also Farquhar 1981; Endicott-West 1986, 1989, 1991.

non-Chinese population of north China, especially in the cities, constituted a sizable minority. These people practiced a diversity of religions: Islam, Judaism, Christianity, Manichaeism, Buddhism, Confucianism, and others. Social values and legal, philosophical, and customary traditions also varied widely across this diverse population. The Yuan government faced the challenge of devising a legal and administrative system that could accommodate this multicultural mix. The Yuan emperors addressed whether to apply different laws to different ethnic groups or to try to impose unified laws on everyone within Yuan territory. They switched back and forth on this policy, as will be seen in the cases in Part II, but they also developed hybrid laws and new legislation unprecedented in Chinese history that exerted much influence on later Chinese law. In this respect they were more successful than their Liao and Jin predecessors.[39]

The Mongol emperors recognized the diversity of their conquest subjects and the need to establish legitimacy across a range of constituencies. As Herbert Franke has described, to the various steppe peoples they had to demonstrate martial prowess and assert charismatic leadership to maintain legitimacy as great khans. The role of the khan included providing booty and other rewards for military followers. To their Chinese subjects, the Mongol rulers needed to fill the role of Confucian sage emperors. Over time, they adopted Confucian state rituals, court ceremonies, and various policies that asserted the Yuan's legitimacy as a traditional Chinese dynasty. These policies included the use of a dynastic title and reign titles, the issuing of a new calendar, the laying out of the capital city based on Confucian symbolism, and so forth. The Yuan rulers' embrace of Lamaist Buddhism helped them rule Tibet. Buddhism, moreover, provided an ideology of divine sanction for Mongol rule and a concept of universal emperorship across cultural and political divides.[40] Multilingual monuments also asserted the authority and legitimacy of the Mongols as universal rulers. A beautiful example is the massive stone arch at Juyong Pass (Juyongguan 居庸關) outside Beijing, still standing today, with inscriptions carved in six languages. (See Figure 1.1.) The arch, built in the 1340s, was part of a Buddhist temple complex in Tibetan style and includes carvings of the Buddhist guardians of the four directions and other Lamaist images. The multi-lingual inscription depicts

39. Aubin 2004; Birge 2008, 2017.
40. Franke 1978.

Figure 1.1 Multilingual arch at Juyong Pass. Located 60 kilometers (37 miles) northwest of central Beijing along the main road to the capital, the inside of the arch contains an inscription in six different languages. (Photograph by author.)

Khubilai as the incarnation of a Buddhist bodhisattva, thereby further serving to legitimize the Mongols as divinely ordained universal rulers.[41]

The Yuan administration itself was multilingual. All documents were issued in Chinese and Mongolian, and sometimes other languages. A large body of translators and scribes were employed to produce these, many of them Khitans

41. On this remarkable monument, see Murata and Fujieda 1955–1958. For an excellent description in English, see Andrew West, "Cloud Platform at Juyongguan," *Diary of a Rambling Antiquarian,* http://babeldiary.blogspot.com/2011/08/cloud-platform-at-juyongguan.html (accessed August 29, 2016). The arch, called the Cloud Platform, included a trio of stupas on top, now gone. In Yuan times it was on the main road to the capital, through which all traffic from the north passed; it is now about 60 kilometers (37 miles) northwest of the city along the road to Badaling on the Great Wall. The six languages are Sanskrit (in Lanydza script), Tibetan, Mongolian (in Phags-pa script), Uighur, Chinese, and Tangut. On the significance of its construction, see Robinson 2009, 20–21. See also Crossley 1999, 263.

or Uighurs.[42] Among the Mongol emperors, some, like Khubilai, had extensive contact with China and certainly spoke Chinese, although they may not have been able to read and write the classical language.[43] But others were raised on the steppe and did not even speak Chinese, let alone write it. The language at the khan's court was Mongolian. Khubilai recruited the learned monk Phags-pa to develop an alphabet for Mongolian that could also be used for other languages, and this script (termed Phags-pa) became the official written language of the empire. All official documents had to be issued in this script. Steles proclaiming the emperor's decrees were erected with Mongolian Phags-pa script on one side and Chinese characters on the other.[44] Edicts issued by Khubilai and other emperors, always in Mongolian, were reproduced in Chinese in a form of direct translation that used Chinese characters to represent Mongolian words but retained Mongolian syntax and grammar. This hybrid language, which I call Sino-Mongolian, is found throughout the cases of the *Yuan dianzhang*.

The Mongols maintained a quota system to ensure that Mongols and Inner Asians dominated the ranks of the bureaucracy. For recruitment into the civil service and other privileges, the Yuan rulers divided the entire population into four ranked classes. At the top were Mongols (*mengguren* 蒙古人), who made up a political and military elite. All Mongol men served in the military and received numerous privileges. Next came Inner Asians and foreigners from the West, including Uighurs, Persians, and even Europeans among others, called *semu* (*semuren* 色目人), "people of various categories." These held many top civil service posts. The third category, called "Han people" (*hanren* 漢人 or *han'erren* 漢兒人), comprised people living in north China who had been subject to Jin rule. These included mostly Chinese but also Jurchens, Khitans, Koreans, and others. In contexts outside the recruitment system, however, such as in the marriage cases of the *Yuan dianzhang*, the term is usually used to designate Chinese speakers in the area of north China. Last, at the bottom of the ranking, were residents of south China (*nanren* 南人), for whom it was most difficult to enter the civil service. When the Mongol emperor Renzong (r. 1311–1320) restarted the Chinese-style civil service examinations in 1315, after a hiatus since the conquest, quotas were set for each of these categories. The

42. de Rachewiltz 1967; Kara 2005; Brose 2005.
43. Franke 1953; Rossabi 1988.
44. On these, see Cleaves 1950, 1951, 1952; Cai 1955.

same numbers of successful candidates were chosen from each group, but many more Chinese sat for the exams in both the north and the south, making the competition among the *hanren* and *nanren* much stiffer than for other groups. Moreover, Mongols and *semu* were given special examinations that were easier to pass.[45]

More important for the population at large, the Mongol rulers enacted a system of household registration, whereby every household was classified as a certain type. This classification determined a household's tax and service obligations to the state, generation after generation. These hereditary classifications numbered more than eighty and included a dizzying array of occupations, such as weaver, goldsmith, falconer, wine maker, entertainer, and so forth. Some of the categories were religious, including Buddhist, Daoist, Muslim, and Nestorian Christian clerics, which were exempted from taxation. Households of the literati elite, designated "Confucian households," also received tax exemption and special treatment. A few categories were ethnic-based, such as Uighur, Jurchen, and Khitan, and some were geographic.[46] Skilled artisan families enjoyed especially favorable treatment, including tax exemptions and government salaries, in particular those who supplied weapons and armor to the military, and luxury goods to the court. Instead of using tax revenues to purchase goods the government needed, the Mongols in many instances requisitioned specific products and services from households designated for that purpose. A plethora of agencies within multiple branches of the administration had the Herculean task of supervising these households. This system of fixed, hereditary occupations ran counter to the highly commercialized and fluid society found in China by this time. The government faced the perennial problem of keeping a sufficient number of households registered in each category to supply the state. Marriage across occupational groups was a prime way for people to fall off the registers or change categories, and the state's concern about this issue is evident in the *Yuan dianzhang*.

---

45. Meng 2006, especially 46–65. The regulations for civil service exams are found in TZTG 5:220–225. For more on the examination system under the Mongols, see Elman 2000, 34ff.; Iiyama 2011. For meanings of the term *hanren* in Yuan legal cases, see Liu Xiao 2013.

46. On this system, see Huang Qinglian 1977, especially 197–215 for a summary chart of all categories. See also discussions in Mote 1994a, 648–656; Mote 1999, 495–497; Chü (1956) 1966; Hsiao 1978a.

Among occupational groups, of paramount importance were military households (*junhu* 軍戶), or hereditary soldier households. These had to supply one soldier to the state, available at all times, together with full equipment. Military households had special privileges but also onerous duties. Several households often shared the burden. One, termed a "regular military household" (*zheng junhu* 正軍戶), would provide the able-bodied male, and the others, termed "auxiliary military households" (*tie junhu* 貼軍戶), gave funds to supply him with a horse, armor, and weapons. These made up between a seventh and a third of total households in a given area, and the Yuan state administered them directly through the Bureau of Military Affairs.[47] Yuan policies on marriage and inheritance reflected concern for keeping these households solvent and preventing families from leaving the military registers. Laws formulated for military households were often extended to all households.

At the bottom of society were large numbers of slaves. Like the Jurchens before them, the Mongols captured and enslaved large numbers of people in the course of their conquests. Vanquished populations in north China, as they had been in Inner Asia, were distributed as slaves to imperial relatives and military leaders. During the conquest of the south, and even afterwards, soldiers, corrupt officials, and human traffickers kidnapped children and others to sell as slaves in northern markets. The capital Dadu (Beijing) had a large market in people.[48] The populations of appanages were also considered to have semi-servile status, at least in the early part of the dynasty. The challenge of maintaining large numbers of people in servile status and preventing them from crossing status boundaries garnered much attention from the Yuan government. Marriage was a means by which to escape servile status, and Khubilai and his top administrators had to address the issue of marriage between slaves and commoners and the disposition of their offspring. As seen in the cases, slaves would escape and pose as commoners to get married. Other times slaves married commoners openly with the expectation that their children would be free commoners. A series of decisions between 1269 and 1288 addressed this problem and estab-

---

47. For details of this system, see Chen Gaohua 1982, 72–90; Hsiao 1978b; Matsuda 1990. Within military households there were several types; see Huang Qinglian 1977, 197–198. The Song had had an army of paid soldiers.

48. Ebisawa 1983. The government tried to prevent the kidnapping and trafficking of commoners, but it remained a problem.

lished that if a free woman married a slave, she had to do so willingly, and her offspring would be slaves.[49]

During the Yuan, theatrical arts developed and flourished. Particularly popular was a form called *zaju* 雜劇, Northern drama, or "variety play." These plays featured singing that alternated with spoken prose passages in vernacular language, as well as acrobats and elaborate costumes and makeup. These shows can be seen as a precursor to today's Peking Opera. Talented men of letters wrote plays, other opportunities for literati being limited, and the Mongol rulers patronized the theatre.[50] A popular genre was courtroom dramas. A large number of surviving plays feature the incorruptible Judge Bao, who stood up to venal officials and relieved the suffering of common people. Corrupt officials and rigged courts appear frequently in these plays. But the story lines usually conclude with matters set right and justice prevailing.[51]

A significant theme discernable in the body of marriage cases is the growing influence of the philosophical school and social movement referred to in English as Neo-Confucianism.[52] Neo-Confucian doctrine presented a new perspective on ethics, which held that one could ascertain a universal moral truth through an understanding of "principle" or "coherence" (*li* 理) that resided in all things. By a sustained process of learning and self-cultivation, one could gain an awareness of this principle, which pervaded the cosmos, "Heaven and Earth," and oneself. Neo-Confucianism, like classical Confucianism, stressed study of the Confucian classics, but it differed from the latter by emphasizing a direct fundamentalist reading of the canon unencumbered by the accretion of more recent commentaries and historical interpretations. Moreover it stressed the need to realize in the contemporary world the moral Way (*dao* 道), as found in the texts, rather than to focus on more superficial forms of cultural expression, broadly termed *wen* (文). Neo-Confucian philosophy linked morality to cosmology and understood the orderly workings of "Heaven and Earth" to be the ultimate source of moral truths. Such cosmological language is evident in certain

49. See Chapter 8, cases 18.67–70.

50. There is a large literature on Yuan drama. See for instance Crump 1980; Idema and West 1982; West and Idema 2010.

51. See Hayden 1978; Idema 2010.

52. For an understanding of Neo-Confucianism, its development, and its significance for Chinese history, see Bol 1992, 2008; Tillman 1992. For the large corpus of studies on various aspects of Neo-Confucianism, see the works cited therein.

of the marriage cases and can serve to tip off the reader to an author's Neo-Confucian sympathies.

The movement had religious significance in that it imbued one's personal existence with transcendent meaning, which was confirmed through moral action and daily ritual practice at home and in public life. The movement had political significance in that it bestowed on individual literati a source of moral authority and intellectual legitimacy independent of the state, and it justified local leadership and community activism by scholarly elites. Key to Neo-Confucian piety was exemplary moral behavior, by men and women, based on a literal reading of the Confucian classics. This included filial piety, loyalty, subordination of juniors to seniors, proper gender roles, and in particular wifely fidelity and widow chastity. Neo-Confucians felt it imperative that the law embody these normative principles, and they saw legal activism as a means to implement a universal code of ethics and bring into effect the moral way of Heaven and Earth among the populace.

The Neo-Confucian movement began during the Northern Song dynasty (960–1127) and flourished in the Southern Song (1127–1279), under the influence of its most important thinker, Zhu Xi 朱熹 (1130–1200). Even while China was divided, and the north was controlled by the Jurchen Jin and then the Mongols, Zhu Xi's thought began to gain adherents in the north. The message of Neo-Confucianism, of moral and political authority that did not emanate from the state, found fertile ground among the frustrated Confucian elites of Yuan times, for whom avenues to official position were greatly reduced. But it also quickly gained followers among officials at the Mongol court, both Chinese and non-Chinese.[53] Already in the ninth month of 1271, the Ministry of Rites proposed that wedding rituals from Zhu Xi's *Family Rituals* (*Zhuzi jiali* 朱子家禮) be adopted as the standard. The Central Secretariat approved the proposal but excised the provision in the text about using a horse and carriage to transport the bride, arguing that poor people could not afford them.[54] When the Mongol

53. On the spread of Neo-Confucian ideas to north China under the Mongols and their influence on the court, see de Bary 1981 and Chan 1982. On Chinese elites and government service under the Yuan, see Jay 1991 and Iiyama 2011, 2014. On Neo-Confucianism and women, see Birge 1989, 2003.

54. YDZ 30:1a–2a. A masterful translation of Zhu Xi's text is found in Ebrey 1991a, *Chu Hsi's Family Rituals*. The *Yuan dianzhang* quotes the seven steps of the marriage rites from Zhu Xi's text, but with minor modifications. Later scholars who reprinted Zhu Xi's text routinely

emperor in 1313 decided to restart the civil service examinations, they were based on Zhu Xi's interpretations of the Confucian classics. Over the subsequent decades, Neo-Confucian adherents, both Chinese and non-Chinese, gained influence at court and in the bureaucracy.[55]

As the cases in the *Yuan dianzhang* reveal, over time, the law shifted in the direction of the Neo-Confucian moral agenda, which aimed to strengthen patriarchal authority and reduce women's autonomy. This shift included limits on married women's property rights, a favoring of the groom's family over the bride's, and laws to encourage widow chastity and penalize widow remarriage.[56] At the same time, we see in the marriage cases women filing lawsuits and appealing to the law to protect their property and autonomy. These women were mostly widows or mothers of brides. The cases indeed reveal a growing influence of Neo-Confucian ideology, but also provide evidence that wives and widows still enjoyed considerable legal and economic prerogatives and many possibilities for exerting agency. Absent are any references to widow suicide, which are found in legal cases in later centuries.[57] The emerging cult of female fidelity had not yet reached the masses whose lives are revealed in the documents.

The cases translated below take place against this background of social ferment, at a time when boundaries of gender, ethnic, and status privilege were getting defined and challenged in the poly-ethnic world of China under Mongol rule.

---

made such modifications to accord more with current practice and their own ideas, as described in Ebrey 1991b.

55. See Dardess 1973, especially chapter 4.

56. For more on these, see Birge 1995, 2002, 2003. A preoccupation with issues of female fidelity and widow chastity was not limited to Neo-Confucians but had taken hold among a large segment of elite men by Yuan times, as seen in literati writings. See Bossler 2013, especially chapter 9.

57. For the Qing, see discussions in Sommer 2000 and Theiss 2004.

CHAPTER TWO

Yuan Administration and the Legal System

The Mongols had to adapt their relatively simple and direct system of govern-ment as practiced on the steppe to the complex and multi-tiered institutional system needed to govern the large, sedentary population of China. The trans-formation was never complete, and many elements of the Yuan administration reflect ideas of rulership that the Mongols brought with them. As they extended their rule over newly conquered parts of China, the Mongols established new branches and offices of their administration, which often combined military and civil functions. New institutions sometimes operated alongside ones previously in place. Different branches of the administration had legal jurisdiction over the same area, and plaintiffs could bring their suits in any number of courts. Khubilai and other emperors freely established new agencies and bureaus to fill perceived needs, and abolished them just as freely. Even offices at the highest level of administration, such as the Secretariat for State Affairs, were established and abolished several times. The resulting system was ad hoc, redundant, and fluid, and yet it managed to administer the largest and most advanced empire known in the world at that time.

The Central Administration

At the pinnacle of government stood the emperor. His word was final, and all legislation was implemented in his name. The Yuan emperors, however, were also great khans of the Mongol empire and brought a distinct ideology of ruler-ship with them from the steppe. Among the Mongols and other steppe peoples, the authority of the ruler was established by charismatic leadership and the personal loyalty of his followers. Authority resided in the person, not in the institution. The Great Khan (later, *khaghan* or *kha'an*) was chosen by a special grand council, called a *khuriltai,* of imperial relatives (both male and female), nobles, and military leaders. The khan maintained his authority by personally leading troops into battle, directing large royal hunts, which were a form of military training, and rewarding his followers with war booty, including the granting of fiefs. The Yuan emperors continued these practices, which explains the proliferation of appanages granted to relatives and generals. These included both lands and subject peoples and were only partially controlled by the central government.

In the early stages of the Mongol state, before the Eurasian conquests, Chinggis Khan and his successors ruled through their personal followers. These were originally the *nököd,* who were later organized into the khan's personal bodyguard, the *keshig* (Chinese *qiexue* 怯薛). The administration of the state was thus an extension of the khan's own household and person. Along these lines, the area of north China first conquered by the Mongols was called *fuli* 腹裏, literally "within the belly" (or as Farquhar labels it, "the guts"), thereby creating an image of Yuan territory as the embodiment of the emperor himself.[1] I translate the term as "Inner Domain." It covered the modern provinces of Hebei, Shandong, Shanxi, and eastern Inner Mongolia. The imperial government was disproportionately concerned with administering this area, also called Central Province (Zhongshusheng 中書省). Many of the fiefs that Khubilai granted were located within this area as well.

In 1260, Khubilai established the Central Secretariat (Zhongshusheng 中書省) as the highest organ of his government to implement his rule. The Chinese term Zhongshusheng refers to both the geographic area (Central Province) and the administrative office (Central Secretariat), the two meanings distinguished by context. The Central Secretariat was the highest decision-making body of the bureaucracy, with the highest possible rank of 1A. (The rank of an office, which dictated what kind of document it could send out, was determined by the highest rank of the officials who staffed it.) Most of the documents translated in Part II below record cases passed up to it for judgments, which had the force of law throughout the realm.

1. Farquhar 1990, 2, 5.

The Central Secretariat consisted physically of a vast array of offices in the capital staffed by an army of bureaucrats.[2] The Central Secretariat existed throughout the entire Yuan dynasty, yet even the authority of this institution was unstable. For three separate periods during the Yuan, an additional body was established at the top of the bureaucracy, the Secretariat for State Affairs (Shangshusheng 尚書省), which was often staffed by non-Chinese. The Secretariat for State Affairs was nominally subordinate to the Central Secretariat, but over the course of the three periods of its existence its power increased, eventually surpassing that of the Central Secretariat.

As Khubilai's armies conquered additional territory, he created branch secretariats (*xingsheng* 行省 or, more formally, *xing zhongshusheng* 行中書省, also translated as "mobile secretariats" or "acting secretariats") to control areas beyond the Central Province. These had a combined military and civil function, for they commanded troops in addition to administering the civilian population in their area. Like Zhongshusheng, the term *xingsheng* could refer to the administrative office or the area under its control. These were variously established and abolished but eventually numbered eleven, and they are the basis for the provinces of modern China, called simply *sheng*. Each branch secretariat replicated the Central Secretariat and was meant to extend the authority of that office. The rank of the branch secretariats was 1B, just under that of the Central Secretariat, although documents passed between these offices were of the type sent between equals, such as a "communiqué" (*zi* 咨). Marco Polo and other Western visitors to China called these branch secretariats "countries," giving the impression of relative independence from the throne. Nevertheless, they could not communicate directly with the emperor but had to pass their memorials through the Central Secretariat. Moreover, as the content of the documents in the *Yuan dianzhang* show, the branch secretariats regularly sent their decisions to the Central Secretariat for approval. In 1296, the military authority of the branch secretariats was greatly reduced when the emperor issued a decree prohibiting them from transferring troops without an order from the court.[3]

---

2. The Persian historian Rashīd al-Dīn writes that the Secretariat in the capital, Dadu, had a staff of "nearly two thousand" and held archives going back "several thousand years" (Boyle 1971, 281).

3. Farquhar 1990, 367–368.

Below the Central Secretariat, Khubilai established six ministries (*bu* 部), namely the Ministries of Personnel, Revenue, Rites, War, Punishments, and Works, each ranked 3A. These did not stand alone at first, but were combined into the Three Ministries of the Left (Personnel, Revenue, and Rites) and the Three Ministries of the Right (War, Punishments, and Works). Over time these were combined differently, under various names, until finally, in 1276, they took shape as six separate ministries.[4] Each ministry handled a separate aspect of governance according to its title, similar to the offices of the same names in Chinese dynasties. All of the ministries handled legal cases, and the cases of the *Yuan dianzhang* are each classified under the heading of one of the Six Ministries. When the Central Secretariat received a legal case, it would send the case to one of the Six Ministries for a judicial ruling. The ministry would send its ruling back to the Central Secretariat for approval, and once approved, the latter would distribute the decision to subordinate offices. This trail of documents is manifest in nearly every case presented in Part II.

The marriage cases from chapter 18 are found in the section of the *Yuan dianzhang* for the Ministry of Revenue (*hubu* 戶部), indicating that the government viewed marriage through the lens of how it affected households and tax revenues. By the late thirteenth century, and especially after the death of Khubilai and the accession of his grandson Temür in 1294, cases came to be handled by the Ministry of Rites (*libu* 禮部), reflecting a Confucian perspective that saw marriage as belonging to the realm of ritual, needed to order society. But cases adjudicated by the Ministry of Rites still appear in the "Marriage" chapter under the Ministry of Revenue section of the *Yuan dianzhang*.[5]

The Ministry of Punishments (*xingbu* 刑部) reviewed capital cases and regulated judicial procedures (including the use of torture), among other duties. Most important, it set punishments, as the name suggests. The other ministries determined what actions were legal or illegal; then the Ministry of Punishments decided what penalty should be applied to offenders. Both the prohibition and

---

4. For details of these changes, see Farquhar 1990, 175–176, 199–200.

5. The "Ministry of Rites" section of the *Yuan dianzhang* includes five marriage-related cases, under the heading "Marriage Ritual" (or "Weddings," *hunli* 婚禮). See YDZ 30:1a–3a. The Ming code, like the *Yuan dianzhang*, includes marriage cases in the Ministry of Revenue section. In the Tang and Song codes, marriage law is under the general heading "Household and Marriage" (*huhun* 戶婚). These earlier codes did not use as headings the names of the Six Ministries.

the penalty were subject to approval by the Central Secretariat, after which the decisions had the force of law. The making of new laws, then, involved the work of both the Ministry of Punishments and another ministry, and we find examples in the *Yuan dianzhang* where the Central Secretariat ordered a ministry to work with the Ministry of Punishments to devise a new law in this way.[6]

Units of Local Government

The primary unit of government below the branch secretariats was the Circuit (*lu* 路). Circuits were administered by an office called the Directorate-General (*zongguan fu* 總管府), whose chief officer was a Director-General (*zongguan*). Circuits began to be established in 1260, and eventually they numbered 184. They were classified as First-class Circuits (*shang lu* 上路), rank 3A, or Second-class Circuits (*xia lu* 下路), rank 3B, depending on their population and strategic location. The circuits were responsible for all the basic administrative functions of local government, such as collecting taxes, keeping order, supervising government schools and manufacturing, and hearing legal cases. In the documents in Part II, some cases originate at the circuit level, while others are passed up from lower courts. After rendering a provisional judgment, the circuit would pass the case up for review. Circuits within the Central Province could send their recommendations directly to any of the Six Ministries; those outside had to send their cases first to the branch secretariat above them, to be passed to the Central Secretariat at the capital.

Below the circuit were three additional levels of local government: the Superior Prefecture (*fu* 府), rank 4A; the Prefecture (*zhou* 州), rank 4B; and the County (*xian* 縣), rank 6B. All three of these performed the traditional functions of local government, including collecting taxes, maintaining order, and handling legal cases. Superior prefectures numbered just 33 and could have any number of households. Prefectures numbered 360 and were divided into First-, Second- and Third-class Prefectures, depending on population. Counties, of which there were 1,125, were similarly divided into three classes on the basis of population. The population level set for each grade of prefecture and county

---

6. See case 18.18 in Part II. See also discussion in Zhang Fan 2007, 58ff. Sometimes a ministry other than the Ministry of Punishments recommended a penalty.

was much higher in south China than in the north, reflecting the much denser population of the south. For instance, in the north a first-class prefecture needed to have at least 15,000 inhabitants, whereas in the south more than 50,000 inhabitants were required. Similarly, in the north a county was designated first-class if it had more than 6,000 residents, but in the south more than 30,000 were needed.[7]

The most salient feature of these geographic and administrative units in the Yuan is that they did not nest uniformly as in other dynasties. There was no neat hierarchy of county–prefecture–superior prefecture–circuit; rather these units were set up at various times for various reasons in an ad hoc manner, sometimes independently and sometimes within the jurisdiction of a higher administrative unit. Thus, a county, the lowest level of administration, might be within the jurisdiction of a prefecture, which in turn answered to a superior prefecture, and up to a circuit, or it could be separate and answer directly to a circuit. In rare instances, a county could be administered directly by a branch secretariat or the Central Secretariat (the latter through the Six Ministries). Similarly, a prefecture could be governed by a superior prefecture above it, or could be under the direct control of a circuit or even a branch secretariat. It might or might not govern a county below it. A superior prefecture might be controlled by a circuit, or it might answer directly to the Central Secretariat or one of the branch secretariats, and it might have prefectures and counties under its jurisdiction or sometimes none. The lines of authority from the central government down to local units were thus inconsistent and non-uniform. Cases could arrive at the circuit level from a superior prefecture, a prefecture, or even a county directly, as is evidenced by the cases in Part II. Likewise, the branch secretariat could receive dispatches from any number of subordinate-level offices. The names of these units, their administrative seats, and geographic areas also changed repeatedly. Such changes occurred in other dynasties as well, but they were more frequent in the Yuan.

In some areas, yet another unit, called the Region (*dao* 道), stood between the branch secretariat and the circuit. Regions were headed by a number of different offices, collectively called Pacification Offices (*xuanweisi* 宣慰司), of which there were eight different kinds, with ranks ranging from 2B to 3A. As their

7. Farquhar 1990, 418–420.

names suggest, these units were originally formed for military operations, and they were used in the conquest of the south and against rebellious districts. After the fall of the Song, however, as Khubilai tried to establish civilian rule, the Pacification Offices were gradually stripped of their military independence and authority and were made subordinate to the branch secretariats. Eventually, the regions became part of the chain of command from the Central Secretariat and branch secretariats down to lower-level offices, though in an irregular and patchwork fashion.[8] Chart 1 illustrates this complicated system.

Another important aspect of the administration that was unique to the Yuan dynasty was the use of agents, called in Mongolian *darughachi* (Chinese *daluhuachi* 達魯花赤).[9] These were installed in offices at every level of government, and their rank and salary matched that of the chief administrator of each office. Thus in a circuit, the *darughachi* ranked 3A and received the same salary as the Director-General. The presence of these agents in every unit of administration resulted in a dual system of government, whereby important decisions could not be made by any one individual. Most important, Khubilai intended the position to be filled by Mongols, as a check on Chinese administrators. His desire to have ethnic-based checks and balances in his rule over China was made clear in 1265, when he announced that "Mongols shall fill the post of Agent (*darughachi*) in all circuits, Northern Chinese (*hanren*) shall fill the post of Circuit Director-General, while Muslims (*huihui*) shall fill the post of Associate Director-General. This shall ever be our fixed policy."[10] Despite this intention, however, in actuality Chinese and Inner Asians frequently filled the position of *darughachi*. Of 299 agents who can be identified by name in the Yuan dynastic history, only 103 had Mongol names, while 47 appear to be Chinese. Of the remainder, 99 had Western Asian or Central Asian names (such as Uighur, Khitan, or Jurchen names), and 42 cannot be identified.[11] If we further consider that many Chinese took Mongolian names, the proportion of Mongols who held the position likely dips below one third of the total. The ethnicity-based agenda

8. On this system, see Shi Weimin 1993 and Li Zhi'an 2003, 91–104. For a brief overview (written before this newer scholarship), see Farquhar 1990, 411–414.

9. On the *darughachi*, see Endicott-West 1989. As with other Chinese transliterations, variant characters were sometimes used for this term.

10. YS 6:106, quoted in Farquhar 1990, 7–8. See also Endicott-West 1989, 79.

11. These figures come from Jagchid Sechin 1980b, 556–594. See also discussion in Endicott-West 1989, 78–83.

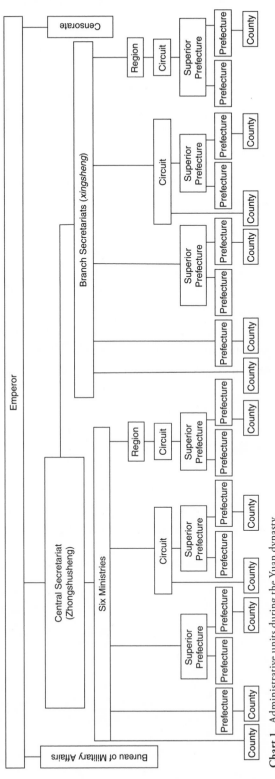

Chart 1. Administrative units during the Yuan dynasty.

that the position of *darughachi* was meant to promote is further indicated by the fact that none of these agents were assigned to Lingbei, the area of the Mongolian heartland. The cases of chapter 18 in the *Yuan dianzhang* do not make any direct reference to the *darughachi,* but there is continual reference to the consultations that were required for every decision by circuit-level or other courts to bring agents into the decision-making process.

The Censorate Establishment

Alongside the bureaucracy of the executive branch under the Central Secretariat was a parallel bureaucratic system under the authority of the Censorate (*yushitai* 御史臺).[12] The Censorate during the Yuan, as in other dynasties, had broad powers of investigation and surveillance, and could impeach both civil and military officials for misconduct. Moreover, it had the power to communicate directly with the emperor. In the *Yuan dianzhang* we find the local representatives of the Censorate reviewing judicial decisions and impugning the verdicts at every level. As seen in the cases, however, the Central Secretariat often upheld the original decision of its own subordinate bureaucrats. The main Censorate was given rank 1B, just under that of the Central Secretariat at 1A. The Censorate was required to communicate with the Secretariat in the form of a "report" (*cheng* 呈), a document sent from an inferior to superior office, thus reinforcing its subordinate position.[13]

The work of the main Censorate was concentrated in the Central Province and the branch secretariats immediately surrounding it, namely Henan-Jiangbei to the south and Liaoyang to the north. As the conquests proceeded, and the empire expanded, the Censorate established two branch censorates (*xing yushitai* 行御史臺, or just *xingtai*) to extend its activities to new areas. These were the Jiangnan Branch Censorate, or Southern Censorate for short (*nantai* 南臺), and the Shaanxi Branch Censorate, or Western Censorate (*xitai* 西臺). The former was established in 1277 and covered the area of the southeast, the prov-

---

12. On this system, see Hung 1982; Niwa 1994; Li Zhi'an 2003, 244–354; Farquhar 1990, 241–245.

13. The relative rank of these institutions was debated early in Khubilai's reign, some officials advocating that the Censorate be allowed to send a "communiqué" (*zi* 咨) to the Secretariat, indicating equal rank. See YS 158:3726–3727.

inces (or branch secretariats) of Jiangzhe, Jiangxi, and Huguang; the latter was created in 1290 and covered the west, namely the Shaanxi, Gansu, Sichuan, and Yunnan branch secretariats.

Beneath the level of the Censorate and the branch censorates was a bureaucracy of lower offices that carried out the work of investigation and surveillance. The territory of the main Censorate was divided into regions (*dao* 道), which eventually numbered eight. The Jiangnan Branch Censorate included ten regions, and the Shaanxi Branch Censorate had four, one for each of the provinces it covered. These "regions" were not the same as the regions of the same name that existed within the executive branch, as described earlier. The Censorate's regions covered the whole country and had different names and geographic areas from those under the Secretariat, though their territories could overlap and they could share similar names. Each region of the Censorate administration was headed by a Regional Surveillance Office (*tixing anchasi* 提刑按察司), first created in 1269. In 1291 the name of these changed to Regional Investigation Offices (*suzheng lianfangsi* 肅政廉訪司). Each of these offices employed armies of surveillance officials who made rounds to administrative offices at both the local and higher levels in order to ferret out corruption and wrongdoing, which they did by conducting audits of local records and reviewing legal decisions. These visits happened on a twice-yearly schedule. Evidence from the *Yuan dianzhang* shows that the censors did not usually communicate directly with the officials they were investigating, but rather sent their reports up the chain of command to the main Censorate, which could then transmit a report to the Central Secretariat. If a decision was to be overturned, the Secretariat would then send its order back down its own chain of command to the local offices. With only a few exceptions, the apparatus for carrying out an impeachment was cumbersome and time-consuming. The work of the Censorate impinged seriously on the operations of governance, both civil and military, but it was highly valued by the rulers, who struggled to keep unscrupulous officials in check.

The Military Establishment

The third branch of Yuan administration was the military, headed by the Bureau of Military Affairs (Shumiyuan 樞密院, sometimes translated as "Privy

Council"). Like the Censorate, its ministers could communicate directly with the emperor without going through the Central Secretariat, but also like the Censorate it was ranked 1B, just below the Secretariat. The Bureau of Military Affairs was created in 1263 to supervise the vast Yuan armies and bring them under tighter control of the court. These armies included regular Mongol troops and the non-Mongol troops from north and, later, south China who were incorporated into the ranks as the conquests progressed. It had many other responsibilities as well, such as supervising agricultural colonies attached to the military.[14] It handled all legal cases involving military households (*junhu* 軍戶). When any lawsuit or criminal offense involved a member of a military household—not necessarily a soldier—the case had to be sent over to the military bureaucracy for adjudication and would be passed up to the Bureau of Military Affairs for review. Special judges served in the Bureau for this purpose. If a soldier committed a crime against a civilian, the matter was handled by separate mixed military-civilian courts. Nevertheless, the Central Secretariat still had the final say in important cases whose rulings became law.[15]

Like the other two branches of government, the Bureau of Military Affairs extended its reach by replicating the main bureau with branch bureaus of military affairs (*xing shumiyuan* 行樞密院). But unlike the other two, the military branch bureaus were only temporary, created to carry out the invasions of the south and west. When the conquests were complete, the branch bureaus were absorbed by the branch secretariats, which oversaw troops in peacetime. In cases of rebellions or other military emergencies, a branch bureau of military affairs would again be temporarily reconstituted.

Mongol, Chinese, and troops of other nationalities were present throughout the territory of the Yuan. Marco Polo comments on how they were feared and detested, and allusions to their presence appear in Yuan drama. These soldiers were organized into military units based on a decimal system, which was famously established by Chinggis Khan originally to break up tribal loyalties. The

14. On the military establishment of the Yuan, see Hsiao 1978b. On the myriad offices within the Bureau of Military Affairs and the translations of these into English, which I follow, see Farquhar 1990, 247–282. The agricultural colonies were sometimes handled by other offices as well. See Endicott-West 1989, chapter 2.

15. Ratchnevsky 1993; Farquhar 1990, 247–248. Minor crimes were handled by local civil authorities.

primary unit was a Chiliarchy (*qianhu suo* 千戶所), led by an officer called a Chiliarch (*qianhu*). As the name suggests, a chiliarchy was originally envisaged as having 1,000 troops, but during the Yuan dynasty, a chiliarchy came in three classes, first, second, and third, made up of varying numbers of troops from 300 to 700 or more. Above this unit was a Myriarchy (*wanhufu* 萬戶府), led by a Myriarch (*wanghu*) and made up of 10 chiliarchies. Again, troop numbers in the unit could vary, and there were three classes. After the branch secretariats absorbed the branch bureaus of military affairs, the myriarchs and chiliarchs answered to the branch secretariats. Below the chiliarch were lower-level units, such as a Century (*baihu suo* 百戶所), led by a Centurion (*baihu*).[16]

The chiliarchs and myriarchs acted like prefectural- and circuit-level magistrates in judging cases involving military personnel. They would then send the cases up for review by the branch secretariat, which would send them to the Bureau of Military Affairs at the capital. We see in case 18.37 in Part II, however, an example where the Bureau of Military Affairs in 1296 merely forwarded such a case to the Central Secretariat without a decision. The Central Secretariat then sent it to one of the Six Ministries for a verdict, as it would for a case from the civilian administrative hierarchy. After approving the Ministry's ruling, the Central Secretariat sent the case back to the Bureau of Military Affairs, which forwarded it back to the branch secretariat, to be distributed back down to the myriarchy. In this way the chain of command crossed over between military and civilian offices. Such mixing of civilian and military duties was not unusual in the Yuan.

The Legal System and Administration of Justice

Legal procedure during the Yuan also reflects the redundant and cumbersome nature of the bureaucracy under Mongol rule. Not unlike under other dynasties, legal cases were heard by magistrates at each level of the executive bureaucracy. But in the Yuan, offices in the different branches of government—the executive, the censorial, and the military—all had authority to try cases. Also, during the Yuan there were special courts for people in any number of specified groups, such as soldiers, monks, or artisans. Separate courts for Mongols operated

16. On these units, see Farquhar 1990, 22, 416–418; Hsiao 1978b, 9–11, 54–57, 72–74.

for the duration of the dynasty. As mentioned earlier, different laws applied to different ethnic groups, however vaguely defined, at various times in the dynasty. Appanage holders in north China also had independent judicial powers within their territories, though over time their legal authority diminished as, beginning with Khubilai's reign, the central government aggressively reasserted more direct control over these areas.[17]

Most of the cases that are presented in translation in Part II start with an accusation filed by a plaintiff in a local government office, such as a county, prefecture, or sometimes a circuit. A box was set up outside the courtroom into which litigants could "throw" their plaints, which were then picked up by the law clerks.[18] In other instances, an offender arrived in court after being apprehended by the authorities. The judge of first instance was responsible for investigating the case, including obtaining witness testimony, and making a judgment on the basis of established law or existing precedents. If the crime called for the guilty party to receive a beating of up to 57 strokes with the light stick, a county magistrate could adjudicate the matter and carry out the punishment without recourse to higher review. If the punishment was a beating of up to 87 strokes, it could be carried out at the prefecture or superior prefecture level and the case would be closed. If the offense called for a beating of 97 or 107 strokes, the Directorate-General of a circuit or a Pacification Office of a region could adjudicate it without further review. But harsher penalties, such as penal servitude, life exile, or death, had to be passed up to the Ministry of Punishments for approval.[19] Thus, minor crimes were meant to be handled at the local level, but more serious matters had to be passed up for a verdict by a higher court. In such cases, the lower court was required to collect evidence and forward the case dossier with a provisional opinion. Each court along the way up also usually issued a provisional judgment, which was to be appended to the case file. As in earlier

17. See Ratchnevsky 1993.

18. Hayden 1978, 209n29.

19. These basic regulations for handling criminal cases are found in the 1291 legal compilation the *Zhiyuan xinge* (New statutes of the *zhiyuan* period [1264–1295]). See Ch'en 1979, 152–156 for a translation (Chinese original, p. 166). They are also found in YDZ 39:1b. See discussions in Hu 2007, 166; Chen (2000) 2005; and Ch'en 1979, 71ff. During the Yuan, there were eleven degrees of punishment by beatings, namely 7, 17, 27, 37, 47, or 57 blows of the light stick and 67, 77, 87, 97, or 107 blows of the heavy stick. By contrast, in other dynasties there were ten degrees in units of 10 (10 to 50 with the light stick, 60 to 100 with the heavy stick). See Ch'en 1979, 48–51.

dynasties, plaintiffs could also bring their cases to a higher court for review if they were unhappy with the verdict of a lower court.[20]

In addition, cases would be passed up the hierarchy for review if the local office could not determine an applicable law, no matter how minor the crime. These are the types of cases found in the *Yuan dianzhang*. One of the most surprising aspects of the *Yuan dianzhang* is the number of seemingly minor cases that get passed up for review, all the way to the Central Secretariat or even the emperor. None of the translated cases resulted in a punishment of more than 107 strokes, and most resulted in considerably less, yet nearly every case was sent up to the Central Secretariat for a decision, with reviews and provisional rulings by offices along the way. In the documents, local judicial authorities express their uncertainty about the law and request a decision by the higher office, and so forth on up. This situation inevitably caused delays and inefficiencies in the legal system, as even relatively minor cases might be judged by many different offices. Khubilai's close advisor Hu Zhiyu 胡祇遹 (1227–1295) commented on this problem. He asserted that the local authorities were in a better position to judge minor crimes, and complained that they were passing up cases unnecessarily, thereby clogging the system:

> If they do not assume this responsibility and push off their work, things get messy and out of hand; cases drag on and cannot be settled.

And he chastised the county magistrates for sending up so many minor cases:

> If there are no serious crimes involved, the county authorities should take care of the cases themselves. It is not suitable for them to send dispatches up to the prefecture, superior prefecture, or circuit level, or to raise them with the [Regional] Surveillance Office.[21]

In the absence of a legal code, judges were insecure about their decisions and frequently abdicated judicial responsibility to avoid reprisals. Hu Zhiyu also notes that local officials (whom he suspects of being corrupt) feared audits of their decisions by the Regional Surveillance Offices of the Censorate.[22] A typical

---

20. Hu (2007, 167) notes that there were no limits stipulated for such reviews. For the situation in the Song, see Birge 2002, 74–75 and Miyazaki 1980, 66. Civil cases in the Song could not be appealed to the emperor, thus no judgment was unambiguously final, a situation not found in the Yuan. On the procedure in earlier dynasties, see Johnson and Twitchett 1993; Barbieri-Low and Yates, 1:111–186.

21. *Zazhu* 23:237–238. See also Hu 2007, 166.

22. *Zazhu* 23:238. For examples of such audits, see cases 18.12, 18.15, and 18.17 in Part II.

Figure 2.1 Courtroom scene. From *Ming Rongyu tang ke Shuihu zhuan tu*. (Original, late Ming. Reprint, Beijing: Zhonghua shu ju, 1965, 22:1a.)

pattern of adjudication and appeals, as seen in the *Yuan dianzhang*, began with a county magistrate, who would record the results of his investigation, including the basic facts of the case and any confession or testimony of offenders, accomplices, plaintiffs, or witnesses. The document might give a provisional ruling and note the lack of clear applicable law on which to base a verdict. The magistrate would then pass the case up to the prefectural or circuit level, depending on which was the next-highest level above the county. These had facilities to keep offenders in detention awaiting trial for long periods, which were lacking at the county level. At the level of a superior prefecture (*fu*) and above, there were also specialized judicial officials, including a Legal Officer (or judge, *tuiguan* 推官), to handle criminal cases.[23] A prefecture would pass the case up to the circuit, with or without a provisional judgment. The circuit authorities would then review the case and issue a provisional ruling. The circuit was the key office in issuing legal decisions at the local level. The Legal Officer carried out the main investigation, including interrogating witnesses, and checked for applicable law, but the ruling itself had to be issued collectively and only after a conference of officials serving in the Directorate-General of the circuit. These included the Director-General and the Agent (*darughachi*), who together headed the office, the Legal Officer, and others of sufficiently high rank. The circuit would then prepare a report describing the facts of the case and their ruling. Phrases in the *Yuan dianzhang* that frequently preface the findings, such as "We the circuit authorities deliberated together and determined that . . . ," refer to this joint conference.[24] If a circuit was within the Central Province (Zhongshusheng), it could send its report directly to one of the Six Ministries requesting a judgment, and the ministry could convey its ruling directly back to the circuit, without passing through the Central Secretariat. Outside the Central Province, however, the circuit had to send its report to the relevant branch secretariat, which would forward the matter to the Central Secretariat, which would in turn send it to one of the Six Ministries for a decision. The ministry would then send its decision back to the Central Secretariat for approval, and the Central Secretariat would send the ruling back out to the branch secretariat and down the chain of administration. Each report, including the final ruling, included the decisions of

23. See discussion in Ch'en 1979, 72–75 and Farquhar 1990, 111, 414, 419.
24. See, for instance, case 18.8, among many other examples.

the subordinate offices. Thus we find that the *Yuan dianzhang* documents as many as five or six verdicts in a particular case, issued at various levels of government, and often conflicting with each other. They reveal dialogue and contention over fundamental questions governing issues of marriage and family relations, making the *Yuan dianzhang* especially valuable to legal and social historians.

The flow of documents is clearly indicated in the *Yuan dianzhang* text. Specialized terms for each document identify what level of office has issued it. Thus a county or prefecture would issue a "dispatch" (*shen* 申) to the circuit above. The circuit would issue a "report" (*cheng* 呈) to one of the Six Ministries or to a branch secretariat. The branch secretariat was allowed to issue a "communiqué" (*zi* 咨) to the Central Secretariat, indicating its equal status with that body. The Central Secretariat would issue a "superior communication" (*zhafu* 札付 or 劄付) to one of the Six Ministries, a term for a document from an office rank 2 and above to an inferior. Each of these documents, and many others, could only be used by an office of a specific rank. Moreover, a different type of document would be issued to a superior than to an inferior. (In Part II, I have indicated in footnotes the particulars of each document type at first mention in the translation.)

Sources of Law and Adjudication in the Absence of a Legal Code

The Yuan is unique among major dynasties in China in that it never promulgated a formal legal code. When the Mongols first conquered parts of north China, they followed the example of the Liao and Jin before them and allowed different laws to apply to different ethnic or cultural groups. In general, Chinese were subject to the old Taihe code of the Jurchen Jin promulgated in 1202, while Mongol customary law continued to be applied to Mongols and other Inner Asians. Muslim western Asians were allowed to follow Muslim law. For instance, in 1268, the authorities of Dadu Circuit (Beijing) consulted a Muslim cleric (*qadi*) to resolve a marriage dispute between two Muslim residents of the city.[25] In the initial stages of the conquest, special Mongol judges called *jarghuchi* (Chinese *zhaluhuochi* 札魯火赤, *zhaluhuachi* 劄魯花赤, and other variations) were put in charge of adjudicating cases, as was the case in Persia and other subject

---

25. Case 18.44, translated in Part II.

areas. Although the Persian historian Rashīd al-Dīn and others praised the work of these judges in west Asia, in China they were widely condemned for their harsh and arbitrary rule. In most areas, local civil authorities gradually took over cases involving Chinese, and within the local administrative offices (called ya-mens), special Law Offices (*fasi* 法司) were maintained for this purpose. These had existed under the Jin and they specialized in deciding cases on the basis of the Taihe code. The *jarghuchi* continued to handle cases involving Mongols and other Inner Asians.[26]

There is no evidence that the Taihe code of the Jin was ever promulgated as a formal code, although it was used in adjudication. Khubilai expressed dissatis-faction with it. He blamed the prevalence of violence and brigandage in north China on the Taihe code and on judges' having too much discretion in using it.[27] The statesman Wu Cheng 吳澄 (1249–1333) wrote that Khubilai wanted to es-tablish his own laws and abolish the codes of previous dynasties as other founding rulers had done.[28] Other advisors criticized the Taihe code as being too harsh or including too many Jurchen customs.[29] The pluralistic legal system, moreover, posed challenges for the Mongol-Yuan, as it had for the Khitan-Liao and Jurchen-Jin before. People under Yuan rule borrowed customs from each other, and we find frequent warnings from judges that people in one group were not to appeal to the laws of another group.[30] Determining a person's cultural identity for the purposes of the law could also be problematic. It is clear that some residents of north China saw themselves as bicultural or multicultural.[31] Chinese frequently adopted Mongol names and sometimes Mongols adopted Chinese ones, and in-termarriage across cultural groups also created confusion over what law should apply to whom.[32]

---

26. The situation was not clear-cut. In instances of serious crimes, Chinese in the north were still subject to the jurisdiction of the *jarghuchi,* and these had wide jurisdiction in the capital cities of Dadu and Shangdu. The issue of their authority was debated throughout the Yuan. Special judges called *jarghuchi* served in other offices as well. See Ratchnevsky 1993; Farquhar 1990, 244, 248, 338, 154; Ch'en 1979, 82–83, 153n145; Jagchid Sechin 1980a.

27. YS 14:289; Birge 2010, 391–392.

28. *Wu Wenzheng gong ji* 11:26a, 232; Ch'en 1979, 13–14.

29. YS 102:2603; *Qingya ji* 4:27; Yao 1986, 118ff.; Ch'en 1979, 13–14.

30. See, for instance, Chapter 7, case 18.57.

31. See the example in Steinhardt 2007.

32. Chen Gaohua 2000; Hung 1997a, 1997b.

In the eleventh month of 1271, Khubilai issued a blanket order to stop using the Taihe code.[33] This came at the same time that he formally established his dynasty and declared its title to be "Yuan," which underscores Khubilai's wish to put into effect his own system of laws, appropriate to his dynasty. But the abrogation of the Taihe code before another system was in place caused serious concern among Khubilai's advisors and top officials. They repeatedly admonished Khubilai to issue a comprehensive code on which judges could base their decisions.[34] They also complained that the absence of clear laws gave rise to corruption and malfeasance on the part of local officials. The translated cases reveal the underlying insecurity that magistrates felt about making decisions without a firm basis in codified law or in the absence of an applicable precedent. Phrases like "There has not yet been a ruling in a similar case to use as a precedent" or "We have not received a universally applicable precedent" appear frequently in the *Yuan dianzhang*. Sometimes even the Central Secretariat issued a ruling that was provisional "until a universally applicable precedent is established."[35] Judges continued to cite the Taihe code of the Jin with relative frequency even after Khubilai rejected its use in late 1271, although it was usually cited for reference, and a different (usually more lenient) sentence was applied than what the code would have mandated. Judges similarly cited the Tang and Song codes in their verdicts.[36] Private legal writings also attest to the importance of earlier codes for literati officials. At least ten commentaries on the Northern Song text *Xingtong fu* 刑統賦 (Ode to the Song code) were written during the Yuan.[37] The original *Xingtong fu* was a prose-poem in rhymed verse that served as a mnemonic device for officials to memorize the Song code (the *Song xingtong* 宋刑統), and it provided guidelines for how to apply the code and adjust punishments when there were mitigating circumstances.

33. See YDZ 18:15b (Chapter 6, case 18.29); *Qingya ji* 4:27a–b; *Yuandai zouyi jilu,* 188–189; YS 7:138.

34. Ch'en 1979, 14–16; Birge 2002, 211.

35. See, for example, YDZ 17:15b, and cases 18.4, 18.10, and 18.23, translated in Part II. See also Birge 2010, 399–400.

36. Birge 2010, 392–394.

37. Langlois 1981, 174ff. The founder of the Ming dynasty, Zhu Yuanzhang, and his Confucian advisors saw the lack of a legal code as a grievous failure of the Yuan dynasty. In response, Zhu promulgated a comprehensive legal code in 1367, even before the official founding of the dynasty. See Langlois 1982; Farmer 1995. These Confucian officials understood law as the embodiment of a cosmic moral order and the foundation of a harmonious society. See Jiang 2011.

Khubilai was not deaf to the appeals for a comprehensive code. Already in 1262 he had ordered two Chinese ministers to compile a code for his dynasty, and in 1273 they presented a complete draft for Khubilai's consideration titled *Da Yuan xinlü* 大元新律 (New laws of the great Yuan). Khubilai gave it to his Mongolian advisors for their suggestions, but in the end no code was promulgated.[38] Instead, Khubilai in 1291 issued a set of ordinances titled *Zhiyuan xinge* 至元新格 (New statutes of the *zhiyuan* period [1264–1295]), drafted in ten short sections by his Chinese advisor He Rongzu 何榮祖 (dates unknown), then head of the Central Secretariat. These mostly addressed administrative matters and official malfeasance, prime concerns of Khubilai's government at this time.[39] After Khubilai's death in 1294, He Rongzu at the command of Emperor Chengzong (Temür, r. 1294–1307) drafted another, more comprehensive, code, titled *Dade lüling* 大德律令 (Laws and statutes of the *dade* period [1297–1308]) which he presented to the emperor around 1305. His death soon afterwards, however, prevented the project from going forward.[40] Other attempts to issue a comprehensive code by Khubilai and the emperors who followed him also failed.[41]

Efforts at establishing a formal legal code having been unsuccessful, the Yuan court turned its attention to compiling collections of imperial edicts and judicial decisions to be used as the basis for adjudication. Emperor Renzong (Ayurbarwada, r. 1311–1320) promoted these efforts, and in 1323, during the reign of his successor, Yingzong (Shidebala, r. 1321–1323), the court issued such a collection with the title *Da Yuan tongzhi* 大元通制 (Comprehensive regulations of the great Yuan). A Ming dynasty manuscript of the "Statutes" section of this work survives and was published in 1930 with the title *Tongzhi tiaoge* 通制條格 (Statutes from the *Comprehensive Regulations*).[42] The *Da Yuan tongzhi* was

38. YS 8:151–152; YS 126:3083.

39. This work largely survives today as reconstructed from fragments. See Uematsu 1972; Ch'en 1979; *Yuandai falü*, 9–34. These are translated into English by Ch'en 1997. On its authorship, see Ch'en 1997, 16. The *Zhiyuan xinge* came out shortly after the purge of the corrupt minister Sangha and his followers, who had been enemies of He Rongzu.

40. Ch'en 1979, 19–20.

41. Ch'en 1979, 14–15.

42. A definitive punctuated and annotated modern edition, based on the original Ming manuscript, was produced by Fang Linggui 方齡貴 with the title *Tongzhi tiaoge jiaozhu* (Beijing, 2001). (All further citations are to this edition, hereafter cited as TZTG.) For an earlier punctuated edition, see Huang 1986. There is also a Japanese translation of the work published in three volumes (Kobayashi and Okamota 1964–1976). On the *Tongzhi tiage* in general, see Birge 2002, 212–213; Ch'en 1979, 24–28.

translated into Mongolian. A fragment of it, excavated at Khara Khoto, survives in the Institute of Oriental Studies in St. Petersburg.[43] In 1346 the court of Emperor Shundi (r. 1333–1368) issued a continuation of this compilation, titled *Zhizheng tiaoge* 至正條格 (Statutes of the *zhizheng* period [1341–1368]). This work was long thought to be lost, but a partial edition was rediscovered in Korea in 2002, in the private library of a family residing near Kyŏngju. It was published in 2007 by the Academy of Korean Studies, in two volumes containing a photoreproduction and a typeset, punctuated edition.[44]

Earlier, in 1332, the court of Emperor Wenzong (Tugh Temür, r. 1328–1332) issued a massive collection of administrative and legal documents titled *Jingshi dadian* 經世大典 (Great compendium for administering the world). One section of this, the *Xiandian* 憲典 ("Judicial Institutions"), collected together the laws that had been established during the dynasty and the punishments for infractions. In this regard it resembled the legal codes of other dynasties, but it was never promulgated as a formal code. The *Xiandian* section was copied into the Yuan dynastic history (*Yuanshi*) as the *Xingfazhi* 刑法志 ("Treatise on Punishments"), where we find it today.[45] Many of the decisions in the *Yuan dianzhang* are mentioned therein.

The *Yuan dianzhang* was produced within this context of a general lack of codified law on which to base the administration of justice. Seen from this perspective, we can appreciate its significance and importance within the legal system of the early fourteenth century.

43. Munkuyev 1970; Kara 2003. My own research on this document confirms Munkuyev's hypothesis that it is a fragment from the *Tongzhi tiaoge,* but I conclude that it comes from a different section than what Munkuyev posits and for different reasons than he suggests.

44. See *Zhizheng tiaoge* (Korean title *Chijŏng chogyŏk*). This work was very influential in Korea, which helps explain why it survived there; see Bourgon and Roux 2016, 39–42.

45. For evidence that the "Treatise on Punishments" is from the *Jingshi dadian,* see Liu Xiao 2004; Abe 1972, 253–271, 304–306. The complete "Treatise on Punishments" has been translated into French and published with annotation in four volumes as *Un Code des Yüan* (Ratchnevsky and Aubin 1972–1985).

CHAPTER THREE

Origins, Contents, and Transmission of the *Yuan dianzhang*

Among the treasures removed for safekeeping from the imperial palace in Beijing prior to World War II, which eventually became the nucleus of the collection of the National Palace Museum in Taipei, is the only extant original printing of the *Da Yuan shengzheng guochao dianzhang* (Statutes and precedents of the sacred administration of the great Yuan dynastic state), known by its abbreviated name *Yuan dianzhang* (Statutes and precedents of the Yuan dynasty). The voluminous work, containing sixty chapters (*juan* 卷) plus a supplement, was produced in 1322, more than a century before Gutenberg's bible, in forty string-bound booklets (known as fascicules) that fit comfortably into one's hand.[1] Between these covers is one of the most remarkable and valuable texts that we have for the study of medieval Chinese history.

Origins and Nature of the Text

The exact origins of the *Yuan dianzhang* remain a mystery. It lacks a colophon with publication details, but the appearance of the work gives us clues to its provenance. Distinct features of each page tell us that it was produced in the commercial printing center of Jianyang, in the northern part of modern Fujian

---

1. Guoli gugong bowuyuan 1971, 69, 88, 107, plate 19; Guoli gugong bowuyuan 1983, 571. The fascicules measure 23.5 by 15 centimeters (about 9 by 6 inches), not unlike a standard book today but much thinner. I had the pleasure and privilege of inspecting the work in person in December 2006. I thank my colleague Lau Nap-yin of the Academia Sinica for the introduction that made this possible.

Province. Like other premodern Chinese books, two pages are printed on one side of a sheet, which is then folded in two and bound into the book at the open edge, creating two pages of the volume. Along the center fold of the sheet (the characters now split between two pages) are found in abbreviated form the title of the whole work, the *juan* number, and the page number within the *juan*.[2] In the *Yuan dianzhang*, these are framed by black highlights, called "fish tails" (*yuwei* 魚尾). A thin black stripe, called a "black mouth" (*heiko* 黑口) or "elephant trunk" (*xiangbi* 象鼻), appears above and below the information along this fold in the sheet, which like the fish tails helped tell the binder where to fold the page. A black line marks the four edges of the printed frame, with a double line on the left and right sides. The characters are in a distinctive, thin style, with eighteen columns and twenty-eight characters per column crowded onto a page, within a frame size of just 19.9 by 13.2 centimeters (7.8 by 5.2 inches).[3] A supplement, bound together with the rest of the text, crams nineteen columns with thirty characters each onto each printed page. In places the text uses simplified forms of characters found in the Yuan, which could speed the process of carving the wood blocks for printing. These features make the *Yuan dianzhang* recognizable as a Jianyang commercial imprint.[4] (See Figure 3.1.) Such imprints were produced for the flourishing book trade in fourteenth-century China, and the market for this substantial work would have extended far beyond its point of production to towns and urban centers all over Yuan territory.

Information about who produced the *Yuan dianzhang* can also be deduced from internal evidence and visual aspects of its pages. The magnitude of the work and its importance for governance have led some scholars to assume that it was produced under official auspices.[5] But we can conclude from the evidence that

---

2. For *juan* 18, the "Marriage" chapter, each page states "Dianzhang Hu 4" (典章戶四), meaning the fourth *juan* of the "Hubu" (Ministry of Revenue) section of the *Yuan dianzhang*, corresponding to *juan* 18 of the whole work. The page number appears further below.

3. These dimensions are from Guoli gugong bowuyuan 1971, 69, 88, 107. Chang (1972, 1) gives the slightly smaller dimensions of 19.5 by 13 centimeters, and the modern online catalog of the National Palace Museum gives the slightly larger measurements of 20.3 by 13.4 (see http://www.npm.gov.tw/exhbition/age1010/m2_mainframe1_8h.htm).

4. See Tian 2003, 2, 217–218, 240–241; Chia 2002, 43–44, 50–51, 106–107.

5. See, for instance, de Pee 2007, 201.

Figure 3.1 Sample pages from the *Yuan dianzhang,* woodblock printed in 1322. The thin, crowded style of the characters and distinctive elements in the margins, such as black highlights, indicate that the work was published in the commercial printing center of Jianyang, Fujian. The titles of cases are flagged by a circle and printed in white on black. References to the emperor start a new line and are elevated above the rest of the text. (From the collection of the National Palace Museum.)

it was not a formal government publication. Rather it was probably a collaboration between an official or member of the local elite with access to government archives and a commercial printing establishment in Jianyang. The aesthetic qualities alone argue against the work being an official state sponsored production. The *Yuan dianzhang* is in the form of a "small-character volume" or "small-format edition" (*xiaozi ben* 小字本), displaying the cramped orthography of the cheaper Jianyang imprints. A more amply financed and lavishly produced official publication would be in the medium- or large-character format with the characters more majestically spaced and more white space showing on the page.[6] The paper also would likely be of higher quality. The copious number of characters squeezed onto each page of the *Yuan dianzhang* is on the high end, even for the commercial productions of Jianyang.[7]

Other evidence also indicates that the work was not produced under official auspices. Most telling is the fact that the "Treatise on Punishments" (*Xingfazhi*) of the Yuan dynastic history (*Yuanshi*) does not list the *Yuan dianzhang* among the legal compilations produced during the dynasty, each of which it describes in its opening pages.[8] Other known Yuan legal compilations, some extant, some now lost, are included in these pages, but the *Yuan dianzhang* is conspicuously missing. Additionally, any work published under official auspices in the Yuan had to be approved by the central government, and the formal document granting approval is usually found at the front of the work.[9] The *Yuan dianzhang* includes no such approval. Instead, it cleverly reproduces on its title page a faux version of such an approval. This is a communication from the Central Secretariat issued in 1303, which states its endorsement of a request from an official in Jiangxi to have "statutes and precedents (*ge li* 格例) from the *zhongtong* era (1260) to the present collected and made into a book, to be distributed throughout the land."[10] The *Yuan dianzhang* fits this description, and its compilers no doubt wanted their book to be seen as responding to this call from the Central Secretariat. The Central Secretariat's communication, however, had no direct connection to the *Yuan dianzhang* per se and did not constitute approval of any particular work. Nevertheless, the text of this communication—appearing

6. For examples of such works compared to the *Yuan dianzhang*, see Guoli gugong bowuyuan 1971, plates 15–22. Plate 19 is the *Yuan dianzhang*. The designation of small or large format was based on the number of columns on the page and characters per column, not on the size of the whole page or the actual book, which was fairly consistent over time in China (Chia 2002, 42–43, 104). Jianyang also produced some high-quality imprints, with official sanction or private funding (see Chia 2002, 104–106). The 1972 and 1976 facsimile reprints of the *Yuan dianzhang* by the National Palace Museum both reproduce the character frame slightly larger than the original and add wide margins all around resulting in larger volumes than the originals, thereby conveying the image of a more imposing work.

7. See Chia 2002, appendix A.

8. YS 102:2603–2604; Ratchnevsky and Aubin 1972–1985, 1:1–3.

9. Tian 2003, 1–2. An example of such a document from the Central Secretariat survives in the Naikaku Bunko library in Tokyo and is reproduced in Miya 2001, plates I, II, III. For other examples, see the opening pages of *Dao yuan leigao*, *Ma Shitian wenji*, *Zhizheng Jinling xinzhi*, and *Guochao wenlei*, in the editions listed in the Bibliography of this volume.

10. YDZ *gangmu*:1a. A complete translation of this document is found in Appendix A.

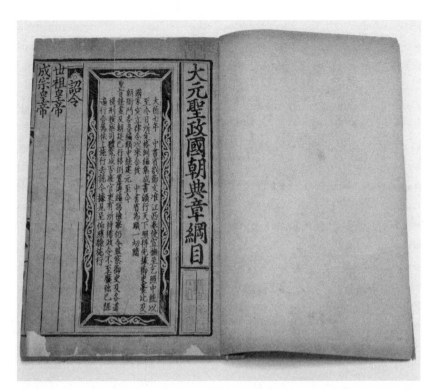

Figure 3.2 Title page of the *Yuan dianzhang*. Set off by a decorative cartouche, the opening page of the *Yuan dianzhang* contains a communication dated 1303 from the Central Secretariat endorsing the publication of a collection of "statutes and precedents" issued since the beginning of Khubilai's reign, in 1260. The seals at the bottom right are in red and indicate that the book once belonged to the famous library of Mao Jin (1599–1659) of Changshu. A third red seal appears at the top right. (From the collection of the National Palace Museum.)

on the very first page of the *Yuan dianzhang* and highlighted by a handsome cartouche with an elaborately decorated border—suggests to readers that the work had the official imprimatur of the government (see Figure 3.2).

The title of the work also skillfully imparts an impression of importance. The term "dianzhang" has the general meaning of "institutions" or "workings of government" and evokes a work of grandiose scale. At the same time, the original request from the Jiangxi official, advertised on the opening page, explicitly names "statutes and precedents" (*ge li* 格例). And the Central Secretariat's communication in response cites an earlier request from the Censorate for the same thing in the same terms, a collection of "statutes and precedents" to be used for making judicial decisions in the absence of a legal code. The term *dian* by itself can mean something like "statute," and the word *zhang* by itself can mean something similar to "substatute" or "precedent," implying something closer to the actual content of the *Yuan dianzhang*. My translation as *Statutes and Precedents of the Yuan Dynasty* is meant to reflect this more accurate description of the contents.[11]

No author's or compiler's name is recorded in the *Yuan dianzhang*, and the exact circumstances of its printing cannot be known, but from internal evidence we can make several conjectures. The scale of the work and the legal documents it contains indicate that its publication involved some kind of collaboration with regional or local officials. We know that officials outside the capital made efforts to collect imperial orders and legal decisions to use as precedents. A funerary inscription for the official Wang Duzhong 王都中 (1279–1341) describes how, around the late 1290s and early 1300s, when he was the Assistant Pacification Commissioner of Zhedong Region (in the northern part of modern Zhejiang Province), he worried that in the absence of official laws and regulations, local officials could easily engage in corrupt practices and make questionable rulings. The inscription recounts: "He collected official regulations and judicial precedents into eighty portfolios, so that officials would have something to follow and not find it so easy to engage in malfeasance."[12] Later Wang was promoted to become a leading official in the Jiangzhe Branch Secretariat (comprising roughly modern Zhejiang and Fujian), whose jurisdiction included Jianyang, giving him all the access and resources needed to compile a work like the *Yuan dianzhang*.

Most likely, an official like Wang Duzhong who had access to official archives and who may have collected materials from a previous posting teamed up with a commercial publishing house in Jianyang to produce the *Yuan dianzhang*. The documents themselves and their arrangement in the collection further suggest this. Each document in the work is a copy of a legal decision, administrative order, or imperial edict sent out by the central government. The originals of such official correspondence were kept in archives in the local yamen, filed under the

11. The full title of the supplement includes the terms *dian* and *zhang* in parallel with *tiao* 條 and *li* 例, which also mean "statutes and precedents," again implying a correspondence between these terms. Quite a few scholars have translated the title as "Institutions of the Yuan Dynasty."

12. *Jinhua ji* 31:8b–9a (315–316). See also *Quan Yuanwen* 30:418–419. This could possibly have been an early version of the *Yuan dianzhang* itself. I thank Liu Xiao for making this suggestion and drawing my attention to this reference.

name of each of the Six Ministries, according to which ministry had issued the document. In the *Yuan dianzhang*, too, the documents are arranged under the names of the Six Ministries, as they would have been archived in the yamen. This suggests that they were copied, at least in part, from one or more local archives. Such material may have then been supplemented with additional legal documents that circulated privately or were even published separately. Many of the documents are addressed to government bureaus in the area of modern Fujian, suggesting that the archive was located in Fujian, perhaps even in Jianyang itself, where the work was published.[13]

Some scholars have conjectured that the *Yuan dianzhang* grew out of an earlier work, the *Dade dianzhang* 大德典章 (Statutes and precedents of the *dade* era [1297–1307]), which would have been produced sometime after 1303 and before 1307. The *Dade dianzhang*, which survives only in fragments, might have been compiled in response to the call for such a collection from the Central Secretariat in 1303, reproduced on the first page of the *Yuan dianzhang*.[14] The *Dade dianzhang* may have been an early edition of the *Yuan dianzhang*. This is supported by evidence suggesting that the *Yuan dianzhang* came out in several editions, each one adding to the one before.[15] Irregularities in the pagination and mismatches between the table of contents and the body of the work suggest that the collection was published several times with new material added into different sections. Some material is also excised. Pages and parts of pages are curiously missing. In a few places, one can make out scrape marks, indicating that passages were excised from the printing blocks. One example of such erasure is in the section on imperial edicts at the beginning of the work. It is possible that edicts published in a previous edition may have been reversed by a later emperor, and the editors did not dare to reprint them.

The circumstances of the publication of the *Yuan dianzhang* explain other errors and lacunae in the text. The commercial printers of Jianyang sought speed

13. See comments in Miyazaki (1954) 1975; Uematsu 1972; Chang 1972. Yuanzhou Circuit has also been suggested as the location of the archive (Uematsu 1992, 58).

14. See discussion in Niida (1940) 1991 and Ch'en 1979, 19–22. Ch'en assumes this was an imperially ordered compilation, but like the *Yuan dianzhang*, it was more likely a private undertaking. The extant fragments of this work survive in the *Yongle dadian;* they are reprinted in *Yuandai falü,* 50–62.

15. Shen Jiaben remarked on this in 1908 (*Yuan dianzhang* [1964], 2:809), as did other early commentators. See also Chang 1972; Niida (1940) 1991; Miya 2006, 438.

and economy in their productions; consequently, the proofreaders were not particularly attentive and the block carvers were not overly meticulous. Characters are sometimes miswritten or left out. Occasionally phrases or whole sentences are missing. These can sometimes be filled in from other places in the text where a passage is repeated, or from another Yuan source that preserves the same document. At other times, one has to surmise from the context what the text should read.[16]

The hasty production, on the other hand, also contributes to the value of the *Yuan dianzhang* as a historical source. The editors made no attempt to rework the documents or make them consistent with each other (other than the few excisions previously described). Decisions recorded in later documents contradict earlier ones. And within the same document, one finds judges at higher levels routinely reversing lower level decisions. It is not unusual to have as many as five or six rulings in one case, all different from each other.

The lack of editing is particularly evident if we compare the *Yuan dianzhang* to a similar legal collection produced by the court at about the same time, the *Da Yuan tongzhi* 大元通制 (Comprehensive regulations of the great Yuan), promulgated in 1323. A part of this work survives in a Ming manuscript under the title *Tongzhi tiaoge* 通制條格 (Statutes from the *Comprehensive Regulations*).[17] The *Tongzhi tiaoge* contains some of the same cases as the *Yuan dianzhang,* but the *Tongzhi tiaoge* cases are heavily edited. Lower rulings and contradictory rulings are deleted, as are redundancies and unnecessary language. Sometimes the basis for a decision recorded in the *Tongzhi tiaoge* is different from that found in the *Yuan dianzhang.* The resulting documents are much shorter than the versions found in the *Yuan dianzhang,* and they serve to obscure the disagreements and discord that preceded the final legal rulings. Taken together, the documents in the *Tongzhi tiaoge* conform to a consistent legal agenda. The *Tongzhi tiaoge* reveals the careful editing of central government legal experts, who thereby produced a coherent legal compendium to serve as a source

16. I have indicated in footnotes every case where my translation incorporates a variant from what appears in the original text. With some exceptions, I have followed the corrections indicated in the punctuated edition (Chen Gaohua et al. 2011) produced by the Yuan Research Group of the Institute of History, Chinese Academy of Social Sciences, Beijing.

17. My citations of this text are to the 2001 edition, punctuated and annotated by Fang Linggui, hereafter cited as TZTG. For an earlier punctuated edition, see Huang 1986; and for a Japanese translation, see Kobayashi and Okamota 1964–1976.

of law. The *Yuan dianzhang* on the other hand presents no such consistency or coherent legal narrative. Rather, the documents reveal disagreements within the bureaucracy over fundamental legal principles and social values. They also reveal the fluidity of the law and allow one to track changes in policy over time. The existence of the *Tongzhi tiaoge*, published by the court at almost the same time as the *Yuan dianzhang*, also points to the conclusion that the latter lacked any imperial commission.

Context, Contents, and Audience

The unusual juridical situation of the Yuan helps explain why the *Yuan dianzhang* would likely have been a commercial success for its publisher. Unlike any other major dynasty in Chinese history, the Yuan did not promulgate a formal legal code. Instead, magistrates and judges at all levels were left to base their judgments on imperial edicts and judicial decisions issued by the central government.[18] In the absence of a code, both officials and local literati made efforts to compile collections of these decisions to serve as precedents in administering the law. The *Yuan dianzhang* was just such a collection. Indeed, the Central Secretariat's communication of 1303 calling for such a compilation, reprinted at the front of the *Yuan dianzhang* as a spurious endorsement, makes this point. It cites an earlier appeal by the Censorate to collect, edit, and compile "imperial regulations and statutes and precedents issued by the court" so that "officials and clerks will have something to follow and government orders will not be disregarded."[19]

Along these lines, the *Yuan dianzhang* is designed as a handy legal reference work. The entire work is divided into ten broad categories. These are: "Imperial Decrees" (*zhaoling* 詔令), "Sage Administration" (*shengzheng* 聖政), "Court Principles" (*chaogang* 朝綱), "Censorate Principles" (*taigang* 臺綱), plus one for each of the Six Ministries: Personnel, Revenue, Rites, War, Punishments, and Works. Under each category are multiple chapters (*juan*), for a total of 60 chapters in all. The first four categories together contain just 6 chapters of the 60. The Imperial Decrees category, for instance, includes only a limited number of edicts of major national importance, such as the announcement of a new reign

18. For the difficulties and inadequacies of this system, see Birge 2010.
19. YDZ *gangmu*:1a.

period or the accession of a new emperor. The bulk of the work, 54 chapters of the 60, is taken up with material found under the six categories for the Six Ministries. In fact, imperial edicts on relevant topics appear in the chapters under the headings for the Six Ministries together with other documents. Within each chapter, the cases are grouped into sections by topic, the titles of which are highlighted in large, bold characters. Within each of these sections, the cases are chronological. Sometimes a case was judged by a different ministry than the one under which it appears, and sometimes a case was judged by more than one ministry. Considerations of topic seem to have taken priority in the arrangement of the cases. Each case is given a title, presumably by the editors, flagged by a circle and set off in white on black characters. (See Figure 3.1.) But these do not always match the content very well (evidence again of the haphazard editing job of the Jianyang commercial press). At the front of the work is a list of "General Contents" (*gangmu* 綱目) with all the category and chapter titles given. This is followed by a detailed "Table of Contents" (*mulu* 目錄) listing the title of every case in the collection (with a few errors). Of particular note is the presence of a chart at the beginning of most chapters that summarizes the legal decisions included in the chapter. The charts present these in the form of general prohibitions with the punishment for violators indicated. These summary charts taken together could be read as a rudimentary law code.

The *Yuan dianzhang* was probably most attractive to magistrates and local officials, who presided over the courts of first instance. But officials at all levels of government would find it a useful handbook. In addition to providing a quasi law code containing precedents to use in deciding legal cases and administering state affairs, the work is filled with practical information that any official would want at his fingertips. These include titles that went with a particular rank, mourning grades and requirements for all manner of relatives, and the type of document to send to any particular office according to the rank of sender and receiver.[20] Beyond officialdom, legal specialists, whose numbers were burgeoning at this time, would also be eager buyers. These precursors to modern lawyers advised people about the law and helped them draw up documents to file lawsuits or petition the government. Their services made the courts available to a broad segment of Yuan society, as we see in the translated cases. More generally, members

---

20. YDZ 29:1a (for document types), 30:1a (for mourning grades).

of the educated elite would likely have been glad to acquire a copy at a local market to have on their bookshelves. People of means had frequent recourse to the law, and might buy such a work to consult. Legal knowledge by Yuan times was no longer confined to officialdom but had spread to the literate populace at large.[21] Books like the *Yuan dianzhang* both reflected that new reality and helped to create it.

Language and Format

A salient feature of the documents in the *Yuan dianzhang* is the mixture of writing styles that they contain. These include three distinct types. The first and most common is a literary, bureaucratic Chinese that is found in legal writings of other dynasties. Within these passages, however, also appear specialized terms used in the Yuan dynasty and sometimes foreign words rendered phonetically. The second type of writing is Yuan dynasty colloquial Chinese. This was used most often to record the testimony of witnesses and plaintiffs, and it suggests that the court scribes attempted to record the actual words of these people.[22] Colloquial language was also used in some official correspondence during the Yuan, a feature that sets the Yuan apart from other dynasties. The third form of writing is the most remarkable, what is termed Sino-Mongolian or "Direct Translation from Mongolian," or in Chinese "Hard Translation" (from Mongolian) (*yingyi wen* 硬譯文).[23] This consists of a direct word-for-word translation of Mongolian sentences, replacing the Mongolian words with Chinese characters, that preserves Mongolian syntax and word order. Mongolian prepositions and postpositions are rendered into Chinese particle characters that if read as regular Chinese make no sense but that are essential to determine the grammar and meaning of a passage. For instance, the Chinese term *gendi* 根底 indicates

21. Miyazaki (1954) 1975 stresses this point of the spread of legal knowledge to a wide populace. Hu Xingdong 2007, 15, also emphasizes that the *Yuan dianzhang* was for use by legal experts and litigants of all stripes.

22. In other dynasties, testimony was re-rendered into either literary Chinese or, as in the Qing, a standardized vernacular based on northern dialects. See comments in Sommer 2000, 26–29, on the recording and editing of witness and plaintiff testimony in legal case documents of the Qing.

23. There is a large literature on this language, especially in Japanese. Among the most useful are Yilinzhen 1982 and Tanaka 1964. See also works cited in Funada 1999.

that the preceding word is in the accusative, dative, locative, or genitive case.[24] In the documents of the *Yuan dianzhang,* these particles are all regularized and used consistently. The translation of the Mongolian words appears also by this time to have been fixed for most words. Dictionaries exist from after the Yuan, and it is likely that some kind of a dictionary existed during Khubilai's time to make these translations consistent.[25]

The Sino-Mongolian language was used to record anything originally in Mongolian, most often the pronouncements of the Yuan emperors, who all spoke in Mongolian.[26] Orders from the councilors of the Secretariat for State Affairs or other central bureaus are also at times in Sino-Mongolian, indicating that the orders were spoken or written originally in Mongolian. The Sino-Mongolian conveys a sense of "listening in" on the actual words uttered by the Mongol khans and their top advisors. The directness of the language and the colloquial Chinese in which it is rendered impart a sense of immediacy, of "being in the room" as it were. Both the straight colloquial Chinese and the Sino-Mongolian can appear quite jarring, and they give the text of the *Yuan dianzhang* a crude, vulgar tone, in contrast to the formal writing of traditional Chinese bureaucratic documents.

This unusual style of the *Yuan dianzhang* was noted by later scholars, who criticized the work for being coarse and inferior, lacking the proper quality for official documents. The Qing dynasty editors of the great imperial literary compendium, the *Siku quanshu* (Complete writings of the four treasuries) are a case in point. They decided not to include the *Yuan dianzhang* in the compendium, which was meant to preserve all worthy literature in the land.[27] But they also did not put it in the banned category, which included books the court deemed to be threatening to the state or otherwise unsuitable to be in print and thus liable for destruction if discovered. The *Yuan dianzhang* fell into a middle category of books that were noted and described in a catalog as part of the *Siku quanshu* compendium but were considered unworthy of tran-

24. On these grammatical constructions, see Poppe 1954.

25. See de Rachewiltz 2006.

26. Herbert Franke (1953) concludes that most of the Yuan emperors were not well versed in Chinese. Although Khubilai understood and spoke Chinese, he did not use it for his pronouncements.

27. The editors did their work from 1773 to 1782, during the Qianlong reign. On this collection, see Guy 1987; Wilkinson 2015, 945–954.

scription and inclusion in the actual collection. These books were given brief catalog descriptions (*tiyao* 提要), in which the editors also explain their reasons for rejecting a work. The words of the editors regarding the *Yuan dianzhang* are telling.

As in other entries, the editors start by noting in their catalog what edition and copy of the work they have examined. For the *Yuan dianzhang* they state: "Copy held in the Imperial Palace Library" (*neifu zangben* 內府藏本). They then go on to describe the book and its contents, naming the section headings, dates covered by the entries, and so forth. From this description we can conclude that the editors without question were handling the same book that now resides in the National Palace Museum in Taipei. They then go on to comment that the *Yuan dianzhang* is not mentioned in the Yuan dynastic history (*Yuanshi*), and they share their puzzled musings as to whether it is the same as the *Da Yuan tongzhi*, concluding that it is not:

> This book is not recorded in the *Yuanshi*, which only records the words of Order of the Golden Belt [*sic*] Censor Li Duan[28] of the second year of *zhizhi* (1322), as follows: "The regulations established from the reign of Shizu [Khubilai, r. 1260–1294] ought to be written down as statutes, so that officials will not be able to engage in malfeasance and those who judge legal cases will have something to follow."[29] Emperor Yingzong agreed. The book was completed with the title *Da Yuan tongzhi* (Comprehensive regulations of the great Yuan) and was promulgated throughout the empire. It contained 2,539 items. If one notes the time when this work was produced, one sees it is just the same as that of the *Yuan dianzhang*, but the number of items, 2,539, does not match the latter. And the communication from the Central Secretariat recorded at the beginning of the *Yuan dianzhang* also does not fit this work. Probably the *Yuan dianzhang* is a separate book, which is not the same as the *Tongzhi* (Comprehensive regulations).

28. The *Siku* editors accidentally include two characters from the previous sentence in the *Yuanshi* as part of the title for Li Duan. There was no such title as "Order of the Golden Belt" in the Yuan.

29. This passage is found in YS 28:625. Interestingly, this sentence uses vocabulary similar to that in the funerary inscription for Wang Duzhong by Huang Jin (cited earlier in this chapter), which would have been written about twenty years later than the ostensible date of Li Duan's words here. The information about the *Da Yuan tongzhi* that follows is also from the *Yuanshi*, though not quoted directly. Li Duan is only known from this *Yuanshi* reference (see Qiu 2000, 342).

The editors then comment on the hastily compiled and sketchy quality of the
Yuanshi and lament that very few legal materials have survived from the Yuan. In
particular, they note that the important late Yuan compendium *Jingshi dadian*
經世大典 (Great compendium on ordering the world) has long been lost, adding:
"Some fragments can be found in the [Ming dynasty compendium] *Yongle
dadian* 永樂大典, but these are scattered and out of order. They cannot be used
to reconstruct the work." In conclusion they give their evaluation of the *Yuan
dianzhang*, weighing its positive and negative features:

> This book takes the laws and statutes of the period and arranges them neatly
> in order under section headings. And the materials it collects together are
> quite detailed and complete. Thus it certainly ought to preserve knowledge
> of matters during the [Yuan] dynasty. Nevertheless, the documents recorded
> [in the *Yuan dianzhang*] are all bureaucratic correspondence. Moreover, in
> seven or eight tenths of these, local dialect and vulgar colloquial language
> are mixed in, or empty verbiage obscures their meaning. Also, the organ-
> ization is confused and unsystematic. Looking at the communication from
> the [Central] Secretariat at the beginning of the work, we find the words
> "copying out into a book." From this we know that these case records were
> transcribed by clerks and minor officials. They do not constitute material
> worthy of evidential scholarship. At first we decided to transcribe the book
> [into the Four Treasuries collection], but in the end we only retained men-
> tion of it here in the catalog.[30]

The *Siku* editors noted the value of the *Yuan dianzhang* as a source for Yuan
history, especially in the absence of other surviving legal works. But they judged
the work unworthy of inclusion in their canon of classical writing precisely for
the reasons that make the *Yuan dianzhang* uniquely valuable as a historical
source for us today. They objected to its use of local dialect and colloquial language. And they found the lack of editing to make the organization "confused
and unsystematic." (They probably noticed the contradictory rulings as well.)
Most significant, they seem not to have recognized the Sino-Mongolian passages, referring instead to "empty verbiage" that "obscures the meaning" of the
documents. And they attribute this to poor writing by undereducated clerks.
Along these lines, they call attention to terms found in the communication from

---

30. *Siku quanshu zongmu* 83:713–714.

the Central Secretariat of the Yuan reproduced in the elegant title-page cartouche, which they interpret to mean that the text was merely "copied" by clerks or functionaries and was not the work of literati officials. Reading such writing that lacked appropriate polish, they imply, was beneath scholars like themselves. Still, the fate of the *Yuan dianzhang* hung in the balance as at first they planned to include it in the compendium, but in the end their professional sensibilities decided its fate. Other scholars of the time expressed a similar low regard for the unpolished and confusing language of the *Yuan dianzhang*.[31]

The *Siku* editors also disparaged the *Yuan dianzhang* for containing unedited "bureaucratic correspondence." Indeed, these documents are written in a complicated and redundant style required by the rules of official dispatches. In particular, each office that handled a document quotes the original document in its response, such that the final dispatch will have quotes of multiple embedded documents. Thus, a case in the *Yuan dianzhang* might start: "We received your report as follows," then quote the report. The quoted report in turn might start, "We received a dispatch as follows," and will quote the contents of the dispatch, on and on until the lowest level of embedded document quotes the original plaint and witness testimony. These quoted documents are run together in the text, but specialized terms for documents from a particular office and other phrases indicate the beginning and end of each quote.[32] This style of embedded documents was not new in the Yuan, and scholars have found examples from as early as the Tang and Song. The style was also used widely in the Ming and Qing dynasties, after the Yuan.[33]

As the *Siku* editors also noted, the documents in the *Yuan dianzhang* were copied from originals found in the archives—indeed, probably by clerks and scribes. Therefore, they do not always contain all the elements found in the original document. We can get an idea of just what is left out of the *Yuan dian-*

---

31. Ch'en 1979, 32. See also comments in Mote 1994b, 697–698.

32. In my translations I indicate these quotations of documents with indentation, as explained in Chapter 4, "Notes on the Translation." For diagrams of this style, see for instance Gendai no hōsei kenkyū han 2007, 150–151.

33. See the important discussion in Wang 2017, 18–28, where the author calls this "layered quotation style." I thank Chelsea Wang for sharing her work on this issue with me.

zhang entries by comparing them with more complete extant versions of similar documents. A transcription of an apparently complete communiqué (*zi* 咨) from the Central Secretariat is contained in a rare Yuan book preserved in the Naikaku Bunko library in Tokyo. This is an order of approval for the official publishing of the book that is included at the beginning of the work.[34] Also, fragments of the actual documents held in the yamen archive of the Yuan city of Khara Khoto, in modern western Inner Mongolia, have survived, and they include bits of documents of the types reprinted in the *Yuan dianzhang*.[35] By comparing these texts, we find that the *Yuan dianzhang* omits stock phrases that begin every document, such as "by the authority of the emperor" (*huangdi shengzhi li* 皇帝聖旨裏). It also omits the names and signatures of the officials who drafted the documents at each level. (These are often in Phags-pa Mongolian script.) Some redundancy in the documents is also eliminated. Nevertheless, the comparison confirms that the *Yuan dianzhang* contains the essentials of each case, and in most cases the entire substantive content of the document.

Transmission and Editions

Clues to the owners and transmission of the only extant Yuan edition of the *Yuan dianzhang*, now in the National Palace Museum in Taipei, also come from within the work itself. Those who once had in their possession the book we have today left evidence of their presence for us to find. The earliest owner was likely a Yuan official from south China. This person had some of the original documents at hand, for he (or she) annotated the book with ink and brush in places, filling in missing dates and other information that could only have been known by someone with another source for the same documents. Our next clue is in the form of several red seal impressions that appear throughout the work. They

34. Miya (2001) discusses the document and reproduces it in plates I, II, and III. See Miya 2006 for a discussion and translation (329–332) and figure 7–1 (330–331) for a reproduction of the text, but in a smaller, less legible format than in Miya 2001.

35. These have been beautifully published in photoreproduction. See *Zhongguo cang Heishuicheng* and *Heicheng chutu wenshu*. The surviving fragments are generally small, reflecting damage the documents suffered as a result of a fire at the yamen. The city of Khara Khoto (in Chinese "Black City" Heicheng 黑城 or "Black Water City" Heishuicheng 黑水城) was visited by Marco Polo, who called it Etzina, from the local Tangut name Ejinai (Yijinai 亦集乃 in Chinese transcription).

proudly announce that the book belonged to the late Ming–early Qing literatus and book publisher Mao Jin 毛晉 (1599–1659) of the city of Changshu, near modern Shanghai, and was part of the collection of his famous library, the Pavilion of Inspiration from the Ancients (Jiguge 汲古閣).[36]

Sometime in the Qing dynasty, the book made its way from Changshu in the south to Beijing, where it entered the imperial library. The compilers of the *Siku quanshu,* working between 1773 and 1782, found it there, but as mentioned earlier, they found it wanting and declined to include it in their great compendium. The exclusion of the work from the *Siku quanshu* greatly reduced its accessibility to readers, and the negative judgment of the *Siku* editors discouraged general interest in the work. Nevertheless, other scholars of the day appreciated the value of the text, for a number of people copied out all or parts of the text in manuscript, and these had begun to circulate by the end of the Qianlong emperor's reign (1736–1795).[37]

The great Qing scholar Qian Daxin 錢大昕 (1738–1804), as a historian of the Yuan, early on appreciated the value of the *Yuan dianzhang.* In a colophon to the work, he recounts his long quest to obtain a copy and his joy at finally securing one:

First I went to the capital (Beijing), where I heard that an old established family possessed this book. I proceeded to their home hoping to borrow and read it. But they kept it privately and would not let me see it. Ten years later, my friend from Changzhou, Wu Qijin, took the manuscript copy that had been kept in his family and presented it to me as a gift. The paper and ink were of splendid quality. It was like receiving a trove of treasure. When I think back on these events, they make me sigh [just as Zhao Mengfu must have] over the two monks Dugu and Dongping.[38]

36. Both the handwritten characters and red seals are described by Chang 1972, 2. They are clearly visible in the National Palace Museum photoreproductions of 1972 and 1976.

37. See Chen Gaohua et al. 2011, 4:2449ff., appendix 3.

38. *Qian yantang wenji* 28:22b; also found in *Yuan dianzhang* (1964), 2:936; Chen Gaohua et al. 2011, 4:2458–2459. The last sentence refers to the great Yuan painter and calligrapher Zhao Mengfu 趙孟頫 (1254–1322), who wrote that he sought to obtain a copy of the renowned calligraphy piece by Wang Xizhi 王羲之 (ca. 303–361) called "Preface to the Poems Collected from the Orchid Pavilion" (*Lantingji xu* 蘭亭集序). The monk Dongping refused to let Zhao view his copy, but the monk Dugu gave Zhao his as a gift. For an account in English, see McCausland 2011, 84. Wang Xizhi's original was so highly prized that it is said to have been buried in the tomb of Emperor Taizong of the Tang (Li Shimin, r. 598–649).

Other scholars of the period describe in colophons and prefaces various manuscript copies they had acquired, but as seen in these accounts these are nearly all incomplete.

As the nineteenth century progressed, manuscript editions also made their way into foreign libraries, especially in Japan. A beautiful, complete manuscript of the *Yuan dianzhang* is held in the Wade collection of the Cambridge University Library. We can surmise that Sir Thomas Wade (1818–1895) acquired it during his years as head of the British legation in Beijing, where he served from 1861 to 1882.[39] In 1996 I had the opportunity to view the manuscript, and I compared chapter 18 word for word with the Yuan edition. It exactly matched, without any errors, and only deviated where a different orthography was occasionally used for a character. It also was written in traditional characters, without the Yuan dynasty simplifications of the original. Without question it was copied from the Yuan edition in the imperial palace library of Beijing, and was copied very carefully.[40] Another notable difference in the Wade manuscript is that it omits the new lines and characters above the line when referring to the emperor or high imperial offices, marks of obeisance to the Yuan court that were mandatory for any book published during the Yuan (as in other dynasties) but which would not always be included when one reproduced the book in a later dynasty.

From this point in time begins a series of events that in hindsight appear like a comedy of errors in the process of making the *Yuan dianzhang* available again to a wide readership. The *Siku quanshu* editors did not mention in their catalog entry that the work they examined was an original Yuan dynasty imprint. Subsequently, the existence of a Yuan printing in the palace library was evidently forgotten. The great Qing jurist and legal scholar Shen Jiaben (沈家本 (1840–1913) wrote in 1908 that "no printed edition" of the *Yuan dianzhang* survived.[41] Therefore, when Shen took on the ambitious task of printing the

39. Giles 1898, 38. As a diplomat in charge of delicate legal negotiations, he was interested in law texts, as he recounts in his letter in which he stated that he was donating the book collection to Cambridge.

40. Herbert Franke (1959) in his description of the manuscript identifies at least five different hands that did the copying. Franke also found occasional deviations from other editions in the parts he checked, but he was comparing it with flawed versions, the Yuan printing not yet having been published.

41. *Yuan dianzhang* (1964), 2:809; Chen Gaohua et al. 2011, 4:2461. This is especially surprising, since in 1905 Shen was in charge of revising the Qing code and must have had access to the palace archives.

Yuan dianzhang, completed in 1908, he overlooked the Yuan edition and used an unreliable manuscript copy. In bold calligraphy at the end of this work, by his colleague Cao Guangquan 曹廣權 (1861–1924), a printer's colophon announces that it is based on a copy that had been held by a well-known book collector in Hangzhou, Ding Bing 丁丙 (1832–1899).[42] In fact, as Shen details in his own extended postface to the work, the picture is more complicated. Shen recounts that his friend Dong Shoujin 董綬金 (1867–1947) made a trip to Japan, during which he saw a manuscript copy of the *Yuan dianzhang* that "supposedly" had been transcribed from Ding Bing's edition in Hangzhou. Dong subsequently had a new transcription of the manuscript made for himself, which he brought back for the library of China's first officially sponsored law school, founded in Beijing in 1906. This copy is what Shen Jiaben used for his printing blocks, and it subsequently became known as the Shen edition (*Shen keben* 沈刻本).[43]

The resulting printed version of the *Yuan dianzhang* is rife with errors and omissions. Sentences are frequently missing, or whole passages are excised from one case and inserted erroneously into another. In one case in the "Marriage" chapter, the word "not" (*bu* 不) is inserted in such a way that the original meaning of the document is exactly reversed. Despite the deficiencies of the Shen edition and its inadequacy as a historical source, however, it was included in the collection *Songfen shi congshu* and reprinted in two volumes in 1964 by Wenhai publishing house in Taiwan.[44] This edition made its way into libraries around the world, and even today citations to the *Yuan dianzhang* in works by Western scholars are often to this edition.

Meanwhile, in the 1920s, officials charged with cataloging the old imperial library rediscovered the Yuan edition. This sparked a flurry of attention and attempts to produce a reprint, but in wartime China such an edition failed to materialize. Instead, the great legal scholar Chen Yuan 陳垣 (1880–1971)

---

42. *Yuan dianzhang* (1964), 2:810. On Ding Bing, see Hummel 1943, 726–727.

43. See *Yuan dianzhang* (1964), 2:809; Chen Gaohua et al. 2011, 4:2463. Shen Jiaben in addition argues rather spuriously that the copy held by Ding Bing was none other than the precious manuscript of Qian Daxin. Ding Bing's famous book collection was purchased by the Nanjing library (then known as the Jiangnan library) in 1907, but no manuscript of the *Yuan dianzhang* survives there.

44. See *Yuan dianzhang* (1964). A second printing was issued in 1974.

produced two works of corrections to the Shen edition of the *Yuan dianzhang*.[45] He also gathered various manuscript editions that were available to him at the time, mostly partial, and compared these to the Yuan edition. He concluded that they were all based on the Yuan edition, probably the very one that was then in the palace library of the former Qing dynasty.

As fighting between Chinese and Japanese forces in north China intensified during the 1930s, many items in the imperial palace, especially the rare books in the imperial library, were transferred to cities in the south. The Nationalist government eventually shipped these to Taiwan as the Nationalist forces retreated from the mainland.[46] The *Yuan dianzhang*, its precious value now widely recognized, found a home in the National Palace Museum of Taipei (Guoli gugong bowuyuan 國立故宮博物院). In 1972, the National Palace Museum issued a beautiful color photoreproduction of the work in sixteen fascicules, using traditional string-bound format. Then in 1976 they published a hardbound edition in three large volumes, making the 1322 work widely available in photoreproduction. My translation is based on this reproduction. By the mid-1990s the work was already sold out, but a reprint subsequently appeared in mainland China in 1998 published by China Broadcasting Publishers, with modern pagination added.[47] Another reprint based on the original 1972 National Palace Museum edition, but with four leaves to a page, was included in the modern collection *Xuxiu Siku quanshu* [Continuation of the *Siku quanshu*], published in Shanghai in 2002.[48]

The work of the Yuan Research Group of the Chinese Academy of Social Sciences in Beijing culminated in a punctuated and annotated edition, published in four volumes in 2011.[49] Earlier they published selected chapters with punctuation and additional annotation.[50] In addition, Dr. Hung Chin-fu of the Insti-

45. Chen Yuan 1931, 1934. In 1990, the Shen edition of the *Yuan dianzhang* was reprinted in Beijing with Chen Yuan's corrective works conveniently appended. See *Yuan dianzhang* (1990).

46. See Wilkinson 2015, 420.

47. See *Yuan dianzhang* (1998). In the translations in Part II, I have supplied the page number of the Yuan original and the cumulative page number found in this work.

48. See *Yuan dianzhang* (2002). This entire collection was published between 1995 and 2002.

49. Chen Gaohua et al. 2011.

50. See Chen Gaohua, Zhang Fan, and Liu Xiao 2004, 2005, 2007, 2008a, 2008b, 2010, 2012. These cover seven chapters of the "Hubu" (Ministry of Revenue) section of the *Yuan*

tute of History and Philology, Academia Sinica, in Taipei, Taiwan, published his own much-anticipated punctuated and annotated edition in four large volumes in the summer of 2016.[51] In Japan, research groups began working on the *Yuan dianzhang* in the 1940s and 1950s and have continued to the present day. This work has resulted in a large number of publications, most notably a punctuated edition of the Ministry of Punishments section in two volumes, among other works.[52] In recent years, the Yuan Law Research Group at the Institute for Research in Humanities (Jinbun kagaku kenkyūsho) at Kyoto University has been working on a Japanese translation of the *Yuan dianzhang*. In 2007 and 2008 they published their first installments, covering the Ministry of Rites chapters from the *Yuan dianzhang*.[53] These recent works are finally making the *Yuan dianzhang* widely accessible as it deserves.

---

dianzhang, including the "Marriage" chapter, translated in Part II. I follow the method of numbering cases as found in these articles.

51. See Hung Chin-fu 2016. I follow the indentation style used in this work. See Hung 1982 for English translations of documents from the *Yuan dianzhang* related to the Censorate.

52. Iwamura and Tanaka 1964. See Zu and Li 2004, for a Chinese version of this work. Other notable works include: Yoshikawa and Tanaka 1964; Tanaka 1965, 2000; Uematsu 1980, 2004. For references to other works, see Uematsu 1992; Mote 1994b, 698n40, Funada 1999.

53. Gendai no hōsei kenkyū han 2007, 2008a, 2008b.

CHAPTER FOUR

Notes on the Translation

Translating legal cases from the *Yuan dianzhang* into English poses many linguistic challenges. Some of these are common to all translations of premodern Chinese into English. Others are specific to Yuan-era texts and the *Yuan dianzhang*. In these pages, I explain the ways I have chosen to handle these challenges and the conventions I am following.

Offices, Geographic Units, and Specialized Terms

For names of Yuan offices and geographic units, I have followed David Farquhar, *The Government of China under Mongol Rule: A Reference Guide* (Stuttgart: Franz Steiner, 1990), with only a few exceptions. For the names of different types of documents, I have chosen one term in English and used it consistently. These are all glossed at first mention in a footnote, as are place names.

The *Yuan dianzhang* uses many specialized legal terms. Many of these are found in legal texts of earlier and especially later periods, but their meanings are often quite different. One can track the evolution of these terms over time, usually in the direction of being more specific and fixed. Where possible, I have used a consistent translation for legal terms and stock phrases but have not tried to explain them. Some terms cannot be mapped onto a single English expression and have therefore been translated differently in different contexts. A discussion of the changing meanings of legal language and my choices of translation will have to await a separate publication.

Numbering of Cases

The translations in Part II make up Chapter 18 (*juan* 18), titled "Marriage," of the *Yuan dianzhang*. I have numbered the documents in consecutive order as they appear in the chapter, then prefaced that number by the chapter number 18. Thus, the tenth case in the chapter is 18.10. For references to cases elsewhere in the *Yuan dianzhang* I have given the chapter (*juan*) number and page number in the 1976 National Palace Museum photoreproduction of the 1322 original. The translation is based on this edition.

Brackets

I have used brackets sparingly. For the most part I have used them only where I am filling in text that is missing from the original owing to printer's error and that must be reconstructed from context and knowledge of similar documents, or in some places to clarify the case for a Western audience. I have not used brackets when filling in words that would be understood by a reader of the time and are therefore not provided in the original text. To take an example from Spanish, the expression *Es profesora* would be translated "She is a professor," not "[She] is a professor." The inflection of the verb and noun indicate the third-person feminine subject, so no brackets are needed. The pronoun "she" (*ella*) is omitted in the Spanish since it is redundant. For a similar example in bureaucratic writing of the Yuan, different words for the English verb "to receive" indicate what kind of document is being sent and whether it is coming from a superior, an inferior, or an equal. To make the English clear, I have repeated the name of the document. For instance, I write "dispatch received" where "dispatch" does not actually appear in the Chinese but would be understood by the reader from the verb used for "received" and other context. To distinguish between different verbs in the Chinese, I have added qualifiers where appropriate, such as "respectfully received" or "humbly received."

Names of Women and Men

The names of Han Chinese women in the *Yuan dianzhang* are consistently given with their husband's surname first, followed by the particle *a* (阿), then their natal family surname. I capitalize these in English to show that they are proper names. Thus the name Liu A-Zhao indicates a woman née Zhao who is married to a Mr. Liu. The common form of maiden surname + *shi* (氏) found in earlier and later dynasties, is quite rare in the *Yuan dianzhang,* and I translate it as "Madam X" or, in this example, "Madam Zhao." Sometimes a woman's full name, both surname and given name, also appears in the text.[1]

Chinese names are made up of characters that have meanings, and a translator must decide whether to render those meanings into English. Names found in the *Yuan dianzhang* are often colorful, especially those of poor commoners. Many of these are apotropaic names—names that use disparaging terms to ward off evil spirits. Reflecting customs in north China, the word "donkey" (*lü* 驢), appears frequently as a man's name, by itself (case 18.56), in colloquial usage, Lü'er (case 18.8), or combined with another word, as in "Midnight Donkey," Choulü (case 18.5), or "Donkey Brother," Lüge (case 18.10).[2] Other names describe characteristics, or include a word that Endymion Wilkinson dubs an "affectionate term of abuse" such as "dog" or "slave."[3] Number names were common for all classes, such as Wang Fourteen, or Zhang Ten Thousand.[4] I have chosen not to translate these and other names for several reasons. The people using them probably did not think of their meanings, any more than calling someone Rose makes one think of the flower. Even if the names were denotative at the time they were given, over time they likely would function as referents rather than words. Chinese characters often have more than one meaning; moreover, the connotation of any word differs between cultures and time periods. It is hard to translate names into words that connote the same thing today as they did for the people in the thirteenth century. By leaving names in romanization, one can also refer back more easily to the original Chinese text. In a few places I translate the names, where this is helpful to make sense of the case, or I indicate the

---

1. This is unusual in later legal writings. See Watson 1986; Sommer 2000, xvii.

2. On the name "Donkey," see Wilkinson 2015, 132. Yan Zhitui 顏之推 in the late sixth century commented on the name "donkey" in particular, finding it comical.

3. Wilkinson 2015, 130.

4. These became especially popular in the Song era and later (see Hung 1987). On naming practices in the Yuan and the large number of Chinese taking Mongol names, see Chen Gaohua 2000. On naming practices in general, see Wu Han 1959; Wilkinson 2015, 125–147, and works cited therein; and on the significance of Han surnames and others adopting them, see Ebrey 1996. On translating Chinese personal names, see Wilkinson 2015, 49–51.

meaning in a footnote to provide some of the flavor of these names—albeit within our modern system of connotations. It is not uncommon for different names to be used for the same person in a case, in which instance I provide an explanatory note. In some places, I prefix a name with Mr. or other title, when no such title appears in the Chinese. This is to clarify the gender for the reader, or to make the sentence read more like a similar document in English. In most cases, though, I have tried to translate only what appears in the original text.

I render names from languages other than Chinese, such as Mongolian, Arabic, or Persian, into their English forms, for example, Fatima or Muhammad, omitting diacritical marks and double vowels. Thus I use Mubarak, not Mubārak or Mubaarak, and Shah, not Shāh or Shaah.[5] Where this is not feasible, I retain the original Chinese version of the name in pinyin romanization.

Romanization and Transliteration

Chinese words and proper nouns are romanized according to the pinyin system. Mongolian is transliterated according to the system used in *The Cambridge History of China*, vol. 6, *Alien Regimes and Border States, 907–1368*, edited by Herbert Franke and Denis Twitchett (Cambridge, 1994). This system follows the standard originally set by A. Mostaert in his *Dictionnaire Ordos*, vol. 3 (Beijing, 1944) and used by Nikolas Poppe and later specialists,[6] with the exception of certain consonants that are modified to avoid diacritical marks. These become sh, ch, and j. In addition, the Greek letter gamma becomes gh, and q becomes kh. Thus I write Khubilai Khan, not Qubilai Qan, and Khanbalikh, not Qanbaliq.

Dates and Ages

As in other Chinese texts, years are counted in the *Yuan dianzhang* by the emperor's reign period. During the Yuan, the reign of each emperor was divided into periods, each with a name, such as *dade* ("Great Virtue"). Dates are given by the number of the year within that period, such as "the second year of the

---

5. The Muslim names can be found in a standard Muslim name dictionary; see for instance Ahmed 1999. I thank Christopher Atwood for his help with deciphering the non-Chinese names.

6. See Poppe 1954, 12. Poppe uses kh not q for proper names such as Khubilai (1954, 5).

dade period." On occasion a year is given by the animal of the zodiac to which it corresponds or by the sixty-year cycle derived from combinations of the traditional Chinese Ten Heavenly Branches and Twelve Earthly Stems. I leave the names of the reign periods in the text in romanization and give the equivalent year by the modern Western calendar in parentheses. The number of the month and the day I leave as in the Chinese. Thus a date might read, "In the sixth year of the *zhiyuan* period (1269), third month, eleventh day." Since the Chinese followed a lunisolar calendar, dates at the end of the year might fall into the next year by Western reckoning. Intercalary months were periodically inserted to keep the calendar accurate.

I leave ages of people as in the Chinese text, namely by Chinese counting (*sui* 歲). Chinese ages were counted as one year at birth with a year added at every New Year. Thus a child born on the last day of the twelfth month of a year would be "two years old" a day after birth. This means that the age given for a person in the text could be anywhere between one and two years older than in Western counting.

Embedded Documents and Indents

The cases in the *Yuan dianzhang* are in a bureaucratic style that quotes extensively from other documents, generally the report or dispatch to which an office is responding. Thus a case might start "We received your report as follows," then proceed to quote the entire report. I indicate each of these by indenting the text that is quoted. The document that is thus embedded usually quotes another document from another office, and so on. Each of these is indicated by an additional indent, sometimes numbering five or more. The indent ends at the end of the quote, and the text returns to being unindented. Sometimes two quotes end in the same place, and in that case the next line will be moved left by two indentation levels. By noting the left margin of a passage, readers can determine which document they are reading and what office is talking.[7]

---

7. On this style, see Wang 2017, and the discussion in Chapter 3 of this volume.

Visuality and Hierarchy

The 1322 printing of the *Yuan dianzhang,* like similar documents in other dynasties, presents a visual image that embodies a system of hierarchy and deference. References to the emperor in terms like "Imperial Edict" (*shengzhi* 聖旨) start a new line and are elevated two character spaces above the rest of the text. The terms "Imperial Amnesty" (*she'en* 赦恩) "Memorial" (*zou* 奏), and "Court" (*chaoting* 朝廷) among others, all get a new line and a one-character space elevation.[8] Whenever the Central Secretariat or the Censorate is named, a space is left before the word to convey respect for the office, or sometimes a new line is started. The names of documents from the Central Secretariat are also preceded by a space. I capitalize these terms to indicate their special status and provide an explanation in a footnote at the first occurrence. The English translation, regrettably, cannot convey the full visual impact of the text.

---

8. For some examples of these, see cases 18.26, 18.42, 18.14, and 18.32, respectively. See Figure 3.1 for an illustration of these features.

PART II

Chapter 18, "Marriage," from the *Yuan dianzhang*

An Annotated Translation

CHAPTER FIVE

Sections 1–2

Marriage Rites and Exchanges; Getting Married

Section 1: Marriage Rites and Exchanges

18.1

This first case, dated 1269, deals with the fundamental problem for the government of how to reduce lawsuits over marriage disputes. The Ministry of Revenue, which in the thirteenth century decided nearly all marriage cases, decides here that for a marriage to be legal, the parties must establish a written contract detailing the betrothal gifts, type of marriage, and other conditions, and have it signed by the go-between and relevant parties.[1] Just one month later, the Ministry of Revenue revisited this issue and prohibited types of betrothals commonly practiced without a written contract or exchange of property, such as while children were still unborn (called "pointing at bellies") or very young (called "cutting the shirt [and exchanging the cloth fragments]").[2] This emphasizes the point, found in traditional Chinese law, that a legal marriage

1. An example of such a contract was excavated at Khara Khoto; see *Zhongguo cang Heishuicheng,* 6:1252; *Heicheng chutu wenshu,* 186 and Plate 18 (1) document F13:W130; Li Yiyou 1992; Zhang and Yang 2015, 311–317. Two copies were written on one page, with the characters for "contract" written on the back. The two parts were then separated, splitting the characters, with one copy going to the bride's family and the other to the groom's. The contract was not to have any slang or obscure language, etc. See *Shilin guangji* (1988), 996; *Shilin guangji* (1999), 124; *Yuandai falü,* 70; and the chart at the beginning of chapter 18 in the *Yuan dianzhang* (YDZ 18:1a, pictured in Fig. I.1). Models for a marriage contract are found in *Shilin guangji* (1988), 289–290. For the use of these contracts, common from the Tang on, see Ebrey 1991a, 51n10.

2. For this decision, see YDZ 30:2a (p. 1141); TZTG 4:166–167 (Art. 76); YS 103:2642; Ratchnevsky and Aubin 1972–1985, 2:116 (Art. 384). On these marriages in the Song (and elite condemnation of them), see Ebrey 1991a, 50.

required the formal handover of property from the groom's family to the bride's.[3] Marriages without such an exchange were invalid. We see in this case how the Yuan government tried to encourage the use of contracts.[4]

The ministry here makes reference to two different kinds of uxorilocal marriage that were practiced legally in the Yuan, permanent and temporary, and cites this type of marriage as a major source of legal contention.[5] In case 18.3, the Ministry of Revenue revisits regulations for uxorilocal marriage. See also cases 18.10 and 18.11 for conflicting policy decisions over uxorilocal marriage and just how far private marriage contracts could go in establishing legally binding prenuptial agreements.

18.1 *When getting married, the parties must establish a written marriage contract*[6]

In the sixth year of the *zhiyuan* period (1269), third month, eleventh day, a document from the Ministry of Revenue of the Central Secretariat states:[7]

3. In Tang, Song, and Ming law, if the bride's family accepted betrothal gifts from the groom's family, it was the same as if a contract had been established, and they could not back out of the marriage. See TLSY 13:254 (Art. 175); SXT 13:213; Johnson 1997, 153; *Da Ming lü* 6:639; Jiang 2005, 82 (Art. 107); Birge 2002, 51–52. For earlier times, see Dull 1978, 42–49.

4. The Yuan government relied on private contracts rather than obsolete government registers to prove property ownership, marriage rights, and so forth. It obtained income from a tax on contracts, which, as Valerie Hansen (1995, 113–146) argues, it was more successful in collecting than previous dynastic governments.

5. In a temporary uxorilocal marriage, a son-in-law lived with his wife's family for a fixed period of time, before leaving with her to return to his own family or to set up a new household. A permanent uxorilocal son-in-law, as the term implies, was expected to stay indefinitely in the home of his in-laws. See *Lixue zhinan*, 76. This and other texts divide uxorilocal marriage into four types, but three are merely different names for variations on temporary uxorilocal marriage.

6. YDZ 18:2a, p. 659. Traditional page numbers are from the 1976 National Palace Museum edition of the *Yuan dianzhang*. Cumulative page numbers are from *Yuan dianzhang* (1998). This case with slight differences and omissions survives in TZTG 3:145–146 (Art. 44). It is dated twelfth month of 1269 rather than third month. The final pronouncement by the Ministry of Revenue at the end of the case also appears in *Shilin guangji* (1988), 996; *Shilin guangji* (1999), 124; and in *Xingtong fushu*, 168 (#14). See also reprint in *Yuandai falü*, 70.

7. Whenever the office of the Central Secretariat is named in the text, a one-character blank space precedes it to show respect. In this instance, this space is filled in by brush writing with the characters for "eleventh day" (十一日). This is one of many oddities in the *Yuan dianzhang*. The National Palace Museum edition of 1322 has numerous brush-written annotations such as this.

We have investigated and note that, regarding the Way of human moral relations, marriage between a son and a daughter is of the greatest importance. It is the case that rites and procedures as currently practiced in different localities are inconsistent and vary one from another. There are those who establish a written marriage contract and formal agreements. But there are also those who do not establish a written contract detailing their original agreement and instead only rely on a go-between to carry out the marriage. After the engagement, if there is the slightest dispute, the groom's family will use the pretext of not having a marriage contract to back out of the original agreement. They will fraudulently insist on increasing or decreasing the marriage payments. Or they will disagree over whether an uxorilocal son-in-law is permanent or temporary, or there will be a discrepancy over how many years he is to stay in his in-laws' home, and the lawsuits end up in court. In the process of the litigation the magistrates are not impartial, and the go-between and other parties are untruthful.[8] The magistrate can only rely on oral testimony, and the litigation never ends. This is a very unbeneficial situation.

We the Ministry of the Secretariat deliberated together and determine: from now on, when one negotiates a betrothal for marriage, one must write out a marriage contract and establish a formal agreement. It must state clearly the amount of betrothal gifts and payments that were originally negotiated. If one is inviting in an uxorilocal son-in-law, one must establish whether he is permanent or temporary, and for how many years. The sponsor of the marriage, the guarantor, the go-between, and others involved must all sign the contract, in order for a legal marriage to take place.[9] In this way, lawsuits will be prevented.

We [the Central Secretariat] in addition [to approving the ruling] order that this be distributed to all subordinate offices and enforced according to the above.[10]

8. The TZTG version attributes both the lack of partiality and the untruthfulness to the go-between, leaving out the criticism of magistrates found here. See TZTG 3:145–146 (Art. 44).

9. The "sponsor of the marriage" (*zhuhun* 主婚) would usually be the parent responsible for the negotiations. Ebrey translates it as "those presiding at the marriage" (Ebrey 1991a, 48; Chinese text, 192). The "guarantor" (保親) and "go-between" (媒妁) are the same, these just being different terms for the same person, used variously. See TZTG 3:146n3.

10. The term *chuwai* (除外) at the beginning of this sentence appears commonly in the *Yuan dianzhang.* It indicates that the Central Secretariat approves the ruling of the ministry and *in addition* is sending out its order to enforce the provisions. This decision is quoted in case 18.10.

18.2

In the second month of 1271, Khubilai issued an imperial edict approving a set of rules from the Central Secretariat regulating marriages. It confronted the problem that the marriage practices of different peoples in the empire were in conflict. The seven items generally reiterated traditional Chinese marriage laws but crucially established that Mongols were exempt from them and that people of different ethnic groups could follow their own customary laws. Each item reaffirms an aspect of Chinese marriage law that contradicted Mongol marriage customs. They prohibited overly lavish betrothal gifts and banquets, the delay of a marriage after the betrothal, same-surname marriage, and having multiple wives. The decree also reiterated the right of widows to return to their natal families, in contrast to the Mongol practice of the levirate, which forced widows to marry a relative of their deceased husband. Khubilai reversed this right of widows just eight months later (see case 18.49, also quoted in 18.26), and the issue of the levirate generated much legal contention over the next decades.[11] The promulgation of these regulations suggests that within a multi-ethnic society, with conflicting marriage practices, there was beginning to be confusion among the populace over what constituted a legal marriage and what legal protections each party had within marriage.

These regulations were widely cited by judges, who used them as the basis for resolving marriage disputes. Their importance is also attested by the fact that they appear in multiple sources that survive from Yuan times.[12] Several of the regulations originated from earlier rulings by the Central Secretariat or other agencies (indicated in notes) and were here elaborated on or issued for the whole country. They were also amended and reiterated over time, as officials struggled to keep up with social evolution and economic development in a culturally diverse population. Imperial edicts could not prevent people from borrowing cus-

---

11. See discussion in Birge 1995; Birge 2002, chapter 4; Birge 2003.

12. All but the last item of this case appears in almost identical wording in *Hanmo quanshu,* 4:3a–3b (169:133), and *Yuan hunli gongju kao,* 151–152. All of them except the first appear in *Shilin guangji* (1988), 297–298, and *Shilin guangji* (1999), 43. Selected items appear in multiple other sources surviving from the Yuan period, as indicated in notes; and a mention of the edict appears in the Yuan dynastic history, YS 7:133. For a discussion of this case, see Birge 2002, 236–238, where I translate the title as "General Rules for Marriage and Betrothal Gifts."

toms from each other or flaunting their wealth, and confusion continued over what laws applied to what people.

18.2 *Regulations governing marriages and betrothal gifts: 7 items*[13]

In the eighth year of the *zhiyuan* period (1271), second month, we [the Central Secretariat] respectfully received an Imperial Edict,[14] stating:

> It is the case that the Central Secretariat has submitted a memorial on "Fixing Rules for Marriages and Betrothal Gifts among the People" and other matters. We approve the memorial.

We order that these regulations be sent out to all circuits to be made known and implemented in their entirety.

Item 1. Betrothal gifts, which can include textiles,[15] head ornaments, and other items, should all be valued in terms of official paper currency.[16] One is permitted

---

13. YDZ 18:2a, p. 659.

14. The term "Imperial Edict" (*shengzhi* 聖旨) always starts a new line and is elevated two character spaces above the rest of the text in the *Yuan dianzhang,* to indicate the highest level of respect for this document above all others. I have rendered the term in capital letters to reflect its special status.

15. *Biaoli* (表裏), literally "outer and inner clothing," refers to bolts of cloth, usually silk, used for clothing, gifts, or sometimes currency. It is also the measure word for a bolt of cloth. See usage in TZTG 3:143 (Art. 43) and discussion in TZTG 3:144n2. In his widely influential manual for wedding ritual, Zhu Xi (1130–1200) of the Song recommended lengths of colored silk for betrothal gifts but also approved of jewelry, wine, and food items. See Ebrey 1991a, 53, 193. All of these items, plus money itself, appear throughout the cases.

16. This paper currency (*yuan baochao* 元寶鈔) was issued by the Yuan government starting in 1260, at the beginning of Khubilai's reign, and it became the universal currency of the empire, the first such wide circulation of paper money in the world. It was convertible into either silver or copper, with no time or geographic limit. Initially its value was relatively stable, but over time problems arose. Sometime after this regulation was issued, Khubilai's advisor Hu Zhiyu 胡祇遹 (1227–1295) warned that no one followed these limits, since inflation had made goods eight, nine, or even ten times as expensive, in terms of paper currency. He recommended that new standards be issued using gold, silver, and silk cloth as the standard (*Zazhu* 22:222). In 1304, the government finally took this step, reissuing these limits denominated in ounces of gold and silver, and bolts of silk. See TZTG 3:143 (Art. 43); *Hanmo quanshu,* 4:3b–4a (169:133–134); *Yuan hunli gongju kao,* 153; *Shilin guangji* (1988), 297; and chart at the head of chapter 18 in the YDZ (18:1a [p. 657]). Hu Zhiyu had earlier advocated limits on marriage payments as part of efforts to stem inflation and control monetary policy generally. See *Zazhu* 22:202. For summaries of Yuan use of currency, see Chan 1990; von Glahn 1996. For more in-depth studies, see Takahashi 2000; Peng 2007, 430–453; Schurmann 1956. The prevalence of paper money in the Yuan was much remarked upon by Marco Polo and other European travelers.

to use goods of equivalent value to make up the amounts. If both sides agree, these rules need not be adhered to.

Ranked Officials   Ranks 1 and 2: 500 strings of cash.[17]

Rank 3: 400 strings

Ranks 4 and 5: 300 strings   Ranks 6 and 7: 200 strings

Ranks 8 and 9: 120 strings

Commoners   Upper-tier households: 100 strings

Middle-tier households: 50 strings

Lower-tier households: 20 strings[18]

Item 2. The lavishness of the wedding banquet is according to the rank of the groom's family.

Ranked Officials   Not to exceed four dishes.

Commoners   Upper- and middle-tier households, not to exceed three dishes.

Lower-tier households, not to exceed two dishes.[19]

17. A "string of cash" (*guan* 貫), originally referring to a string of one thousand copper coins, was used as a denomination for paper currency. Images of such strings of cash appear on Yuan currency notes. See Peng 2007, plates 64 and 65; von Glahn 1996, 59; Farquhar 1990, plate 1.

18. The Yuan government ranked households on the tax registers into these three categories, according to their wealth.

19. The text reads "three," but we can conclude this is an error for "two" on the basis of other sources. See *Hanmo quanshu,* 4:3b (169:133); *Yuan hunli gongju kao,* 151–152; *Shilin guangji* (1988), 298; *Shilin guangji* (1999), 124; and YDZ 18:1a–b (the chart at head of chapter 18). The Central Secretariat based these sumptuary laws on an earlier ruling of 1270, fourth month, by the Ministry of Revenue, on behalf of Taiyuan Circuit in Shaanxi. The circuit authorities complained that wedding feasts of twenty or thirty courses, lasting all night in drunken reverie, were causing fights and lawsuits and bankrupting commoner families. The Ministry ruled that wedding banquets had to be during the day and not last past curfew, and they articulated limits on the number of courses for wedding feasts among commoners, repeated here. They ordered the circuit authorities to advertise the regulations through placards and wall postings. See YDZ 30:2a–b; TZTG 27:634 (Art. 523). In this reissue of the ruling, the Central Secretariat adds limits for ranked officials and extends the regulations to the whole country. Nevertheless, lavish weddings continued, as seen in a report of 1284, ninth month, from the local office of the Censorate in Handong Region of Shaanxi about how lavish weddings and funerals were devastating households, which prompted the Ministry of Rites and the Central Secretariat to reaffirm these rules and order the local officials to enforce them. See YDZ 30:9a–b. A similar complaint from the same region in 1297 impelled the Ministry and the Central Secretariat to again reiterate these rules and outlaw a local custom of providing large quantities of dried mutton as part of the engagement negotiations (suggestive of steppe influences). See TZTG 4:169 (Art. 80).

[Item 3.][20] Once the marriage has been contracted, when the girl is fifteen years or older, if for no legitimate reason the marriage is not concluded within five years (a legitimate reason would be on the order of if either the bride or groom had not reached marriageable age, or if they were in mourning; if there are such reasons, then the years and months during which they apply are not counted),[21] or if the groom runs away and does not return within five years, then the marriage can be annulled, and the betrothal gifts are not returned.[22]

Item 4. People of the same surname may not marry each other. This regulation will begin in the eighth year of *zhiyuan* (1271), first month, twenty-fifth day. Those who were married before this date may remain married. Those married after will be liable for prosecution according to the law, and the marriage will be annulled.[23]

Item 5. If one who has a wife already marries another wife, even if there has been an amnesty, the marriage is annulled.[24]

20. This item is combined with the previous in the *Yuan dianzhang,* but we can determine from other sources that it is a separate item, thus bringing the total to seven as in the title. See TZTG 4:162 (Art. 68); *Hanmo quanshu,* 4:3b (169:133); *Yuan hunli gongju kao,* 152; *Shilin guangji* (1988), 298, 996; *Shilin guangji* (1999), 43, 124; *Yuandai falü ziliao,* 70.

21. The words in parentheses are given as commentary to the text, in reduced-size characters. The latter phrase is mistakenly given as part of the main text instead of the commentary in the *Yuan dianzhang.* The correction is based on TZTG 4:162 (Art. 68), which also adds two characters that clarify the meaning. The Tang code prohibited marriage during the mourning period and prescribed the harsh punishment of three years' penal servitude. See TLSY 13:257 (Art. 179); Johnson 1997, 157–158. But during the Yuan, the mourning period was unevenly enforced, and violators were not harshly punished. See cases 18.5, 18.15, 18.24, 18.29, 18.43, 18.73, 18.74, 18.75; discussion in Birge 2002, 257–261, and Birge 1995, 130–131.

22. Song law allowed a fiancée to break the engagement if the marriage was not carried out within just three years, or a wife could remarry if her husband disappeared and did not make contact for three years. See QMJ 9:349–351, 9: 353; Birge 2002, 132–133; Niida (1964) 1991a, 398–399; McKnight 1996, 112–113. Ming law, like the Yuan, specified a five-year limit between betrothal and marriage, but, following the Song, it allowed for a wife to remarry if her husband disappeared for three years. It also required that a certificate be filed with the local government. See *Da Ming ling* 1:6a–b (pp. 19–20); Farmer 1995, 159.

23. This item is also found in *Hanmo quanshu,* 4:3b (169:133); *Yuan hunli gongju kao,* 152; *Shilin guangji* (1988), 298, 996; *Shilin guangji* (1999), 43, 124; *Yuandai falü,* 70.

24. See similar prohibition in the Tang code, punishable by one year of penal servitude, in TLSY 13:255 (Art. 177); Johnson 1997, 154–155. Amnesties were more common in the Yuan than in other dynasties. See Ch'en 1979, 46; Birge 2008, 474–476. This item is also found in TZTG 4:162 (Art. 68); *Hanmo quanshu,* 4:3b (169:133); *Yuan hunli gongju kao,* 152; *Shilin*

Item 6. If a woman whose husband has died wishes to stay chaste after the mourning period is over, or moreover wishes to return to her natal family, she should be allowed to do so. Her father- and mother-in-law may not on their own initiative arrange a remarriage for her.[25]

Item 7. When people of the various ethnicities marry within their group, they should each follow their own customary laws. Those who marry across ethnic groups should follow the customs of the husband.[26]

Mongols are not subject to these regulations.[27]

18.3

In this decision, dated the seventh month of 1271, the Ministry of Revenue follows up on the Regulations Governing Marriages and Betrothal Gifts issued in the second month of that year (case 18.2), and establishes comparable regulations for uxorilocal marriages, those where the groom moved to the bride's home instead of vice versa. It also responds to the problems of uxorilocal marriages cited in their general decree of 1269 (case 18.1).

Marriage exchanges for uxorilocal marriages were not symmetrical with patrilocal marriages. The three items in the ruling establish reduced payment scales for temporary and permanent uxorilocal marriages, with payments coming

---

guangji (1988), 298, 996; *Shilin guangji* (1999), 43, 124; *Yuandai falü*, 70; YDZ 18:1a–b (chart at head of chapter 18).

25. This item is also found in TZTG 3:147–148 (Art. 47), and in *Hanmo quanshu*, 4:3b (169:133); *Yuan hunli gongju kao*, 152; *Shilin guangji* (1988), 298; and *Shilin guangji* (1999), 43. It is quoted in cases 18.24, 18.26, and 18.60.

26. The Tang code, article 48, includes the general rule that non-Chinese people follow their own law, and that when the offenders are of different ethnic groups they follow Chinese law. See TLSY 6:133; Johnson 1979, 252. Khubilai's advisor Hu Zhiyu 胡祇遹 (1227–1295) had earlier proposed this rule, saying that the Mongol "northerners" (*beiren* 北人) and Chinese "southerners" (*nanren* 南人) should follow their own marriage law and that the customs of the husband be followed in mixed marriages; see *Zishan daquanji* 21:9a–b (1196:366). This item of the case is also found in TZTG 3:143 (Art. 42); TZTG 4:169 (Art. 80); *Shilin guangji* (1988), 298; *Shilin guangji* (1999), 43; *Xingtong fushu*, 171 (the last incomplete).

27. Some scholars apply this last line only to item 7, but other sources establish that it applies to all the items. See TZTG 4:163 (Art. 68). Moreover, the practices outlawed in the preceding items, like same-surname marriage, multiple wives, and the levirate, were legal for Mongols throughout the Yuan dynasty.

in some cases from the bride's family, not the groom's.[28] The decision also details government attempts to have go-betweens registered with local authorities. Only such registered matchmakers had formal authority to contract a legal marriage, and through them the government collected a contract tax. The case addresses the problem of corruption and abuses in the government registration system and of government-registered go-betweens charging exorbitant fees. There is a brief mention here of military households, but the sensitive issue of uxorilocal marriages of military personnel is revisited in 18.34, dated 1273.[29] This text reveals a remarkable degree of intrusion attempted by the Yuan government into private marriage arrangements.

18.3 *Rules for marriage payments for uxorilocal sons-in-law*[30]

In the eighth year of the *zhiyuan* period (1271), seventh month, Pingyang Circuit[31] respectfully received a certified document[32] from the Ministry of Revenue of the Secretariat for State Affairs,[33] as follows:

We note that regarding marriage and betrothal payments among the people and related matters, we have already respectfully received an Imperial Edict fixing the regulations.[34] In addition, regarding both permanent and temporary invited-in sons-in-law, in the third year of the *zhiyuan* period (1266), fifth

28. For the similarly inconsistent and irregular system of marriage payments for uxorilocal marriages in the Song, see Ebrey 1992. For a very negative view of these marriages from a Yuan writer, see Smith 1998.

29. Military households (*junhu* 軍戶), or hereditary soldier households, were required to provide one soldier and his equipment to the government from generation to generation. Sometimes several households shared the onerous obligation, one or more providing equipment and horses and another supplying the fighting man. For good overviews, see Hsiao 1978b, 17–25; Chen Gaohua and Shi Weimin 2000, 520–525.

30. YDZ 18:2b, p. 660.

31. Modern Linfen City, in southwest Shaanxi Province on the Fen River. In the Yuan it was part of the Central Province. In 1305 the circuit name was changed to Jinning.

32. *Fuwen* 符文. This is a specialized term for a document issued from one of the Six Ministries to inferior offices such as a circuit, as in this case.

33. The Secretariat for State Affairs (Shangshusheng 尚書省) existed during three periods of the Yuan dynasty, for approximately one to four years at a time, in conjunction with the Central Secretariat. It stood between the Central Secretariat and the Six Ministries, and although nominally subordinate to the Central Secretariat, it gradually gained power over time at the expense of the Central Secretariat. (See discussion in Zhang Fan 1997, 21–27.) A space appears in the text before the name of this office, just as with the Central Secretariat, to manifest the prestige of the office.

34. This is case 18.2.

month, we received a superior communication[35] from the Central Secretariat, which reads in part as follows:

> One should follow the original marriage contract. Permanent uxorilocal sons-in-law should be permanent. Temporary uxorilocal sons-in-law may leave at the appointed time. Each should pay taxes and assume labor duties as a military or civilian household according to their place of residence, whether with their in-laws permanently or in a new place to which they leave.

Moreover, we have in recent times respectfully received Imperial Regulations[36] that include fixed rules for permanent and temporary uxorilocal sons-in-law. Nevertheless, because there are no fixed rules governing marriage payments, the parties frequently demand excessive amounts or delay payment, thereby inciting lawsuits, which are very unbeneficial. Because of this, we the Ministry of the Secretariat[37] deliberated together and arrived at the following provisions. We have carefully considered them and recommend that they be enforced in their entirety. We sent up this report,[38] and respectfully received a superior communication from the Secretariat for State Affairs, saying:

> We sent this to the Central Secretariat and received their communiqué[39] in return, saying: "We approve the recommendation for enforcement. If both sides agree, however, they may do otherwise." We the Secretariat Office[40] [agree with what the Central Secretariat has decreed and] in addition order that you have this widely enforced.

35. *Zhafu* (札付 or 劄付). This is a specialized term for a communication from an office of the second rank or above to subordinate offices. The Central Secretariat was rank 1A, the highest other than the emperor himself.

36. *Shengzhi tiaohua* 聖旨條畫. These are regulations from top offices of government that have been approved by imperial edict. The term, like that for "Imperial Edict," is raised two character spaces above the top of the text to show the utmost respect. Here, these may refer to the vague rules on uxorilocal marriages included in case 18.1.

37. *Shengbu* 省部. This is a short name used by the Six Ministries to refer to themselves.

38. A report (*cheng* 呈) was a document sent from an inferior to a superior office. An example can be found in *Sitanyin disanci zhongya kaogu*, 1:210.

39. A communiqué (*zi* 咨) was a document sent between equals, in this case between the Secretariat for State Affairs and the Central Secretariat, which were nominally of equal rank.

40. *Shengfu* 省府. This term is generally used by the branch secretariats to refer to themselves, but in this early period, before the branch secretariats were set up, we find it used by the Central Secretariat and the Secretariat for State Affairs to refer to themselves. Here, it is the latter using the term.

Superior communication respectfully received. We the Ministry of the Secretariat investigated and found that go-betweens are getting registered in excessive numbers and are taking too much money. We order that the following provisions, itemized herein and sent out, be distributed widely to all subordinate offices, and that they be posted for the public and enforced.

Item 1. When inviting in a permanent uxorilocal son-in-law, the betrothal gifts should be one half of the amounts previously fixed for a regular marriage.[41] One must engage a [registered] go-between and establish a clear marriage contract to complete the marriage.

Item 2. When inviting in a temporary uxorilocal son-in-law, each party should follow what has been agreed to. They should engage a go-between and establish a clear marriage contract. Whether the payments are prepared by the male side or the female side, they should be based on the agreed-upon time limit [for residence in the bride's home]. The betrothal gifts should be calculated at not more than two thirds of the amounts previously fixed for a regular marriage.[42]

Item 3. It is the case that there are now fixed regulations governing marriages and betrothal gifts for both regular and uxorilocal unions. From now on, local leaders under the appropriate jurisdictions, such as commune chiefs, ward chiefs,[43] and local elders, must recommend and guarantee trustworthy women to become

41. These are the amounts specified in the edict of 1271, second month, case 18.2. In the case of permanent uxorilocal marriages, the bride's family usually made these payments, not the groom's, as specified in the chart at the beginning of chapter 18 in the *Yuan dianzhang*, added by the editors. See YDZ 18:1a. But see cases 18.5 and 18.8 for exceptions.

42. The chart at the beginning of chapter 18 indicates that in this case of a temporary uxorilocal marriage, the groom's family should pay the betrothal gifts (YDZ 18:1a), which we can understand to be reduced by one third to compensate for the time the groom spends laboring in the home of his in-laws. Nevertheless, the previous sentence suggests that payments could go in either direction, and indeed such examples are found in Yuan texts.

43. Commune chiefs (*shezhang* 社長) and ward chiefs (*xiangzhang* 巷長) were unpaid officers chosen locally in rural and urban areas, respectively, who operated under the supervision of government officials. As described in Yuan sources, the commune chiefs were responsible for such things as promoting agriculture, education, and security and for minor dispute resolution, and we can infer that ward chiefs had similar responsibilities. Khubilai's code of official conduct promulgated in 1291, the *Zhiyuan xinge*, gave commune chiefs explicit jurisdiction over marriage disputes. See Ch'en 1979, 124, 161 (original text). They were not supposed to collect taxes but in fact often got involved with such activities. See YS 93:2354–2355; Yang

go-betweens, and the local authorities will register their names. This will be strictly enforced in all cases. Go-betweens may not as was previously done demand too much money or be registered in excessive numbers.[44] Violators will be liable for prosecution.

Section 2: Getting Married

18.4

This is one of many remarkable and to a modern reader amusing cases in the *Yuan dianzhang*. Here, three men are trying to marry the same woman, Zhao Su'er. Her mother engages her to one man, her brother to another, and she herself elopes with a third. The Ministry of Revenue supports the mother's authority to arrange the marriage and invalidates the betrothal arranged by the brother. In this, the ruling is consistent with Song and Jin law, and law after the Yuan, all of which gave mothers authority over sons in property and marriage decisions.[45] It rules that, if the fiancé arranged by the mother, Wang Er, still wants to marry Zhao Su'er after her elopement, he may do so. But if he chooses not to, the betrothal gifts must be returned to him, and she is evidently free to marry someone else. It is strongly suggested that the latter will be the outcome, since Wang has already found another wife in the course of the lawsuit. The ruling does not mention any punishment for Zhao Su'er herself or her partner in adultery, and the case leaves open whether her marriage to him will stand (which the circuit authorities seem to support). A confusion in the name of the partner with whom Zhao Su'er elopes also leaves some doubt as to the final details of the case.

Ne 1975; Okamoto 1965; Schurmann 1956, 43–48; Ch'en 1979, 93–94, 121–124, 161; Farquhar 1990, 215–216.

44. This last injunction was reissued in 1282 in a ruling by the Regional Surveillance Office of Dongxi Region, Shandong Province, which also forbade go-betweens from charging a cut of the designated betrothal gifts. See TZTG 4:171 (Art. 83). The injunction against excessive fees charged by go-betweens is also repeated in the "Treatise on Punishments" in the Yuan dynastic history. See YS 103:2642; Ratchnevsky and Aubin 1972–1985, 2:118 (Art. 386).

45. QMJ 9:301; Shiga 1967, 427; TZTG 3:153–154 (Art. 60); *Da Ming ling* 1:6a (p. 19); Farmer 1995, 159; Ch'ü 1965, 99–102.

18.4 *While the mother is still living, the son cannot arrange a marriage*[46]

In the fifth year of the *zhiyuan* period (1268), tenth month, a document from the Ministry of Revenue of the Central Secretariat states:

We received your dispatch,[47] as follows:

> Tian Ying and Wang Xiucai each arranged a betrothal to the daughter of Zhao A-Wang,[48] Zhao Su'er. They sued each other, but before the case was decided, she went and got married to Meng Er. We could decide to give Zhao Su'er to Tian Ying to became his younger brother's wife, but it must be noted that Zhao Su'er's second older brother, Zhao Ding, arranged the marriage. He drank betrothal wine to confirm the engagement, yet he is not a person authorized to arrange the marriage. Or, we could decide to let Wang Xiucai have her to be his son's wife, then equally we must note that at this time Wang Xiucai has already obtained another wife for his son. We are left allowing her to become the wife of Meng Er. There has been no previous ruling in a case like this to use as a precedent. We humbly request that you consider this matter.

We the Ministry of the Secretariat deliberated the matter. Zhao Su'er has a mother who is still living, but her brother went outside the family and drank betrothal wine. It is not appropriate for a son to act on his own authority in this way. We cannot allow a betrothal arranged by the brother to stand.[49] Now,

---

46. YDZ 18:4a, p. 663.

47. A dispatch (*shen* 申) is a document from a subordinate office of the third rank or below to a superior office. It was used routinely for these petitions for legal review from a circuit (*lu* 路) up to the central government. The dispatch typically lays out the case and ends with a request for a ruling from the higher office, as here. The originating circuit is usually named, though here it is not. Circuits within the Central Province (Zhongshusheng) could send their dispatches directly to one of the Six Ministries, and before the creation of the branch secretariats other circuits could as well. After the creation of the branch secretariats, circuits outside of the Central Province could send documents only through their branch secretariat, which would pass them along to the Central Secretariat, which would send them to one of the Six Ministries for consideration.

48. The names of wives in the *Yuan dianzhang* are given almost without exception in this form, namely, the husband's surname, followed by "A-" (阿), then the wife's maiden surname. I have used a hyphen and capitalization to indicate that these are both surnames.

49. The ministry here uses the term *nan* 難, literally "hard to," to express this negative. This is a common expression in the *Yuan dianzhang* used to convey a negative in documents addressed to either superiors or, as in this case, inferiors. I translate it here as "cannot" to convey both the euphemistic softening of the negative and the legal authority it carried.

Zhao Su'er's mother, A-Wang, says that she accepted betrothal gifts from Wang Xiucai and arranged for his son Wang Er to marry her daughter. They should have gone ahead with the marriage. But before the marriage took place, Zhao Su'er had illicit sex with Little Li[50] and ran away with him. They were apprehended and brought before the authorities. Henceforth, if Wang Xiucai is no longer willing to marry Zhao Su'er to his son, then the betrothal presents that he originally gave to A-Wang should all be returned to him. We order you to give this ruling your careful consideration and enforce it accordingly.

18.5

In this interesting case from 1268, widow A-Li remarries, leaving her daughter behind in the home of her deceased husband, then later arranges the marriage of her daughter to the son of her second husband. When this son dies, A-Li and her husband accept betrothal gifts and arrange a second marriage for the daughter by inviting in an uxorilocal son-in-law. A-Li's former brother-in-law, Liu Heng, files suit to be involved in the marriage, objecting that the daughter's second marriage was during the mourning period for her first husband. In her testimony, widow A-Li reveals that she paid betrothal gifts to her former brother-in-law for the first marriage of her daughter, and no doubt Liu Heng wants to share in the second round of payments (though he says in his suit that A-Li herself received the first betrothal payments, a rather odd possibility, since they came from her husband).

As in 18.4, the Ministry of Revenue upholds the authority of the mother, A-Li, to arrange the marriage or remarriage of her daughter, noting that she is both the mother and mother-in-law in this case. It even chides the circuit authorities for sending the case up for review, something rarely found in the documents of the *Yuan dianzhang*. But in the final verdict, the ministry issues a mixed ruling that nevertheless orders the daughter to wait until the mourning period is over before remarrying and instructs A-Li to consult with her brother-in-law before arranging the uxorilocal marriage.[51]

---

50. It is not clear if this is the same man as Meng Er, mentioned earlier. This could be yet a fourth man who tried to marry Zhao Su'er.

51. The Taihe code of the Jin set the mourning period of a wife for her husband at twenty-seven months (see case 18.24), and the ministry seems to be accepting that as the law currently in effect, although their enforcement is not very strict, merely delaying rather than annulling the marriage. Such relatively mild consideration of the mourning period is typical of the early Yuan

This case contains an unusual example of the groom's family, not the bride's, paying betrothal gifts for a permanent uxorilocal marriage. Although contrary to the chart at the head of chapter 18 in the *Yuan dianzhang* (YDZ 18.1a), which specifies that the bride pay in these cases, this is consistent with the language in 18.3 referring to payments going in either direction. In this case perhaps the groom is willing to pay to enter another family because it will allow him to escape from the onerous military service owed by his father's hereditary soldier household. We will see in case 18.34 (dated 1273) that the government later forbade sons in these military households to marry out as uxorilocal husbands and thereby escape military service.[52]

18.5 *When a mother takes her daughter into a remarriage, she has authority over the daughter's marriage*[53]

In the fifth year of the *zhiyuan* period (1268), tenth month, a document from the Ministry of Revenue of the Secretariat for State Affairs[54] states:

We received your dispatch,[55] as follows:

Liu Heng of a civilian household registered in the Municipal Affairs Office[56] filed a plaint, stating:

Previously, my sister-in-law A-Li accepted betrothal gifts and arranged the marriage of my niece Po'an to Choulü, the son of Administrative Officer Zhang.[57] In the ninth month of the third year of *zhiyuan* (1266), the husband Choulü died. Before a year had passed, I learned that her father-

---

(see Birge 2002, 257–261). See case 18.15 for later developments in consideration of the mourning period.

52. In this case, 18.5, the new father-in-law, A-Li's second husband, holds an administrative post within the Yuan military system, so his household would presumably still count as a military household, although it would not have to supply in addition a soldier for the army.

53. YDZ 18:4a–b, pp. 663–664.

54. This should read "Central Secretariat." The Secretariat for State Affairs (Shangshusheng 尚書省) did not exist at this time. It was first established only in the first month of 1270.

55. We learn from the text below that this dispatch comes from a circuit. As in the previous case, the name of the circuit is omitted, but we know it is within the Central Province, since the dispatch is going directly to the Ministry of Revenue.

56. The Municipal Affairs Office (*lushisi* 錄事司) was a police office established in the urban seat of most circuits, responsible for registering the population, keeping order, and so forth. It was also found in some prefectures. See Farquhar 1990, 416, 419.

57. An Administrative Officer (*zongba* 總把) served within a chiliarchy, one of the decimal military units founded by the Mongols, consisting nominally of one thousand households. The post was abolished in 1284. See Farquhar 1990, 23; YS 98:2508; Hsiao 1978b, 72.

in-law Mr. Zhang had sold out her mourning,[58] by obtaining forty strings worth of paper money from Zhang Xiaoyi of a military household and inviting in his son to be her uxorilocal husband.

On account of this, we questioned Administrative Officer Zhang's wife, A-Li, who testified:

> Originally I was the wife of [Liu] Run, the older brother of the plaintiff, Liu Heng, and I gave birth to Po'an. Later, my husband the elder Liu died, and I, A-Li, got remarried to Administrative Officer Zhang. In the year *gengxü* (1250)[59] I paid betrothal gifts and obtained my daughter Po'an, who was left behind in the home of my first husband, the elder Liu, and I married her to Choulü, the son of my second husband, Zhang Yong [Administrative Officer Zhang]. In the ninth month of the third year of *zhiyuan* (1266), my son-in-law [Choulü] died. While my daughter was in mourning, in the fourth year of *zhiyuan* (1267), because our family was poor and we had no other son to take care of us, we accepted betrothal gifts of five bolts of silk from Zhang Xiaoyi, with the intention of inviting in his son Zhang Er to be the permanent uxorilocal husband of Po'an. But as yet, the marriage has not taken place.

We the circuit authorities[60] could decide to return Liu Po'an to her natal lineage, or we could allow her mother A-Li to arrange a remarriage. But there has been no previous ruling in a case like this to use as a precedent. We humbly request that you consider this matter thoroughly.

We the Ministry of the Secretariat deliberated the matter. We note that A-Li is Po'an's legal mother and moreover is her mother-in-law, thus one need not send up a dispatch to ask for a ruling. We order that Po'an observe mourning according to legal principles.[61] When it is completed, A-Li may arrange an uxorilocal marriage in consultation with the uncle Liu Heng.

---

58. *Maifu* 賣服, "to sell the mourning" or "sell out the mourning," refers to a relative's accepting betrothal gifts and arranging the marriage of a woman while she is still in mourning.

59. A-Li gives the year using the sixty-year cycle, *gengxu* 庚戌, corresponding to 1250. But 1250 seems a little early for the marriage (since the remarriage takes place in 1266), and this could be a mistake for another date, such as 1260 (*gengshen* 庚申).

60. *Fusi* 府司. This is a short term for the personnel of the Directorate-General (*zongguanfu* 總管府), the main administrative office of a circuit, at the head of which was a Director-General (*zongguan*).

61. *Yili* 依理. This term is used widely in the *Yuan dianzhang,* and is often interchangeable with *yili* 依例, "according to the regulations / precedent" or *yifa* 依法, "according to the law,"

18.6

This case involves an underage girl who is adopted into a family as the future bride for the family's son. Here the girl runs away at age fifteen, two years after the formal marriage to her adoptive brother, and manages to marry a man in a neighboring circuit to whom she bears a son. The first husband sues to get her back. The circuit posits that, since offspring have already been born to the couple, she be allowed to stay in her second marriage, but that the second husband must make restitution by repaying the original betrothal gifts.[62] The Ministry of Revenue disagrees and orders the young mother back to her original marriage.

These "little daughter-in-law" marriages remained common in China into modern times. Research on Taiwan in the twentieth century shows that they could be abusive and that they generated fewer offspring than marriages between mature partners.[63] This case suggests a similar situation in the Yuan.

18.6 *A man gets married to a runaway wife*[64]

In the sixth year of the *zhiyuan* period (1269), the fifth month, twenty-sixth day, Zhangde Circuit[65] sent up a dispatch and received back a certified document from the Ministry of Revenue of the Central Secretariat, as follows:

> [We received your dispatch, as follows:][66]
>
> > Li Banjie of Anyang County[67] filed a plaint, stating:
> >
> > > Hu Da'an of an ordinary household[68] in Fuyang County, Ci Prefecture,[69] and others snatched away my runaway wife Gao Huannu.

and often simply means "according to law." (Compare 18.43, where *yili* 依例 is used instead.) I have translated it variously according to the context. In earlier judicial usage, terms like *li* and *fa* were more clearly distinguished, meaning "principle" and "law," though in Southern Song times they were already used sometimes in combination. See MacCormack 2011, especially 170–171; Birge 2002, 195–196.

62. These were usually minimal in cases of future-bride adoptions.

63. See, for instance, Arthur Wolf 1981; Margery Wolf 1968, 1972; Wolf and Huang 1980.

64. YDZ 18:4b, p. 664.

65. In modern Henan Province, with the seat at modern Anyang, north of Zhengzhou.

66. This phrase is omitted in the original text but can be inferred from what follows.

67. A county in Zhangde Circuit, the site of modern Anyang.

68. *Renhu* 人戶. This term referred to households in the Yuan that were not of servile status.

69. This prefecture and county were in Guangping Circuit in the Yuan, just north of Zhangde, in modern Hebei. The two circuits mentioned in this case were both within the Central Province, so their dispatches went directly to the Ministry of Revenue without passing through the Central Secretariat. The text mistakenly gives Gan 淦 for Fu 滏, in the name of Fuyang County.

In consultation with our counterparts [in Guangping Circuit][70] we learned upon questioning that the parents of Li Banjie arranged his marriage. They hired a go-between, paid betrothal gifts, and adopted the child Gao Huannu into the family as a future bride for their son. When she reached the age of thirteen,[71] the actual marriage took place; and when she turned fifteen, she ran away. The testimony we obtained from Gao Huannu plus the go-between and others was the same. The defendant in the case, Hu Run, stated:

> I relied on Zhu A-Tang as the go-between, paid betrothal gifts, and obtained Gao Huannu as my wife. Now a son has been born to us. I absolutely did not know the situation that Li Banjie was betrothed to her already.

Since there has already been a son born to the couple, why not with Hu Run as a guarantor, have Gao Yuanshi come into the yamen and make him return the original betrothal gifts paid by Li Banjie? We humbly request that you consider this matter.

We the Ministry of the Secretariat deliberated the matter. Seeing that the go-between testified that, and the neighbor Fang A-Yao and others confirmed that, the parents of Li Banjie indeed paid betrothal gifts and adopted Gao Huannu into the family as a bride for their son, and that she ran away, we cannot allow Hu Run to contract a go-between, pay betrothal gifts, and marry her. In the end she is the wife of Li Banjie, and the situation should be rectified. We order that you take Gao Huannu and give her as before to Li Banjie to be his wife.

18.7

In this case, a man engages his daughter to be married, but eleven years have gone by, and the groom has still not come to pick up the bride and carry out the marriage. The Ministry of Revenue cites one of its earlier rulings as a precedent in determining that the groom has thirty days from the date of the ruling to carry out the marriage or else the bride is free to marry someone else. The

70. Since the crime was outside the circuit where the plaint was filed, the officials are required to consult with the authorities of the other circuit on the case.

71. All ages in the translation are given by Chinese counting (*sui* 歲), which results in an age on average one and a half years older than in Western reckoning.

decision is confirmed by both the Secretariat for State Affairs, which was in existence at this time, and the Central Secretariat above it. (The case initially goes directly to the Ministry of Revenue, since it comes from a circuit within the Central Province.) This case may have inspired the item of Khubilai's "Regulations Governing Marriages and Betrothal Gifts" of the following year (1271, second month; see 18.2) that specified a five-year limit between the betrothal and the marriage. This is one of many examples of a seemingly minor and straightforward matter getting passed up to the central government for a decision.

18.7 *If a man gets engaged to a woman but does not marry her, she may marry someone else*[72]

In the seventh year of the *zhiyuan* period (1270), fourth month, a document from the Ministry of Revenue of the Secretariat for State Affairs[73] states:
We received your report, as follows:

> Liu Quan filed a plaint, saying:
>
>> Yuan Kai through the services of a go-between negotiated the betrothal of his son to my daughter Banyi, and she has been thus engaged, unable to marry anyone else, for eleven years. Now my daughter Banyi is twenty-four years old, past marriageable age, but he has still not come to marry her.
>
> We humbly request that you consider this matter.

Report received. We have investigated and found that previously Taiyuan Circuit[74] submitted a dispatch about the plaint of Wu Gui, and these two cases are analogous. [In the earlier case] we sent an official report to the Central Secretariat and received a Secretarial decree[75] from the Central Hall[76] approving our decision, which reads as follows:

---

72. YDZ 18:4b–5a, pp. 664–665.
73. No space precedes the characters for this office in the text, as nominally required.
74. Modern Taiyuan, Shaanxi Province. This circuit was within the Central Province.
75. *Junzhi* 鈞旨. This is a specialized term for an order issued by officials of the first rank, such as the councilors of the Central Secretariat, rank 1A (as in this case), the heads of the Censorate and Bureau of Military affairs, rank 1B, or some imperial sons-in-law. For an early Ming gloss, see *Liwen jilan,* in Maema and Suematsu 1975, 335.
76. *Dutang* 都堂. This term is a commonly used synecdoche referring to the Central Secretariat, and a space always precedes it.

Within thirty days of when the certified document [with the decision] from this Ministry arrives, the fiancé must submit betrothal gifts and complete the marriage. If he does not carry out the marriage within the time limit, the bride may go and marry someone else.

Now, in the dispatch currently before us, the legal situation is analogous. We sent a report to the Secretariat for State Affairs and received back a juridical communication,[77] stating:

We received a Secretarial decree from the Central Hall, stating: "We approve the decision."

Distribute this to all subordinate offices, and enforce it according to the above.

18.8

In this case a man arranges the betrothal of his daughter. But before the marriage takes place, he arranges for his daughter to marry another man, who is invited into their home as an uxorilocal husband. The father of the first fiancé sues to have the first marriage carried out, and since the bride's father had accepted the betrothal gifts, the plaintiff wins his case. Oddly, in the *Yuan dianzhang* record, the two fiancés share the same given name, Lü'er, meaning "donkey."

This ruling reinforces the law, found in Tang, Song and earlier codes, that the acceptance of betrothal gifts constituted an irreversible commitment to go through with a marriage. (See 18.1 annotation, and cases 18.18, 18.44, and 18.45.)

18.8 *A woman who is already betrothed marries someone else*[78]

In the tenth year of the *zhiyuan* period (1273), fourth month, a document from the Ministry of Revenue of the Central Secretariat states:

A dispatch from Dadu Circuit[79] reads:

Guo Bocheng filed a plaint, stating:

Li Zhonghe took his daughter Chouge, who was originally betrothed to my son, and went and married her to Lü'er as his uxorilocal son-in-law.

---

77. *Pansong* 判送. This is a document from the Secretariat to one of the Six Ministries. It is in the form of a brief note appended to another document, usually asking for a decision or approving a decision contained in the document, as in this case. See the example in Miya 2001.

78. YDZ 18:5a, p. 665.

79. This was the capital, modern Beijing.

We obtained testimony from the various parties. We the circuit authorities deliberated together and determined that, in the eighth month of the sixth year of *zhiyuan* (1269), Li Zhonghe, through the services of a go-between, arranged the betrothal of his daughter Chouge to Lü'er [the son of] Guo Bocheng. He accepted betrothal payments of thirty-five ounces worth of paper money,[80] wedding gifts,[81] and other items to conclude the engagement. But before the marriage was carried out and they had brought her to their home, [Li Zhonghe] in the seventh year of *zhiyuan* (1270) further accepted betrothal payments of fifteen ounces worth of paper money from Shi Lü'er and invited him into their home as an uxorilocal son-in-law.[82]

We have considered the circumstances and decided the punishment according to the crime to which the protagonist has confessed, to be carried out after the protagonist recovers from illness. Shi Lü'er did not know of the situation that Guo Bocheng had arranged a betrothal to Li Chouge, but based on legal principles his marriage should be annulled. Li Chouge should be given to Guo Bocheng's son, Lü'er, to be his wife. There need be no further payment of betrothal gifts beyond the thirty-five[83] ounces already paid. The betrothal gifts worth fifteen ounces that Li Zhonghe accepted from Shi Lü'er should be returned to him. Since this ruling will stand as a precedent for a long time to come, we humbly request that you render a clear decision.

We the Ministry of the Secretariat received your report and deliberated the matter. We order that you investigate the matter further, and if there has been no mistake, we approve the decision for enforcement. In addition, regarding the

---

80. An "ounce" (*liang*), nominally of silver, was a denomination of paper currency. It was equivalent to a "string" (*guan*) of one thousand cash, another denomination of paper money (seen in case 18.2). Its actual conversion was to half an ounce of real silver (see Chan 1990, 446).

81. Reading *huahong* 花紅 for *honghua* 紅花. *Huahong* (literally "flowery red things"), referring originally to red silk, was a general term for items given as betrothal gifts. (*Honghua*, the red-flowering plant safflower, was used for medicine or dye.)

82. Note that these payments for a permanent uxorilocal marriage are coming from the groom's side, not the bride's, contrary to the chart at the beginning of chapter 18 in the *Yuan dianzhang*. Nevertheless, they are approximately one half of the amount that Li Zhonghe accepted for the patrilocal marriage of his daughter, as specified in the regulations of 1271, seventh month (case 18.3).

83. The text mistakenly omits the character for "three" (*san*) and thus reads "fifteen" (*shiwu*) ounces instead of "thirty five" (*sanshiwu*).

betrothal payments of fifteen ounces that Shi Lü'er made, only if the said person truly did not know of the situation should the full amount be returned to him.

18.9

This case offers an early example of the problems that could arise in uxorilocal marriages. Case 18.10 offers a litany of similar complaints about uxorilocal husbands absconding and abandoning the families they had married into. In fact, legal handbooks of the Yuan included sample plaints for filing a lawsuit against an uxorilocal son-in-law who refused to support the family.[84] Here, a mother, presumably widowed, arranged a temporary uxorilocal marriage for her daughter, until her son "was grown up." But a year later, the husband ran away and married another woman. Fourteen years later, the mother brought a lawsuit. The circuit authorities arrived at a compromise solution. Noting that the mother and son-in-law could no longer be expected to live together, but finding nothing to justify annulling the marriage, they ruled that the son-in-law should pay the full complement of betrothal gifts and take the daughter into a new home in a virilocal marriage. The Ministry of Revenue approved the decision, but neither ruling addressed the fact that the man would now have two wives.

The mother and son-in-law were both sojourning far from Dadu (Beijing) in Qianzhou, a non-Han area in Central Asia on the northwest edge of Khubilai's khanate, possibly as part of a program forcibly to settle artisans there.[85] The lawsuit was filed back in Dadu, after they had both returned from Qianzhou. Such circumstances may explain why the suit came so late, probably after the natal son had grown up and the time period during which the son-in-law was obliged to labor for his mother-in-law had been exceeded, and why the Ministry was still willing to consider it.

84. See *Yuandai falü*, 224–225.
85. Qianzhou 欠州 (also written 謙州, and other variants) is the site of modern Kyzyl, the capital of the Tuva Republic in southern Russia, along the upper reaches of the Yenisei River (it claims to be the exact center of Asia). It was approximately five hundred miles northwest of Khara Khorum in Yuan times and was inhabited by Mongols, Uighurs, and Kirgiz. The Yuan dynasty history refers to artisan and agricultural families being settled there, though the people in this case evidently stayed only temporarily. They may have been part of a group allowed to return to Han territory in 1265. See YS 63:1574–1575 and YS 6:105. On Yuan administration of the area, see Zhou 2001.

18.9 *An uxorilocal husband abandons his wife and marries someone else*[86]

In the tenth year of the *zhiyuan* period (1273), sixth month, a document from the Ministry of Revenue of the Central Secretariat states:

A dispatch from Dadu Circuit reads:

We respectfully received your juridical communication.[87] Liu A-Gao filed a written plaint, stating:

In the year *yiwei* (1259) when I was sojourning in Qianzhou through the services of Sister Gao and others as go-betweens, I paid engagement gifts[88] and arranged to invite in Zhang Shilü to marry my daughter Sinu as an uxorilocal husband. We agreed that he would live with us until my son was grown up, at which time he would be allowed to leave our home and live elsewhere. In the second month of the year *gengshen* (1260) he stopped supporting the family; moreover, he abandoned my daughter Sinu and went and married another woman, Zhi Xian'er, and he no longer comes to our house.

We the circuit authorities obtained through interrogation the testimony of Zhang Shilü, whose given name is Rong, as follows:

In the year *yiwei* (1259), I went to Qianzhou to live in the home of my mother-in-law Liu A-Gao, as an uxorilocal son-in-law. It is indeed true that we agreed I would take on the taxes and labor duty of the household.

We the circuit authorities carefully examined the matter and determined that, Liu A-Gao paid engagement gifts and arranged to invite in Zhang Rong as an uxorilocal son-in-law. He lived in her home for one year, then left and married another woman, Zhi Xian'er. He lived with her elsewhere for fourteen years without providing any food or clothing to Sinu. If we make him go back to being an uxorilocal son-in-law, it seems likely that the parties will not be willing to live together. Nevertheless, there is also no legal basis for annulling the marriage. We rule that Zhang Rong should prepare betrothal payments worth fifty ounces,

---

86. YDZ 18:5a–b, pp. 665–666.

87. This phrase has been inserted erroneously, or perhaps a part of the text is missing, since a "juridical communication" (*pansong*) is a document from the Central Secretariat to one of the Six Ministries and cannot have been received by a circuit.

88. Literally "red engagement gifts" (*hongding* 紅定). This is another term for betrothal gifts.

corresponding to a middle-tier household,[89] and that he marry Liu Sinu and take her into a separate household. We humbly request that you consider this matter.

We the Ministry of the Secretariat deliberated the matter. We order that you investigate the matter further, and if there has been no mistake, we approve the decision for enforcement.

18.10

Uxorilocal marriages, where the husband was "invited-in" and lived in his wife's parents' home, were common in the Yuan, but as the document in this case illustrates, in a Confucian-oriented, patrilocal society, they raised significant social and legal problems concerning the balance of power between the wife's and the husband's side in a marriage. This text, dated 1273, provides a remarkable example of how women and their families in north China used prenuptial contracts to manipulate the law in their favor and circumvent Confucian social structures that otherwise privileged the male side.

Parents of an uxorilocal son-in-law expected him to follow their orders and work to support the family, and as testimony recorded in this case suggests, some may have treated their sons-in-law harshly and as little more than bondservants. At the same time, as the complaints reveal, the son-in-law might refuse to work, while away hours getting drunk, and wantonly spend or outright steal the family's money. Moreover, if the son-in-law ran away, the wife could not legally remarry unless she obtained a letter of divorce from her husband. This left the wife's household deprived of the male labor they needed from an uxorilocal husband. In anticipation of this problem, legally savvy parents of the bride might insert clauses into the marriage contract stipulating that if the husband refused to work, disobeyed his in-laws, or ran away, the marriage would be null and void. The nearly identical wording of these clauses in different instances suggests that they came from model contract books compiled by local legal experts.[90]

In five lawsuits described in this case, we find relatives of the wife of an uxorilocal husband who has absconded bringing a plaint to allow the wife to di-

---

89. This indeed corresponds to the fifty strings worth of paper currency specified in Khubilai's Regulations of 1271 (case 18.2) for a middle-tier household, fifty ounces of silver being equivalent to fifty strings of cash.

90. Similarly, model plaints for a lawsuit against a wayward son-in-law can be found in surviving Yuan legal handbooks. See *Yuandai falü*, 224–225.

vorce her husband in his absence and marry someone else, thus regaining male labor for the household. The suits describe how sons-in-law have refused to work and run away without returning, sometimes stealing valuables or even beating their in-laws before leaving. In several instances the wayward husband has been captured by the authorities, given a beating, and returned to his wife's family, only to run away again. Significantly, the plaintiffs all assert that their original marriage contracts have clauses stipulating that in such cases the wife will be free to remarry on her own initiative. Nevertheless, they still feel the need to go to court to have these prenuptial agreements in private contracts sanctioned.

The Ministry of Revenue here sides with the female plaintiffs, and the Central Secretariat confirms their decision. In response to a case sent up from Taiyuan Circuit in 1268, the Ministry rules that the government should honor privately negotiated marriage contracts and allow the wives in these cases to divorce and remarry. They build a careful argument, citing four earlier lawsuits to illustrate the frequent bad behavior of uxorilocal husbands and arguing that the parties should be held to the contracts they have negotiated. Their ruling gives enhanced legal privileges to the wife, in essence granting her the right of unilateral divorce, as the husband would have in a patrilocal marriage. Responding to a significant source of local disputes and lawsuits, the ruling also gives private prenuptial agreements the force of law, thus backing away from any centrally imposed, universal vision of marriage. This document reveals two instances, one earlier than the other, when the Ministry of Revenue deliberated and issued a ruling on this matter. Both supported the wife's family, and both won approval from the Central Secretariat. This is noteworthy, for less than two years later in the following case (18.11) the Ministry was to reverse itself completely on this issue.

18.10 *When a live-in son-in-law runs away, adjudicate a divorce based on the original marriage contract*[91]

In the tenth year of the *zhiyuan* period (1273), twelfth month, a document from the Ministry of Revenue of the Central Secretariat states:

We respectfully received a juridical communication from the Central Secretariat. The original report from this Ministry reads:

A dispatch from Taiyuan Circuit reads:

Song Derong filed a plaint, stating:

91. YDZ 18:5a–7b, pp. 666–670.

In the fifth year of the *zhiyuan* period (1268), seventh month, we established a marriage contract and invited in Shi Huhu, the younger brother of Shi Xian from the north suburb of the administrative seat, to [marry] my niece Xiaomei. The contract we established said that, [if he runs away] and she remarries on her own initiative,[92] Shi Xian and Shi Huhu may not contest the remarriage in court. In the seventh month of the seventh year of *zhiyuan* (1270), our son-in-law Shi Huhu[93] ran away. On the fifteenth day of the same month, our son-in-law Shi Huhu was found in the home of our relative by marriage [his brother] Shi Xian, and on the seventeenth day, Commune Chief Miao of this suburb sent him back to our home. On the eighteenth day, he went and ran away again, and we don't know where he is.

We [the circuit authorities] apprehended all the people involved to give evidence, and their testimony was all the same. It is the case that Shi Huhu ran away three years ago. A search was mounted, but he could not be found. We could adjudicate this on the basis of the contract that was originally established, but we have not seen a ruling in a case like this to use as a precedent. We humbly request that you consider this matter.

Report received. This Ministry investigated and found numerous previous dispatches submitted from circuits such as Dadu[94] and Weihui,[95] including the cases of Yang A-Wang and other families, who filed plaints claiming that an uxorilocal son-in-law had run away. We summarize some examples as follows:

[Example 1] Yang A-Wang filed a written plaint, stating:

In the ninth month of the second year of *zhiyuan* (1265), with the services of a go-between I established a written marriage contract, which read:

We are inviting in Shige, the son of Ma Dexin, to be the permanent uxorilocal husband of my daughter Zhangge. If Ma Shige refuses to work or will not maintain the family enterprise, this document will stand as

---

92. That is, without a letter of divorce from the husband, which would release the wife to remarry legally. Some characters are missing from the text here, but the meaning is clear from what follows. See Hayden 1978, 146–147, for an example in the Judge Bao play *Houting hua* (*The Flower of the Back Courtyard*), where a wife's lover forces her husband to sign a divorce document.

93. The text erroneously reads Shi Huyi.

94. Text reads Taidu for Dadu.

95. In modern Henan Province, just north of Zhengzhou and Kaifeng. It was in the southern part of the Central Province during the Yuan.

a letter of divorce, and he will additionally be fined fifty ounces worth of paper money.

He lived with us until the twenty-third day of the fourth month of the sixth year of *zhiyuan* (1269), when our son-in-law Ma Shige ran away, taking with him money and property from our family. Then on the twenty-third day of the sixth month of the eighth year of *zhiyuan* (1271), Ma Dexin and his wife, together with the go-between Zhao Niang, brought our son-in-law Ma Shige back to our home. They established a new contract vowing on pain of death that he would not abscond again, and he went back to living with us as before. Then on the sixth day of the tenth month, Ma Shige ran away again, this time stealing gold and silver hairpins and jewelry.

[Example 2] Zhang Rong filed a plaint, stating:

We established a marriage contract, which read:

We invite in Zhang Xiaoxing, the son of Zhang A-Feng, to marry my niece Fuxian, as a permanent uxorilocal husband. If he [does not obey] the instructions of his father- and mother-in-law or does not maintain the family enterprise, or if he runs away and does not return within sixty days, then this document will stand as a letter of divorce.[96] And if Zhang Fuxian gets remarried to someone else, he cannot contest it in court. If he on the contrary does contest the remarriage in court, he will willingly pay a fine of one hundred strings worth of paper currency to be confiscated by the government, to which he cannot object.

We thus wrote the marriage contract. On the twenty-eighth day of the seventh month of the fourth year of *zhiyuan* (1267), our son-in-law entered our house. On the eighteenth day of the fifth month of the seventh year of *zhiyuan* (1270) our son-in-law Zhang Xiaoxing, without any reason or being reprimanded, ran away. In the ninth month, we filed a plaint in this circuit. In the twelfth month, the authorities of Qi Prefecture[97] forced Zhang Xiaoxing's older brother Zhang Er to search for our son-in-law Zhang Xiaoxing and bring him into court. They punished our son-in-law Zhang Xiaoxing with a beating of 27 strokes and told him to go back and live in my, Rong's,

96. In Song law, a wife could remarry if her husband left and did not return for three years (QMJ 9:353). See also Birge 2002, 132–133; Niida (1964) 1991b, 398–399; McKnight 1996, 112–113.

97. Modern Qi County, in the northern part of Henan Province. It was part of Weihui Circuit in the Yuan.

household and work to support our family. On the seventeenth day of the
sixth month [of the next year], Zhang Xiaoxing ran away again. This time, on
the contrary, the Supervisor and Bandit Control Officer[98] of the prefecture
summoned me, Rong, to court for questioning. They received a document
from the Municipal Affairs Office of Nanjing Circuit[99] stating that our son-
in-law Zhang Xiaoxing had become a bandit and at present had run away.

[Example 3] An Lin filed a plaint, stating:

In the eighth month of the second year of *zhiyuan* (1265) I had Meng Delu
act as go-between to invite in Wang Lüge of the same hamlet,[100] the stepson
of Li Da the Lamb Roaster by his wife's previous marriage, to marry my
daughter Xiuge as a permanent uxorilocal husband. We established a
marriage contract, which read:

If our son-in-law Lüge is lazy and indolent, wasteful and profligate, does
not maintain the family enterprise, or does not obey the orders of his fa-
ther- and mother-in-law, this document will stand as a letter of divorce.

After the marriage, in the seventh month of the fifth year of *zhiyuan* (1268),
Wang Lüge refused to work to maintain the family enterprise. He jumped
into the well [and attempted] to kill himself. He violently attacked his
mother-in-law, knocking her down, then ran away. We filed a plaint in
Wanping County[101] and with the authorities of this appanage.[102] We established another contract, on pain of death, which read:

If from now on Lüge acts the least little bit perversely, or does not attend to his father- and mother-in-law, then Li Da the Lamb Roaster
will himself willingly accept all responsibility. And if Lüge after this

---

98. For these offices see Farquhar 1990, 20, 419; YS 91:2317. Being a low-level prefecture,
these two offices were combined in Weihui.

99. Modern Kaifeng in Henan. It was part of the Central Province during the Yuan.

100. A hamlet (*du* 都) was the lowest-level administrative unit in rural areas during the
Yuan. It was inherited from the Song and Jin dynasties, and during the Southern Song it
gradually replaced the *li* (里) as the lowest level of rural administration, as part of the *dubao*
security system. As in the Song, the units were primarily responsible for taxes and security,
among other matters. See McKnight 1972, 75–77.

101. This county was part of the capital circuit (modern Beijing), and controlled the area
outside the gates to the west.

102. Certain territories and individual households within Yuan territory belonged to private appanages (*touxia* 投下), which were granted by Yuan emperors to their relatives and close
allies. These had their own separate administration. One of the parties in this case must have
belonged to an appanage, and thus the plaint also had to be filed with the appanage authorities. On appanages, see Farquhar 1990, 17–18; Ratchnevsky 1993.

acts wickedly, as he did before, and does not maintain the family enterprise, then this document will stand as a letter of divorce,[103] and he cannot contest it in court.

After this, our son-in-law Wang Lüge just as before refused to work to support the family. He ruined our household through his wicked business plans. Thus we [again] brought a plaint to the authorities of Wanping County. In the second month of the eighth year of *zhiyuan* (1271), they sent up a dispatch and respectfully received back a certified document from the Ministry of Revenue of the Secretariat for State Affairs. They gave Wang Lüge a beating of 27 strokes and ordered him back to our home to be our son-in-law as before. They said that if thereafter he again disobeyed as before and did not work to maintain the family enterprise, we could go to court and report the facts and would be allowed to obtain a divorce. Thereafter, he harbored a grudge. He falsely accused our daughter Xiuge of adultery and hatched a nefarious plan to sell her to a brothel.[104] Moreover, he became violent and hit his mother-in-law in the left eye, causing her serious injury.

Such was the plaint. Dadu Circuit obtained the confession of the said person and was about to sentence him to punishment when he again ran away.

[Example 4] Wang Delin filed a plaint, stating:

In the fourth month of the third year of *zhiyuan* (1266), I invited in Meng Yelü, the son of Meng Fu of this circuit, to marry my daughter Wage and live in our home for fifteen years as her uxorilocal husband. We established a marriage contract, which read:

From here on in, he may absolutely not be wasteful or profligate. If he does not tend to the family enterprise or does not work for his upkeep, this document will stand as a letter of divorce.

We thus established the marriage contract. On the nineteenth day of the fifth month of the fifth year of *zhiyuan* (1268), our son-in-law Meng Yelü without any reason or being reprimanded, ran away.

[End of examples]

---

103. Reading *xiu* 休 for *fu* 伏.

104. Literally "have a brothel buy her as a prostitute." In the Yuan, an adulterous woman could be sold legally into another marriage but not into prostitution. See YS 104:2644, 2654. The text uses the term *maixiu* 買休, "to buy a divorce," a common term for buying a wife from someone already married to her, in essence wife-selling on the part of the husband. The term appears in Yuan drama and legal texts of the Yuan, Ming, and Qing.

In response to these dispatches from various circuits, we have provisionally decided that these cases should be adjudicated on the basis of the marriage contract. But we note that, there has been no previous ruling to use as a precedent. This Ministry has already sent out decisions in response to the dispatches sent up from the various circuits. Moreover, we note that in the second month of the sixth year of *zhiyuan* (1269) [we] the Ministry of Revenue of the Secretariat for State Affairs[105] [previously] issued a decision, as follows:[106]

> It is the case that marriage practices among the people are inconsistent. There are those who establish a written marriage contract and formal agreements. But there are also those who do not establish a written contract detailing the betrothal payments they originally agreed upon and [instead only] rely on a go-between to carry out the marriage. After the engagement, they will use the pretext of not having a written marriage contract to increase or decrease the marriage payments. They will dispute how long an uxorilocal son-in-law should stay in his in-laws' home, and the litigation never ends. We deliberated and decided: from now on those who get married must write out a marriage contract and establish a formal agreement. [It must state] the amount of betrothal payments that were originally negotiated and whether an uxorilocal son-in-law is permanent or temporary, and for how many years. The sponsor of the marriage, the guarantor, and the go-between, must all sign the contract, in order for a legal marriage to take place. In this way, lawsuits will be prevented. Have this regulation distributed to each circuit and enforce it according to the above. We present this report to the Central Secretariat for their thorough consideration.

In addition, in the sixth month of the eighth year of *zhiyuan* (1271), we respectfully received a superior communication from the Secretariat for State Affairs, which reads:[107]

105. This should read "Central Secretariat." The Secretariat for State Affairs did not exist at this time; moreover, the end of this decision and case 18.1 make clear that the Ministry was operating here under the Central Secretariat. See case 18.5 for the same error.

106. What follows is nearly an exact quote of the decision recorded in case 18.1, requiring that a written marriage contract be established for a marriage to be legal. Case 18.1 has a date of third month of 1269, when the circuit received the decision.

107. What follows is nearly an exact quote of the first regulation recorded in case 18.3, the "Rules for Marriage Payments for Uxorilocal Sons-in-Law." Note that the Ministry of Revenue attributes this regulation to the Secretariat for State Affairs, which approved it.

When inviting in a permanent uxorilocal son-in-law, the betrothal gifts should be one half of the amounts previously fixed for a regular marriage. One must engage a [registered] go-between and establish a clear marriage contract to complete the marriage.

We also sent out this ruling to each circuit telling them to enforce it. Now, with regard to the dispatch from Taiyuan Circuit currently before us, on the matter of the plaint from Song Derong that his son-in-law ran away in disregard of the original marriage contract, and such matters, it is the case that [Song Derong] invited in his uxorilocal son-in-law before the second month of the sixth year of *zhiyuan* (1269).[108] His son-in-law subsequently did not maintain the family enterprise and willfully violating the original marriage contract ran away. This Ministry could adjudicate this case on the basis of the actual marriage contract, but there is no established precedent for this. Therefore we laid out a summary of dispatches from various circuits containing plaints about uxorilocal sons-in-law who had run away. On the basis of these, we deliberated and conclude: families among the people who invite in an uxorilocal son-in-law, whether they have no male heir, or whether they have a son who is still young, it is because they have no one to care for them. Among them are families with daughters who pay betrothal gifts and invite in a permanent uxorilocal son-in-law, with the plan of obtaining his labor [to support the family]. There are also families with sons who have no property and therefore [arrange for their son] to be a temporary uxorilocal son-in-law. The two families of the bride and the groom together negotiate and establish a clear marriage contract to secure a guarantee of the marriage. They write such lines as "If our son-in-law does not maintain the family enterprise and runs away, etc., [this contract] will stand as a letter of divorce." This is simply to control their uxorilocal sons-in-law and make them willing to work for the wife's family according to the law, and [prevent them from] unlawfully getting drunk, being lazy and indolent, being wasteful and profligate, not maintaining the family enterprise, and not obeying the orders of their father- and mother-in-law. And there are those who write, "If [our son-in-law] runs away and does not come back to this family for one-hundred days or sixty days, this marriage contract that has been

108. That is, the event happened before the ruling of 1269 quoted above and in case 18.1 requiring a written marriage contract with certain details.

established will stand as a document of divorce, and [the wife] is at liberty to
marry someone else." Moreover, there are those who, because the son-in-law
previously did not maintain the family enterprise but seeks permission to stay
in his wife's family, establish a new contract. They write such lines as "If as in
the past he does not maintain the family enterprise, this document will stand
as a letter of divorce." In response to all of the cases that have come before us in
dispatches as laid out above, we have already sent down decisions to the various
circuits, but up to now the lawsuits cannot be stopped.

As a matter of course, those who become uxorilocal sons-in-law, after they
get married and move to their wife's home, if their parents are living, they
long to return to their own homes. If their parents and grandparents have
passed away, they still scheme to live separately. Even though they have these
intentions, their plans cannot be carried out. So instead they just refuse to
work in the wife's family. They unlawfully get drunk, are lazy and indolent,
steal money, and run away. The lawsuits all arise from this. The wife's family
files a plaint with the authorities, and after many years it is still unresolved.
These suits disrupt government offices and are extremely unbeneficial.

In light of this we have carefully examined the matter and note: if we do
not rely on the privately negotiated marriage contract to adjudicate these
cases, there is nothing on which to base a decision. Thus we rule that all
cases from the various circuits regarding uxorilocal sons-in-law should be
adjudicated according to the marriage contract, which was willingly established by the two parties themselves. A divorce should be allowed, and the
wife should be permitted to marry someone else, to warn those who come
afterwards. This should prevent sons-in-law from being unwilling[109] to work
to support the wife' family according to the law, eradicate past abuses, and
gradually make customs pure and honest.[110]

We submitted this report, and respectfully received a Secretarial decree from
the Central Hall sent to this Ministry, which reads:

If families whose sons have married out as uxorilocal sons-in-law have no
objections, then we approve the decision for enforcement.

---

109. The text reads "willing," but clearly a negative is missing here.

110. Here ends the long quote of the ministry's original report to the Central Secretariat,
mentioned in the first line, with their ruling on the Song Derong case from Taiyuan and the
other four examples used to support their decision. What follows includes the approval from
the Central Secretariat of the decision and a second decision by the ministry.

This Ministry went and analyzed the matter further, and we conclude: In ruling on the dispatches from the various circuits, we could adjudicate according to the originally established marriage contract, but there has been no previous ruling in a case like this to use as a precedent. In addition, one does not have testimony or explanations from both the husband's and wife's family. Therefore, after many years the suits are still unresolved. Moreover, when the son-in-law has run away at the time of the suit, if one does not rely on the privately negotiated marriage contract to adjudicate the case, there is nothing on which to base a decision. Now regarding the [Secretarial decree] that we have respectfully received, in these cases, the son-in-law and his family have already violated the original agreement, and they make up all sorts of deceptive excuses, thus there cannot but be objections from them. In light of this we have carefully examined the matter, and we rule that the original decision of this Ministry should stand. These cases should be adjudicated according to the privately negotiated marriage contract, which was willingly established by the two parties themselves, and a divorce should be allowed. In this way, there is a basis for adjudication, and this should prevent lawsuits so that they do not disrupt government offices. We submitted this report, and respectfully received a Secretarial decree from the Central Hall sent to this Ministry, which reads:

We approve the decision. Have it enforced.

18.11

Less than two years after the order in 18.10 was promulgated, in the third month of 1275, a county magistrate from Shandong Province named Du Run submitted a strenuous objection. What is most remarkable about his plea is that it represents a completely different approach to governance and law than that seen in the 1273 decision of the Ministry of Revenue. The earlier reasoning of the Ministry of Revenue was that local practices negotiated through private contracts between two opposing parties could be supported by law. In the case of uxorilocal marriage, this government support of prenuptial contracts gave the wife's family new legal and social leverage. Magistrate Du on the other hand argued that the role of government was precisely to *change* local customs and provide moral instruction to enforce a state-determined vision of ethical behavior. It was the job of the government to intervene in local society and impose a universal moral vision on the com-

munity. His discourse is thoroughly Neo-Confucian, invoking cosmic principles and the Confucian classic the *Book of Changes* to support his argument.
And his perspective on the role of government further betrays his Neo-Confucian
lens; he argues for a state-led moral and religious transformation that goes
beyond mere law but that uses law to force behavioral changes. Du argues
that a wife cannot be allowed to set prenuptial conditions that give her the
power of unilateral divorce, but rather that marriage is a sacred and eternal
bond between a man and a woman with wide cosmic significance. (Du does
not address the point that the husband was legally allowed to divorce his wife
unilaterally.)

Magistrate Du's petition was forwarded on by the circuit (see Chart 2),
which added its own endorsement and accused wives of switching husbands
freely in search of selfish personal gain. When the proposal reached the Ministry of Revenue it found strong support. The approval by the ministry openly
acknowledged that this was an exact reversal of their earlier ruling on the subject, which they even quote at the outset. The Central Secretariat in their further confirmation of the new ruling highlighted the reversal directly also, by
quoting their earlier words: "One may not as previously done include in a marriage contract words or phrases such as 'If an uxorilocal son-in-law runs away,
etc., then [this contract] will stand as a letter of divorce.'" In adopting Magistrate Du's proposal, the ministry and the Secretariat of State Affairs were em-
bracing a new vision of government as the keeper of Confucian values and the
enforcer of patriarchal authority, even if these went against long-standing local
practices. Gone was the previous sympathy for the wife's family and the dilemmas they faced within the legal system. The contradictions represented by
these two decisions would continue to plague the Yuan dynasty in the following decades.

18.11 *Uxorilocal husbands who run away*[111]

In the twelfth year of the *zhiyuan* period (1275), third month, a document from
the Ministry of Revenue of the Central Secretariat states:

Previously, when members of civilian households invited in an uxorilocal son-
in-law, they established marriage contracts and wrote phrases like "If before his
term of residence is completed he runs away for one hundred days or sixty days,

---

111. YDZ 18:7b–8a, pp. 670–671. A short paraphrase of this case appears in TZTG 4:166
(Art. 75), which omits any indication that this is a reversal of an earlier decision.

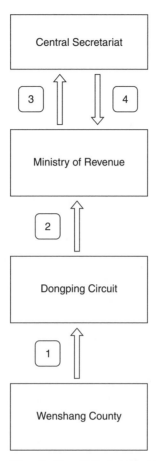

Chart 2. Case 18.11, document flow.

then [this contract] will stand as a letter of divorce, and the wife is allowed to re-marry." We submitted a report, and respectfully received a Secretarial decree from the Central Hall, approving our decision that these cases should be adjudicated according to the marriage contract willingly established by the two parties, and a divorce allowed.[112] After we sent out this order, we now note [a dispatch] from Dongping Circuit,[113] which reads:

112. This is a paraphrase of the decision as recorded at the end of case 18.10.

113. Dongping Circuit, which contained Wenshang County, is in modern Shandong Province, southwest of modern Tai'an. The circuit was part of the Central Province in Yuan times, thus the dispatch goes directly to the Ministry of Rites without passing through a branch secretariat or the Central Secretariat.

A dispatch from Wenshang County reads:

A memo[114] from County Magistrate Du Run reads as follows:

After careful consideration I humbly note that Heaven and Earth are the foundation of all things, and the alternation of movement and quietude is their constant principle. Husband and wife are the basis of human moral relations, and enduring permanence is their constant principle. What is meant by the constant principle is none other than to hold to permanence without deviation, namely not ever changing. For this reason, the "Sequence of Hexagrams" chapter of the *Book of Changes* says: "The way of husband and wife cannot but be one of perseverance. Therefore the hexagram for 'constancy' follows."[115] When one considers the matter from this perspective, it is clear that the way of husband and wife cannot include divorce. Nowadays, even before they get married people plan for their marriage not to be permanent. How can this constitute pure and honest customs? Rather it is debauched and stingy practice. Why not therefore restrain it [by law]? The original reason to establish a marriage contract is fundamentally to prevent either the groom's or bride's side from deceiving the other, to verify the amount of betrothal payments, and to preclude illicit relations.[116] It is not for the bride or groom to set up conditions for whether the marriage will be permanent or not. In later generations, customs became debauched, thus such calculations transpired. This must be forbidden and cannot be abided. If an uxorilocal son-in-law does not work to support the family enterprise or is lazy and indolent, there are already as a matter of course long-standing laws to deal with the situation. One cannot comply with selfish calculations and harm moral relations, or transform ancient moral traditions into debauched customs. It is better to return to the orthodox way and

114. A "memo" (*guan* 關) was a communication between equals of the third rank or below, such as between the Six Ministries. Here the magistrate is writing a memo to his own office, which it then passes up to the circuit.

115. This is a quotation from the *Book of Changes* (*Yijing* 易經), Ninth "Wing," "Sequence of Hexagrams" (序卦傳), commentary on Hexagrams 31 and 32. For the complete passage, see Legge (1899) 1963, 433 (Appendix VI). Du Run gives the character *chang* 常 instead of *heng* 恒 for Hexagram 32. He would seem to be citing a Song edition that changes the *heng* to *chang* to avoid a taboo character from the name of Emperor Zhensong, which was Zhao Heng 趙恒. See Chen Gaohua, Zhang Fan, and Liu Xiao 2007, 264n4.

116. Reading *yuan* 原 for *hou* 厚 at the beginning of the sentence.

follow ancient moral traditions.[117] Thereby one can eradicate debauched traditions and turn them into virtuous customs.

We [Wenshang County] humbly request that you consider this matter thoroughly.

We the circuit authorities carefully examined the matter. When it comes to the way of human moral relations, the duty of husband and wife is paramount. In life they share the same livelihood, in death they share the same grave. The expectation of permanence is an enduring principle of the ages. The simple people of the alleys and lanes do not distinguish between fragrant and foul.[118] Rather they indulge their daughters' likes and dislikes. They allow her to choose noble or base, accept or reject rich or poor. When she deceitfully hatches crafty plans and seeks to remarry over and over, they do not consider it shameful. Anyone with discerning eyes truly cannot be at peace. Now, we note that the words of Wenshang County Magistrate Du Run respect ancient principles and seem fitting. Their intent is to make customs virtuous and sincere and immediately to aid in government. The moral mind of this official is brightly displayed for all to see. We submit this dispatch and humbly request that you consider this matter thoroughly.

Dispatch received. We submitted a report, and respectfully received a Secretarial decree from the Central Hall, which reads:

We approve the decision. Have this prohibition sent to all subordinate offices. One may not as previously done include in a marriage contract words or phrases such as "If an uxorilocal son-in-law runs away, etc., then [this contract] will stand as a letter of divorce." In addition, order the local authorities frequently and thoroughly to instruct and exhort those who are uxorilocal sons-in-law to behave carefully in accordance with the law and each work to support their particular family enterprise. If there are those who are lazy and indolent or who unlawfully run away, they will be dealt with severely.

18.12

This document recounts two instances where a betrothed couple got together and had illicit sexual relations before all the betrothal gifts had been exchanged and

---

117. Reading 返 for 反.
118. Reading 辨 for 辯.

the actual wedding had taken place. As in many other cases in the *Yuan dian-zhang*, it reveals differences of opinion between different branches of government. In the earlier instance, the Censorate branch, represented locally by a Regional Surveillance Office, considered the couple in violation of parental authority, and impeaching the circuit's handling of the case, it ruled that the marriage should be annulled, even though the bride was already pregnant. The circuit appealed to the Ministry of War and Punishments (these two ministries combined into one at this time) to overturn the ruling of the Regional Surveillance Office, which it did. The Ministry argues that this is not the same as regular adultery and rules that the couple should each get a light beating but that the betrothal gifts should be paid in full and the marriage should be allowed to stand. The document below first recounts the later case (involving an exchange of daughters between two families, thus two marriages), which the Central Secretariat has asked the Ministry of War and Punishments to decide. The Ministry draws on the precedent of the earlier case, in which it overturned the Regional Surveillance Office, to support its ruling. The Central Secretariat approves this decision. Here we read the document that the Ministry is sending out, probably to the prefecture, to notify them of this final decision.

18.12 *When a couple who are already betrothed have illicit sexual relations and elope, allow the marriage to stand*[119]

In the twelfth year of the *zhiyuan* period (1275), eleventh month, a document from the Ministry of War and Punishments[120] states:

We respectfully received a Secretarial communication.[121] Our original report reads:

[We the Ministry of War and Punishments received a dispatch from De Prefecture, which reads:][122]

119. YDZ 18:8a–b, pp. 671–672.
120. From 1271 to 1276 the Ministry of War and the Ministry of Punishments were combined. As described in Chapter 2, the ministries were configured in varying ways in their early years when the central government was taking shape under Khubilai, but after 1276 they had taken their final form of six separate ministries. See YS 85:2142–2143; Farquhar 1990, 175–176, 199–200.
121. *Shengpan* 省判. This is short for a juridical communication (*pansong* 判送) from the Central Secretariat (Zhongshusheng 中書省). A blank space precedes the term in the *Yuan dianzhang* text to show respect to the Central Secretariat, indicated in the translation by capitalization.
122. We can surmise this missing line from what follows, which must be the contents of the original dispatch from the prefecture (see example in case 18.10). We learn that the prefec-

Dou Heisi confessed to a crime as follows:

> My daughter Yijin traded places in marriage with Bangu,[123] the daughter of Hao Jin, who was to become my concubine. We had the go-between Second Sister Liu deliver only three feet of thin, cheap yellow silk [as a betrothal gift], and we each wrote up a marriage contract. [Before the actual marriage] I enticed the girl Bangu into having illicit sex with me. Her older brother Da then threatened my daughter Yijin and forced her to hand over the marriage contract. He then sent Hao Bangu over to my home prematurely to be my concubine.[124]

Additionally, Hao Bangu and the others all [confessed to] their crimes. We respectfully received a Secretarial decree from the Central Hall sent to this Ministry, stating:

> Reconsider and make a decision on this case, then submit to us, the Secretariat, a report with your conclusions.

Secretarial decree respectfully received. We have investigated and found a dispatch from Pingluan Circuit[125] of the eleventh year of *zhiyuan* (1274), sixth month, twenty-ninth day, which reads:

Shi Yanshou testified as follows:

> In the third month of the ninth year of *zhiyuan* (1272) I secretly played around with my wife-to-be Liu Ruige. We repeatedly had illicit sex and ran away.

Liu Ruige confessed to the same events. We the Circuit decided to confiscate from Shi Fuchu any unpaid remainder of the original betrothal gifts and hand them over to the possession of the father of Liu Ruige, and we sentenced Shi Yanshou to a beating. In addition, Liu Ruige, who has become pregnant, was taken into the custody of the Municipal Affairs Office to await trial. Then on the ninth day of the sixth month of the tenth year of *zhiyuan* (1273), we respectfully received an Imperial Edict, which

---

ture is Dezhou, which at this time was administered directly by the Central Secretariat, so that its dispatches went straight to the Ministry of War and Punishments without passing through a circuit in between. Dezhou was located in what is now northwest Shandong Province.

123. Reading *gu* 姑 for *du* 妬 in this name, as indicated elsewhere in the text.

124. In other words, she came before the final exchange of betrothal gifts and formal wedding.

125. This is in modern Hebei Province, east of Beijing. It was part of the Central Province in the Yuan and so its dispatches could go directly to one of the Ministries.

we sent down to the Municipal Affairs Office for their careful consideration.[126] After we sent down the edict, the Regional Surveillance Office[127] audited the documents of the case and wrote a verdict, as follows:

> We note that a dispatch from the Municipal Affairs Office reads:
>
>> This Circuit extracted testimony from Shi Yanshou to the fact that he made off with his fiancée Liu Ruige, had illicit sex, and eloped with her. The details of the case are consistent with each other. A couple who were already engaged did not wait for the betrothal gifts to be paid in full and the bride to be welcomed into her new home. Instead they recklessly indulged their lewd passions and behind their parents' backs had sexual relations and eloped. This violates the moral way to become husband and wife. The marriage should be annulled.
>
> We [Pingluan Circuit] humbly request that you render a clear decision.

This Ministry deliberated and concludes: the crime committed by Shi Yanshou was to make off with the wife to whom he was betrothed. It is not the same as just anyone committing the crime of illicit sexual relations. Moreover, [the Circuit] has confiscated from Shi Fuchu, the father of Shi Yanshou, the unpaid remainder of the original betrothal gifts and handed them over to the possession of Liu Liuzhu, the father of Liu Ruige, and they sentenced Shi Yanshou to a beating. It seems inappropriate to annul the marriage. In addition, we note that the defendant Liu Ruige is not currently in custody and also has not come to Dadu [for questioning]. We rule that Pingluan Circuit should consider the circumstances and enforce this. We submitted this report, and respectfully received a Secretarial decree from the Central Hall, which reads:

> We approve the decision. Have it enforced.

---

126. It is not exactly clear how this imperial edict is related to the case, but it was probably some kind of amnesty or order for the release of prisoners, which was not unusual. This suggests that Liu Ruige was released; indeed we learn later in the case that she is no longer in custody.

127. The area under the main Censorate (the Central Province, plus Henan, Jiangbei, and Liaoyang Provinces) was divided into regions (*dao* 道), eventually numbering eight. Each of these had, starting in 1269, a Regional Surveillance Office (*tixing anchasi* 提刑按察司) to carry out the Censorate's surveillance duties. In 1291 the name of these offices changed to Regional Investigation Offices (*sucheng lianfangsi* 肅政廉訪司). See YS 36:2180; Farquhar 1990, 242. The officials from these offices were required to conduct audits of government records and review decisions by the offices of civil administration (as here), as well as ferret out corruption and wrongdoing on the part of local officials (Hung 1982, 5–7; Niwa 1994). Here the Regional Surveillance Office is auditing this particular decision by the circuit within its jurisdiction.

Secretarial decree respectfully received. We already sent down this decision to Pingluan Circuit and ordered them to enforce it according to the above. At present, this Ministry further deliberated together and determined that the offense to which Dou Heisi and Hao Bangu confessed is the same as that of Shi Yanshou and the others. It therefore seems inappropriate to annul the marriage. It is merely the offense of not waiting for the betrothal gifts to be paid in full and the bride to be welcomed into her new home before engaging in sexual relations. In light of the circumstances we rule that each party should be punished with 27 strokes of the stick and the marriage be allowed to stand. In addition, regarding the matter of the corresponding marriage between Dou Heisi's daughter and Bai'er, the son of Hao Jin, they also should marry according to the terms of the marriage contract that was originally established, and each party should deliver the betrothal gifts originally agreed upon. As for the others implicated in the affair, it would be appropriate for De Prefecture to consider the circumstances of the case and enforce a ruling.[128]

We submitted this report, and respectfully received a Secretarial decree from the Central Hall sent to this Ministry, which reads:

We approve the report. Have it enforced.

18.13

Men from military households might be away for long periods on campaign, and under such conditions the government was concerned about their wives committing adultery. In this case, when a soldier did not return from the Yuan campaigns into Yunnan, his wife, with the help of a go-between, arranged to invite in a new husband to live with her uxorilocally. The circuit authorities gave them both a beating and annulled the marriage, but the wife sought the services of another go-between and the couple married again. The second offense was adjudicated by the Regional Surveillance Office, the local representative of the Censorate branch of government, which ordered the relatively light punishment of 37 strokes of the stick. Other cases of adultery found in Yuan records are likewise punished relatively lightly, despite the punishment of death for both partners

---

128. Here ends the original report from the Ministry referred to at the beginning of the case. What follows is the record of the Central Secretariat's approval of the Ministry's final decision.

that Chinggis Khan is reputed to have prescribed for adultery during the early Mongol conquests.[129]

18.13 *An adulterous marriage must be annulled*[130]

In the twenty-third year of the *zhiyuan* period (1286), eighth month, a document from the Regional Surveillance Office of this region[131] states:
A document from Yuanzhou Circuit reads:[132]

> We interrogated Zhao A-Ye of a military household from Yichun County[133] and determined that: initially, on the pretense that her husband Zhao Shi had gone off on a military campaign to Yunnan and absconded, the said woman did not wait for her husband Zhao Shi to return, but rather engaged the go-between Tenth Sister Zhao to negotiate an agreement, and invited in Yi Qiansan to be her uxorilocal husband. Her case already came before the authorities for sentencing, and they annulled the marriage. But again, the said woman let Yi A-Peng negotiate an agreement. She accepted twenty-five ounces worth of paper money and one bolt of fancy silk and went and got remarried again.

We the Censorate Office[134] considered the matter carefully. Zhao A-Ye and Yi Qiansan married adulterously. The authorities annulled their marriage, but they went and illegally married again. Moreover, the said woman already has a husband. In light of these circumstances we rule that each party be punished with 37 strokes of the stick and the marriage be annulled. We rule that the gifts and money be confiscated by the government. The go-between Yi A-Peng on account of her age is exempted from punishment. Here is our censorate communication [for your consideration].[135] Enforce this prohibition widely.

---

129. See Birge 2009.

130. YDZ 18:8b, p. 672.

131. We can conclude from what follows that this is the Jiangxi Hudong Region, which at this time was one of eight administered by the Jiangnan Branch Censorate, covering south China. Later these regions numbered ten. See YS 36:2179; Farquhar 1990, 242–243.

132. Yuanzhou Circuit was in northwest Jiangxi Branch Secretariat, southwest of modern Nanchang and east of Changsha.

133. Modern Yichun City, in Jiangxi Province. This was the administrative seat of Yuanzhou Circuit during the Yuan.

134. *Xiansi* 憲司. This was an informal name for the Regional Surveillance Office.

135. A censorate communication (*die* 牒) was a document sent to or from offices of the Censorate administration. The expression here is a paraphrase of a longer expression that often ends these documents.

18.14

Throughout the Yuan era there was tension and disagreement among government officials over having different marriage laws for different ethnic groups. In this document of 1288, the Secretariat for State Affairs, which had been established for the second time in 1287 (second intercalary month) and existed until 1291 (fifth month), recommends to Khubilai that he reconsider his ban on same-surname marriage. On the basis of a report from the Liaoyang Branch Secretariat—which covered the entire northeast of modern China plus parts of eastern Siberia and eastern Inner Mongolia—they argue that couples of the same surname are using the ban as an excuse to get divorced whenever they want, by merely claiming their marriage is illegal. But Khubilai emphatically rejects this recommendation and insists that his earlier decree of 1271 (see case 18.2) banning same-surname marriage must stand. His words suggest that he is applying this only to Han Chinese (he notes at the end that same-surname marriage is allowed among Inner Asians), moreover his original ban never applied to Mongols or other Inner Asians. This case provides a glimpse of the problems arising from different marriage law being applied to different ethnic groups. Liaoyang covered an area populated largely by non-Han peoples, and we can surmise from this case that same-surname marriage was practiced among Han Chinese there. At this point at least, Khubilai chose to preserve separate laws for different peoples in his realm.[136]

This case is noteworthy for its use of Sino-Mongolian, the direct translation of Mongolian words into Chinese characters, preserving the Mongolian syntax of the original. Both the words of the Secretariat for State Affairs and those of Khubilai are recorded in Sino-Mongolian, indicating that their pronouncements were originally in Mongolian. The language provides a sense of "listening in" on the original Mongolian of Khubilai and his ministers.

---

136. At the same time, Khubilai's edicts specify no punishment for same-surname marriage other than annulling the marriage. In Tang law it was harshly punished with two years' penal servitude, and in Ming and Qing law by a beating of 60 strokes.

18.14 *People of the same surname may not marry*[137]

In the twenty-fifth year of the *zhiyuan* period (1288), tenth month, sixteenth day, a document from the Secretariat for State Affairs states:

We submitted a Memorial to the throne,[138] an item of which reads:

The Liaoyang Branch Secretariat sent us a document, which says:

The daughter of a man named Liu Yi from Yi Prefecture[139] invited in a man surnamed Liu to be her permanent uxorilocal husband. They have lived together ten years and have borne two children. At this time, there is no law allowing people of the same surname to be husband and wife.

Thus said the document. When these words arrived, the personnel of the Ministry of Rites adjudicated and determined that,[140] an Imperial Edict of the year of the sheep (1271) states:[141]

Those wives and husbands[142] who were married before the first month of this year may remain married as before. Those who marry after the first month, in accordance with the regulations of this Imperial Edict, must annul their marriage.

If a wife and husband fight with each other and cannot get along, they just say "We're of the same surname," and use this as an excuse to end the marriage and leave. How would it be if we did not make wives and husbands of the same surname annul their marriages?

When we thus memorialized, we received an Imperial Edict, stating:

I have not forgotten these words of mine: those wives and husbands who got married before should not have their marriages annulled. But from now

---

137. YDZ 18:8b–9a, pp. 672–673. This case appears in almost identical form in TZTG 3:146–147 (Art. 45).

138. Communications to the throne in China were always communicated by a document called a memorial (*zou* 奏). The text of the *Yuan dianzhang* starts a new line and elevates the character for "memorial" one space to show respect for this document. I have capitalized the term to replicate the special treatment of the word on the page. Only the term for an imperial edict is given more exalted treatment, getting a new line and two spaces of elevation.

139. Modern Yi County in Liaoning Province. It was in Daning Circuit during the Yuan, which was located in what is today eastern Inner Mongolia and western Liaoning Province.

140. We can understand from this line that the Secretariat for State Affairs sent the case to the Ministry of Rites for advice, after receiving it from the Liaoyang Branch Secretariat. The Ministry of Rites over time gradually took over marriage cases from the Ministry of Revenue.

141. This is the edict recorded in case 18.2. The Secretariat is paraphrasing what must be Khubilai's original Mongolian version of the edict, recorded here in Sino-Mongolian.

142. The term "wives and husbands," or "wife and husband" 妻夫, appears repeatedly in this document. In the TZTG version, these are all changed to "husbands and wives."

on, wives and husbands of the same surname are forbidden to marry. In the regulations for Huihui non-Chinese,[143] this is not forbidden.

Thus said the Imperial Edict. We humbly respect it.[144]

18.15

In the first of two lawsuits recorded in this case, a young widow, Li Xingnu, invites in a new husband to live with her uxorilocally. But when this second husband dies and she tries to marry a third time, the mother of her first husband sues to force her to marry the eight-year-old brother of her first husband in a levirate union. The suit, filed in 1290, also charges that the third marriage was undertaken during the mourning period and thus should be invalidated.

The law surrounding these two issues of the levirate and the mourning period was highly fluid during the Yuan. Adding to the confusion was a complex and redundant legal system with overlapping jurisdictions, as this case illustrates. The document is a reexamination of the case by censorate officials from a Divisional Office of the local Regional Surveillance Office.[145] It demonstrates the detailed surveillance and scrutiny of local records carried out by the Censorate branch of government in the Yuan, which was unprecedented in Chinese history. The Divisional officials in their ruling (which we can infer disagreed with the circuit's original judgment of the case) reject the levirate because of the age disparity—the widow is thirty, the levir eight—but rule that the widow must wait until after the mourning period before she can remarry. Moreover, they order that the betrothal gifts be confiscated. But the main Censorate in the capital upon review disagrees. They cite as a precedent a ruling from 1275 by the Central Secretariat, in response to a similar lawsuit, that the mourning period "has not been fixed," and thus marriages ostensibly during the mourning period can stand. Following this, they rule that the third

---

143. *Huihuijia* 回回家. During the early Yuan, the term *huihui* could be used for any Inner Asian—similar to the term *semu* 色目—including Persians, Arabs, Khitans, Uighurs, and others. (For this usage, see for instance YS 6:106 and comments in Qiu 2000, 275.) These people could be Muslim, Jewish, Christian, or of other religions, but later the term was applied primarily to Muslims. Khubilai here seems to be using the term to mean any non-Chinese.

144. *Qinci* 欽此. This expression comes at the end of an imperial edict. It indicates the respectful reception of the edict by those other than the emperor and is not part of the edict itself, as it is often misread. It is commonly mistranslated as "Respect this." See Hung 1988.

145. These divisional offices served as headquarters for officials from the Regional Surveillance Office on their local tours of inspection, which took place every year between the eighth month and the fourth month of the following year. See Hung 1982, 5–7; Niwa 1994.

marriage of widow Li Xingnu is valid and that the betrothal gifts should *not* be confiscated. They also reject the levirate, here concurring with the Divisional Office.

These two rulings on the mourning period of 1275 and 1291, by the Central Secretariat and the Censorate, respectively, illustrate the legal problems generated by Khubilai's abrogation of the Taihe code in 1271. In the absence of any clear codified law, offices of the central government were unwilling to enforce provisions such as that for the mourning period. The Taihe code specified twenty-seven months of mourning by a wife for her husband (see 18.24 below), but during the decades after its abrogation, no mourning period was enforced.[146]

The title of this piece is misleading. It refers only to the first remarriage of Li Xingnu, which is irrelevant to the plaint and the issue of marriage during the mourning period adjudicated here. This earlier, uxorilocal marriage was evidently contracted with the blessing of the mother-in-law, who no doubt appreciated the male labor while her younger son was still a toddler. Widow Li's third marriage presumably took her out of the household, which is probably why her mother-in-law filed her unsuccessful lawsuit. The desire to keep a woman's labor in the family was often the reason for attempting to force her into a levirate union.

18.15 *An older brother dies and his widow invites in a new husband*[147]

In the twenty-eighth year of the *zhiyuan* period (1291), sixth month, sixth day, a document from the Yannan Regional Surveillance Office[148] states: We received a censorate communication from our Guangping Divisional Office, which reads:

---

146. For another example, dated 1282, see case 18.29. Compare cases 18.5 and 18.43, where in 1268 the Ministry of Revenue upheld the mourning period. Not until the fourteenth century did the central government begin to issue regulations on the mourning period, and in 1320 they settled on a punishment for marriage of a woman during mourning for her husband at 67 strokes for the woman and 57 for her new husband (YDZXJ *hunyin*:3a–b; Birge 2002, 257–261). This was significantly more lenient than Tang law, which prescribed three years of penal servitude, and Ming and Qing law, which each gave 100 strokes of the heavy stick.

147. YDZ 18:9a–b, pp. 673–674.

148. Yannan was one of the eight regions under the main Censorate. It was administered from Zhending Circuit, which was just east of the modern city of Shijiazhuang in southern Hebei Province, about 200 kilometers (125 miles) south of Beijing.

We audited this document of Guangping Circuit,[149] of the seventh month of the twenty-seventh year of *zhiyuan* (1290), where Chen A-Shuang filed a plaint, stating:

> My son's father-in-law Li Xin acted as the marriage sponsor and together with others arranged the remarriage [of my daughter-in-law], but she currently has a younger brother-in-law, Chen Baijialü, whom she should marry in a levirate union. Instead, during the mourning period my deceased son's widow Li Xingnu got remarried to Prison Warden Wang, and her father received betrothal gifts containing paper money, silk and satin, gold and silver hairpins, and jewelry.

We deliberated and determined that Li Xingnu originally married Chen Yuanseng. Yuanseng died, and she went and invited in Sun Fuxing to be her uxorilocal husband. By so doing, she had already violated her vows[150] to Chen Yuanseng. Sun Fuxing also passed away, and she again [married someone] of a different surname from Chen Yuanseng.[151] Moreover, Chen Baijialü is eight years old, and Li Xingnu is thirty. The disparity between their ages is too great. It would thus be appropriate to let Li Xingnu return to her natal family when the mourning period is over. We note that, the betrothal gifts which Li Xin obtained from Wang Yü [Warden Wang] constitute illegal property obtained from a marriage contracted during the mourning period and should be confiscated by the government. We request that you render a decision in this case.

Censorate communication received. We [the Regional Surveillance Office] submitted a dispatch to the Censorate and respectfully received a superior communication in return, which reads:

> We have investigated and found that in the twelfth year of *zhiyuan* (1275) we respectfully received a communication from the Secretariat, as follows:
>
> > Xu Kuan filed a plaint stating that, A-Geng, the widow left behind by his younger brother Xu Bao, accepted betrothal gifts during the mourning

---

149. Just north of the modern city of Anyang in Hebei Province.

150. *Yijue* 義絕, literally "violated duty." This term denotes violations within a marriage that necessitate a divorce. The original definition in the Tang code was confined to physical abuse of a spouse or his or her relatives (TLSY 14:267 [Art. 189]), but by Song times the term was used for a wide range of behaviors that a judge found to necessitate a divorce (McKnight 1996). In this case the term is being used somewhat rhetorically to strengthen the argument that Li Xingnu's marriage to Chen Yuanseng is void and she has no obligation to marry his brother.

151. That is, she did not marry a relative of her first husband Chen in a levirate union.

period and got engaged to marry Li Bin. The Regional Surveillance Office recovered the betrothal gifts and annulled the marriage. We [the Secretariat] note that at this time the length of the mourning period has not been fixed. The couple is already married and they have borne children. The marriage should be allowed to stand. We order you to enforce this as above.

We respectfully received the communication. Now regarding the dispatch that is currently before us, we [the Censorate] deliberated the matter: Li Xingnu got engaged to Wang Yü during the mourning period. The legal situation is analogous to the above. The betrothal gifts originally paid should not be confiscated. As for the rest, we approve the decision [of the Divisional Office]. Have it enforced.

18.16

We saw above in case 18.8 how in 1273 the Ministry of Revenue in a case from Dadu (Beijing) upheld the traditional Chinese marriage provision that once betrothal gifts had been accepted by the bride's family, they could not renege on a marriage and marry their daughter to someone else. But in a similar case brought in 1297 in Pingjiang Circuit (modern Suzhou), as described in the document below, the Jiangzhe Branch Secretariat rejected the suit of the first fiancé on the grounds that too much time, nine years, had elapsed before he brought his plaint and that by then children had been born to the second marriage. In consideration of long-standing law that established the first marriage as final once betrothal gifts were accepted, the judges ordered that a younger sister of the bride be offered to the first fiancé and if there were no such sister that both his original betrothal gifts and those from the second marriage be given to the first fiancé in compensation. The Central Secretariat confirmed the ruling, and three years later, in 1300, the same branch secretariat used this as a precedent to decide a similar case from Shaowu in Fujian. The later ruling of 1300 frames the document, which is addressed to Shaowu Circuit to inform them of the branch secretariat's decision, in response to their report requesting a review of the case.

This document presents a nice example of the use of precedents in Yuan adjudication and the principle that lawsuits must be brought in a timely fashion. It is also noteworthy that the judges express explicit concern for separating a mother from her young children, a sentiment similar to the reluctance of judges to annul a marriage when children were already born, as seen in 18.15 above.

18.16 *Cases of a man who accepts betrothal gifts from one person then marries his daughter to someone else*[152]

In the fourth month of the fourth year of the *dade* period (1300), Secretariat Scribe of the First Class[153] Shi Zhongshi of the Jiangzhe Branch Secretariat prepared a superior communication as follows:

We received your report, which reads:[154]

> Mr. Xu Hui of Shaowu Circuit in the twenty-fifth year of *zhiyuan* (1288) through the services of a go-between arranged for Hejie the daughter of Huang Sanqi to be his wife. Later, because Xu Hui left town, Huang Sanqi in the twenty-eighth year of *zhiyuan* (1291) acted as sponsor and married off his daughter for a second time, to be the wife of Zhu Alao. Since then, nine years have passed, and the couple have a son who is six years old. If we rule that Huang Hejie should be given back to her first husband, Xu Hui, and hand over her son to his father, Zhu Alao, to raise, we are afraid it would not be appropriate. We humbly request that you consider this matter thoroughly.

Report received. We have investigated and found [the following precedent]:

> In the first year of *dade* (1297), sixth month, eleventh day, Pingjiang Circuit[155] submitted a dispatch, as follows:
>
>> Mr. Yang Qianliu of an ordinary household from Changzhou County,[156] in the twenty-second year of *zhiyuan* (1285) engaged the services of Sister Li Qiansi as go-between and arranged the betrothal of his daughter Yang

---

152. YDZ 18:9b–10a, pp. 674–675.

153. *Shengyuan* 省掾, short for *Xingsheng yuanshi* 行省掾史 (Scribe of the First Class working in the Branch Secretariat). These elite scribes were subofficials who handled drafting and clerical work at the highest levels of the Yuan government, such as in the Central Secretariat and the Censorate (Farquhar 1990, 31–32). Their names are routinely listed at the end of these documents but are usually omitted from the reprinted versions as found here in the *Yuan dianzhang*.

154. We can surmise from what follows that the report comes from Shaowu Circuit (modern Shaowu in northern Fujian Province).

155. This is another circuit within the Jiangzhe Branch Secretariat, centered at modern Suzhou City in Jiangsu Province.

156. Modern Suzhou City, in Jiangsu Province. The text mistakenly writes *zhou* 州 for *zhou* 洲. See YS 62:1494 for the names of counties in Pingjiang Circuit. Changzhou County together with another county made up the seat of the Pingjiang Circuit administration.

Fuyiniang to be the wife of Lu Qianwu the son of Lu Xiyi. He received two complements of betrothal gifts, but because of the poverty of each household, the marriage was never carried out. In the eighth month of the twenty-fourth year of *zhiyuan* (1287), Yang Qianliu went to live in Liyang Prefecture.[157] It is the case that in the tenth month of that same year he engaged as go-between the services of Yang Wanshiwu, a resident of that place, and hiding the fact that he had already received betrothal gifts from Lu Xiyi, he married off his daughter Yang Fuyiniang to be the wife of Chen Qianshi'er. We humbly request that you render a decision.

Dispatch received. We sent this to the Judicial Proceedings Office,[158] which deliberated and determined:

Yang Qianliu confessed that in the third month of the twenty-second year of *zhiyuan* (1285) he first accepted betrothal gifts from Lu Xiyi and betrothed his daughter Yang Fuyiniang to be the wife of Lu Qianwu. Then in the tenth month of the twenty-fourth year of *zhiyuan* (1287) he accepted betrothal gifts from Chen Qianyi[159] and again married off his daughter, this time as the wife of this man. According to legal principles, we should rule that the wife be given back to her first husband. But it must be noted that Yang Fuyiniang and Chen Qianshi'er have already been married for ten years, during which Lu Qianwu never brought any plaint to court. Only in the first month of the first year of *dade* (1297), when he ran into Yang Fuyiniang on the road, did he snatch her away and then file a lawsuit. Yang Fuyiniang already has two children, a son and a daughter. If we are to allow the marriage to stand and send out such a ruling to the subordinate offices, we recommend that, if Yang Fuyiniang has a younger sister who is not yet married then let Lu Qianwu be allowed to pay betrothal gifts according to the law and marry her. If she has no sister, then order Chen Qianshi'er and others to prepare betrothal gifts to

---

157. Modern Liyang, southeast of Nanjing City in Jiangsu Province, about 120 kilometers (75 miles) from Yang's home prefecture of Changzhou on the other side of Lake Tai. The text mistakenly writes Piao (漂) for Li (溧) in this place name. In 1287, when Yang Qianliu moved there, Liyang had been elevated to a circuit, but it was back to being a prefecture by 1300 when this ruling was issued. See YS 62:1502.

158. This office existed in each of the branch secretariats to handle judicial affairs. They were ranked 4A and included two judicial affairs officers, two assistants, and support staff. For the Jiangzhe Branch Secretariat, see Farquhar 1990, 372.

159. This is the same person as Chen Qianshi'er referred to elsewhere in the text.

give to Lu Qianwu so he can marry someone else. This will prevent mother and children from being separated.

Ruling received. In the twelfth, intercalary, month of the first year of *dade* (1297) we sent this to the Central Secretariat and received their communiqué, as follows:

> We the Metropolitan Secretariat[160] deliberated and conclude: if Yang Fuyiniang has a younger sister who is not yet married then we approve the ruling and Lu Qianwu should be allowed to marry her. If she has no sister, then recover from Yang Qianliu the clothes, piece goods,[161] and other items he originally received from Lu Qianwu plus the money and gifts paid by Chen Qianshi'er, and give them to Lu Qianwu so he can seek someone else to marry. We send you this communiqué and request that you enforce it as above.

Communiqué received.

This ruling was already sent out to the subordinate offices to be enforced according to the above. Now regarding the report that is currently before us, we have deliberated the matter. Xu Hui filed a plaint against Huang Sanqi claiming that he took his daughter Huang Hejie and arranged for her to remarry Zhu Alao. This is the same as the case of Lu Qianwu filing a plaint against Yang Qianliu for taking his daughter Yang Fuyiniang and arranging for her to be remarried. We the Secretariat Office[162] order the subordinate office to give this their careful consideration. If upon further investigation and clarification there is no mistake, then adjudicate the case according to this precedent.

18.17

This document presents another example of the Yuan government's relatively lax enforcement of traditional marriage prohibitions, and in the absence of a legal code the need to reissue previously long-established provisions of Chinese marriage law. It also demonstrates the redundant workings of the Censorate branch of the Yuan government and the multiple jurisdictions and overlapping agencies with layers of review that dealt with legal and administrative matters under the Yuan. In this case, a man from Linjiang Circuit, just south of the

---

160. *Dusheng* 都省. This was an informal term that the Central Secretariat used to refer to itself in these internal communications.

161. Reading *duan* 緞 for *duan* 段, which was a common variant of the character in the Yuan.

162. *Shengfu* 省府. This is an informal term used by the Branch Secretariat to refer to itself.

Yangzi River (modern Jiangxi), adopted a son but later had five additional sons and two daughters by birth. When he married his adopted son to one of his birth daughters, his own brother reported him to the authorities, out of fear of later legal trouble. The prefecture and the circuit noted that since the adopted son was born to a different surname the marriage should be legal, but they acknowledged the complication that the official registers listed his wife as his sister and thus passed the case up for a decision by the Jiangxi Branch Secretariat. The branch secretariat approved the marriage, but an auditor in its own office challenged the ruling and proposed that the son be required to return to his birth lineage and resume his original surname, thereby making the marriage legal. Meanwhile, a surveillance official from a division of the Regional Investigation Office (the local branch of the Censorate), during his regular audit of Linjiang Circuit's records, also singled out the ruling for censure and prescribed the same remedy as the branch secretariat's own auditor. The circuit passed up his demand for a correction to the branch secretariat, which decided to request a review by the Central Secretariat in Dadu, noting that the ruling would establish a precedent for marriage law. The Central Secretariat approved the ruling by both the auditor and the surveillance official allowing the marriage to stand, and it released the father from any punishment by citing a recent amnesty. Nevertheless, this final decision by the Central Secretariat once again caught the attention of Censorate officials, this time an Investigating Censor from the Jiangnan Branch Censorate reviewing the records of the branch secretariat.[163] While noting that it was impractical to reverse the ruling in this particular case, he nevertheless expressed alarm that the case established a precedent allowing brother-sister marriage between legal adoptees and advocated that a general prohibition be issued on such marriages in the future. The branch censorate agreed, and in an unusual move—inconsistent with other Yuan sources—they transmitted the request for a prohibition to the civil administration not up through the capital but down through their own subordinate offices, which were asked to notify the circuits in their jurisdictions, which in turn were to pass the request up to the branch secretariat. The opening of the document reveals this unusual paper trail, beginning with the final receipt of

163. This branch censorate was established in 1277 to oversee surveillance of officials in the southern regions, then newly conquered from the Song (YS 86:2179; Farquhar 1990, 242–243). Such branch censorates were technically at the same level as the main Censorate in the capital, rank 1B, but in practice, as seen in the *Yuan dianzhang*, the main Censorate was dominant.

the request by the branch secretariat from the circuit. Note that the branch secretariat receives it from Longxing Circuit, a different circuit than Linjiang, where the case was initially judged. Of interest also is the long testimony reproduced in colloquial language but dotted with formal legal terms, and the multiple names of the protagonists, evidence of the Chinese custom of using different names in different contexts or at different stages of life.

18.17 *Hu Yuanyi and his sister get married*[164]

On the [blank] day of the fourth month of the sixth year of the *dade* period (1302), a document from the Jiangxi Branch Secretariat states:

A dispatch from Longxing Circuit[165] reads:

We received a censorial communication from the Regional Investigation Office for the Jiangxi Hudong Region,[166] which reads as follows:

We have respectfully received a superior communication from the Branch Censorate,[167] which reads:

A report from our Investigating Censor[168] reads:

Having examined the records of the Jiangxi Branch Secretariat, among them is found the following item:

On the twenty-second day of the fourth month of the fourth year of *dade* (1300), a document from Linjiang Circuit[169] states:

A dispatch from Xinyu Prefecture reads:

On the twenty-first day of the first month of the fourth year of *dade* (1300), Hu Xinfu, chief of the sixteenth commune in the fifth hamlet, wrote a dispatch, stating:

On the sixth day of the twelfth month of the third year of *dade* (1299), Hu Yuansan, a householder of this commune, came to me,

---

164. YDZ 18:10a–11a, pp. 675–677. The first few indents are omitted here to make this case more readable.

165. Modern Nanchang City in Jiangxi Province.

166. This was one of ten regions in the Jiangnan Branch Censorate, each overseen by a Regional Investigation Office (*suzheng lianfangsi* 肅政廉訪司, name adopted in 1291). See YS 86:2179. For this office, see Li Zhi'an 2003:282–354; Hung 1982, 58–63; Farquhar 1990, 242–243.

167. That is, the Jiangnan Branch Censorate. By this time it was located in Jiankang City, modern Nanjing (YS 86:2179; Farquhar 1990, 242–243). A space appears in the text preceding its name to show respect.

168. There were twenty-eight of these officials in the Jiangnan Branch Censorate, and they carried out its main surveillance activities.

169. Southwest of modern Nanchang in Jiangxi Province.

Xinfu, and said: "My own younger brother Hu Qianqi married his daughter named Yuanqiniang to his eldest son Hu Yuanyi. I am his own older brother, but he refused to listen to my warnings. I humbly request that you report this to the officials."

Dispatch received. We [Xinyu Prefecture] apprehended Hu Yuansan, whose given name is Daju, and obtained his testimony as follows: "Hu Qianqi, the person being reported, plus Hu Qianba and me, Daju, are all brothers by birth. In the year *gengwu* of the defeated Song dynasty (1270),[170] I don't remember the month or day, my younger brother Hu Qianqi adopted Li Gengli, the son of Li Cengsan of the seventh hamlet,[171] into his home to be his own son. He changed the boy's name to Hu Jili and raised him in his family. He is now Hu Yuanyi. Later, my brother Hu Qianqi gave birth to sons of his own Hu Gouli, Hu Nüli, Hu Maoli, Hu Dili, Hu Zhengli, and to one daughter, Hu Ximei, who is now Hu Yuanqiniang. In the thirtieth year of *zhiyuan* (1293), in the fifth month, my brother Hu Qianqi gave birth to another daughter, Chengu. In the third year of *dade* (1299), on the sixth day of the twelfth month, my brother Hu Qianqi spoke to me, Daju, and said, 'I've decided that on the eighth day of this month I will marry my daughter Yuanqiniang to Hu Yuanyi.' I, Daju, said to him, 'Hu Yuanyi calls Yuanqiniang his sister. I fear this wouldn't be right.' But my brother Hu Qianqi refused to heed my warnings, and on the eighth day my brother Hu Qianqi invited me, Daju, to drink nuptial wine and preside over the marriage of his daughter Yuanqiniang to his son Hu Yuanyi. I, Daju, said to him, 'I don't dare drink your wine!' After I'd spoken, I went away for a while. On the tenth day I came home, and my wife, A-Zhang, said to me, 'Your brother Hu Qianqi on the eighth day already carried out the marriage of his daughter Yuanqiniang to his son Hu Yuanyi.' I, Daju, feared that later if there was trouble, I would be implicated, so I went and informed the commune chief, and he made a report to notify the authorities. This is the truth." We then obtained the testimony of Hu Qianqi (whose real name is

170. He gives the name of the year by the sixty-year cycle of Heavenly Stems and Earthly Branches.
171. Reading *qi* 七 for *bi* 比.

Da'an), Hu Qianba, Hu Yuanyi (whose childhood name is Jili), and Hu Youqiniang (who actually is Hu Yuanqiniang), and it was all consistent. We the prefectural authorities considered the matter carefully. We note that even though Hu Yuanyi is the son by birth of Li Cengsan, he was adopted to be the heir of Hu Da'an, which makes him the older brother of Hu Youqiniang.[172] We could decide to issue a ruling to annul the marriage, but this humble prefecture notes that there previously has been no ruling in a case like this to use as a precedent. We submit this dispatch and humbly request that you examine the matter. Dispatch received. We the circuit authorities considered the matter carefully. We could issue a ruling to annul the marriage; however, since Hu Jili in the end is the son of Li Cengsan who is of a different surname, this cannot be considered a case of same-surname marriage. We could allow the marriage to stand; nevertheless, we note that Hu Da'an already registered Li Gengli under the name of Hu Jili, thus he and Hu Youqiniang are brother and sister as attested in the official records. We submit this dispatch and humbly request that you examine the matter.

Dispatch received [by Jiangxi Branch Secretariat]. This is a case of allowing the marriage to stand. It would be hard to adjudicate otherwise. We sent a superior communication to the circuit for their careful consideration. After we sent it, we found a report from an auditor in our office,[173] as follows:

We have inspected the records and conclude that, whereas Hu Jili and Hu Youqiniang are brother and sister as attested in the official records, if we allow the marriage to stand, it would violate human moral relations. Hu Da'an already has sons of his own, thus we rule that Hu Jili should be ordered to return to his original lineage, then become a regular son-in-law. This seems most expedient.

In the fifth year of *dade* (1301), on the tenth day of the first month, we [the Branch Secretariat] again received a dispatch from Linjiang Circuit, which reads:

172. Again, reading *qi* 七 for *bi* 匕.

173. These were service officials, rank 7A, within the Central Secretariat and the branch secretariats, whose job it was to audit records and investigate delays or lost documents, especially in the work of the scribes. See YS 85:2125; YS 91:2308; YS 102:2616; Ratchnevsky and Aubin 1972–1985, 1:133; Farquhar 1990, 174. In this example they seem to be doing work similar to the Censorate in reviewing an actual decision by the branch secretariat.

We received a censorial communication from the Divisional Office of the Regional Investigation Office,[174] which reads as follows:

Regarding the above matter,[175] Hu Qianqi already has five sons of his own to be his heirs. If according to the communication from the Secretariat the marriage is allowed to stand, then according to legal principles clearly Hu Yuanyi should be ordered to recognize his rightful surname as Li. If this is not corrected, it would contravene the ethical rule that brother and sister cannot become husband and wife.

We submit this dispatch and humbly request that this be corrected.[176] Dispatch received. We the Branch Secretariat considered the matter carefully. We could order Hu Yuanyi to recognize his rightful surname and return to his lineage, then become a regular son-in-law. But since this is a precedent-setting case that affects human moral relations, we have sent a communiqué to the Metropolitan Secretariat for their thorough examination and sent a superior communication to Linjiang Circuit for their careful consideration. We received in reply a communiqué from the Central Secretariat, which reads as follows:

Regarding the above matter, we sent this to the Ministry of Rites, which deliberated and determined: "Hu Yuanyi is the foster son of Hu Da'an and has gotten married to Hu Qiniang.[177] We have carefully examined the matter and conclude that one should approve the ruling of the auditor in the Branch Secretariat and that of the Regional Investigation Office and order Hu Yuanyi to revert to his original surname. He can remain married to Hu Qiniang as before and return to the Li family. This would be appropriate. Regarding the crime of Hu

---

174. As described in case 18.15, the surveillance officials from these divisional offices were charged with reviewing the records of lower-level administrative units, such as the circuit.

175. This phrase confirms that the circuit is not quoting the entire document, which must preface the finding of the Divisional Office by a presentation of the Central Secretariat's decision.

176. This sentence is highly unusual, as it appears that the circuit is issuing an order to its superior, the branch secretariat. Evidently the order of the local surveillance officials is being transmitted up to the branch secretariat through the circuit, rather than first going up to the main Censorate and then over to the Central Secretariat in the capital and back down to the circuit. See also introductory comments to this case.

177. The text leaves out one character of the sister's name.

Da'an of Doing What Ought Not to be Done,[178] we note that there has been an Imperial Amnesty issued, thus there need be no further adjudication. We present this report for your thorough consideration." We send you this communiqué and request that you enforce it as above.

Communiqué received [by the Branch Secretariat].

At present, this humble official[179] has considered this matter carefully. Hu Da'an married his daughter by birth Hu Yuanqiniang to his foster son Hu Yuanyi. From the perspective of ethical principles, this is extremely contrary to what is right. Nevertheless, the Metropolitan Secretariat has already approved the ruling [in this matter], thus it cannot be considered further. But from now on, if we do not issue a general prohibition, I respectfully fear that this practice could become an entrenched custom that would harm civilized traditions. Moreover, this case will stand as a precedent. I submit this report and humbly request that you examine the matter.

Report received. We [the Branch Censorate] order all offices of this [Branch] Censorate and below to give this their careful consideration and transmit it to the local authorities. These in turn should send dispatches to the relevant superior offices to have this prohibition enforced.[180]

18.18

This document is in the form of a communiqué, dated 1313, from the Central Secretariat to the Jiangzhe Branch Secretariat (and, we can assume, sent to all branch secretariats) reestablishing the traditional Chinese law that once the

178. *Buying zuifan* 不應罪犯. This was a general category in the Tang code for crimes not covered specifically under any of the articles in the code. See TLSY 27:522 (Art. 450); Johnson 1997, 510. In the Yuan the punishments given for crimes under this category could vary widely, contrary to the 40 strokes specified in the Tang code. In the Qing there were two designations within this category, light and heavy, punished by 40 and 80 strokes, respectively (see, for instance, Bodde and Morris 1967, 159n3, 178–179, 440–441).

179. This is the Investigating Censor from the beginning of the case, who initiated this final review.

180. Note how this decision of the Branch Censorate, with its long quote from the report of the Investigating Censor, has been sent out by the Regional Investigation Office to Longxing Circuit (not the circuit where the events took place) and then to the Jiangxi Branch Secretariat (whose records were being examined to begin with) as per these instructions. This unusual transmission of the decision from a lower to a higher office is documented at the beginning of the case.

bride's family has agreed to a betrothal, either by returning a marriage contract or accepting betrothal gifts, they may not back out of the marriage. The proposal to issue the prohibition and a set of punishments for violators comes from the Director-General of Jinning Circuit sent by the circuit directly to the Ministry of Rites, which it can do since the circuit is within the Central Province. The Ministry approves the idea, then is asked by the Central Secretariat to confer with the Ministry of Punishments to determine a penalty. This they do, and the two ministries issue a joint report confirming the punishments proposed by the Director-General, and this document is what the Central Secretariat sends out. The ruling cites the Tang code but decides on penalties considerably less severe than those of the Tang or Song, illustrating the leniency of Yuan law in general.[181] The case also makes reference to amnesties issued by the Mongol court, which were frequent and served to exempt past violators from punishment. The ruling establishes a new precedent with the force of law. The groom's family can cancel a betrothal without punishment, but they will forfeit the betrothal gifts, as in Tang and Song law. The Yuan ruling makes an exception if five years have passed and the groom's family has not yet carried out the marriage, under which conditions the bride's family can go to the authorities and apply for a certificate granting permission to remarry. Note that, the Jinning Circuit Director-General complains that judges have been allowing illegal marriages to stand when children have already been born into them, as seen in cases 18.16 and 18.17 above. His proposal herein reflects the Neo-Confucian attempt to enforce stricter and more consistent marriage laws as the cornerstone of a stable, ethical society. As in case 18.11, the result is to restrict the freedom of the bride's family. The last part of the case, articulating the final law, is found in the "Treatise on Punishments" in the Yuan dynastic history, among other Yuan texts.[182]

---

181. See discussions in Ch'en 1979, especially 43–51; Birge 2008, 474–477. It should be noted, however, that Tang and Song judges often imposed penalties more lenient than what the codes prescribed. In a similar case from the Southern Song, a judge in his verdict cited the harsh penalties of the codes but merely urged the parties repeatedly to negotiate a mutually acceptable resolution to avoid punishment. There is no record that any beating or other punishment was administered. See QMJ 9:346–348; McKnight and Liu 1999, 338–340.

182. YS 103:2643; Ratchnevsky and Aubin 1972–1985, 2:122–123 (Art. 391). The law as formulated here was copied into the *Da Yuan tongzhi* and preserved in the *Shilin guangji;* see *Shilin guangji* (1988), *bieji* 3:995–996; *Shilin guangji* (1999), 124; *Yuandai falü,* 70.

18.18 *Once the betrothal is fixed, the bride's family may not renege*
       on the marriage[183]

In the second year of the *huangqing* period (1313), the fifth month, [blank] day, the Jiangzhe Branch Secretariat received a communiqué from the Central Secretariat,[184] as follows:

A report from the Ministry of Rites states:

> We respectfully received your Secretarial communication. Our original report is as follows:
>
> A dispatch from Jinning Circuit[185] reads:
>
>> We received a memo from Director-General Shi, Grand Master for Excellent Counsel,[186] as follows:
>>
>>> It is my humble understanding that marriage between a man and a woman is the foundation of the five moral relations. First there is the relation between husband and wife, and only then can there be parent and child. There is the relation between parent and child and only then can there be senior and junior. The joining in harmony of two surnames creates the parental relations of a [new] family. And thus the lineage received from one's ancestors can be passed down to future generations. Nowadays when families among the common people first arrange a marriage, if the family means are abundant, then relations between the two sides are cordial and harmonious. But if later, the groom's family should unfortunately suffer a decline and not be able to provide the full amount of

---

183. YDZ 18:11a–12a, pp. 677–679. This title is given in slightly longer form in the Table of Contents as "Once the betrothal is fixed, the bride's family may not renege on the marriage and marry their daughter to someone else" (YDZ *Mulu*: 14a). The same case appears with this longer title in the 1322 supplement to the *Yuan dianzhang* (YDZXJ *hunyin*: 1a–b).

184. The text here starts a whole new line for the characters "Central Secretariat" to show respect, rather than leaving just one blank space as elsewhere in the *Yuan dianzhang*.

185. Northwest of modern Loyang in southern Shaanxi Province. Before 1305 it was called Pingyang Circuit. This circuit is within the Central Province, so its dispatch can go directly to the Ministry without first passing through the Central Secretariat.

186. The Director-General was the highest official in the circuit, responsible for all its operations. After his name, the text reads *jiayi* (加議), short for *Jiayi dafu* (嘉議大夫). This is an honorary, or prestige, title (*sanguan* 散官), which confers rank and salary on an official. This title indicates a rank of 3A and thus matches Mr. Shi's assignment as Director-General of a first-class circuit, which Jinning was (Farquhar 1990, 22–25, 414). Such correspondence between rank and office was usually but not always the case.

betrothal payments originally negotiated, the bride's family does not honor the marriage. If by good fortune the bride's relatives prosper, they turn their back on the original agreement and go and arrange a marriage to someone else. There are even instances where, after the marriage, parents have summoned their daughters back home and subsequently betrothed them to someone else.[187] Such disputes arrive at the magistrate for adjudication, and the lawsuits drag on for days and months. By then children are born into the new marriage, and thus the verdict is to allow the second marriage to stand. When setting out on the road to prosperity becomes a despicable practice of avarice and greed, it not only disrupts local government but truly damages civilized traditions. The moral principle of a wife is not to remarry. Once she is united with her husband, she must stay faithful for the rest of her life. This official notes that in Tang law it states: "When a daughter is betrothed to be married and the marriage contract has already been returned or there has been a private agreement between the parties, if the family reneges, the punishment is 60 strokes of the heavy stick. Even if there is no marriage contract but the bride's family has accepted the betrothal gifts, it is the same as if there were a marriage contract. In cases where the bride in addition has been betrothed to someone else, the punishment is 100 strokes. If the second marriage has already taken place, the punishment is one and a half years of penal servitude. If the second husband knew of the situation, he is punished one grade less. The daughter is returned to her first husband."[188] Now, if we take a brief look at this matter, we find that more than ten active lawsuits have come before the authorities of this circuit. These practices in the prefectures and counties have already become entrenched custom. In light of this, I have carefully examined the matter and recom-

187. Reading *yinqu* (姻娶) for *yinqu* (因取).

188. This is a quote from the Tang code, and it is also found in the Song code; see TLSY 13:253–255 (Art. 175); SXT 13:212–214; Johnson 1997, 152. This passage is quoted by a judge in the Southern Song, who interprets the exchange of "engagement cards," common at the time, to meet the test of an irrevocable engagement; see QMJ 9:346–348; McKnight and Liu 1999, 338–340. The person being punished is the sponsor of the marriage (*zhuhun* 主婚), usually the father of the bride. Note that in the absence of a contract the acceptance of betrothal gifts constituted agreement of a legally binding marriage. See cases 18.1 and 18.3 for more on these marriage contracts in the Yuan.

mend: in cases where five years have passed and for no legitimate reason the groom's family has not yet carried out the marriage, the bride's family should be allowed to go to the authorities and petition to receive a certificate permitting them to arrange a remarriage. In all other cases, with the exception of those whose cases have already come before the authorities and have been excused from punishment on the basis of an Imperial Edict of amnesty, the matter should be adjudicated on the basis of the Tang code. Hereafter, those who dare to offend against the law should by analogy be punished two degrees less than as prescribed in the Tang code, and the daughter should be returned to her first husband. In this way, one can eradicate the tradition of greedily seeking fortune, and it would be most expedient. Nevertheless, since this is a precedent-setting case, we should give it careful consideration and in turn send a dispatch to our superior office to adjudicate the matter and send down a clear decision.

Memo received. We the circuit authorities submit this dispatch to humbly request that you consider this matter thoroughly and at your earliest convenience bestow upon us a clear decision. When it is passed down we will respectfully enforce it accordingly.

Dispatch received.[189] This Ministry has carefully examined the matter. Husband and wife embody the way of unchanging ethical values, the utmost of human moral relations, and a most important aspect of propriety.[190] In recent years, lawsuits among the people over marriage have proliferated. This is because people vainly seek the path of prosperity and disregard chastity and duty. They wantonly create enmity and distrust, while despising the groom's family. Thus they go back on the original marriage agreement such that matters have arrived at this state. It truly damages civilized traditions. Now, what Mr. Shi, Grand Master for Excellent Counsel of Jinning Circuit, has proposed verily accords with ethical principles. If our report receives your approval, this Ministry will adhere to it as a legal precedent, and it would be appropriate to promulgate it widely. We present this report for your thorough consideration. [end of original report of the Ministry of Rites]

---

189. The text mistakenly writes "received" as *zhun* 准 instead of *de* 得. Since a dispatch is from a lower office, the verb "to receive" cannot be *zhun*, which is for offices of equal rank.

190. This is an allusion to the *Mencius* 5A:2; see Legge (1895) 1960, 345.

We [the Ministry of Rites] respectfully received a Secretarial decree from the Central Hall [in response to our report], stating:

> We send this to you, the Ministry of Rites, and request that you confer together with officials from the Ministry of Punishments to come to a decision.

Secretarial decree respectfully received. This Ministry deliberated together with Minister Xie of the Ministry of Punishments,[191] and we jointly conclude: the union in marriage between a man and woman represents the utmost in human moral relations. The common people are ignorant of this and frequently renege on marriage agreements to marry someone else. This leads to lawsuits and is unbeneficial. If we do not establish a law to prohibit this behavior, we will not be able to promote honest customs. From now on, when a daughter is betrothed to be married and the marriage contract has already been returned or there has been a private agreement between the parties, or the bride's family has accepted the betrothal gifts, if the family reneges, the punishment is 37 strokes of the light stick.[192] In cases where the bride in addition has been betrothed to someone else, the punishment is 47 strokes of the light stick. If the second marriage has already taken place, the punishment is 57 strokes. If the second husband knew of the situation, he is punished one grade less. The daughter is returned to her first husband. If the groom's family reneges, they are not punished, but they may not recover the betrothal gifts.[193] In addition, in cases where five years have passed and for no legitimate reason the groom's family has not yet carried out the marriage, in accordance with the Old Regulations,[194] the bride's family should be allowed to go to the authorities to receive a certificate permitting them to arrange a remarriage. We think

---

191. Minister Xie can be identified as Xie Rang 謝讓 (1252–1317), whose biography in the Yuan dynastic history confirms that he was a minister in the Ministry of Punishments at this time (YS 176:4110). After 1300, three of these ministers, rank 3A, directed the Ministry of Punishments (Farquhar 1990, 200).

192. Reading *bao* 報 for *zhao* 招, on the basis of the same passage above and in the Tang code. The corrected line is also found in *Shilin guangji* (1988), 995; *Shilin guangji* (1999), 124.

193. Reading *bu* 不 for *zhi* 只. This corrected version of the line is found in the Tang code, the Song code, and the Yuan dynastic history (YS 103:2643). The same case in the supplement to the *Yuan dianzhang* writes both *zhi* and *bu* (YDZXJ *hunyin*: 1b).

194. There is general agreement that the term "Old Regulations" (*jiuli* 舊例) refers to the Taihe code of the Jin when used before 1271, the date Khubilai abrogated the Taihe code and forbade its use in deciding cases (see case 18.29 below). For dates later than 1271, there is disagreement among scholars, but in this instance it is likely still referring to the Taihe code, since this provision

it would be appropriate that, if you approve of what we have proposed and promulgate it widely, you send this Ministry a superior communication, to which we will adhere as a legal precedent. We hereby present this report.

Report received. We the Metropolitan Secretariat send you [the Jiangzhe Branch Secretariat and all branch secretariats] this communiqué and request that you enforce it.

18.19

This case of 1319, one of the later ones in the *Yuan dianzhang*, concerns whether a marriage forced on a woman against the wishes of her and her family can stand. Two fathers who each have a son and a daughter arrange to marry their two sons to their two daughters, but when a flood in the region brings financial hardship, the fathers decide to cancel the betrothals, even though betrothal gifts have already been paid. Nevertheless, when one father later betroths his daughter to someone else, the other father kidnaps the girl and forces her into a marriage that his son promptly consummates. The Judicial Proceedings Office of the Jiangzhe Branch Secretariat tentatively rejects the precedent of 1313 by the Ministry of Rites (see 18.18), which stated that the bride's family may not back out of a marriage once betrothal gifts have been accepted, and instead applies a precedent of 1284 by the Ministry of Revenue that stated that a forced marriage is unlawful and must be annulled. (I do not find this case in the *Yuan dianzhang*.) But it expresses concern about forcing a woman to marry twice and declines to make a final decision, passing the case up for review at the capital. The Central Secretariat sends the case to the Ministry of Rites, which by this time had taken over most marriage cases from the Ministry of Revenue. In a show of Neo-Confucian concern for a woman marrying twice, and in deference to their own decision of 1313, the Ministry of Rites rules that since the forced marriage has already been consummated, it should not be annulled, because that would force a woman into two successive marriages. The two families should go back to their original agreement for a double marriage exchange. In a somewhat contradictory statement, however, they rule that in the future forced marriages should be annulled. The Central Secretariat approves the ruling, but in the order sent

---

is not found in the Tang and Song codes and the Tang code is referred to explicitly by name in this document. See Kobayashi 1977; Ye Qianzhao 1972; discussion in Birge 2010, 392–394.

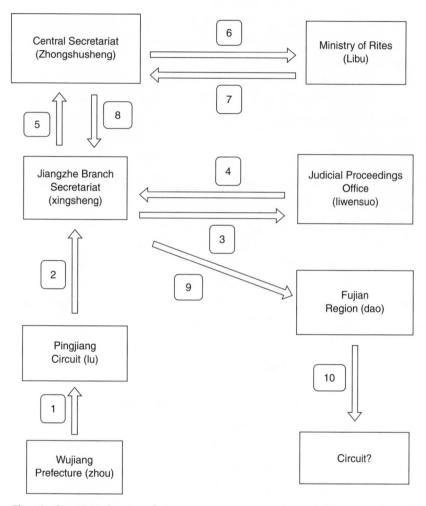

Chart 3. Case 18.19, document flow.

out universally, they take the opportunity to reemphasize the 1313 precedent upholding original betrothal agreements. The opening of the document shows the paper trail of the order from the Central Secretariat, to each branch secretariat, to the region, and then presumably the circuit (see Chart 3).

This case demonstrates the difference between thirteenth-century rulings by the Ministry of Revenue that upheld more narrow legislation and private marriage agreements, which often favored the bride's side of a marriage, and early fourteenth-century rulings usually by the Ministry of Rites that tried to enforce what they saw as universal Confucian values such as female loyalty and fidelity, often at the expense of the bride's family and her independence, in this case even allowing for kidnapping and rape.

18.19 *Ding Qingyi contests his daughter's marriage*[195]

In the sixth year of the *yanyou* period (1319), the fourth month, we respectfully received[196] a document from the Pacification Commission and Military Command of Fujian Region,[197] as follows:

We respectfully received a document from the Jiangzhe Branch Secretariat, stating:

We received a communiqué from the Central Secretariat, which reads:

We received your communiqué, as follows:[198]

Pingjiang Circuit passed up a dispatch from Wujiang Prefecture,[199] which reads:

In the first year of *huangqing* (1312), second month, Xu Qiansan through the services of Zhou Qian'er as go-between arranged the betrothal of his son Xu Bange to Ding Anü,[200] the daughter of Ding Qingyi. At the same time Xu Qiansan betrothed his own daughter Xu Erniang to the

---

195. YDZ 18:12a–b, pp. 679–680.

196. It is not clear exactly what office is receiving this document, whence it was gathered into the *Yuan dianzhang*. It would logically be one of the eight circuits (*lu*) under the jurisdiction of Fujian Region (*dao*). Note that the case originates from Pingjiang Circuit in the far north of Jiangzhe Branch Secretariat, which is not within the jurisdiction of Fujian Region in the south of Jiangzhe. This is an example where a verdict is sent out widely as a general precedent, not just to the office that sent the case up.

197. *Xuanwei shuaifu* 福建道宣慰帥府. This is one of eight different types of Pacification Offices (*xuanweisi* 宣慰司), which administered regions (*dao* 道) under the Yuan. The title is short for "Pacification Commission and General Regional Military Command" (*xuanwei shisi duyuan shuaifu* 宣慰使司都元帥府). One of two regions within the Jiangzhe Branch Secretariat, Fujian Region, was headed by this type of office. Regions were a unit of executive administration that existed in some areas between the branch secretariats (*xingsheng*) and the circuits (*lu*), which helped propagate orders down to smaller units of government. These "regions" headed by a Pacification Office did not exist everywhere and were different from the "regions" (*dao*) that were founded as local units of the Censorate, as encountered previously in other cases (Shi Weimin 1993; Li Zhi'an 2003, 91–104; Farquhar 1990, 411–412).

198. What follows is the original communiqué from the Jiangzhe Branch Secretariat. After that is the decision by the Central Secretariat, which gets sent out to the branch secretariat, then to the region, and then to the unnamed circuit at the beginning of the case, as indicated by the opening lines of the case.

199. This prefecture was just south of the seat of Pingjiang Circuit, which is modern Suzhou City.

200. Reading *nü* (女) for *ding* (丁), based on the name of the bride given later in the text.

son of Ding Qingyi, Ding Asun. Each side accepted betrothal gifts and agreed to exchange their children in marriage, but the final marriages did not actually take place. Then in the first year of *yanyou* (1314) a flood destroyed the crops, and in the midst of hardship and famine both families established documents of divorce to cancel the marriages. In the third year of *yanyou* (1316), ninth month, Ding Qingyi took Ding Anü and betrothed her to Ni Fuyi. But before the final marriage took place and she had moved in with his family, in the twelfth month of the same year, on the seventh day, Xu Qiansan, together with his wife A-Qiu, his son Xu Bange, and others, got on a boat and snatched away Ding Qingyi's daughter Ding Anü. They forced her onto the boat with them and took her back to their home, where the marriage was unlawfully consummated.

We [the Jiangzhe Branch Secretariat] sent this to the Judicial Proceedings Office, which concluded: "We have examined this matter carefully. If we adjudicate this case according to the decision of the twenty-first year of *zhiyuan* (1284), third month, by the Ministry of Revenue of the Central Secretariat, where Bai Yü filed a plaint against Hu Xing for snatching away his daughter Bai Man'er and forcing her to marry Hu Huijin, then we should order the marriage annulled. Nevertheless we note that, in the second year of *huangqing* (1313), seventh month, the Ministry of Rites of the Central Secretariat established the marriage-law precedent proposed by Director-General Shi of Jinning Circuit,[201] which states: 'We have deliberated together and conclude: from now on when a daughter is betrothed to be married and the bride's family has accepted the betrothal gifts, if the family reneges, they should be punished according to this precedent, and the daughter returned to her first husband.' Now,[202] regarding Wujiang Prefecture, we have deliberated and decide that the case of Xu Bange forcing Ding Anü to have sexual relations with him to consummate their marriage is not equivalent to the precedent of reneging on a marriage where the couple is ordered to reunite. Examining the crime committed by Xu Bange, there has been an amnesty exempting him from punishment. Nevertheless, we fear that the bad traditions of the Wu and Yue regions[203]

---

201. This is case 18.18 just above, although the date there is given as the fifth month rather than the seventh.

202. Reading *jin* 今 for *ling* 令.

203. Wu and Yue are the names of ancient states located in southeast China. The names continued to be used to refer to the area.

could be transmitted and imitated in other places. If we rule that the marriage be annulled on the basis of the precedent of Bai Man'er, might Ding Anü prefer to avoid entering a second marriage? Moreover, this matter concerns a universal precedent." We send you this communiqué and request that you consider it thoroughly.

Communiqué received. We [the Central Secretariat] sent this to the Ministry of Rites, whose report is as follows:

We have deliberated and conclude: Ding Qingyi and Xu Qiansan accepted betrothal gifts from each other and agreed to exchange their sons and daughters in marriage. Afterwards, because of a famine, they wrote out letters of divorce. Xu Bange went ahead and carried out the marriage. In the end he did not know that he should not have snatched Ding Anü and forced her back to his home, then on his own have unlawfully consummated the marriage. Regarding his crime, there has been an amnesty exempting him from punishment. If we were to rule that the marriage be annulled, it would compel a woman to marry two different men in succession, which would be extremely contrary to what is right. We considered the matter carefully and conclude that, the two families should be ordered to carry out the marriage exchange according to the earlier agreement. As for the betrothal gifts paid by Ni Fuyi, they should be paid back to him according to their full value. From now on, if there are cases similar to this, they should be adjudicated according to the precedent of Bai Man'er and the marriage should be annulled. We think it would be appropriate to send a communiqué to the Branch Secretariat asking that they enforce this as above. We present this report for your thorough consideration.

Report received. We the Metropolitan Secretariat deliberated and conclude: in the case of Ding Qingyi and Xu Qiansan contesting a marriage, we approve the decision of the Ministry. But from now on, when a daughter is betrothed to be married and the marriage contract has already been returned or there has been a private agreement between the parties, or the bride's family has accepted the betrothal gifts, all such cases should be adjudicated according to the universal precedent of the second year of *huangqing* (1313), which stipulates that the original marriage be preserved. Violators will be prosecuted according to the law. We send you [the Branch Secretariat] this communiqué requesting that you consider it carefully and enforce it as above.

18.20

This next case is the first in a series of four that address the issue of wife-selling. It was illegal for a man to marry off his wife to someone else in return for betrothal payments, but this case, from 1271, suggests that people in north China at this time widely accepted the behavior and did not always realize it was prohibited. (Note that the language used in these transactions was that of marriage, where the betrothal payments made by the groom to the bride's family constituted the "price" of the wife.) This first case is of particular interest, because the man selling his wife was an official of fairly high rank, which prompts the circuit to send the case up for adjudication by the central government. Moreover, the purchaser goes to court to complain that this official is trying to bully him into making additional payments for the wife. Neither protagonist seems to have anticipated any trouble from the law for wife-selling or wife-purchasing itself.[204] Also of interest is that the wife in question has a Jurchen name, revealing the existence of intercultural marriages in the north.[205] At this date, eighth month of 1271, four months before the abrogation of the Taihe code, the court follows this code of the Jurchen Jin to arrive at a sentence, including the Jin system of redemption payments in lieu of beatings. But it also applies the considerable reduction of punishments ordered by Khubilai in 1269. The court collects the redemption payment from the first husband, but in the end it declines to punish the second husband, the plaintiff, and allows the second marriage to stand, in contradiction to the Tang, Song, and Jin codes.

18.20 *A husband himself marries off his wife to someone else*[206]

In the eighth year of the *zhiyuan* period (1271), eighth month, a document from [a Ministry of][207] the Secretariat for State Affairs states:

---

204. There was even a special term for the payments, which appears here and in later legal documents: *maixiuqian* 買休錢, literally "money to buy a divorce," or "payment to buy out the marriage."

205. The name is found in slightly longer form in the list of Jurchen surnames in the Jin dynastic history (*Jinshi* 55:1230).

206. YDZ 18:12b–13a, pp. 680–681.

207. We can discern from the text that this document is from one of the Six Ministries, which until the twelfth month of 1271 operated under the Secretariat for State Affairs.

A dispatch from Dadu Circuit reads:[208]

> Xu Shuncheng filed a plaint, stating:
>
>> Zhang Taige brought some people whom he knew to my house and de-manded of me, Shuncheng, additional payment to buy out his marriage to my wife, Hesushi, whom I married [properly] through the services of a go-between.
>
> We apprehended Zhang Tai[ge], whose given name is Shirong, the go-between A-Zhao, and others and obtained detailed written confessions from each. Leaving aside other matters to be dealt with separately, it is the case that Zhang Shirong has confessed to the crime of "a husband himself marrying off his wife to someone else."[209] We could adjudicate this accord-ingly; but we the circuit authorities respectfully note that according to Zhang Shirong's testimony, he has received the Imperial Decree of office with the Golden Insignia tablet, charged with supervising rice-growing households.[210]
>
> Thus we humbly request that you pass down a clear decision.

Dispatch received. The Old Regulations state: "One who by consent marries an-other man's wife and the one who gives the wife in marriage are each punished by three years of penal servitude. If a husband himself marries off his wife to someone else, he is punished the same and the marriage is annulled."[211] We the Ministry of the Secretariat deliberated over the matter. It is the case that Zhang Shirong has

208. At this date, Dadu Circuit was still called Zhongdu Circuit. See YS 58:1347; YS 90:2300. The name changed to Dadu in 1272. The compilers of the *Yuan dianzhang* likely changed the original to match contemporary usage.

209. This infraction is found in the Tang and Song codes punished by two years of penal servitude. See TLSY 14:266 (Art. 187); SXT 14:223; Johnson 1997, 166.

210. The Imperial Decree of office (*xuanming* 宣命) was granted to officials of the fifth rank and above, whose posts were technically conferred by the emperor, while the Golden Insignia tablet (*jinpai* 金牌) was granted to officials of rank 4 or 5 (YS 83:2064, 91:2311). Marco Polo describes these tablets that granted special privileges, and one of these golden tablets was listed in his will (Komroff 1930, 123–124; de Rachewiltz 1997). For a reference in Yuan drama, see Hayden 1978, 51. The text starts a new line with the term "Imperial" and elevates it one char-acter space to show respect. We can surmise from the information in this sentence that Zhang Shirong was a Superintendent (*tiju* 提舉), rank 5B, for special households who owed goods or services to the state, in this case rice-growing households. Such officials served in the special establishments of the Emperor and Empress (YS 88:2234; Farquhar 1990, 20, 146, 327–328). Because of Zhang's status, the circuit does not dare pass judgment on him.

211. We can understand "Old Regulations" here to mean the Taihe code of the Jin, in which the provision is the same as that in the Tang and Song codes. The text states the punishment as three years of penal servitude rather than two years, as found in the Tang and Song codes, but we can determine that this must be a misprint, since Zhang's reduction of punishment given

received the Imperial Decree of office with the Golden Insignia tablet, charged with supervising rice-growing households. He is a person of official rank. According to the Old Regulations, officials of the seventh rank and above who commit crimes punishable by life exile or less have their sentences reduced by one degree. Thus he should be sentenced to one and one half years of penal servitude. Now, there has been a previous legal regulation issued in the sixth year of *zhiyuan* (1269), seventh month, eighth day, reducing the sentences for criminal offenses, which reduces the sentence five grades. Thus the sentence should be 80 blows of the heavy stick. He can redeem this sentence with a fine of sixteen catties of copper.[212] Each catty is equivalent to 200 pieces of cash, thus his total redemption payment is three strings and 200 cash in paper money to be collected by the government.[213] In addition, Zhang Shirong has already broken off his marriage with Hesushi, thus Xu Shuncheng is allowed to marry her in accordance with the law, and his marriage should be allowed to stand. The original payment to buy out his marriage demanded by Zhang Shirong should be confiscated by the government, but since there has been an Imperial Amnesty reducing sentences, this need not be collected.

18.21

This case of wife-selling takes place in south China, sixteen years later than the previous case, and the protagonists clearly knew they were breaking the law. After eighteen years of marriage, a man sells off his wife to another, using the pretense that she is his younger brother's widow. Unlike the previous case, where the central government allowed the second marriage to stand, here the Jiangzhe Branch Secretariat annuls both marriages and allows the woman to return to her natal

---

later in the case is calculated on the basis of an initial two years' penal servitude, in accordance with Tang and Song law (TLSY 14:266 [Art. 187]; SXT 14:223).

212. The Tang code allowed redemption of 80 blows with only eight catties of copper (TLSY 1:4 [Art. 2]; Johnson 1979, 57). On those eligible, the young, the old, the infirm, and officials, see TLSY 2:34, 4:80–83 (Art. 11, 30); Johnson 1979, 93, 169. The Yuan compilers of the Jin dynastic history noted the increased punishments in the Taihe code (*Jinshi* 45:1024). The decree of 1269 reducing punishments is referenced in YS 6:122. The punishment here of 80 blows is similar to the 100 blows that a judge in the Southern Song meted out to all parties in lieu of penal servitude in a case of wife selling. The Song judge also annulled the two marriages and confiscated the betrothal gifts. See QMJ 9:352–353; McKnight and Liu 1999, 343–344.

213. Each string was worth 1,000 cash, so this computes accurately.

family to marry again from there. Citing one of the frequent amnesties in the Yuan, the branch secretariat metes out no further punishment to either husband.

18.21 *A wife who is married off by her husband is allowed to divorce and marry someone else*[214]

In the first year of the *dade* period (1297), seventh month, a document from Yuanzhou Circuit states:

Duan Wanshisi[215] took A-Pan as his wife and was married for eighteen years, when in the second year of *yuanzhen* (1296), in the twelfth month, he pretended his wife, A-Pan, was the widow of his younger brother and sold her off to be the wife of Tan Xiaoshi. He received four ingots worth of paper money for himself.[216] We submitted this dispatch and respectfully received a superior communication from the Jiangxi Branch Secretariat, which reads as follows:

> Duan Wanshisi falsely claimed that his wife was the widow of his deceased younger brother. He accepted betrothal payments and married her off to Tan Xiaoshi. This constitutes a violation of his marriage vows. Although there has been an amnesty that absolves him from punishment, according to legal principles the marriage should be annulled. The wife should be allowed to return to her natal lineage and from there go and marry someone else.

18.22

In this case, also from Yuanzhou Circuit and just one year later than the previous case, 18.21, a man marries his wife off to a soldier in exchange for two ingots worth of paper money as betrothal gifts. The circuit authorities try to confiscate the betrothal gifts paid, but the first husband is so indigent that the funds are no longer retrievable. The Jiangxi Branch Secretariat annuls both marriages and sends the woman back to her natal family, as they did in the previous case. In addition, they note a recent amnesty on the occasion of an imperial birthday and recommend that on that basis the circuit forego confiscation. The Ministry of Rites at the capital agrees, and the Central Secretariat (using its informal name, Metropolitan Secretariat) approves the ruling.

---

214. YDZ 18:13a, p. 681.

215. The character for the surname Duan (段) in the *Yuan dianzhang* uses a common Yuan variant.

216. Reading *ding* 錠 for *ding* 定. One "ingot" (*ding*) was worth fifty ounces of silver (*liang*) and was a standard unit of paper money (see Chan 1990, 446).

In its ruling, the Ministry of Rites acknowledges the prevalence of wife-selling in Jiangnan (literally "south of the [Yangzi] river," referring to southeast China) and reveals considerable sympathy for the poverty that contributed to it, which may explain the lenient treatment meted out in these cases compared to the penalties specified in the Tang, Song, and Jin codes. We also see again how judges could take advantage of the frequent amnesties issued by the Yuan court to gain flexibility in their application of the law.

18.22 *A husband marries off his wife to someone else, but the betrothal gifts are not confiscated*[217]

In the second year of the *dade* period (1298), eighth month, [blank] day, a document from the Jiangxi Branch Secretariat states:

A [dispatch] from Yuanzhou Circuit reads:

> We investigated and learned through interrogation that Guo Ji'er claimed his wife, Peng Mingsigu, was his younger sister and married her off to Soldier Wang Er. He received in payment two ingots worth of paper money, one silver hairpin, red fancy silk, and twenty strings of cash for the go-between.[218] We repeatedly attempted to recover these items, but Guo Ji'er is impoverished, and we were unable to collect them from him. How would it be to forego confiscation?

We the Secretariat Office considered the matter carefully. These events were prior to the Imperial Amnesty decreed on the twenty-seventh day of the second month of the first year of *dade* (1297).[219] Nevertheless, if we forego confiscation, we note that the ruling would become a universal precedent. Therefore, we sent this to the Metropolitan Secretariat and received back a communiqué, which reads as follows:

> We sent this to the Ministry of Rites, which investigated the matter and issued a ruling, as follows:

>> Guo Ji'er married off his wife Peng Mingsigu to Wang Er. This is contrary to the law. The Branch Secretariat has already ruled that the wife should return to her natal lineage, and there need be no further adjudication of this aspect of the case. Regarding the disposition of the betrothal

---

217. YDZ 18:13a–b, pp. 681–682.

218. Reading *duan* (緞) for *duan* (段).

219. This amnesty is recorded in the Yuan dynastic history (YS 19:409). The term starts a new line and is elevated one space to show respect.

gifts that were originally accepted [by Guo Ji'er], even though Wang Er claims he absolutely did not know the situation, in the end he was married for a year. Thus his statement cannot be believed. In addition, Guo Ji'er married off his wife because his household was impoverished. This is due to long-standing tainted customs of the Jiangnan region and cannot be helped. We have carefully examined the matter and note that, these events were prior to the Imperial Amnesty. If you approve our proposal to forego confiscation, then we recommend that you send a communiqué to the Branch Secretariat telling them to enforce this as above.

We the Metropolitan Secretariat approve the report.

18.23

This last case in this series on wife-selling takes place in 1310 in Hunan Region (*dao*), whose seat was at the modern city of Changsha. This region was part of the Huguang Branch Secretariat, which encompassed a small bit of modern Hubei, plus modern Hunan, Guangxi, the western part of Guangdong, most of Guizhou, and Hainan Island. The Pacification Office, the ruling body of the region, applies an earlier precedent of 1301 from their own region in the case, but they don't seem to know of precedents generated from other branch secretariats or feel that these would be applicable. In particular, they ask for permission to forego confiscation of the betrothal gifts, as approved by the Ministry of Rites and the Central Secretariat in the 1298 case, 18.22 above, from Yuanzhou Circuit. But this time the Ministry of Rites, under the Secretariat for State Affairs (which was in existence at this time), rejects foregoing confiscation, despite an imperial amnesty having taken place, thereby contradicting their own previous ruling of 1298. Both rulings are referred to in their respective case documents as "universal precedents" (*tongli* 通例). The Ministry approves the rest of the Pacification Office's decision to annul both marriages and send the wife back to her natal family, the same action taken in the two Yuanzhou cases above. We see here once again that an amnesty can be applied flexibly, or as in this case, not at all. By this time, the illegality of wife-selling seems to have been well-established, and the second husband agrees to pay hush-money to keep the matter away from the authorities, though in the end he suffers no punishment beyond the annulment of his marriage. This was to change later in the dynasty. The "Treatise on Punishments" from the Yuan dynastic history contains a final ruling, not found in the *Yuan dianzhang*, that establishes a beating of 67 strokes, annulment of both marriages, and confiscation of the betrothal gifts as punishment in cases of wife-selling.[220]

18.23 *A man accepts betrothal gifts and marries off his wife to someone else*[221]

In the third year of the *zhida* period (1310), eleventh month, the Hunan Pacification Office[222] respectfully received a superior communication from the Huguang Branch Secretariat, as follows:

We received your report, which reads:

> Liu Ziming pretended his wife Guo Erniang was his younger sister, and through the services of a go-between he accepted betrothal payments from Wang Wansi and married his wife to this man. Later, when he found out about the situation, Wang Wansi paid an additional forty ounces worth of paper money to keep the matter quiet.[223] These actions are indeed contrary to the law. If we follow the precedent in the case of Tan Bashiyi marrying off his wife,[224] then we should order Guo Erniang back to her natal lineage, and the sons born to her should go to their respective fathers.[225] The payments and betrothal gifts originally received should all be confiscated. We tried to recover the betrothal gifts from Liu Ziming but were unable to. We could forego confiscation, but we have not yet received a universal precedent to apply in such a case.

We [the Branch Secretariat] sent this to the Secretariat for State Affairs[226] and received their communiqué in return, which reads in part as follows:

> We sent this to the Ministry of Rites, whose report reads:
>
> > We examined this matter thoroughly. Liu Ziming accepted betrothal gifts and married off his wife Guo Erniang to Wang Wansi. Both the wife

---

220. YS 103:2643; Ratchnevsky and Aubin 1972–1985, 2:126 (Art. 397).

221. YDZ 18:13b, p. 682.

222. This Pacification Office for Hunan Region was located at the seat of Tianlin Circuit, modern Changsha City.

223. *Maihe* 買和, literally "pay to keep things amicable," refers to payments to settle matters out of court, in this case to keep things quiet, away from the attention of the authorities.

224. This case is described in case 18.40 and took place in 1301, also in Hunan Region. It would have been handled by this same Hunan Pacification Office. The name of the protagonist Tan is written there slightly differently as 譚, not 潭.

225. Reading *sheng* 生 for *zhu* 主, as earlier in the sentence.

226. This case takes place within the third time period when the Secretariat for State Affairs was in existence during the Yuan, namely eighth month of 1309 to first month of 1311.

giving and wife taking are unlawful and should be punished as a warning. Although these events were prior to an Imperial Amnesty and the offenses are exempted from punishment, the situation must be corrected. We recommend that you approve the decision by the Pacification Office of the said region and order Guo Erniang back to her natal lineage. The sons born to her should each go to their respective fathers. The payments and betrothal gifts originally received should be confiscated. This would be appropriate. We present this report for your thorough consideration.

We the Metropolitan Secretariat[227] send you this communiqué and request that you enforce it as above.

18.24

In this case, dated 1271 eleventh month, the plaintiff is a grandmother who wants to force her son's widow to invite in an uxorilocal husband to take the place of her son and support the household. She is asking the court to allow the marriage during the mourning period for her son, marriage during the mourning period being illegal in traditional Chinese law. As part of her appeal, she argues that without an able-bodied man in the house she cannot meet her tax and labor obligations. The court rejects her suit on two counts. The Ministry of Revenue upholds Khubilai's edict of 1271, second month, just nine months before this case, which includes the provision that a widow cannot be forced by her in-laws to remarry and may return to her natal family after the mourning period is over if she so chooses. It also enforces the mourning period and cites the Taihe code of the Jin (still in operation at this time), which fixes the mourning period of a wife for her husband at twenty-seven months. The court declares that the widow can do what she wishes after this time. In response to the household's predicament, the Ministry orders the circuit to consider some tax and corvée relief. The text does not give a place for the suit, but we can surmise that it comes from a circuit within the Central Province, since the Ministry of Revenue communicates directly with the circuit.

This ruling and Khubilai's edict behind it provided widows with significant personal autonomy. Such legal support of widows was reversed in 1309, when the Secretary for State Affairs ruled that a widow could not return to her natal

---

227. Note that in this case this term refers to the Secretariat for State Affairs (Shangshusheng), not the Central Secretariat.

family, nor could she remarry on her own initiative, but had to have the permission of her in-laws, who would thenceforth keep the betrothal gifts paid for the remarriage. This decision is recorded in 18.26 just below.[228] Also noteworthy here is the enforcement of the mourning period, based on provisions of the Taihe code of the Jin. Within weeks of this ruling, Khubilai abrogated the Taihe code and thereby ushered in a period of inconsistent application or even rejection of the mourning period (as seen in cases 18.15 and 18.29 among others) and general instability in the law.[229]

18.24 *A father and mother may not marry off their son's widow*[230]

In the eighth year of the *zhiyuan* period (1271), eleventh month, a document from the Ministry of Revenue of the Secretariat for State Affairs states:
We received your dispatch, which reads:

Xu A-Du filed a plaint, stating:

In the twelfth month of the sixth year of *zhiyuan* (1269), my son Mianhe died, leaving behind his children with no one to support them. I cannot meet my tax and labor obligations. I want to have my son's widow, A-Liu, invite in a foster son for me, who will be her husband. But since the mourning period for my son Mianhe is not yet complete [and my daughter-in-law cannot remarry], I am truly suffering extreme hardship.

We the circuit authorities do not dare make a decision on our own in the absence of a precedent. We humbly request that you pass down a clear decision. With regard to this case, we investigated and found that we have humbly received a set of Imperial Regulations, one item of which reads as follows:

If a woman whose husband has died wishes to stay chaste after the mourning period is over, or moreover wishes to return to her natal family, she should be allowed to do so. Her mother- and father-in-law may not on their own initiative arrange a remarriage for her.[231]

---

228. For a discussion of the context and significance of these rulings, see Birge 2002, chapter 4, especially 264–268; Birge 1995, 128–139.
229. For a discussion of these changes in the application of the mourning period, see Birge 2002, 257–261.
230. YDZ 18:13b–14a, pp. 682–683.
231. This is an exact quote of the edict of 1271, second month, recorded in case 18.2, Item 6 (with the exception that the order of "mother-in-law" and "father-in-law" is switched).

We the Ministry of the Secretariat deliberated over the matter. We could approve the request made by Xu A-Du in her plaint; nevertheless, we have investigated and found that the Old Regulations state that, the mourning of a widow for her husband is formally three years, but in practice it's actually twenty-seven months.[232] We rule that the plaintiff should wait until the mourning period is over, then respect the wishes of A-Liu. It is the case that the father- and mother-in-law may not arrange an uxorilocal marriage for their son's widow. We order you humbly to respect the intent of the Imperial Edict previously issued and have this enforced. As for the taxes and labor duties of Xu A-Du's household, they should be assessed and some relief provided.

18.25

Similar to the four cases concerning wife-selling above, a father was not allowed to sell his daughter-in-law into another marriage. Only a girl's parents or grand-parents, or other natal family members in their absence, were permitted to arrange her marriage. In this interesting example, an official in the circuit administration of Wenzhou sells off his son's wife to another official. The Ministry of Punishments sets a relatively mild punishment of a beating of 47 blows. They find the wife-purchaser guilty of collusion in the crime, since he knew of the circumstances, but he suffers from a serious illness so they excuse him from punishment until he recovers. Both officials receive a black mark in their performance dossiers. The verdict does not explicitly state what happens to the wife, though we can assume she is returned to her natal family. The case comes up to the central government through the Censorate administration, but the main Censorate at the capital sends it to the Central Secretariat for final adjudication.

18.25 *A man accepts betrothal payments and marries off his son's wife*[233]

In the thirtieth year of the *zhiyuan* period (1293), ninth month, a document from the Censorate states:

We received your communiqué, which reads:[234]

---

232. The Taihe code of the Jin contained eleven regulations on the mourning period, and we can assume that this was one of them; see *Jinshi* 45:1024. Here the content is cited in very colloquial language that would not have been found in the code itself.

233. YDZ 18:14a, p. 683.

234. This would be from one of the branch censorates, since the document is in the form of a "communiqué" (*zi*).

Associate Director-General Gu Wenkui of Wenzhou Circuit improperly accepted betrothal gifts and married off his son's wife Li Yuansiniang to Supervisor Dawu.[235] Dawu is afflicted with the wind illness, thus we cannot hold him liable for punishment.[236] Associate Director-General Gu is guilty of the offense of Doing What Ought Not to be Done, and we sentence him to a beating of 47 strokes.[237]

We submitted a report to the Central Secretariat and respectfully received a superior communication in return, as follows:[238]

The Ministry of Punishments deliberated and concluded:

Based on the testimony of Gu Wenkui, we approve the sentence of a beating of 47 strokes. In addition, we note that Supervisor Dawu clearly knew of the circumstances that he was illegally seeking to marry the wife of Associate Director-General Gu's second son, thus he is guilty of collusion. We recommend that the authorities wait until he has recovered from his illness, then, based on the testimony collected by the said region, proceed with adjudication according to the regulations. Moreover, it would be appropriate to record in each official's performance dossier a notation of their having committed this private offense.[239]

We the Metropolitan Secretariat approve the ruling.

---

235. These two officials served in the main administrative office of the circuit, the Directorate-General. Associate Director-General Gu was rank 4B, second only to the Director-General himself, and Supervisor Dawu was rank 6A (Farquhar 1990, 22). Dawu was a foreign name, perhaps Mongol or Jurchen. Wenzhou Circuit was part of Jiangzhe Branch Secretariat and had its seat at modern Wenzhou City, on China's southeast coast.

236. The "wind illness" (*fengbing* 風病) could refer variously to paralysis from a stroke, leprosy, or even mental illness.

237. For this catchall name for a crime, see note under case 18.17.

238. Note the language of inferior to superior in this sentence. The Censorate was ranked 1B and the Central Secretariat 1A, thus the Censorate "humbly receives" (*feng*) a "superior communication" (*zhafu*), and issues a "report" (*cheng*) to the Central Secretariat. The relative ranking of these offices was debated at the beginning of the Yuan. See YS 158:3726–3727.

239. During the Yuan, dossiers were kept on everyone assigned to office, which were used for performance reviews and consideration for promotion at the end of one's term. They included a special section to record any criminal offenses. For references to this system, see YDZ 11:16b (p. 436); TZTG 6:295 (Art. 171). Crimes committed by officials were classified as either "public" or "private" offenses, depending on whether they involved official public duties or officials' private lives, though the distinction was not always clear. This classification goes back to the Tang code. See TLSY 2:44 (Art. 17); Johnson 1979, 112–113.

18.26

As clearly indicated by the title, the ruling of 1309 in the case below, confirmed by Emperor Khaishan (r. 1307–1311), exactly reverses the ruling of 1271 in 18.24 above that gave widows the freedom to return home and remarry of their own choice, without interference by their former in-laws. Traditional Chinese marriage law granted considerable autonomy to a widow and her natal family, giving her the legal right to return to her natal family, to remarry, and to keep her dowry property with her person. Her natal parents, moreover, could keep the betrothal gifts from a second marriage. The ruling below, by contrast, shifts the balance of power away from a widow and her natal family and grants it to the husband's family. This new law, unprecedented in Chinese history, strips wives of their right to return home when widowed, and strips their natal parents of the right to preside over a remarriage and keep the betrothal payments.

The Secretariat for State Affairs, which had just been reconstituted one month before this ruling, was well aware that they were overturning previous dynastic law, for they carefully cited previous rulings on the issue. But they argued that parents-in-law were left destitute when their son died and his widow returned home, while the widow's natal parents could arrange a remarriage and collect the lucrative betrothal gifts a second time for the same daughter. It thus ruled that a chaste widow should be forced to stay in the home of her in-laws. If she wished to remarry, she had to marry any eligible levir within the family, and in the absence of a levir, only her in-laws had the power to arrange a remarriage and could keep any betrothal gifts collected.

This ruling transferred rights to a woman's body from herself and her natal parents to the parents of her first husband. It incorporated into Chinese imperial law the Mongol steppe idea that a woman's body and assets were transferred upon marriage to her husband's family for life. The new law below demonstrates a remarkable confluence of interests between Neo-Confucian fundamentalists, who were gaining influence at court in the early fourteenth century, and steppe-oriented emperors. Emperor Khaishan had spent his years as a military commander on the steppe and had little interest in or knowledge of Confucianism. But his policies on marriage that implemented steppe ideas whereby a woman's ties to her natal family were largely severed upon marriage overlapped with the Neo-Confucian agenda to promote widow chastity and strengthen the authority of the husband and his family.

This case is just one of a number of new policies in the early fourteenth century implemented not only by emperors who embraced Confucian reforms but also by an emperor who came out of the steppe and was uninterested in Confucian ideas. These policies profoundly changed Chinese marriage law, shifting it away from support of the legal and customary rights that Chinese women had traditionally enjoyed.[240] This case is written in Sino-Mongolian, thus giving the language an informal, almost vulgar, feel. The use of Sino-Mongolian indicates that the original document was in Mongolian and reflects the dominance of Mongols and Inner Asians in Emperor Khaishan's Secretariat for State Affairs.

18.26 *A father and mother may marry off their son's widow*[241]

In the second year of the *zhida* period (1309), ninth month, a document from the Secretariat for State Affairs states:[242]

We submitted a Memorial to the throne, an item of which reads:

> In the twenty-eighth year of *zhiyuan* (1291) we respectfully received an Imperial Regulation, which states:[243]

>> If a woman whose husband has died wishes on her own volition to stay chaste after the mourning period is over or to return to her natal family, she is allowed to do so. Her father- and mother-in-law may not arrange a remarriage for her.

> We humbly respect the Imperial Regulation. We have investigated and found that in addition we respectfully received an Imperial Edict, which reads in part as follows:

>> Quickly have this order sent out: a younger brother should take his sister-in-law in levirate marriage.[244]

240. For a full analysis of this case and its significance, see Birge 1995, 137–138; and Birge 2002, 165–166.

241. YDZ 18:14a–b, pp. 683–684.

242. The table of contents of the entire *Yuan dianzhang* gives the date of this text as *zhida* third year (1310) instead of second.

243. What follows is a quotation of Item 6 in case 18.2, with slightly different wording. The date given here of "twenty-eighth year of *zhiyuan*" (1291), must be a mistake for "eighth year of *zhiyuan*" (1271), since the year of this edict is 1271.

244. This is a quotation with slightly different wording of the edict in case 18.49, which is Khubilai's momentous edict of 1271, twelfth month, legalizing levirate marriage for all peoples.

Thus said the Edict. In addition to humbly respecting these Edicts, we note that the various branch secretariats have sent us communiqués saying that: Wives whose husbands have died do not stay chaste in the home of their husbands. Rather, they go to the home of their natal father and mother. During the mourning period they accept meat, wine, and paper money from other men and on their own initiative go and get remarried. We all deliberated and conclude: The natal father and mother are getting betrothal payments twice. First they take in mutton, wine, silk cloth, and paper money from their daughter's father- and mother-in-law in her original marriage. When this boy dies, they again demand betrothal payments and arrange the remarriage of their daughter to someone else's son. Because of this, the households of a wife's father- and mother-in-law are gradually becoming impoverished. How would it be if, from now on, a woman whose husband has died who wishes on her own volition to stay chaste must do so in the home of her first husband? If she wants to remarry and there is no younger brother-in-law to inherit her in a levirate union, she must obey her father- and mother-in-law, who will accept the betrothal gifts and arrange the remarriage.

When we thus sent this memorial to the throne, we respectfully received an Imperial Edict, stating:

Do it like that![245]

We humbly respect the Edict.

---

245. This Sino-Mongolian expression appears routinely in the *Yuan dianzhang*, recording the emperor's order to carry out the proposal before him. I have intentionally translated it with a peremptory tone to preserve the timbre of the words in the context of the *Yuan dianzhang*. The phrase appears in the Chinese interlinear text of the *Secret History of the Mongols* in several places, though in a different context. See *Menggu mishi jiaokan ben* 2:103, 105, 5:360; de Rachewiltz 2004, 1:24, 1:86.

CHAPTER SIX

Sections 3–5

Marriage between Officials and Commoners; Marriages of Military Personnel; Divorce

Section 3: Marriage between Officials and Commoners

18.27

The first case in this section concerns an official serving in a circuit office who takes as his concubine the daughter-in-law of a man in custody. This crime is similar to the cases of wife-selling in the previous chapter, and here the official is a knowing purchaser of someone else's wife. The official is fined one month's salary and gets a black mark in his dossier, which is a very light punishment compared to the heavy beatings or even exile prescribed for similar offenses in the Tang, Song, and Ming codes.[1] The father-in-law does not incur punishment, presumably because the authorities understand him to have been coerced, and neither do the others involved in the case. The offense was discovered by the Regional Surveillance Office of the Censorate and passed up to the main Censorate, which sought a draft decision by their Law Office before appealing to the Central Secretariat for a final ruling.

---

1. These prescribe beatings of up to 100 strokes, or exile if the marriage was forced. See TLSY 14:265–266 (Art. 186); Johnson 1997, 164–165; SXT 14:221–222; *Da Ming lü* 6:684; Jiang 2005, 86 (Art. 116). The chart at the beginning of chapter 18 of the *Yuan dianzhang* cites a decision not included in the main body of the chapter that gives beatings of 37 and 47 strokes to low-level officials for this crime. See YDZ 18:1b.

18.27 *A ranked official takes as his concubine the daughter-in-law*
      of a man in custody[2]

In the sixth year of the *zhiyuan* period (1269), tenth month, a document from
the Central Secretariat states:

A report from the Censorate reads:

A dispatch from the Regional Surveillance Office of Shanbei Dongxi Region reads:[3]

A document from Beijing Circuit states: "Zhang Yu was taken into custody
by the Directorate-General on account of some government grain provisions
going missing. While the matter was being pursued, Overseer Qiao of this
circuit had his servant Little Liu together with the go-between Miao Niang-
niang and others go to the prison to seek the hand of Zhang's daughter-
in-law to be his concubine." We obtained the confession of Overseer Qiao
Dejian together with the testimony of all those involved in the case.

We [the Censorate] sent this to the Law Office,[4] which investigated the matter
and after deliberation determined:

The marriage between Qiao Dejian and his concubine should be annulled,
and the betrothal gifts should not be returned. Since the crime involved
a salaried official, one should weigh the circumstances of the case and
impose an appropriate reduction in his salary.

This Office [the Censorate] sends up this report and humbly requests that
you consider it thoroughly.

We the Secretariat Office deliberated together and determined that, the crime
committed by Qiao Dejian should be punished by a fine of one-month's salary.
In addition, the relevant ministries should be notified and a notation made in
his performance dossier of his having committed this offense. The concubine

---

2. YDZ 18:15a, p. 685.
3. This was one of the regional offices under the main Censorate, with its seat at Beijing
Circuit, approximately 300 kilometers (186 miles) northeast of the Yuan capital of Dadu
(modern Beijing). This circuit was later called Daning, and was within Liaoyang Branch
Secretariat.
4. These law offices (*fasi* 法司) existed within the Censorate and the Six Ministries and were
charged with looking up laws and drafting decisions. They were associated with the use of the
Taihe code of the Jin, and after this was abrogated in 1271, they were gradually abolished.
See Miyazaki (1954) 1975, 163–166; Yao Dali 1986, 125–129.

whom he married, Li Xingge, should be granted a divorce, and the betrothal gifts should not be returned. Notify the other people who gave testimony that they do not incur punishment. We order that this be sent out to the subordinate offices and enforced according to the above.

18.28

Every Chinese dynasty confronted the problem of local officials allying with rich and powerful families within their jurisdictions against the interests of the common people and those of the central government. For this reason, Tang, Song, and Jin law all prohibited local officials from forming marriage alliances with families in the jurisdictions where they served.[5] But in this document, the Secretariat for State Affairs in 1270 declines to extend such a ban into Yuan law. It asks the Ministry of Revenue to consider a proposal from an unknown circuit to ban officials from forging marriage alliances with families living within the area where they served or from affiliating with rich and powerful locals who used their undue influence to oppress and bully the people. The Ministry concludes that marriages within jurisdictions should *not* be banned, since such a ban would leave officials with the difficult task of having to negotiate marriages across long distances only with families known to them back in their home districts. To counter the problem of influence, it reiterated that showing any kind of favoritism in the execution of one's duties was punishable by law. But the Ministry did recommend that officials be ordered to associate only with those of good character or relatives by marriage within their jurisdictions. The Secretariat for State Affairs shows reluctance to rule on either issue. It provisionally approves the Ministry's ruling allowing local marriages, but only "until a decision is issued to serve as a universal precedent." Moreover, it tables for another time any ruling on the matter of restricting a government official's ability to fraternize with local elites. Later in the Yuan dynasty the problem of officials building regional power bases through local alliances became severe, and we do find in the "Treatise on Punishments" of the Yuan dynastic history a provision to restrict such alliances.[6]

5. For the Tang statute, carried over into the Song, see SXT 14:222. The item from the Taihe code of the Jin is cited in *Qiujian wenji* 88:848. Ming and Qing law also prohibited these marriages; see Bodde and Morris 1967, 256–258 (case 59).

6. For these restrictions, see YS 102:2611; Ratchnevsky and Aubin 1972–1985, 1:56 (Art. 32). For references in the Yuan to the problems of local elites allying with and influencing local officials, see YDZ 57:23b–27a; Chen Gaohua et al. 2011, 3:1918–1924.

18.28 *Officials forming marriage alliances within their jurisdictions*[7]

In the seventh year of the *zhiyuan* period (1270), eleventh, intercalary, month, a document from the Secretariat for State Affairs states:

We recently received a report, as follows:

> Officials who are sent out to serve in the various circuits often associate with the rich and powerful in their jurisdictions and form marriage alliances with them. They are continuously paying respects to relatives by marriage and having contact with these families. As a result, these families can bully and oppress the poor and the weak. Why not issue a universal prohibition of such practices?

We sent this to the Ministry of Revenue, which after investigation and deliberation, concluded:

> When it comes to human moral relations, marriage is of the utmost importance. Officials who are sent out to serve are of all different backgrounds and circumstances. They serve at different distances from their home districts, both near and far, and they are of unequal financial circumstances, both rich and poor. If they could only associate with and form marriage alliances with people in their home districts or the neighboring areas, given that the families have to be well matched, the boy and girl have to be compatible, and that the go-betweens would then have to travel great distances to negotiate the marriage, it would be most inconvenient to complete a marriage. If the marriage is delayed for one or two terms of office, one's son or daughter will have passed marriageable age, and this would be extremely unbeneficial. If on account of a marriage alliance an official took advantage of the circumstances and showed favoritism, and this was truly the case, then his behavior would constitute a crime in itself. In addition, regarding the issue of officials currently serving who associate with the rich and powerful, and continuously pay respects to relatives by marriage and have contact with these families, we think it would be appropriate to prohibit all such associations, except with those who are relatives by marriage or are learned gentlemen who are filial and upright, honest and trustworthy. We humbly request that you consider this matter thoroughly.

We the Secretariat Office deliberated and conclude: we will separately deliberate and make a decision about the matter of prohibiting associations. As for the issue

7. YDZ 18:15a–b, pp. 685–686.

of officials forming marriage alliances within their jurisdictions, we provisionally approve the ruling of the Ministry of Revenue to be in effect until a decision is issued to serve as a universal precedent. We order you to give this ruling your careful consideration and enforce it accordingly.

18.29

As we just saw, in 1270 the Secretariat for State Affairs made marriages of officials within their jurisdictions legal, but in 1282, in this next case, the Regional Surveillance Office of Jiangnan Zhexi Region, seated at Hangzhou, under the Censorate branch of government, dismissed a county magistrate from office for marrying a woman under his jurisdiction who was in mourning for her first husband. The Pacification Office of Zhexi Region, also seated at Hangzhou, under the administrative branch of government headed by the Central Secretariat, disagreed.[8] It noted that the mourning period was not at the time fixed in law and ruled provisionally that the magistrate should divorce and pay a fine but could remain in office. It then appealed to the Branch Secretariat for a final ruling, which in turn sent the case to the Central Secretariat. The latter rejected any penalty for the magistrate. It ruled that he be allowed to marry the woman and be reinstated in his job, with no punishment incurred, noting that no law prohibited either marrying during the mourning period or marrying within one's jurisdiction. (The Central Secretariat's refusal here to annul a marriage during the mourning period after the abrogation of the Taihe code is consistent with their earlier ruling of 1275, in case 18.15.)

This case demonstrates the conflict that could arise between overlapping jurisdictions in the Yuan and different offices within the bureaucracy. Here, two regional offices of two different branches of government, both seated in the same city, disagreed over a legal decision. The Central Secretariat had the final word, trumping the Censorate bureaucracy. This text also makes an interesting reference to the woman becoming a "secondary wife" or "second wife" (ci qi 次妻), a term usually used in the context of Mongol marriage practices where a man could take more than one "wife." By contrast, in Chinese marriage law, only one woman in a marriage could be the legal "wife" (qi 妻), whereas other women were relegated to

---

8. These two offices both headed "regions" (dao), but they were part of different branches of administration, and the regions they headed were distinct from each other.

"concubine" (*qie* 妾) status. As seen in the *Yuan dianzhang*, the Yuan government wrestled with the contradictions between these two marriage regimes.[9]

18.29 *A local official marries a woman residing within his jurisdiction*[10]

In the nineteenth year of the *zhiyuan* period (1282), first month, a document from the Pacification Office of Zhexi Region[11] states:

We recently submitted a report about the matter in Hangzhou Circuit of Yuqian County Magistrate Liu Jiao, who married Zhao Yuanyiniang, a widow in mourning residing within his jurisdiction. We respectfully received in return a communiqué from the Branch Secretariat, which reads in part as follows:

We received your report, which reads:

Liu Jiao sought to marry Zhao Yuanyiniang, a widow in mourning, as his secondary wife. The Surveillance Office of this region[12] obtained his confession that he "should not have sought to marry a girl who had not yet completed her mourning," and they ruled that the marriage be annulled. Moreover, they dismissed Liu Jiao from office. It is the case that in the eighth year of *zhiyuan* (1271) we respectfully received an Imperial Edict, which reads in part:

The Taihe code is no longer to be in effect. Stop applying it![13]

We humbly respect the Imperial Edict. In addition, at this time the mourning period is not yet fixed. This humble office[14] deliberated and

9. See especially 18.65 and 18.66. In a decision dated 1276, six years before this case (found in case 18.66 below), the Central Secretariat declared that taking a "secondary wife" did not violate Khubilai's earlier provision against a man having two wives (case 18.2). The Central Secretariat is seen to be following that earlier ruling here. This category of "secondary wife" existed among the Jurchen Jin as well. See discussion of these statuses in Bossler 2013, 333–335.

10. YDZ 18:15b, p. 686.

11. This Pacification Office was located at this time at Hangzhou Circuit, modern Hangzhou.

12. This would be the Regional Surveillance Office of Jiangnan Zhexi Region, within the Censorate bureaucracy, which like the Pacification Office also had its seat at Hangzhou Circuit.

13. A record of this edict abolishing the Taihe code is found in the Yuan dynastic history, on the same day that Khubilai declared the dynastic title of "Yuan," day *ihai* of the eleventh month of 1271 (*zhiyuan* 8); YS 7:138. The text of the edict can also be found in a memorial of Wei Chu 魏初 (1226–1286), who gives the date of receiving it more precisely as the twelfth month of 1271, twenty-fifth day. See *Qingya ji* 4:27a–b (p. 757); *Yuandai zouyi jilu*, 188–189. The wording in Wei Chu's memorial is very slightly different, perhaps due to copyist error.

14. That is, the Pacification Office of Zhexi Region.

concludes: Liu Jiao is the magistrate of Yuqian County; he is a local official caring for the people. The offense he has committed is that he should
not have gotten engaged to Zhao Yuanyiniang, a woman residing in his
jurisdiction, to be his secondary wife. Later he learned that this woman
was still in mourning for her previous husband. Although the final marriage
did not take place and she had not yet entered his home, in the end he is
still at fault. We could apply the ruling of the Regional Surveillance Office to dismiss him from office and moreover annul his marriage to Zhao
Yuanyiniang, but we feel this would be too severe. Our decision is to annul
the marriage, according to the Regional Surveillance Office, but have Liu
Jiao reinstated in office and return to work. As for his crime of Doing What
Ought Not to be Done,[15] we rule provisionally that he be fined as redemption. We humbly request that you consider this matter thoroughly.

[We the Branch Secretariat sent a communiqué to the Central Secretariat,
and in reply they sent a communiqué, which reads:][16]

We the Metropolitan Secretariat deliberated and conclude: at this time
the mourning period is not yet fixed. We rule that this should be communicated to the Pacification Office of the said region: given that Zhao
Yuanyiniang accepted engagement gifts from Liu Jiao, and that the matter
has been investigated by the authorities and the testimony is clear, he is allowed to marry her according to the law. Moreover, we order that Liu Jiao
be reinstated in office and return to work. Have this enforced.

18.30

This case is the earliest of a series of government rulings, handed down in the
early years of the fourteenth century, that together severely restricted the legal
rights and autonomy of widows.[17] Here, the Ministry of Rites and the Central

15. Reading *ying* 應 for *yin* 因.

16. This sentence is missing in the text, which skips directly to the answer from the Central
Secretariat. Some argue that "Metropolitan Secretariat" (*dusheng* 都省) should read "Branch
Secretariat" (see Chen Gaohua et al. 2011, 2:640n2), but the ruling seems rather to be aimed
at the Branch Secretariat from the Central Secretariat. Moreover, this kind of decision where
definitive law was lacking would certainly have been passed up to the capital.

17. For these other rulings, see cases 18.47 (dated 1303), 18.26 (dated 1309), and 18.32 (dated
1311). The Yuan government also issued rewards for widow chastity. In 1304 it ordered local officials to help support meritorious chaste widows to prevent them from remarrying (TZTG
3:148). Also in 1304 it instituted a system of rewards for households with a verified "meritorious

Secretariat approve a proposal originating from a local arm of the Censorate, the Regional Investigation Office for the far south region of Haibei Guangdong, that prohibited widows of officials serving in that area from remarrying. The proposal claimed that officials from the north died in high numbers while serving in the malaria-plagued regions of Guangdong and Guangxi, and that their widows, both principal wives and concubines, could scoop up the family property and take it all into a remarriage together with any children, other dependents, and household servants. The ruling declares that widows and other household members, together with any family property, are to be sent back north by local authorities through the government transportation network and returned to the custody of the deceased official's relatives up north. Any remarriage contracted by the widow of an official in the south was to be annulled.

It is hard to know how well this was enforced, and we have no case records pertaining to the enforcement of this new law. At this time, 1299, widows still had the right in Yuan law to remarry on their own initiative in the absence of an eligible levir, and traditional Chinese law and custom granted them this right as well. This decision, nevertheless, represents a major shift in government attitudes toward the financial and legal autonomy of women.

18.30 *Regulation on wives and concubines of officials in Guangdong and Guangxi getting remarried*[18]

In the third year of the *dade* period (1299), eleventh month, the Branch Secretariat for Huguang and Other Places[19] received a communiqué from the Central Secretariat, as follows:

A report from the Censorate states:

We received a communiqué from the Branch Censorate, as follows:

A dispatch from the Regional Investigation Office for the Haibei Guangdong Region[20] reads:

---

chaste widow" (YDZ 33:13a–b). See case 18.32 note 33. For discussion of these cases and their significance in Chinese history, see Birge 1995, 128–143; Birge 2002, 253–272.

18. YDZ 18:15b–16a, pp. 686–687.

19. This appellation is close to the official name of this branch secretariat, which was the Branch Central Secretariat for Huguang and Other Places. As already encountered in case 18.23, it comprised the southern part of modern Hubei, Hunan, Guangxi, the western part of Guangdong (including Hainan Island), and most of Guizhou.

20. This was one of ten Regional Investigation Offices in the Jiangnan Branch Censorate. It had its seat at Guangzhou Circuit, modern Guangzhou City.

Li Tong and others filed a plaint, stating:

> My older brother Li Rong served as the Commissioner for the
> Paper Currency Exchange Bank of Huizhou Circuit.[21] He died
> because of illness, leaving behind his wife, A-He. During the
> mourning period she got remarried to Guo Keren, the Files Su-
> pervisor of the same circuit.

Leaving aside our investigation of this particular case, we humbly
observe that Guangdong is a malarial and pestilent area. Officials
who come from the north are separated from their families by ten
thousand *li*. They cannot adjust to the water and soil, and those who
die of disease are too many to count. The wives and concubines they
leave behind are unable to stay chaste but get remarried to other
men. They gather up all the property and people of the household
rightfully belonging to their first husband and take them away. Even
before the bones and flesh of the deceased official have grown cold,
the assets and people of his household already belong to someone
else. Furthermore, for the dependents young and old of officials who
pass away in Guangdong, there are already established regulations
for supplying transport ships for them to leave Guangdong.[22] We
suggest that you issue to the subordinate offices a strict prohibition:
From now on, when officials serving in Guangdong pass away, the
dependents young and old they leave behind must obey the local
authorities of the area who will send them back to their families in
accordance with the regulations. They may not on their own initiative remarry. If there are those who violate the law, and the matter
comes before the authorities, they are liable for prosecution and the
marriage will be annulled. If any of the household assets of the first

---

21. Huizhou Circuit was on the south China coast within the Jiangxi Branch Secretariat,
just across the border of Huguang Branch Secretariat. It was under the jurisdiction of the
Censorate's Haibei Guangdong Region (and the Central Secretariat's Guangdong Region). Its
seat was at today's Huizhou City, approximately 120 kilometers (100 miles) east of Guangzhou Circuit. Paper Currency Exchange Banks (formal name, Stabilization Exchange Banks)
were established in various circuits around the empire, both to exchange silver and gold for
bank notes and to replace worn notes (Farquhar 1990, 179–180, 415). For this system and its
many problems, see Chen Gaohua and Shi Weimin 2000, 436–446.

22. These regulations are found in YDZ 36:27b–28b. See Chen Gaohua, Zhang Fan, and
Liu Xiao 2008a, 288.

husband are missing or lost, the wife or concubine will be forced to make restitution. This prohibition will make it possible to stop lawsuits at their source. Moreover, it will correct human moral relations and improve one aspect of traditional customs.[23]

We [the Censorate] present this report for your thorough consideration.

Report received. We [the Central Secretariat] sent this to the Ministry of Rites, who investigated and made a decision, then sent back a report, as follows:

We examined this matter thoroughly. In the case of officials sent out to serve in Guangdong and Guangxi who pass away, we approve the decision of the Regional Investigation Office. The local officials of the area will take the dependents and assets of the household left behind and in accordance with the transport regulations send them back to their families. Their wives and concubines may not remarry. Violators will be prosecuted according to the above, and the marriage will be annulled. This would be appropriate.

We the Metropolitan Secretariat approve the decision. Have it enforced.

18.31

The following document from 1304 once again addresses the issue of officials marrying women within their own jurisdictions, seen in cases 18.28 and 18.29. This time, the Censorate forwarded to the Central Secretariat a proposal to ban such marriages sent up from their Regional Investigation Office in Shandong. The Office argued that local officials were taking advantage of their position to coerce girls and women into marriage or concubinage without paying betrothal gifts or setting up legal marriage contracts. The Central Secretariat sent the matter to the Ministry of Punishments and the Ministry of Rites, which together ruled to continue allowing such marriages, but only for those officials whose principal wives had died or who had no male heir, and who followed proper procedures through negotiations by a government-registered go-between. Once again they cited the inability of officials to return home to marry, to justify this break from previous Chinese law.

---

23. This is the end of both the dispatch from the Regional Investigation Office and the communiqué from the Branch Censorate to the main Censorate.

18.31 *Ranked officials seek to marry wives and concubines within their jurisdictions*[24]

In the eighth year of the *dade* period (1304), third month, twenty-seventh day, the Jiangxi Branch Secretariat received a communiqué from the Central Secretariat, as follows:

A report from the main Censorate states:

> A dispatch from the Shandong Regional Investigation Office[25] reads:
>
>> We have thoroughly investigated and conclude that, ranked officials when they take up office do not distinguish between virtuous traditions and contemptible customs.[26] Rather, they wantonly bully and deceive the people in their jurisdictions. They request to get engaged to girls and women but then write fake marriage contracts and fail to deliver the betrothal gifts. In this way, acquiring a wife truly harms public morals and damages traditional customs. It would be better to prohibit such action and from now on not allow officials to marry in the districts where they serve.
>
> This office [the main Censorate] considered the matter carefully. When officials are appointed to office, their main purpose is to nurture the common people and clearly instill in them civilized teachings. But nowadays, many ranked officials do not accept this task. After they take up office, they follow their lustful passions and abandon their official duties. We think it would be appropriate to decide on a regulation prohibiting this behavior. We present this report for your thorough consideration.

We [the Central Secretariat] sent this to the Ministry of Punishments, which deliberated together with the Ministry of Rites and concluded:

> We could issue a general prohibition not to permit officials to marry in the districts where they serve with the exception of those officials assigned to office who have no principal wife or who lack a male heir and are seeking to obtain a concubine. We note however that, officials who are transferred around in office are not able on a regular basis to return to their home villages, thus we fear such a prohibition would be unbeneficial. In light of this we have carefully ex-

---

24. YDZ 18:16a–b, pp. 687–688. Most of this case is also recorded in TZTG 4:172–173 (Art. 84).

25. This was one of eight Regional Investigation Offices under the jurisdiction of the main Censorate in Dadu.

26. Reading *bian* (采) for *cai* (采).

amined the matter and recommend the following: From now on, ranked officials whose wives are indeed deceased or who have no male heir and who wish to take a wife or a concubine are permitted to have a government-registered go-between come and negotiate a marriage and establish a clear marriage contract.[27] They may thus marry an appropriate woman [in their district] without doing harm.[28] Violators will be liable for prosecution and their marriages will be annulled. Any betrothal gifts paid will be confiscated. We think this would be appropriate.

We the Metropolitan Secretariat approve the decision. Have it enforced.

18.32

The following document records yet another one of the legal inducements for widows to remain chaste, which the government instituted in the early fourteenth century, this one promulgated in 1311. Based on a proposal from a prominent official serving in Shangdu,[29] the northern capital of the Yuan, the Ministry of Rites instituted a regulation to prohibit widows who received titles of enfeoffment by virtue of their husband's position from remarrying after this husband died. The regulation was seconded by the Central Secretariat. The official argued that women with such titles of nobility had to be held to a higher standard than the wives of mere commoners and could not be allowed to remarry when widowed, as was all too commonplace among the populace. In 1317 the government further decreed that women who had remarried were not eligible for titles of enfeoffment.[30]

18.32 *Wives invested with titles of enfeoffment are not permitted to remarry when their husbands die*[31]

In the fourth year of the *zhida* period (1311), eighth month, the Jiangxi Branch Secretariat received a communiqué from the Central Secretariat, as follows:

A report from the Ministry of Rites states:

We respectfully received your Secretarial communication, as follows:

27. The registration of these go-betweens is addressed in case 18.3, Item 3, in a regulation of 1271.

28. The word "marry" (*qu* 娶) is missing from the text but can be found in the TZTG version (4:172 [Art. 84]).

29. Shangdu was located in modern eastern Inner Mongolia. It was described by Marco Polo and made famous in later Western literature by Samuel Taylor Coleridge as Xanadu, in his poem "Kubla Khan." See discussion in Rossabi 1988, 31–34.

30. YDZ 11:24a–b.

31. YDZ 18:16b, p. 688.

A report from Protector Wang of Shangdu, Grand Master for Palace Counsel,[32] reads:

> It is my humble understanding that men maintain the ethical standard of respecting marriage, while women preserve the cultural tradition of not remarrying. When they are alive, they share the same room. When they die, they share the same grave. This is a universal ethic of ancient and modern times. Wives who preserve their chastity after their husbands have died are granted official recognition with door insignia by the local authorities, and the Imperial Court issues a Decree of Imperial Favor [granting exemption from labor service].[33] Righteous husbands and virtuous wives will without fail receive official rewards and recognition. This is the genesis of improving civilized traditions. In recent years, those widows who preserve their chastity after their husbands have died are extremely few. Those who remarry appear over and over, such that even before their tears of mourning have dried, they are again enjoying the splendor of dragon-phoenix candles at their wedding banquet. Nothing harms public morals and damages traditional customs more than this. It is now the case that the Secretariat for State Affairs sent a Memorial to the throne and received approval to confer honorary titles on the parents and wives of ranked

32. *Zhongyi* (中議), short for *Zhongyi dafu* (中議大夫), reading *zhong* (中) for *zhong* (忠), as later in the text. This is another prestige title (*sanguan*), rank 4A. This rank matches the post of Assistant Protector (*fu liushou* 副留守), not Protector (*liushou* 留守), and Wang can be identified as Wang Gui 王桂, who was the Assistant Protector of Shangdu beginning in 1310 (YS 26:579). See Chen Gaohua, Zhang Fan, and Liu Xiao 2008a, 291. On this office and prestige title, see Farquhar 1990, 25. For the translation of the prestige title I am following Hucker 1985, 191 (#1569).

33. The term "Decree of Imperial Favor" (*deyin* 德音) is an archaism from previous dynasties referring to a decree granting tax or labor relief. The two terms capitalized here ("Imperial Court" and "Decree of Imperial Favor") each start a new line in the *Yuan dianzhang* and are elevated one and two spaces above the top of the text respectively to exalt the emperor. The order to grant door insignia and exemption from labor duty to chaste widows was issued in 1304, eighth month, and is found in YDZ 33:13a–b. For discussion and analysis see Birge 1995, 136; Birge 2002, 264–265. This order also placed limits on who qualified as a "chaste widow" (she had to be widowed before the age of 30 and stay chaste until after age 50), and specified procedures for local officials to verify their eligibility for rewards. By this time in the Yuan, elite families in large numbers were petitioning to receive labor exemptions for meritorious behavior such as filial piety and widow chastity, so this order both codified government support of widow chastity (the first such law in Chinese history) and served to stem the flood of dubious claims. On the abuse of these rewards, see Bossler 2013, 370–373.

officials.[34] They have now promulgated the policy across the realm. These wives on account of their husbands and sons receive county and prefectural titles of enfeoffment. They are not the same as wives of ordinary commoners. After they have received such an Imperial investiture, if their husband or son should unfortunately pass away, they should not be permitted to marry again. This should be established as a fixed rule. If they do not obey this rule, then the Imperial Edict of investiture should be retracted, and they should be liable for prosecution and the marriage annulled. In the event that you approve my proposal, it will not only help the Imperial Court a little to promote the honorable intentions of the enfeoffment system, but will also improve public morals and traditional customs and reinforce one aspect of human moral relations. I present this report for your thorough consideration.

We [the Central Secretariat] are sending this to you, the Ministry of Rites, to examine and make a decision and return a report to us, the Secretariat.

Secretarial communication respectfully received. This Ministry examined the matter thoroughly, and we think it would be appropriate to approve the proposal of Grand Master for Palace Counsel Wang. We present this report for your thorough consideration.

We the Metropolitan Secretariat approve the report. We send you this communiqué for your careful consideration and request that you enforce it accordingly.

18.33

This case of 1312 concerns a marriage between a nephew and his maternal uncle's wife. Marriage of a man to the wife of a relative within certain degrees of mourning was unlawful in all Chinese dynasties and harshly punished. The Tang, Song, and Ming codes punished marriage to the wife of one's uncle, as in this case, by one year of penal servitude.[35] Yuan law was more complicated. After 1271, when Khubilai made the levirate legal for all peoples, a man could inherit his uncle's widow in a levirate union. But in 1304 the Central Secretariat, following a ruling by the Ministry of Rites, outlawed all such aunt-nephew

---

34. This policy was instituted in 1309. A record of it is found in YDZ 11:21a. Officials of the fifth rank and above could receive honorary titles for their parents and principal wives.

35. TLSY 14:264 (Art. 183); Johnson 1997, 162–163; SXT 14:220. The Ming added a beating of 60 strokes (Da Ming lü 6:677–678; Jiang 2005, 85–86 [Art. 115]).

marriages for Chinese.[36] Here, an uncle divorces his wife because she has borne no children, then marries her off to his nephew, a low-level official. Both the local Censorate and the Ministry of Punishments condemn the practice as immoral and declare it illegal.

Since the case involves a ranked official, it is included in this section. The nephew loses his job and the marriage is annulled, but because of an amnesty, the central government imposes no other punishment. This amounts to very lenient treatment compared to the codes of other dynasties. The document contains some corruptions of place names and a missing phrase, but they are all easily sorted out from context.

18.33 A nephew marries his uncle's wife[37]

In the first year of the *huangqing* period (1312), fourth month, the Branch Censorate[38] received a communiqué from the main Censorate, as follows:
We received your communiqué, which reads:
A report from our Investigating Censor reads:
Mr. Gao Fu of Jiangning County[39] filed a plaint, stating:
My older brother Gao San took his wife A-Cheng and his nephew Dong Zhen and went around to places in Jiangning[40] looking for work. On the nineteenth day of the first month of the ninth year of *dade* (1305), I went to the market town of Jiangning Garrison in Jiangning County[41] and found my sister-in-law A-Cheng and my nephew Dong Zhen. He told me that my brother Gao San had divorced A-Cheng because she had no children and had married her to him.
We examined this matter thoroughly. A-Cheng is the wife of Dong Zhen's mother's younger brother, his maternal uncle Gao San. Even if Gao San divorced his wife because she had no children, it is not lawful for his nephew to marry her. The offense has been exempted from punishment

---

36. TZTG 3:152 (Art. 58); Birge 2002, 255–256.

37. YDZ 18:16b–17a, pp. 688–689.

38. From the text this can be identified as the Jiangnan Branch Censorate.

39. Jiangning County was the seat of administration of Jiankang Circuit, at modern Nanjing.

40. Reading Jiangning (江寧) for Pingjiang (平江). We can surmise from the context that this should read Jiangning, where this case takes place.

41. Reading Jiangning (江寧) for Pingning (平寧). There is no such county as Pingning in the Yuan, whereas Jiangning Garrison (*zhen* 鎮) was a market town located in Jiangning County during the Yuan.

due to an amnesty; nevertheless, according to legal principles the situation should be corrected and the marriage annulled. Moreover, the offense that Police Officer[42] Dong Zhen has committed truly damages civilized traditions. We cannot let him continue in office. We rule that his name should be removed from the service rolls.

Because this is a precedent-setting case, [we send you this communiqué and request that you consider it thoroughly].[43]

Communiqué received. We submitted a report and respectfully received a superior communication from the Central Secretariat, as follows:

We sent this to the Ministry of Punishments, which deliberated and concluded:

Police Officer Dong Zhen of Jiangning Garrison in Jiankang Circuit unlawfully got married to A-Cheng, the wife of his mother's younger brother Gao San. Although the marriage has already been annulled, this is an offense that corrupts public morals and damages traditional customs; moreover, this person is a police officer on the rolls of official service. Thus we find it appropriate to approve the ruling of the investigating censor that, his name should be removed from the service rolls and a notation made in his official performance dossier. We present this report for your thorough consideration.

We the Metropolitan Secretariat order you [the Censorate] to enforce this as above.

Section 4: Marriages of Military Personnel

18.34

This case concerns the problem of maintaining on the government registers hereditary soldier households in north China who owed military service to the state. A son in one of these households who was liable for military service could marry uxorilocally into a civilian household and thus escape conscription. This order, dated 1273, from the Bureau of Military Affairs,[44] prohibits such mar-

42. Police officers headed Police Offices, which were set up in administrative units below the county level to maintain security and extend the authority of the magistrate to outlying areas. A police officer held the lowest grade of ranked officials, grade 9B. See Farquhar 1990, 421; YS 91:2318.

43. This bracketed phrase (missing in the text) would normally end such a communiqué.

44. Shumiyuan 樞密院. This office of the central government, rank 1B, was established in 1263 to administer military units and oversee matters of military personnel throughout the empire. Like the Censorate (rank 1B) it was technically subordinate to the Central Secretariat,

riages for men who are in line to become the household head in a military household and thus liable for soldier duty. In addition, the first part of the order reiterates for military personnel the ruling seen in case 18.3 that parties to an uxorilocal marriage must establish a clear contract delineating whether residence in the bride's home is permanent or temporary and for how long it is to be. This document reveals that the problem of frequent lawsuits over these marriages afflicted the military as well as the civilian population.

18.34 *The head of a military household may [not] marry out as an uxorilocal son-in-law*[45]

In the tenth year of the *zhiyuan* period (1273), sixth month, a document from the Bureau of Military Affairs states:

We have investigated the issue of military households inviting in uxorilocal sons-in-law. Imperial Regulations have already been issued for distribution to each circuit, and we have respectfully sent these out accordingly.[46] Now, it is the case that, dispatches from every locale report that when military households invite in permanent and temporary uxorilocal sons-in-law, there are many disagreements and lawsuits, and the matter often ends up in court. Of these marriages, many have no marriage contract. Even if the family originally engaged a go-between or guarantor, these are sometimes dishonest or may have already passed away, thus making it very hard to resolve the case. This is extremely unbeneficial. We the Military Office[47] deliberated and conclude: From now on, if a military household invites in an uxorilocal son-in-law, the sponsors of the marriage and relatives

---

rank 1A, but it communicated directly with the emperor. These three offices together made up the top echelon of Yuan central administration. The Bureau of Military Affairs handled lawsuits involving military personnel, but in cases involving both civilians and military, they were to confer with civil judicial organs. See Farquhar 1990, 247ff.

45. YDZ 18:18a, p. 691. The *Yuan dianzhang* title omits "not" (*bu* 不), but an edited version of this case appears in the *Tongzhi tiaoge*, and from this and the content of the document itself, the title can be corrected to include "not." Also following the *Tongzhi tiaoge*, I read *ming* 名 for *min* 民. See TZTG 4:177 (Art. 90).

46. These imperial regulations could be the same ones cited in case 18.3. Case 18.3 also cites an order from the Central Secretariat of 1266 that uxorilocal husbands must pay taxes and provide corvée or military service according to the household into which they marry.

47. *Shufu* 樞府. The Bureau of Military Affairs uses this informal name to refer to itself. It is similar to *shengfu*, used by the Central Secretariat and branch secretariats to refer to themselves.

from both households must establish a written marriage contract.[48] It must include the words "permanent" or "temporary," and the sponsor of the marriage, the go-between, and others must all sign it. In this way, matters will be clear and there will be no mistakes. In addition, in both regular and auxiliary military households,[49] he who will succeed to the position of head of household and take over the military service may [not] become a permanent or temporary uxorilocal son-in-law in someone else's family.[50] We order that you enforce this as above.

18.35

This document, dated 1285, discusses finding wives for southern Chinese soldiers who were incorporated into the Yuan military from the conquered Song armies. These soldiers were put into special units called "Newly Attached Armies" and were not part of the hereditary soldier household system of the north. The record describes a perceived problem that these soldiers, who were mostly unmarried when they first entered the Song army, had not been able to find wives and might thus desert. It also reveals how Chinese women captured in war could become virtual sex slaves, distributed as "wives" to men in the military, as happened in steppe custom. In this document, the Bureau of Military Affairs approves a proposal from one of its branch bureaus in the south that addressed the problem by restricting the remarriage of army widows. Those who were war captives and thus of servile status were reassigned as wives to other soldiers, that is, forced into remarriages by military officers. Those who had married through proper channels with a go-between and exchange of betrothal gifts were forbidden to remarry outside of their late husband's army unit, but after waiting a year could contract a remarriage with an appropriate soldier in the unit. The Bureau of Military Affairs also agreed to support widows of soldiers until they could arrange to get remarried to other soldiers in the unit, thus increasing the supply of brides for soldiers to marry. Such a policy is reminiscent of the Mongol custom of the levirate, legalized

48. Reading *hu* (戶) for *min* (民).

49. The obligations of a military household were usually shared between several households (and sometimes more). The one who supplied the actual soldier was called a "regular military household" (*zheng junhu* 正軍戶); the others, which provided weapons, horses, and supplies, were called "auxiliary military households" (*tie junhu* 貼軍戶). See YS 98:2508; Hsiao 1978b, 18–19, 73.

50. As in the title, following the TZTG this sentence is corrected to include "not," and I read *ming* 名 for *min* 民. See TZTG 4:177 (Art. 90).

for all peoples under Yuan law beginning in 1271, which forced widows to remarry within a kinship group. There is no reference to widow chastity in this case,
however, which by this time had emerged as a way for women to escape levirate
unions among the civilian population (see Section 8, "Levirate Marriage Rejected," in Chapter 7 of this volume). Rather, the Bureau assumes that widows
will remarry. This document illustrates the concern of the Yuan government for
maintaining fixed status groups and keeping marriages within them, and their
willingness to curtail aspects of women's personal autonomy upheld previously in
Chinese law. Note that case 18.37 shows that the policy was discontinued in 1296
and general regulations on the levirate were applied to military personnel.

18.35 *Pairing off wives of Newly Attached Army troops*[51]

In the twenty-second year of the *zhiyuan* period (1285) the Branch Secretariat
for Huguang and Other Places received a communiqué from the Bureau of Mil-
itary Affairs, as follows:
We received a communiqué from the Branch Bureau of Jinghu and Other
Places,[52] stating:
[We received a report, which reads:][53]

> We deliberated and conclude: as for the widowed single women who are
> left behind by deceased soldiers in the Newly Attached Armies, some were
> taken as war captives by various army units, and others were married with
> a go-between and the payment of betrothal gifts. If we allow them to leave
> the military registers and remarry on their own volition, then many sol-
> diers in the Newly Attached Armies of Jiangnan who are single will be
> unable to find someone with whom to join in marriage, and they will
> desert. At present we have deliberated and conclude that, wives who were
> war captives should be married off to single unmarried soldiers by the of-
> ficials in charge of their military units. In addition, those who were mar-

---

51. YDZ 18:18a, p. 691.

52. This was one of several branch bureaus of military affairs that existed in the early part of
the Yuan dynasty. This one was set up in the first month of 1284 at Ezhou (modern Wuhan City,
Hubei) and dissolved in 1286 when it was absorbed into the Huguang Branch Secretariat. The
others were similarly incorporated into the branch secretariats. See YS 13:264; Farquhar 1990,
270–271.

53. We can infer this line or something like it, since what follows is clearly in response to a
report sent from an office subordinate to the Branch Bureau of Military Affairs. The corruptions
of the text make it difficult to discern the exact flow of documents here, but the ruling is clear.

ried with a go-between and the payment of betrothal gifts should wait one year, then be allowed to negotiate a proper marriage with the exchange of betrothal gifts only to soldiers within their military units who are suitable matches for them. While they are waiting to get married, each month local officials should give them grain and salt rations, as determined by the regulations, to provide them succor. This would seem to be most beneficial.

Report received. We transmitted this to the Bureau of Military Affairs and received their communiqué in reply, as follows:

Carefully investigate this further, and if there are no complications, then enforce it accordingly.

See section on "Military Service" for a related item.[54]

18.36

In case 18.13 we saw how the wife of a soldier off on campaign got married to a new husband, who lived with her uxorilocally. In this document, the government addresses the problem of a woman getting married off to a new husband when a soldier did not return from campaign. The document, dated 1289, makes explicit reference to the campaigns against the state of Annam, in modern Vietnam, which the Yuan mounted in 1284 and 1287. The Yuan were defeated in both campaigns, and many soldiers died or went missing in action.

The marriage of a daughter could generate revenue from betrothal gifts, and her natal parents had considerable incentive to arrange a remarriage if the first marriage did not work out. (See cases 18.10 and 18.11 for such scenarios involving uxorilocal marriages.) The wife's parents-in-law might also benefit from a remarriage under some conditions—for instance, if the natal parents had died and the in-laws could keep the betrothal gifts. The wording of this case leaves the ruling open to apply to both natal parents and in-laws, although in most circumstances the natal parents would be arranging such a remarriage, and Yuan law at this time gave them the right to keep the betrothal gifts. (Case 18.26, dated 1309, records a new ruling allowing the parents-in-law to keep the betrothal payments.)

The ruling in this case shows the Ministry of Rites anxious to preserve marriages for soldiers and maintain the traditional Confucian ideal of permanent marriage,

54. This line is added by the editors of the *Yuan dianzhang* at the end of this document. It evidently refers to a case titled "Military wives without husbands should be matched to soldiers without wives," which records the same policy decision by the Bureau of Military Affairs, though in largely different wording. See YDZ 34:4b; Chen et al. 2011, 2:1162–1163.

against local customs. In this regard it also shows the government's willingness to limit a woman's ability to remarry. In Song law, a woman could divorce and remarry on her own volition if her husband left and did not return for three years.[55]

18.36 *Wives of soldiers on campaign may not be remarried off*[56]

In the twenty-sixth year of the *zhiyuan* period (1289),[57] fourth month, the Ministry of Rites of the Secretariat for State Affairs respectfully received a superior communication from the Secretariat for State Affairs, as follows:

A communiqué from the Huguang Branch Secretariat reads:

A report from the Guangnan Pacification Office[58] states:

Of the soldiers who went off on the southern campaigns into Annam,[59] many got cut off from their units and went missing in battle. Each family sees that the soldier has not come back for a long time, and the parents marry off his wife to someone else, so that she no longer lives in his home. This dangerously imperils human moral relations.

We send you this communiqué and request that you adjudicate the matter.

We sent this to the Ministry of Rites, which deliberated and concluded:

When a soldier goes out on campaign and his family does not know whether he is alive or dead, the parents may not on their own initiative marry off his wife who is left behind. A communiqué should be sent to the Branch Secretariat to correct this. Moreover, we think it appropriate that the sponsor of the marriage and others involved be liable for prosecution.

We the Metropolitan Secretariat approve the report. We order all subordinate offices to distribute this widely and enforce the prohibition.

18.37

This case revisits the issue of restrictions on remarriage of the widows of soldiers, as seen in case 18.35. In that case, dated 1285, the Bureau of Military

---

55. See QMJ 9:353; Birge 2002, 132.
56. YDZ 18:18b, p. 692.
57. The table of contents of the *Yuan dianzhang* gives the date of this case as 1291.
58. This was the Pacification Office of the Guangnanxi Region, with its seat at the modern city of Guilin, Guangxi Province.
59. The text reads Jiaozhi 交趾, the old Chinese name for the area, which in earlier times was controlled on and off by Chinese dynasties. During the Yuan it was the independent country of Annam 安南, in what is now Vietnam.

Affairs ruled that military widows in Huguang could only remarry within their husband's military unit, and must stay on the military registers. In this ruling, eleven years later, in 1296, the Ministry of Rites reverses the earlier ruling and allows a military widow to marry a civilian. The Ministry follows a provisional verdict by the Jiangxi Branch Secretariat citing an earlier ruling affecting the Central Province that stated that, if there was an eligible levir in the widow's household she had to marry him, but if there was not, she could remarry on her own volition and leave the military registers. (The case of a military daughter, which instigated the decision, is not clearly addressed in the final ruling, but one can infer that she could also marry a civilian freely.)

The flow of documents in this case is interesting. By this time, the branch bureaus of military affairs (*xingshumiyuan*) had been absorbed by the branch secretariats; accordingly, the Longxing Myriarchy, within the military hierarchy, sends its dispatch to the area's Branch Secretariat, which makes a provisional ruling, then sends the case to the central Bureau of Military Affairs in Dadu. But the Bureau of Military Affairs simply passes the case along to the Central Secretariat, which requests the Ministry of Rites to review it, then passes it back to the Bureau of Military Affairs. The Bureau finally sends the approval back out to the Branch Secretariat (see Chart 4). The insertion of the Bureau of Military Affairs (which did not make an independent ruling, according to what is recorded here) between the Branch Secretariat and Central Secretariat was presumably done because the case involved military personnel.

18.37 *Regulation governing the marriage of a deceased soldier's wife and daughters*[60]

In the second year of the *yuanzhen* period (1296), the Branch Central Secretariat for Jiangxi and Other Places received a communiqué from the Bureau of Military Affairs, as follows:[61]

---

60. YDZ 18:18b, p. 692. The final decision of this case is recorded in the TZTG 4:176 (Art. 87) in edited form (as usual for this text). This shortened version leaves out all mention of the Jiangxi Branch Secretariat, which in fact formulated the ruling that gets approved, and it leaves out the record of the original case from Longxing, among other things.

61. The TZTG gives the date of the Central Secretariat's decision as twelfth month of the first year of the *yuanzhen* period (1295); TZTG 4:176 (Art. 87). It is possible that the Branch Secretariat did not receive the ruling, passed along by the Bureau of Military Affairs, until a month later in 1296.

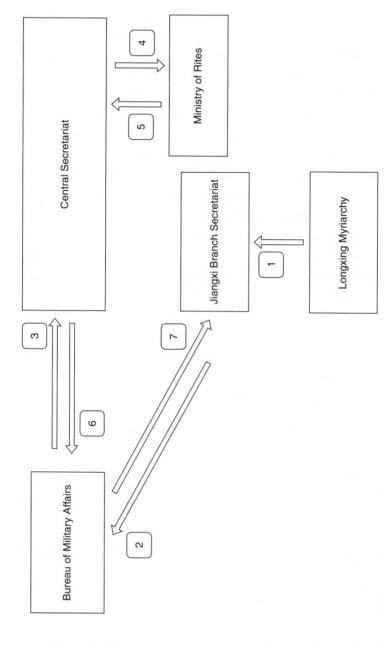

Chart 4. Case 18.37, document flow.

We received a notification from the Central Secretariat, which reads:

We received your report, which states:

A communiqué from the Jiangxi Branch Secretariat reads in part:

A dispatch from Longxing Myriarchy[62] states:

A-Wang, the wife of Cui Fu, a soldier in the Newly Attached Armies, took her daughter Meigu and married her to Director Zhang of a civilian household.[63] We humbly note that daughters in the household of a soldier are fixed on the registers as military dependents.

This Branch Secretariat examined the matter thoroughly. When a soldier himself dies, a nephew or son in the household by law must take over his military service. As for his widow whom he leaves behind, if there is someone who is eligible to inherit her in a levirate union, he should marry her according to the regulations. If there is no such levir,[64] then we rule that it would be appropriate to let her do as she likes, in accordance with the regulations issued for the Inner Domain[65] regarding the marriage of wives and daughters of soldiers.

We [the Bureau of Military Affairs] present this report for your thorough consideration.

Report received. We sent this to the Ministry of Rites, which investigated the matter and issued a ruling, as follows:

We recommend following the ruling of the Jiangxi Branch Secretariat. This would be appropriate.

---

62. A myriarchy (*wanhufu* 萬戶府, Mongolian *tümen*) was a military unit at the level of a circuit, within the decimal organization of the army originally set up by Chinggis Khan. It technically contained 10,000 households, but could be as few as 3,000 (Farquhar 1990, 22, 416–417; Allsen 1994, 403). Longxing Myriarchy was seated at modern Nanchang in Jiangxi Province, just south of the Yangzi River and Lake Poyang.

63. "Director" (*tiling* 提領) was a term for a low-level official in the local government who could hold one of several positions, including director of a smaller station in the courier or postal system (Farquhar 1990, 219–220).

64. Reading *wu* 無 for *you* 有, according to the context and as in the TZTG version (4:176 [Art. 87]).

65. *Fuli* 腹裏, literally "within the belly," was another term for the Central Province, sometimes also used for north China in general. This earlier ruling may have been issued before the conquest of the south, and thus did not automatically apply to south China.

Section 5: Divorce

18.38

Confucian moralists frowned on divorce, but it was legal in all periods of Chinese history. Only the husband could initiate a divorce, and he could unilaterally expel his wife, but traditional Chinese law offered her some protection from arbitrary expulsion by requiring the husband to draw up a letter of divorce, which had to be approved by the local authorities. A divorced woman generally returned to her natal family who could in turn accept betrothal gifts and arrange a remarriage for her.

The following document addresses the problem of illegal divorces, where men married off their wives directly to someone else in exchange for "betrothal gifts," in essence wife-selling. In a proposal dated 1271, the Censorate reiterates provisions found in Song law for a legal divorce. These required the husband to draw up a letter of divorce, which had to be registered with the local authorities. The wife received a copy, and this document gave her the legal right to return to her natal family and remarry. Without it, a woman could be accused of abandoning her husband, which was harshly punished in Chinese law. The husband did not receive remuneration, though in Song practice he could seek the return of his betrothal gifts from the wife's parents.[66] The Secretariat for State Affairs sends the Censorate's proposal to the Ministry of Revenue, which in turn approves it after getting from the Law Office detailed citations of divorce law from the Taihe code of the Jin. These spell out the "Seven Conditions for Divorce" (qi chu 七出), one of which had to be met for a divorce to be legal, and the "Three Circumstances Prohibiting Divorce" (san bu chu 三不去), any one of which could putatively prevent a divorce.[67] The ruling in this case also explicitly allows divorced women to return to their natal family and remarry.

This case is included in the Tongzhi tiaoge, dated 1271 fourth month, and in a rare instance this text reveals some details not found in the Yuan dianzhang. We learn, for instance, that the Censorate's proposal originated from the Re-

66. See discussion of divorce law in the Song in McKnight 1996; Ebrey 1993; Birge 2002, 130–134.

67. These principles, also cited by the Censorate, date back to the early imperial era in China and are found in the law codes of successive Chinese dynasties (Ch'ü 1965, 118–123, especially n155). In evidence from the Song, these conditions were almost never cited in actual divorce adjudication. It is also not clear whether the letter of divorce had to state one explicitly (see Birge 2002, 131–132; McKnight 1996).

gional Surveillance Office of the Shanxi Sichuan Region, regarding the prefecture of Jingzhao, the modern city of Xi'an in Shanxi Province.[68] Case 18.40 makes reference to this ruling as a precedent, and the prohibition on buying and selling divorces is included in the "Treatise on Punishments" in the Yuan dynastic history.[69]

18.38 *Regulations on annulling marriages and buying divorces*[70]

In the eighth year of the *zhiyuan* period (1271),[71] fifth month, the Ministry of Revenue of the Secretariat for State Affairs respectfully received a superior communication from the Secretariat for State Affairs, as follows:

A report from the main Censorate states:

> We understand that there are those husbands and wives who are mutually incompatible, and consequently there have arisen cases of buying and selling divorces. If we do not outlaw this, it will damage human moral relations and corrupt traditional customs. At present we have investigated the Old Regulations[72] and found therein that, for all those who expel a wife, there are seven conditions for divorce but also three circumstances under which a divorce may not be obtained. In light of this we have carefully examined the matter and recommend the following: if a husband wants to expel his wife or concubine, he must write a clear and concise letter of divorce, then go to the authorities to register it and have it certified.[73] Subsequently his wife may return to her natal family and remarry according to the law. This should rectify the moral way of husband and wife. This is a precedent-setting case; we humbly request that you consider the matter.

---

68. TZTG 4:174–176 (Art. 86).

69. YS 103:2644.

70. YDZ 18:19a, p. 693. *Maixiu* 買休. This term, encountered in cases 18.10 and 18.20, refers to a divorce in exchange for payment. The first husband is said to be "selling the divorce" (*maixiu* 賣休), and the new husband "buying the divorce," in essence wife-selling or wife-buying. On this practice in later dynasties, see Sommer 2000, 57–64, and Sommer 2015, Part Two.

71. The table of contents of the *Yuan dianzhang* has the date of this case as 1291.

72. This refers here to the Taihe code of the Jin.

73. Similar requirements for a formal divorce document and approval of the authorities existed in Song law. See QMJ 9:352; 10:380–381; Birge 2002, 130–132. A woman could not remarry without it. See TZTG 4:173 (Art. 85) for the opposite situation in 1303, where a husband tried to get his wife back after divorcing her. The Ministry of Rites ruled that in the future the finger-notch print he made on the letter of divorce was not sufficient for a legal document, but it allowed the wife to remain in the second marriage that her parents had already arranged for her.

Report received. We [the Secretariat for State Affairs] sent this to the said Ministry, which analyzed the matter and reported as follows:

> We sent this to the Law Office, which investigated and found that the Old Regulations state:[74] "When one divorces a wife, one of the Seven Conditions must be met. These are: (1) having no children; (2) licentiousness; (3) not serving one's parents-in-law; (4) talking too much; (5) committing theft; (6) jealousy; and (7) having an incurable illness. Although there are these conditions for divorce, there are the Three Circumstances under which one may not divorce. These are: (1) when the wife has mourned her parents-in-law; (2) if the family was poor when she married but later became rich; (3) she was received from her family but now has no family to go back to. If one of these applies, one may not obtain a divorce. If the wife has committed adultery, this law does not apply." Another item states: "If one commits an offense that constitutes a Violation of Duty, then the marriage must be annulled.[75] Violators are punished by a beating of 100 strokes.[76] If the husband and wife are mutually incompatible and separate amicably, then the punishment does not apply." We recommend that it would be highly appropriate to follow the ruling of the Censorate.

We the Secretariat Office approve the decision. Have it enforced.

18.39

This interesting case from the early Yuan shows the relatively lenient treatment of a wife's adultery by Yuan courts. A woman who is engaged to be married commits adultery with another man. The local arm of the Censorate, the Re-

---

74. The following rules governing divorce are also found in the Tang and Song codes. The only difference is that the conditions that invalidate the Three Circumstances under which one may not divorce include both adultery and having an incurable disease in the earlier codes but only adultery here in the Jin code. The language framing the rules is also slightly different in the Jin code quoted here. See TLSY 14:267–268 (Art. 189, 190); SXT 14:223–224.

75. "Violation of duty" (*yijue* 義絕) was a legal term referring to a particular class of crimes that mandated divorce. These mostly consisted of violence by a wife or husband against members of the other's family. They are defined in the Tang and Song codes, which assign the much harsher punishment of one year of penal servitude for violating this law (TLSY 14:267 [Art. 189]; SXT 14:224). Nevertheless, the beating of 100 strokes prescribed here is the same as that meted out by a judge in the Southern Song for selling a wife into another marriage. See QMJ 9:352–353; McKnight and Liu 1999, 343–344.

76. Note that beatings in the Yuan always ended in the number 7 (47, 107, etc.). This number of 100 reflects the Jin system of punishments, and interestingly, the figure is omitted from the TZTG version of the case.

gional Surveillance Office, rules that the woman's family must return the betrothal gifts and the bride must marry without them. On appeal, the Ministry of Punishments issues a general ruling that again imposes only a monetary punishment, and a lighter one than the lower court. It declares that in such cases the groom's family may call off the marriage and get back all the betrothal gifts, or go ahead with the marriage in exchange for one half of the original betrothal payments. (Recall that normally, once the betrothal gifts are paid, both sides are legally obligated to go through with the marriage. See 18.8 and 18.18.) This case is recorded elsewhere in the *Yuan dianzhang,* which reveals that here a passage is missing. The passage shows the Ministry of Revenue agreeing with the Regional Surveillance Office that the betrothal gifts should all be returned. It writes: "If we have the groom's family pay the betrothal gifts and go ahead with the marriage, then an unmarried daughter will have no incentive to remain chaste."[77] The Ministry of Punishment's final ruling is not included in this later entry, but when the two cases are read side by side, it seems clear that the Ministry of Punishments makes the final decision and overrules the Ministry of Revenue. This result is in keeping with other lenient sentences for adultery in Yuan law, mostly issued by the Ministry of Punishments.[78] See also case 18.13, where a married woman who twice runs off with another man is punished with a relatively mild beating of 37 strokes.

We see here as in other examples in this time period that the Secretariat for State Affairs, when it was in existence, was technically if not in fact subordinate to the Central Secretariat and thus had to get nominal approval from the Central Secretariat for its decisions.[79]

18.39 *When a woman betrothed to be married commits adultery, the marriage can be called off* [80]

In the ninth year of the *zhiyuan* period (1272), a document from the Censorate states:

A report from the Regional Surveillance Office[81] reads:

---

77. YDZ 45:13a; Chen Gaohua et al. 2011, 3:1534–1535.
78. See Birge 2009.
79. See discussion in Zhang Fan 1997, 21–27.
80. YDZ 18:19a–b, pp. 693–694.
81. From the other version of this case, we learn that this is the Regional Surveillance Office of Hedong Shanxi Region, headquartered at Taiyuan, which made the first ruling and

The fiancée of Lü Cheng's son, Wu Meimei, committed adultery with Chen Jun'er. We adjudicated the case and ruled that the groom's family does not need to pay betrothal gifts, and the bride has to marry in exchange for nothing.

We submitted this report to the Secretariat for State Affairs, and respectfully received a superior communication in reply, as follows:

The Ministry of Punishments analyzed the matter and concluded:

When adjudicating cases where a woman who is engaged to be married commits adultery, we recommend that if the groom's family wishes to cancel the engagement they may get back all of the betrothal gifts. But if they choose not to cancel the engagement, then the groom's family need pay only one half of the original betrothal gifts to complete the marriage. This would be appropriate.

We [the Secretariat for State Affairs] sent this to the Central Secretariat and received their communiqué in return, as follows:

We approve the decision of the Ministry of Punishments. Have it enforced.

18.40

This document revisits the problem of wife-selling, here again in the form of divorce in exchange for payment. This case originated in south China, in Guiyang Circuit,[82] and was passed up through the Huguang Branch Secretariat to the Central Secretariat, which sent it to the Ministry of Rites for a ruling in 1301. The Ministry made reference to an earlier ruling, and on that basis it ruled that the second marriage be dissolved and the wife returned to her natal family, despite the fact that two children had been born to the second couple. They also ruled that the betrothal gifts received by the first husband be confiscated, but they declined to impose further punishment, owing to an amnesty. Details of the earlier precedent are excised from the text by the original editors, who refer the reader to an unnamed previous case, which we can surmise to be case 18.38, with the same title, decided by the Ministry of Revenue thirty years earlier, in 1271, and originating in north China, modern Xian. (Recall that in the course of these thirty years, the Ministry of Rites had taken over most mar-

---

sent the case up for review (YDZ 45:13a). (The text mistakenly writes Hexi for Hedong.) The date is also given in more detail as 1272, second month, twenty-eighth day.

82. Modern Guiyang City, in southern Hunan Province.

riage cases from the Ministry of Revenue.) The ruling recorded herein is in turn cited explicitly as a precedent in case 18.23, from the same region, dated 1310. Taken together, these cases reveal that the problem of wife-selling persisted across time, both in the north and the south, throughout the Yuan empire.

18.40 *Regulations on annulling marriages and buying divorces*[83]

In the fifth year of the *dade* period (1301), eighth month, a document from the Huguang Branch Secretariat states:

A report from the Pacification Office of Hunan Region reads:

A dispatch from Guiyang Circuit states:

We investigated the plaint of Tan Bashiyi, which said:

I was enticed by Chen Si to marry off my wife, A-Meng, to Tan Sishisan.

We interrogated Tan Sishisan and obtained his confession of the crime as follows:

I should not have married Tan Bashiyi's wife A-Meng.

We could rule that the marriage be annulled, but there have already been two children, a son and a daughter, born to the couple. We humbly request that you pass down a clear decision.

Report received. We sent this to the Central Secretariat and received their communiqué in return, as follows:

We sent this to the Ministry of Rites, who examined and ruled on the matter, and returned a report as follows:

We have investigated and found (see precedent above)[84] ... Now regarding the case that is currently before us, this Ministry deliberated and concludes: Tan Bashiyi, because of poverty and distress, wrote out a letter of divorce and received money from Tan Sishisan. He thereupon took his wife, A-Meng, and married her off to said person. It should be noted that Tan Bashiyi has already violated marital duty toward his wife. Moreover this constitutes buying and selling a divorce. Both of these acts are illegal. We have examined this matter thoroughly and rule that the

---

83. YDZ 18:19b, p. 694.

84. These words appear in small type and were evidently added by the editors, who felt it unnecessary to reprint the text of the earlier ruling. As noted in the introductory comments, the reference seems to be to case 18.38, dated 1271, which carries the same title as this case. Such editorial comments are rare in the *Yuan dianzhang*.

marriage between Tan Sishisan and A-Meng should be annulled and A-Meng should return to her natal family. An amount of money comparable to what Tan Bashiyi originally received as a betrothal payment should be confiscated from him. This would be appropriate. The crime that each of these people has committed has been subject to an amnesty from the court, so there need be no further prosecution. We submit this report for your thorough consideration.

We the Metropolitan Secretariat approve the report. We send you this communiqué and request that you enforce it as above.

18.41

This intriguing case describes the efforts of a son to redeem his mother, who fourteen years earlier was sold into slavery by his father after she committed adultery, for which she was punished by the local government with a beating of 47 strokes. The local county originally sides with the son and orders the father to return the money and redeem his wife back to freedom, but the circuit overturns the ruling and sends her back into bondage, where she has been married off to one of the other slaves in her master's household. Nevertheless, the circuit notes that a son and a daughter have been born to the new couple and orders that these two be made free commoners but for the time being remain living with their slave parents. The circuit sends this ruling to the Ministry of Revenue for review, and the Ministry concurs with the decision.

The son then appeals to the Regional Surveillance Office, the local branch of the Censorate, which disagrees strongly with the earlier decision. They censure the circuit for having the woman stay in the illegal marriage with the slave husband, and the plot thickens when the text reveals that the person to whom the mother was sold was none other than the Director-General of the circuit (which may explain why the circuit overturned the county ruling). The Regional Surveillance Office orders instead that the marriage be annulled and that the woman remarry someone else, or go and live with her son by the first husband who brought the suit for her freedom. The Censorate passes the case to the Central Secretariat, which seeks a ruling from the Ministry of Punishments. The Ministry of Punishments agrees with the Regional Surveillance Office that the marriage be annulled and the woman sent to live with her older son, the plaintiff in the case. They agree that the children born to the woman and the woman herself should be returned to free commoner status. But in an unusual move, the Central Secretariat disagrees with the Ministry and issues a new ruling overriding it. The Central Secretariat mostly concurs with the earlier ruling by the Ministry of Revenue but asserts that both the woman and her children be given free commoner status (guaranteed by a certificate) and that they remain in the home of the second husband. It argues that a son has been born and too much time has gone by to annul the marriage and break up the family. The first husband escapes punishment because of an amnesty, and no punishment is mentioned for the official who purchased the woman and made her the wife of one of his slaves.[85]

This document records seven different verdicts in response to the lawsuit and reveals the extent to which different offices and branches of Yuan government could disagree over matters of gender and servitude. The different rulings reveal different emphases on such issues as protecting commoner status, keeping a family together, the amount of time that has elapsed, and the issue of whether children were born to the second marriage. In the end, the Central Secretariat emphasized the elapsed time and birth of a son and thus declined to annul the illegal marriage. (Note case 18.40, thirty years later, where the Central Secretariat annulled a marriage despite the similar birth of two children.) It added that after the slave husband died, the mother and her children should be registered as a free commoner household and assessed taxes and corvée. The case makes reference to several interesting aspects of Yuan government and society: a foreign, Muslim, name of a local official, a royal hunt household, and the use of a government-issued certificate to prove the free status of a woman and her children. It also reveals the corruption of local officials, who from the evidence herein could resist the law with considerable impunity in cases like this, though not necessarily indefinitely.

18.41 *A wife who commits adultery is sold into slavery*[86]

In the ninth year of the *zhiyuan* period (1272), a superior communication from the Central Secretariat states:

---

85. In comparison to this lenient treatment, the Tang code prescribed one and a half years of penal servitude for arranging the marriage of a free commoner woman to a slave and life exile 3,000 li away, or even death, for selling a free commoner into servitude (TLSY 14:269–270 [Art. 191]; TLSY 20:369–370 [Art. 292]; Johnson 1997, 164–165, 307–310). Other codes had similar regulations.

86. YDZ 18:19b–20b, pp. 694–696.

We received your report, as follows:[87]

A dispatch from the Regional Surveillance Office of Hebei Henan Region reads:[88]

Zhou Tudang, the son of Zhou Lin of a military household in Hui Prefecture,[89] filed a plaint, stating:

My father Zhou Lin apprehended my, Tudang's, mother A-Deng, because she ran away. She was then punished by Master Hasan[90] with a beating of 47 strokes and sent back to live with us as before. But my father Zhou Lin went and married another woman, Meng Dajie. He followed her inducements and secretly accepted 1,100 ounces worth of silk [notes][91] in payment to establish a contract and sell my mother off as a slave in the household of Commissioner Zhou.[92] There she was married off to be the wife of his slave Little Su. Ji County[93] issued a ruling ordering my father Zhou Lin to produce the original money paid so as to redeem my mother A-Deng and return her to free commoner status. The Directorate-General of Huizhou Circuit, however, took my mother A-Deng and gave her back to Commissioner Zhou to be a slave as before.

We herein transmit the testimony of Zhou Lin, which we obtained in the course of investigation:

My wife Deng Xian'er committed adultery and ran away, so I apprehended her and took her to the authorities. They obtained her confes-

---

87. This report is from the main Censorate, as seen from what follows.

88. This was another one of the eight regions in the territory administered by the main Censorate (as opposed to one of the branch censorates), established to carry out local surveillance work (see case 18.12). At this time it was headquartered in Zhangde Circuit, modern Anyang in Henan Province, though later it moved to Bianliang Circuit, modern Kaifeng.

89. This prefecture was in the far south of the Central Province, in Huizhou Circuit. Hui Prefecture is modern Hui County in Henan Province, north of Kaifeng.

90. This is an Arabic name (Chinese: Asan 阿散). It is preceded by the term of respect *guanren* (官人) with the diminutive *xiao* (小), literally something like "young Mister." He is evidently a local official.

91. The text reads simply "silk," but we learn below that this refers to "silk notes," a form of paper currency issued in 1260 with silk yarns as reserve. As with other paper currency, they came in denominations of "ounces" (*liang*). See Chan 1990, 446.

92. Also called "General Distribution Commissioner," this official was in charge of administering the local government salt monopoly and other fiscal matters. The office existed at various times and places and was constantly changing (Farquhar 1990, 187–189). It is not clear when the protagonist here held the post or where he served in office.

93. This county was the administrative seat of Huizhou Circuit (also called Weihui Circuit), just north of modern Kaifeng.

sion and sentenced her to a beating. At the time, in order to clear my debts related to a lawsuit, I took my wife Deng Xian'er and sold her as a slave to Zhou Er, the son of Commissioner Zhou. I received as payment 1,100 ounces worth of silk notes. This man then took Deng Xian'er and married her off to be the wife of his slave Old Su.[94]

Huizhou Circuit adjudicated the matter as follows:

Deng Xian'er is a free commoner. Even though she betrayed her husband by running away and committing adultery, for which she was punished, her first husband Zhou Lin should not have taken his wife A-Deng and sold her to Commissioner Zhou, who in turn married off A-Deng to be the wife of Little Su. As of today, it has been fourteen years, and a son and daughter have been born. They should each be free commoners but should all remain living together with her current husband, Old Su. We submitted this dispatch to the Ministry of Revenue and respectfully received in reply a certified document, stating: "We approve the decision."[95]

We the Regional Surveillance Office deliberated and conclude: Deng Xian'er was originally a free commoner. She committed a crime, which was dealt with by the authorities. Nevertheless, her husband Zhou Lin took Deng Xian'er and of his own volition established a contract and sold her as a slave to Director-General Zhou Er. He has already committed the offense of violating marital duty. Director-General Zhou Er clearly knew at this time that this woman was a free commoner. But he privately colluded with the sale and married off Deng Xian'er to be the wife of Old Su, another slave in his household. It is clear that his devious intention was to make her a slave permanently. A lawsuit was filed with the authorities. Even though Deng Xian'er has been the wife of Old Su for more than ten years at this point, and a son and daughter have been born to them, in the end the marriage is still unlawful. Their marriage should be annulled, and Deng Xian'er should return to free commoner status and marry someone else. If she is not willing to remarry, then her son Zhou Tudang should care for her for the rest of her life. The original payment received for her by rights should be confiscated by the authorities. The

94. Earlier this slave is called Little Su.

95. Since Huizhou Circuit is within the Central Province, it can send dispatches directly to one of the Six Ministries and get direct replies. As noted earlier, a "certified document" can only come from one of the Six Ministries.

circuit in question ruled that Deng Xian'er should remain with Old Su as his wife. This constitutes a serious error.

This office [the main Censorate] examined the matter thoroughly. This ruling will stand as a precedent for a long time, therefore [we submit this report and humbly request that you consider the matter thoroughly].[96]

Report received. We [the Central Secretariat] sent this to the Ministry of Punishments, which rendered a decision and sent back a report, as follows:

We have deliberated and conclude: Deng Xian'er was originally the daughter by birth of Deng Yishan, of a hunting household.[97] She was betrothed to Zhou Lin and became his wife. Even though she betrayed her husband by running away and committing adultery with another man, the authorities have already adjudicated this woman's crime and punished her. Afterwards, if Zhou Lin did not want to take her back as his wife, he could have divorced her and sent her back to her lineage. He should not have established a contract and sold her as a slave to Director-General Zhou Er. At that time, this official clearly knew that this woman was a free commoner. He should not have agreed to purchase her and moreover gone and married her off to Old Su to be his wife for more than ten years. Even though a son has been born to the couple, in the end this is in error and does not comply with the statutes. We cannot rule that she remain living with her current husband. Following the ruling of the Regional Surveillance Office, the situation should be corrected and she should be returned to free commoner status. The marriage should be annulled. Deng Xian'er should be given over to the custody of her son Zhou Tudang, who can take her back to her lineage and care for her. Moreover, the son obtained by the second husband Old Su should be entered on the registers as a free commoner and allowed to remain living with his father. This would be appropriate.

We the Metropolitan Secretariat deliberated and conclude: Zhou Lin's wife Deng Xian'er ran away and committed adultery for which she was punished, and because of this, he sold her to Zhou Er to be married off to his slave Old Su. Fourteen years have now gone by, and a son has already been born to the couple. We cannot rule that the marriage be annulled. We order that Deng

---

96. This last phrase is missing from the text but can be filled in from the context.

97. More formally called "hunting and falconer households" (*dabu yingfang hu* 打捕鷹房戶), these were one of more than eighty types of specially classified households that provided specified products and services to the government. See Huang 1977, 200; Mote 1999, 495–497; Farquhar 1990, 6.

Xian'er and the son that she bore be returned to free commoner status and be given a certificate to that effect, but that they remain living with her current husband. After Old Su passes away, they should register as a new household and be assessed for taxes and corvée. In addition, as for the offense to which Zhou Lin has confessed and the money received from the original sale, there has already been an Imperial Amnesty so there need be no further adjudication. We have already issued a superior communication to the Six Ministries, for them to transmit to their subordinate offices. Additionally, have this enforced as above.

18.42

In the two lawsuits described in this next document, we learn that adultery by the wife of an uxorilocal husband had much more serious consequences than the mere beatings given to wives in other marriages. In both suits, a court ruled that the husband no longer had to abide by the terms of his uxorilocal marriage agreement to reside in his father-in-law's home, but could leave with his wife. In the earlier case, the father-in-law sued, and upon review the Ministry of War and Punishments (which existed at the time) ruled that the son-in-law should pay some compensation to his father-in-law for the loss of the son-in-law's labor. In the later case, which opens the document, the Ministry of War and Punishments rules this time that the son-in-law be allowed to leave without paying compensation. The Regional Surveillance Office of Hebei Henan Region, the local branch of the Censorate, disputes this verdict and recommends following the earlier precedent of forcing the departing son-in-law to provide compensation. They pass their recommendation up to the main Censorate in the capital, which sends it to the Central Secretariat, which sends it to the Ministry of Revenue for a decision. The Ministry of Revenue sides with the Ministry of War and Punishments, and in its ruling rejects the use of the precedent and allows the son-in-law to leave without compensation. The Central Secretariat approves this decision. The wife's transgression could thus potentially lead to disastrous consequences for the well-being of her parents' household.

The case shows once again different branches of government disagreeing on matters of marital ethics and men's and women's legal rights. When read together with similar cases (such as 18.12, 18.39, and 18.41) we can discern the tensions between the Censorate branch of government, represented locally by a Regional Surveillance Office, and the circuits and ministries whose judgments they audited. The Regional Surveillance Offices seem to take a more conservative approach, striving to preserve rigid status boundaries and upholding Confucian ideas of the sanctity of marriage, while the circuits and ministries usually display a less consistent ethical stance in attempting to consider individual circumstances. In every case, the Central Secretariat has the final word in this tangle, usually agreeing with the ministry in question.

The text of the *Yuan dianzhang* in this instance has some omissions and errors; nevertheless, the basic facts of the cases are clear, and my rendering seems the most plausible interpretation of the entire document. Chart 5 presents the order of verdicts and details of events as I read them. References to names of ministries in the central government that existed only temporarily during the early years of Khubilai's reign help date the various rulings.

18.42 *The wife commits adultery, and the couple leaves her father's home*[98]

In the twelfth year of the *zhiyuan* period (1275), a superior communication from the Central Secretariat states:

We received your report, as follows:[99]

A dispatch from the Regional Surveillance Office of Hebei Henan Region reads:

Gao Sun'er was the uxorilocal husband of Hao Jinlian. Because his wife committed adultery, it was ruled that the couple leave her father's home.[100]

[We note a record of an earlier precedent as follows:][101]

We submitted a report, and received [*sic*][102] a communication from the Secretariat, which states:

We sent this to the Ministry of War and Punishments, which investigated the matter and issued a ruling, as follows:[103] "Qi Shou'an of

---

98. YDZ 18:20b, p. 696.

99. This is from the Censorate, as in case 18.41 preceding this.

100. In other words, the marriage would no longer be uxorilocal, and the couple would leave and set up their own household or move in with the husband's family. We can surmise from what follows that this ruling is from the Ministry of War and Punishments and thus dates to between 1271 and 1275, although the initial ruling would have come from a circuit.

101. Some such phrase is missing here. In what follows, the Regional Surveillance Office is quoting an earlier ruling by the Ministry of War and Punishments that was issued in response to what would be one of its own reports sent up through the Censorate. The situation is similar to the adultery case in 18.41 and case 18.12, where the Regional Surveillance Office reverses (or tries to reverse) a ruling made by a circuit.

102. There is a mistake in the text here, which should read in this context "respectfully received" (*feng* not *zhun*).

103. The reference to the Ministry of War and Punishments means the case dates most likely to 1268–1270, when these two ministries were combined. (See Farquhar 1990, 175–176.)

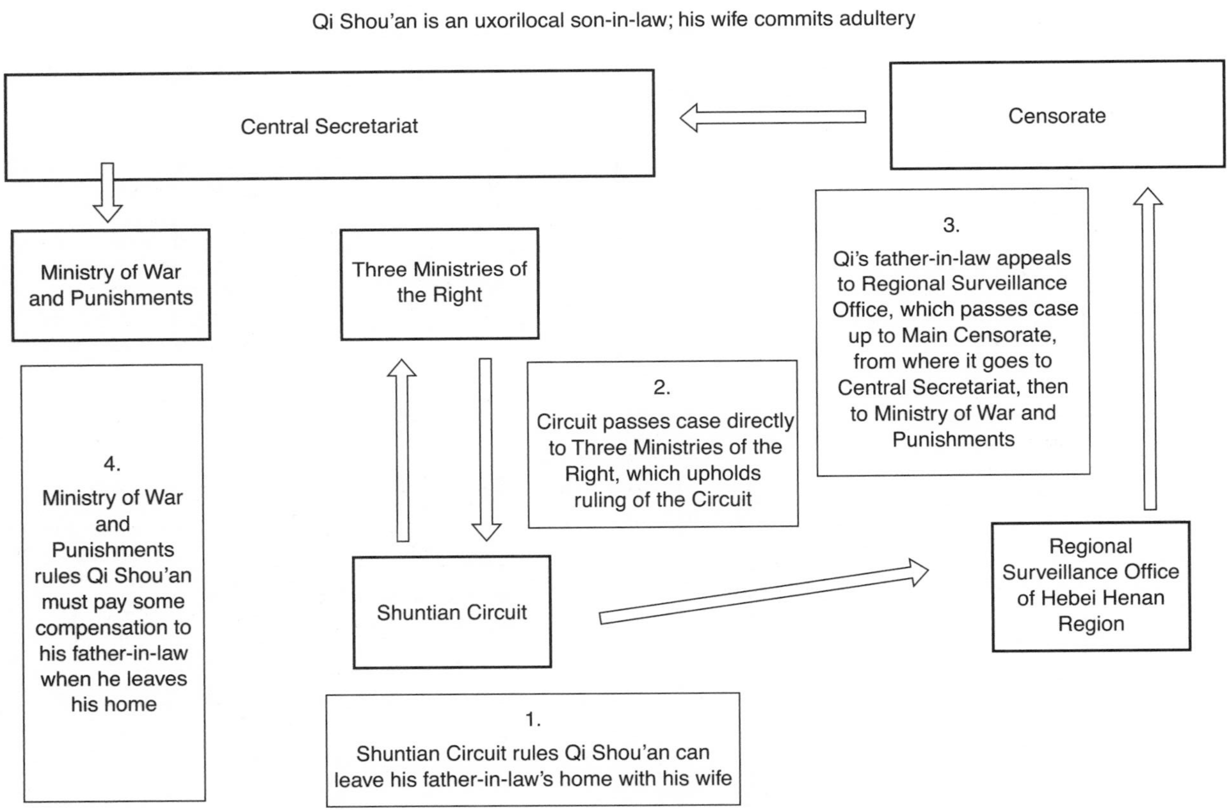

Qi Shou'an is an uxorilocal son-in-law; his wife commits adultery

Chart 5. Case 18.42, outline of verdicts and events.
Chart 5a. 18.42 Outline of verdicts and events, Case A (earlier case): compensation paid.

Gao Sun'er is an uxorilocal son-in-law; his wife commits adultery

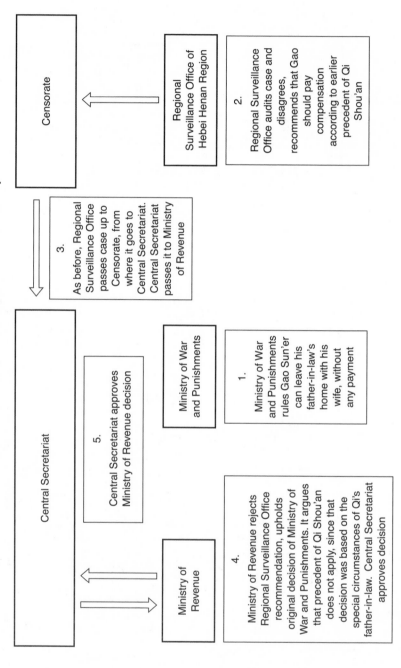

Chart 5b. 18.42 Outline of verdicts and events, Case B (later case): no compensation paid.

Shuntian Circuit[104] was the uxorilocal husband of Chouge, the daughter of Xu De. He caught his wife committing adultery, and she was prosecuted for the offense. It was ruled that the couple should leave her father's home. Nevertheless, Xu De filed a plaint stating that he was old and blind and had no other able-bodied person in the household. In consideration of the circumstances, we rule that Qi Shou'an should provide twenty-five ounces worth of paper money and pay it over to Xu De.

We [the Regional Surveillance Office] note that, if Gao Sun'er takes his wife and leaves her father's home according to the verdict already issued, it will impoverish his wife's family. Therefore, why not adjudicate this case according to the earlier precedent? Consider the time limit for uxorilocal residence originally agreed upon at the time of the marriage and calculate the amount of the betrothal gifts that should be repaid to the wife's family.

We [the main Censorate] humbly request that you consider this matter thoroughly.

Report received. We [the Central Secretariat] sent this to the Ministry of Revenue, which investigated the matter and issued a ruling, as follows:

When the Three Ministries of the Right originally ruled on the case of Qi Shou'an, they initially did not require him to repay the betrothal gifts.[105] As for Hao Mingding, the father of Gao Sun'er's wife, the situation of his physical strength and his family property is not the same as that of Qi Shou'an. We cannot use the precedent and order him to provide payment. We rule that the case should be adjudicated according to the decision already made by the Ministry of War and Punishments. This would be appropriate.

We the Metropolitan Secretariat approve the report. We order all subordinate offices to give this ruling their careful consideration and enforce it accordingly.

---

104. Modern Baoding in Hebei Province. The Yuan Circuit was part of the Central Province, thus it could send its rulings directly to a ministry for review without going through the Central Secretariat. The name changed to Baoding Circuit in 1275.

105. This reference to the Three Ministries of the Right indicates that this early ruling in the case of Qi Shou'an dates to 1266–1268. The Three Ministries were the Ministries of War, Punishments, and Works. In 1268, the Ministry of War and Punishments was separated off, so when the father sued, the case came to them.

CHAPTER SEVEN

Sections 6–8

When the Husband Dies; Levirate Marriage; No Levirate Marriage

Section 6: When the Husband Dies

18.43

This case concerns a fundamental question regarding widows that was repeatedly addressed in Yuan law, namely, where should a wife physically reside when her husband has died? This early ruling, dated 1268, orders the wife to stay in the home of her husband during the mourning period (twenty-seven months, according to Song and Jin law). This is consistent with case 18.5, decided by the same office in the same year and month, where a widow was also ordered to observe mourning, although in other cases, especially after the abrogation of the Taihe code in 1271, judges declined to enforce any mourning period.[1]

The lawsuit that precipitated the ruling reflects the tensions surrounding widow chastity during this period. A young woman, Han Zhaonu, married Mr. Guo Si in the seventh month of 1266. When he died, her mother brought Zhaonu back to her natal home. Guo's older brother sued to keep her in their household "to observe mourning," and the Ministry of Revenue sided with him, on the basis of "the regulations." The ruling was made on behalf of the Ministry of Revenue by the Law Office, which suggests that the regulations to which they refer were found in the Taihe code of the Jin dynasty. (Recall that the Law Offices were tasked with adjudication based on Jin law, and they were gradu-

---

1. See Birge 2002, 257–261, and discussion in cases 18.5 and 18.15. This judgment does not place restrictions on the widow after the morning period, and it is likely that at that time she would be free to return to her natal family and remarry, as seen in case 18.2 (Item 6) and other Yuan rulings around this time.

ally abolished after the Taihe code was abrogated in 1271.) Note that the judges cite the payment of betrothal gifts as proof that the daughter was legally married and owed mourning to her husband. Language such as "fulfill her duty as a wife" and "encourage public morals" suggests that the authors of the ruling were adherents of Neo-Confucianism, which may explain their strict stance on the mourning period and widow behavior.

18.43 *When the husband dies, a widow should observe mourning*
in the home of her husband[2]

In the fifth year of the *zhiyuan* period (1268), tenth month, a document from the Ministry of Revenue of the Central Secretariat states:

We received your dispatch, which reads as follows:[3]

> Guo Congxun, of a civilian household in Pingyang Circuit, filed a plaint stating:
>
>> Han A-Gong of Henan Prefecture, Yiyang County,[4] Shi Village,[5] won't let Zhaonu, the wife of my younger brother, observe mourning for my younger brother Guo Si.
>
> We humbly request that you consider this matter.

We [the Ministry of Revenue] sent this to the Law Office, which analyzed the matter and concluded:

> Han Zhaonu in the seventh month of the third year of the *zhiyuan* period (1266) entered the home of her husband Guo Si. Moreover, her parents received two complements of betrothal gifts; according to the law, she is rightfully married. She has also paid obeisance to her husband's parents.[6] Now that her husband has died, she should observe mourning in the home of her husband in accordance with the regulations,[7] to fulfill her duty as a wife and encourage public morals. This seems appropriate.

---

2. YDZ 18:21a, p. 697. This case is found in truncated form in TZTG 3:147 (Art. 46). The TZTG version omits the crucial reference to the Law Office and gives the date as second month.

3. From what follows, we know this is from the authorities of Pingyang Circuit, in modern Shanxi Province, north of modern Luoyang.

4. Modern Luoyang, in Henan Province.

5. Reading *cun* 村 for *fu* 付.

6. As in a wedding ceremony.

7. The term "regulations" (例) here likely refers to the "Old Regulations" (舊例), namely the Taihe code of the Jin.

We the Ministry of the Secretariat order Han Zhaonu to observe mourning in the home of her husband in accordance with the regulations.

18.44

This case is of particular interest, because it directly addresses the problem of cultural difference among the residents of the Yuan empire and the court's willingness to apply different laws to different ethnic groups. In this case, dated 1269, the Ministry of Revenue chooses to apply Muslim law in a marriage dispute between two Muslim families, probably Arab traders. A man named Muhammad (Chinese, Mahema) pays betrothal gifts to cement the engagement of his twenty-year-old daughter Aisha to the son of another man, named Ali. But Ali's son dies before the actual marriage takes place. Ali wants his younger son, fifteen years old, to marry Aisha in a levirate union. Muhammad sues to prevent the levirate marriage. Remarkably, Dadu Circuit, which judges the case initially, appeals to a Muslim judge, a qadi, to render a decision according to Muslim (Huihui) law.[8] The qadi declares that without the consent of the bride's parents, no levirate should take place, but that in such a case the bride's family must return half the betrothal gifts. The circuit also cites traditional Chinese statutory law (quoting presumably the Taihe code of the Jin), which states that once the betrothal gifts have been paid, the marriage is final, and even if the bride or groom dies, the betrothal gifts are not returned. This law is applied to Chinese in the very next case below. The Ministry of Revenue concurs with the circuit to adjudicate the case according to Muslim law and orders that half the betrothal gifts be returned. The presence of a qadi attests to well-established Muslim communities in Yuan China.[9]

8. A qadi was a Muslim judge charged with adjudication according to Islamic law, among Muslim communities around the world. A qadi judged both religious and temporal matters, and although his decisions could not technically be appealed, in non-Muslim states such as the Yuan, the qadi were dependent on the secular authorities' upholding their decisions, as in this case.

9. On these communities, see Yang Xiaochun 2012; Liu Yingsheng 2013; Chaffee 2006, 2008, 2009.

18.44 *The husband dies before the marriage takes place and half the betrothal gifts are returned*[10]

In the sixth year of the *zhiyuan* period (1269), third month, a document from the Ministry of Revenue of the Central Secretariat states:

A dispatch that we received from Dadu Circuit reads:[11]

> Muhammad[12] filed a written plaint, stating:
>
>> During the first month of the second year of the *zhiyuan* period (1265), I engaged the go-between Fatima to negotiate the marriage of my daughter Aisha to Gou'er, the son of Ali. Then in the seventh month of last year, my son-in-law Gou'er died. And Ali said, "Let Gou'er's younger brother marry your daughter instead."
>
> We apprehended the go-between Fatima and obtained her testimony as follows:
>
>> In the first month of the second year of the *zhiyuan* period (1265), I negotiated the marriage of Muhammad's daughter Aisha to Gou'er, the son of Ali. Ali paid Muhammad [betrothal gifts consisting of]: a pair of jade bracelets with gold rims, a roll of red damask silk, two rolls of plain silk, one bonnet, two head of sheep, one picul of flour, and thirty bottles of wine. Later on, the groom died. At this time, Aisha is twenty years old, and her younger brother-in-law Luoluo is fifteen.
>
> We then questioned the Muslim cleric Buluxi, who stated:[13]
>
>> In Muslim law, when the boy dies before the girl has married into the household, if the girl's parents are willing to let the younger brother marry the girl in a levirate union, then he should marry her. If they aren't willing to let him marry her, then they should give back half the betrothal gifts that were paid. The law is like this.

10. YDZ 18:21a–b, pp. 697–698.

11. At this time Dadu Circuit was still named Zhongdu Circuit. See YS 58:1347; YS 90:2300; and case 18.20.

12. This name and those that follow are all common Muslim names. They are, respectively, the name of the Prophet, the daughter of the Prophet, a wife of the Prophet, and the son-in-law of the Prophet (see Ahmed 1999). Only the names Gou'er and Luoluo are common Chinese names in the Yuan without any obvious Arabic equivalent. Amusingly, they mean "dog" and "little mule."

13. The following is in Sino-Mongolian and highly colloquial, which suggests that his testimony was given orally in Mongolian. The name Buluxi might be the Turkic Burqi.

We have further investigated and found the following [regulation]:[14]

> When taking a wife, if the betrothal gifts have been paid in full but the
> marriage has not yet taken place, even if the boy or girl dies, the betrothal
> gifts are not returned.

We would like to decide this case according to Muslim law. But there has
been no previous ruling in a case like this to use as a precedent. We truly fear
there may be some mistake. We humbly request that you pass down a clear
decision.

We the Ministry of the Secretariat received the dispatch. We order you to investigate this further, and if there is no mistake, have the plaintiff return half
the betrothal gifts, according to [Muslim] law.

18.45

This case presents a formal ruling that once betrothal gifts have been paid, a
marriage is considered final, and the gifts are not returned even if the bride or
groom dies before the marriage is consummated.[15] This contrasts with the
ruling of 1269 in 18.44, based on Muslim law, where the family of the deceased groom was able to get back half the betrothal gifts paid, but it is consistent with the regulation quoted in 18.44, likely the Taihe code of the Jin. The
plaint as recorded herein indicates that the bride's family returned a portion of
the gifts, which suggests that in practice families considered it reasonable to
return some of the betrothal gifts if the marriage did not actually take place. In
law and practice after the Yuan, if the fiancé died before the marriage, the bride
might live as a chaste widow the rest of her life, allowing her deceased husband's family to benefit from government rewards bestowed on chaste-widow
households.

14. This is most likely from the Taihe code of the Jin. Similar regulations existed in Tang and
Song law that once the betrothal gifts were paid, they were not returned even if the marriage did
not take place, though without specific reference to the bride's or groom's dying (TLSY 13:254
[Art. 175]; SXT 13:213). See also cases 18.8 and 18.18. Ming law addresses the case of the bride
or groom dying, as here (*Da Ming ling* 1:6a [p. 19]; Farmer 1995, 159 [Art. 23]).
15. For a later application of this law by the Ministry of Rites, dated 1284, see TZTG 4:167
(Art. 77).

18.45 *Regulation that if the groom dies before the marriage, the betrothal gifts are not returned*[16]

In the ninth year of the *zhiyuan* period (1272), sixth month, twenty-eighth day, a document from the Ministry of Revenue of the Central Secretariat states: We received your dispatch, as follows:

> Ma Li of Hedong County[17] filed a plaint, stating:
>
>> During the tenth month of the seventh year of the *zhiyuan* period (1270), I arranged the engagement of my younger son, Ma San, to the sister of Yang Da of this same prefecture. But on the seventeenth day of the fifth month of the eighth year of the *zhiyuan* period (1271), my son Ma San died. Except for three pieces of jewelry and five articles of clothing, they [the bride's family] are not willing to return the jewelry and garments[18] originally paid as betrothal gifts.
>
> We humbly request that you pass down a clear decision.

We the Ministry of the Secretariat deliberated over the matter. Ma San, the son of Ma Li, was engaged to be married. But before the marriage could take place, Ma San died. The betrothal gifts originally paid should not be returned.[19] We order you to give this ruling your careful consideration and enforce it accordingly.

18.46

This seminal verdict, dated 1273, establishes the right of a widow to resist a forced levirate marriage to one of her husband's younger male relatives if she certifies that she will stay chaste. It is one of the first of several judgments that tempered the application of the levirate to Chinese under Mongol rule, which had been harshly enforced since Khubilai decreed the levirate legal in the eleventh month of 1271 (case 18.49).[20] In this instance, the woman was married

16. YDZ 18:21b, p. 698.

17. Located in Jinning Circuit, in the far southwest corner of the Central Province, in modern Shanxi, roughly equidistant from Xi'an and Luoyang.

18. Reading *biao* 表 for *lai* 來.

19. Reading *xia* 下 for *bu* 不. The correct character *xia* is found in the Shen Jiaben edition of the *Yuan dianzhang* (*Yuan dianzhang* [1964], 18:33b).

20. For these rulings, see the next two sections in this chapter. For a discussion of the conflicting and changing enforcement of the levirate under the Yuan and its significance, see Birge 1995; Birge 2002, 238–245; Birge 2003.

uxorilocally, and after her husband died, she had cared for her natal mother together with her children, staying chaste for five years. When her husband's
younger brother demanded the right to marry her in a levirate union, the mother
took him to court. The circuit authorities initially sided with the brother, in accordance with Khubilai's decree of 1271, even though the woman was widowed before the levirate was legal for Chinese. But the Ministry of Revenue took
note of the mitigating circumstances and ruled that the widow be allowed to
stay chaste and not remarry at all. It demanded a signed certificate from the
widow vowing not to remarry. In later rulings, the Ministry further clarified that
a widow could avoid a levirate marriage only if she vowed to remain chaste, usually affirmed by a formal certificate of chastity, as here. If she broke her vow, any
eligible levir could force her to marry him. These rulings laid the groundwork for
subsequent legal support of widow chastity and limits on remarriage, but they
also reinforced for the time being the legality of levirate marriage under the right
conditions for all peoples under Yuan rule.

18.46 *When the husband dies, his wife is allowed to stay chaste*[21]

In the tenth year of the *zhiyuan* period (1273), [blank] month, a document from
the Ministry of Revenue of the Central Secretariat states:
We received your dispatch, as follows:[22]

> Xiao A-Wang filed a written plaint, stating:
>
>> My daughter Yuge invited in Wang Da to be her permanent uxorilocal
>> husband. He died of an illness. His younger brother Wang Er wants to
>> take my daughter Yuge in a levirate marriage, but I don't want to allow
>> it. We filed a plaint with the authorities of Puyang County, who judged
>> that Wang Er could marry her. But my daughter Yuge wants to stay
>> chaste and is not willing to remarry.
>
> We obtained the testimony of all those involved. We the circuit authorities
> considered this matter carefully, and we note that this is a precedent-setting
> matter. We humbly request that you consider this matter thoroughly.

We the Ministry of the Secretariat deliberated the matter. Xiao Yuge's husband
died, and she already completed the mourning. Five years have passed since
then. She is staying chaste and has vowed not to remarry. Together with the

---

21. YDZ 18:21b, p. 698.

22. From the context that follows, we know this is Daming Circuit, in modern Hebei
Province.

children left behind by her late husband, she is caring for her mother A-Wang. We cannot allow her younger brother-in-law Wang Er to take her in a levirate union. We order further that you obtain from Xiao Yuge a signed certificate attesting that she is staying chaste and has vowed not to remarry. Enforce this as above.

18.47

This is one of the most dramatic and significant cases in the entire *Yuan dianzhang*. Remarkably, it overturns two millennia of traditional Chinese law, which had allowed women to keep their dowry property, including landed property, and take it with them out of their first marriage if they were widowed or divorced. In this ruling approved by the Central Secretariat in 1303, the Ministry of Rites deprived widows of these long-held property rights and declared that the first husband's family could from then on take over a woman's dowry lands and other assets. As seen in such phrases as "from now on," or "as was formerly done," the Ministry was aware that it was overturning centuries of established law. This major policy shift originated from a suggestion by the Director-General of Huizhou Circuit in the south, and it represents the growing influence of Neo-Confucianism at the Yuan court. Neo-Confucians were opposed to widow remarriage and private property rights within marriage, and this is one of a number of decisions in the *Yuan dianzhang* from the first decade of the fourteenth century that overtly promoted their agenda.[23] The foreign name of the director-general, Dorchi, shows that non-Chinese administrators were among those coming to embrace Neo-Confucian ideas at this time.

18.47 *Dowry land should be taken over by the husband's family*[24]

In the seventh year of the *dade* period (1303), [blank] month, the Jiangzhe Branch Secretariat received a communiqué from the Central Secretariat,[25] as follows:

We received your communiqué, which reads in part:

---

23. For these cases, see Birge 2002, 253–273 (this case is discussed on 263). See also Birge 1995, 128–143, especially 133–135, and Holmgren 1986, 182–183, for this case.

24. YDZ 18:21b–22a, pp. 698–699.

25. The text provides here a new line for the characters "Central Secretariat" to show respect.

A report from the Pacification Office of Zhexi [Region] states:[26]

> The Director-General of Huizhou Circuit[27] Dorchi has said:
>
>> Regarding dowry lands and other goods that a woman brings into her marriage: from now on if a woman who has once been married wishes to get remarried, whether she is divorced while her husband is alive or living as a widow after her husband has died, all of the dowry property and other assets that she originally brought into her marriage should be taken over by the family of her former husband. She is absolutely not permitted to take the property with her, as was formerly done.
>
> We the Branch Secretariat examined the matter thoroughly, and we feel it would be appropriate to approve what is said.

We [the Central Secretariat] sent this to the Ministry of Rites, who deliberated and concluded:

> We recommend that the decision be approved, with the exception that if one expels a wife without due cause this regulation will not apply. This would be appropriate.

We the Metropolitan Secretariat approve the report. We send you this communiqué for your careful consideration and request that you enforce it accordingly.

Section 7: Levirate Marriage

18.48

This is an early example of a forced levirate marriage by the Yuan authorities, and if the date is recorded correctly, it is inconsistent with other rulings of the Central Secretariat in these years, which allowed Chinese to follow their own customs and reject levirate marriages (for instance, see ruling in case 18.2).[28] This case is complicated by the triple circumstances that (1) the husband lived in the wife's home in a temporary uxorilocal marriage with a term of seventeen years; (2) the wife's father belonged to a military household; (3) the wife had previously committed adultery, for which she received some unknown punishment. As recorded in the text, the

---

26. For this office and region, see note under case 18.29. Some sources say the region was abolished in 1289, but this case demonstrates that it must have been reinstated.

27. In the southern part of modern Anhui Province, southwest of the city of Hangzhou.

28. There is also the possibility that the principals were Jurchen or other non-Chinese, despite the Chinese-sounding names, which could explain the application of the levirate.

uxorilocal husband died just three years after the marriage, and one of his younger brothers wanted to marry the widow in a levirate union, taking her into a separate household. When her father refused the marriage, citing as a reason that the term of the uxorilocal marriage was not yet up, the older brother of the deceased husband filed a lawsuit. The case went to the Bureau of Military Affairs, since it involved a soldier household, which sent it to the Central Secretariat for a decision. The Central Secretariat ruled against the wife's father, and in an uncharacteristically harsh verdict, ruled that the younger brother could marry the widow and in addition take her out of her father's home into a separate household. The fact that the wife had earlier committed adultery may explain this decision. As seen in case 18.42, in later years the punishment for a wife's adultery in an uxorilocal marriage was for the couple to leave the wife's father's home. The text contains several obvious lacunae and therefore may be missing other crucial details.[29]

18.48 *A husband's younger brother takes his sister-in-law in levirate marriage and leaves with her to live in a separate household*[30]

In the sixth year of the *zhiyuan* period (1269), the Bureau of Military Affairs respectfully received a superior communication from the Central Secretariat, as follows:
[We received your report, which reads:][31]

Liu Congzhou filed a plaint, stating:

Xu Yingxian, the wife of my younger brother, committed adultery and was punished but went back to being his wife, as before. Now, my younger brother has died of an illness. He has two younger brothers who ought to be able to marry Xu Yingxian in a levirate union. But her parents aren't willing to give her away.

We sent this down to the relevant circuit, which questioned the father of Yingxian, Xu De, who stated:

I am registered in this county as a military household. In the third month of the third year of the *zhiyuan* period (1266) I invited in Liu Shouhan to

29. Oddly, the name of the wife's father in 18.42 is also Xu De, as here. Other aspects of the cases do not match, however, so the two documents must refer to two separate lawsuits, unless they are both considerably corrupted.

30. YDZ 18:23a, p. 701. For a discussion of these levirate cases in this section and the next, see Hung 1992 and Ratchnevsky 1968.

31. This line is missing in the original.

live with my daughter Yingxian as my uxorilocal son-in-law for a term of seventeen years. We had established a formal marriage contract. Because my son-in-law Liu Shouhan had not yet finished his term as an uxorilocal son-in-law [when he died], I would not let my daughter Yingxian leave [to remarry].

We humbly request that you consider this matter thoroughly.

We the Secretariat Office rule in this case as follows: allow Liu Jianjian, the younger brother of the late Liu Shouhan, to marry his sister-in-law, Xu Yingxian, in a levirate union in the home of Xu De and [subsequently] leave with her to live in a separate household. In addition, distribute this to all subordinate offices, and enforce it according to the above.

18.49

This document records the dramatic and unprecedented edict from Khubilai Khan that legalized the levirate for all peoples under Yuan rule at the end of 1271. Khubilai issued his order in the twelfth month of 1271, just one month after he abrogated the Taihe code of the Jin dynasty and proclaimed the title Yuan for his dynasty. It came just ten months after Khubilai had reiterated that different peoples should follow their own customary laws and that Chinese were therefore forbidden to practice the levirate, which constituted incest in traditional Chinese law (see case 18.2). Interestingly, Khubilai's edict was in response to a memorial from two close advisors who recommended that he outlaw the levirate for all peoples. Khubilai disagreed and on the contrary legalized it for all peoples. Khubilai's ruling unleashed a torrent of lawsuits, since the operation of the levirate conflicted with many aspects of Chinese marriage law. Some of these are recorded in the cases immediately following.[32] It is unclear why Khubilai chose to overturn earlier policy and impose this steppe custom on the Chinese, but there is evidence that the earlier strategy of applying different laws to different ethnic groups was becoming untenable, as both customary laws and ethnic identity became harder to define. The Sino-Mongolian of Khubilai's order captures some of the blunt decisiveness of his speech.

---

32. For more on this edict and the legal battles surrounding it, see Birge 2002, 238–245; Birge 1995, 120–122. On the incompatibility between Chinese and Mongol marriage law in the context of the levirate, see also Holmgren 1986.

18.49 *Regulation on taking a father's secondary wife or one's sister-in-law in levirate marriage*[33]

In the eighth year of the *zhiyuan* period (1271), twelfth month, the Central Secretariat memorialized the throne, as follows:

> On the eighth day of this month, we received a missive sent by the two messieurs Dashman and Sangha,[34] which in translation reads in part: "One should not take a father's secondary wife or one's sister-in-law in levirate marriage."

In response to the memorial, the Emperor issued an Imperial Edict, stating:

> Quickly have this order sent out: One should take a father's secondary wife or one's sister-in-law in levirate marriage.

Thus said the Imperial Edict. We humbly respect it.

18.50

This case illustrates nicely both the enforcement of Khubilai's edict on levirate marriage in 18.49 and the complications in implementing it. We see that local officials did not immediately know of or understand the new rule, and a full year after Khubilai's decree they continued to regard levirate unions as illegal for Chinese. As recorded in this document, a young widow, Wang Yinyin, gets pregnant with her brother-in-law Zheng Wowo, and the two run away together. In an attempt to make the relationship into a legal marriage, Yinyin's mother accepts betrothal gifts worth twenty-eight ounces of silver, and meanwhile the go-between extracts an additional forty ounces worth of hush-money gifts from the Zheng family to keep the matter away from the authorities. Indeed, when the local circuit authorities find out, they arrest Zheng and put him in a canque,

---

33. YDZ 18:23a, p. 701.

34. Two famous advisors to Khubilai had these names and may well be the officials named here. Dashman (Chinese, Dashiman [1248–1304]) was a Mongol from the Kereit tribe who served Khubilai from an early age. Sangha (Chinese, Xiangge; Mongolian, Senge [d. 1291] "monastic congregation") was a Uighurized Tibetan notorious for his corruption and harsh fiscal measures, who was executed in 1291. The identity of these two cannot be certain, since others had the same or similar names, but the life circumstances of these two make them likely candidates, and they were both at Khubilai's court in 1271. See YS 205:4570; *Xin Yuanshi* 133:573c, 223:868a; *Mengwu'er shiji* 50:384b, 106:665a; *Mu'an ji* 13:112–114; de Rachewiltz et al. 1993, 559–583. For other people named Dashman, see Yang Zhijiu 1985. "Dashman" was also a general term for a Muslim cleric.

then confiscate the hush money, worth forty ounces. They then pass the case up to the Ministry of War and Punishments for higher consideration. The Ministry cites Khubilai's edict of 1271, twelfth month (case 18.49), and orders that Zheng be released and allowed to marry Wang Yinyin in a levirate union. In a nice example of how the levirate operated, they order that the various gifts and money exchanged all be returned to their original owners.

18.50 *Regulation that a husband's younger brother may take his sister-in-law in levirate marriage*[35]

In the ninth year of the *zhiyuan* period (1272), tenth month, a document from the Ministry of War and Punishments of the Central Secretariat states:

We received your dispatch, which reads:[36]

Zheng Wowo confessed to a crime, as follows:

My older brother Zheng Nunu died in the fifth year of *zhiyuan* (1268), leaving behind my sister-in-law Wang Yinyin, who together with my nephew Sheshe lived with me in my home. I, Wowo, was not yet married, and my sister-in-law Wang Yinyin moreover was young and widowed. Subsequently, on the eighth day of the tenth month of the eighth year of *zhiyuan* (1271) we had illicit sex. Afterwards, she got pregnant, and we ran away together.

The testimony we obtained from Wang Yinyin was the same. Moreover, we obtained the confession of Qin Er, who arranged the marriage of Wang Yinyin, as follows:

I originally gave Wang Qing[37] gifts to secure the engagement equivalent to paper money worth twenty-eight ounces. I should not, however, have secretly received from Zheng Xin[38] gifts to settle the matter privately equivalent to paper money worth forty ounces.

The go-between Wang Yü and others also testified. We put Zheng Wowo into a canque. And in addition we recovered the goods, equivalent to paper money

---

35. YDZ 18:23a–b, pp. 701–702.

36. The text does not name the place, but we can surmise that it is a circuit within the Central Province, since the dispatch goes directly to the Ministry. At this time the Ministries of War and of Punishments were combined.

37. From the text that follows this appears to be Wang Yinyin's brother. Later, the circuit authorities say the payment went to her mother, which would be the legally proper procedure to arrange a remarriage.

38. This must be Zheng Wowo's father or elder brother.

worth forty ounces, that were illegally obtained by Qin Er. These are waiting in court. As for the gifts to secure the engagement that Wang Qing's mother, A-Zhang, received from Qin Er, equivalent to paper money worth twenty-eight ounces, should we not also confiscate them? We humbly request that you consider this matter.

We the Ministry of the Secretariat have investigated and found the Imperial Edict respectfully received in the eighth year of the *zhiyuan* period (1271) twelfth month, which reads in part:

One should take a father's secondary wife or one's sister-in-law in levirate marriage.[39]

Thus said the Edict. We humbly respect it. We order you humbly to respect the intent of the Imperial Edict. Take Zheng Wowo and set him free. Then take Wang Yinyin and give her to Zheng Wowo to be his wife in a levirate union. Moreover, take the money and goods obtained from Qin Er that he originally received from Zheng Xin and return them to the original owner [Zheng Xin]. As for the money and goods equivalent to paper currency worth twenty-eight ounces that Wang A-Zhang received from Qin Er, return these to Qin Er.[40] Have this enforced.

18.51

This is an example of a widow suing her brother-in-law for rape, one of a number of such legal battles that arose after Khubilai's blanket legalization of the levirate in 1271 (case 18.49). This suit in 1273 is of particular interest because (1) the brother-in-law already had a wife, (2) his own parents objected to the levirate marriage, (3) the widow wanted to stay chaste and care for her son (as the Ministry allowed in another case the same year; see 18.46), and (4) we can surmise that her natal parents supported her and also objected to the levirate remarriage. Marriage under any of these four conditions violated long-standing Chinese marriage law, and this case demonstrates the legal contradictions and difficulties that came with imposing the levirate on Chinese families. Here the brother-in-law also files a counterplaint to force his widowed sister-in-law into a marriage with him. From the language of their dispatch, the circuit authorities, from an unnamed locality, seem to have sided with the widow, naming the rape in

---

39. For this edict, see case 18.49.

40. This sentence confirms that in a levirate marriage no betrothal gifts or other payments were exchanged.

terms that make it a crime by Chinese law. They portray the widow in positive terms, moreover, and carefully lay out the reasons for not allowing the levirate marriage to go forward. But despite the mitigating circumstances, the Ministry of Revenue issues a harsh verdict and orders the levirate marriage to stand, as per Khubilai's edict. They even suggest that the fact of the rape itself, which has already "sullied" the widow, adds justification to their verdict in denying her the right to stay chaste. In these years, Khubilai's levirate decree overrode all previous marriage law, resulting in a flood of lawsuits, as seen here and in other cases in this section.

18.51 *A husband's younger brother takes his sister-in-law in levirate marriage*[41]

In the tenth year of the *zhiyuan* period (1273), a certified document from the Ministry of Revenue of the Central Secretariat states:

We received your dispatch, as follows:[42]

> Fu Wangbo filed a plaint, stating:
>
>> My older brother Fu Er died of an illness, leaving behind his wife, A-Niu. I, Wangbo, asked permission from my parents and took my sister-in-law A-Niu in levirate marriage in accordance with the regulations.
>
> In addition, Niu Wang'er filed a written plaint, stating:
>
>> Fu Wangbo took me, Wang'er, and violated me. I only wanted to stay at home and observe mourning.
>
> We obtained the testimony of all those involved. We the circuit authorities investigated and found: Fu Wangbo currently has a wife. When he originally told his parents that he wanted to take A-Niu in levirate marriage, they refused to give permission. Then, when his parents were not at home, Fu Wangbo forcibly raped A-Niu, causing her to flee back to her natal family. As for the intent of the father-in-law, Fu Yi, and mother-in-law, A-Qiu Yixu, they did not tell their son Fu Wangbo to take [A-Niu] in a levirate union. They only asked of A-Niu to stay chaste in their home and care for their grandson. This is a precedent-setting case. We do not dare make a decision on our own authority. We humbly request that you consider this matter thoroughly.

41. YDZ 18:23b, p. 702.

42. We know this must be from a circuit within the Central Province, since the dispatch goes directly to the Ministry of Revenue. The circuit remains unnamed.

We the Ministry of the Secretariat deliberated over the matter. Even though Niu Wang'er wants to stay chaste and care for her son, Fu Wangbo has already raped and sullied her. Moreover, Fu Wangbo is the younger brother of Niu Wang'er's deceased husband. We must humbly respect the intent of the Imperial Edict previously issued and allow the marriage to stand. Let the husband's younger brother take Niu Wang'er as his wife in a levirate union.[43] We order all subordinate offices to give this ruling their careful consideration and enforce it accordingly.

18.52

This is another in a series of rulings in 1273 that harshly enforced the levirate. A man engaged to be married died before the actual marriage took place. His father wanted a younger son to take the fiancée in a levirate union, but her father refused. The groom's father filed a lawsuit to force the marriage. Citing Khubilai's edict of 1271, the Ministry of Revenue ordered the levirate marriage to go forward over the objections of the bride's father.

18.52 *Levirate marriage when one is only betrothed*[44]

In the tenth year of the *zhiyuan* period (1273), third month, twenty-second day, a certified document from the Ministry of Revenue of the Central Secretariat states:

[We received your dispatch, as follows:][45]

> Zhao Yong of Hua Prefecture[46] filed a plaint, stating:
>
>> I arranged a marriage exchange with Zhang Zhu. My son Zhao Lian'er was engaged to marry his daughter Yue'er. But before the marriage could take place, my son died of an illness. I want to have my second son, Zhao Zidang, marry in a levirate union, but they are unwilling.

We the Ministry of the Secretariat deliberated over the matter. In the end, the woman is already engaged to be married. And we must humbly respect the Imperial Edict establishing the regulation that a husband's younger brother

---

43. The verb "to take" (*jiang* 將) is missing in the text.

44. YDZ 18:24a, p. 703.

45. This line is missing in the text.

46. Modern Hua County in Henan Province. In the Yuan it was part of Daming Circuit in the Central Province.

should take his sister-in-law in levirate marriage. Have the levirate marriage enforced.

18.53

In a case similar to the previous one, the Ministry of Revenue in 1273 again harshly enforced the levirate despite strongly mitigating circumstances. A man engaged to be married died before the actual marriage took place. His mother wanted the bride to marry her younger son in a levirate union, but the bride's father refused. The mother sued to force the marriage. In clear sympathy with the bride's family, Dadu Circuit noted: (1) the actual marriage had not yet taken place, (2) the groom's mother had not paid the formal betrothal gifts but only the initial engagement fee, (3) the bride was seventeen years old, but the levir was only twelve, not yet of marriageable age, and (4) the bride's father had already accepted a full complement of betrothal gifts from another family and had betrothed his daughter to someone else. But when the case was passed up for a decision, the Ministry of Revenue sided completely with the groom's mother, ruling that the levirate union should go forward in accordance with Khubilai's edict of 1271. It ordered the groom's mother to pay the remaining betrothal gifts and the bride's father to return the other betrothal gifts he had received. This dramatic ruling swept aside many aspects of traditional Chinese marriage law and deprived a Chinese bride and her family of much of the legal autonomy they had previously enjoyed.[47]

18.53 *The groom dies after the engagement, and his younger brother marries the bride after additional betrothal gifts are paid*[48]

In the tenth year of the *zhiyuan* period (1273), fifth month, a document from the Ministry of Revenue of the Central Secretariat states:

A dispatch from Dadu Circuit reads:

Guo A-Qin filed a plaint, stating:

My son Qilü was engaged to be married to E'er, the daughter of Li Da. Qilü died, and I wanted to have my younger son, Dong'er, marry her in a levirate union. But Li Da on his own improperly took his daughter E'er

---

47. For further discussion of this ruling, see Birge 2002, 240–241; Birge 1995, 122–123.
48. YDZ 18:24a, p. 703.

and betrothed her to Chen Lü'er, the son of Chen Dechun, a slave of Military Commissioner Pei.

We the circuit authorities considered the matter carefully. We could have Guo Dong'er marry Li E'er in a levirate union. But Guo A-Qin's deceased son Qilü was not yet formally married to her. Moreover, Guo A-Qin only made the initial engagement payment. Even after the engagement was finalized, she did not pay the regular betrothal gifts. E'er is seventeen years old, while Guo Dong'er is only twelve years old. He has not yet reached marriageable age. In addition, Li Da has already accepted bolts of silk gauze as gifts to secure the engagement from Chen Dechun, the slave of Military Commissioner Pei. These two people are truly married. We humbly request that you pass down a clear decision.

We the Ministry of the Secretariat deliberated over the matter. We note that Guo Dong'er is the actual younger brother of Guo Qilü. And even though Li E'er is engaged to marry someone else, the actual marriage has not yet taken place. In the end she is the wife of Guo A-Qin's son, and we must humbly respect the Imperial Edict already issued. Have Guo A-Qin pay the rest of the betrothal gifts originally agreed upon, and according to the law have her son Dong'er marry Li E'er in a levirate union. In addition, the betrothal gifts that Li Da received from Chen Dechun should be returned to Chen Dechun. We order you to enforce this as above.

18.54

This case, again dated 1273, dramatically illustrates how Khubilai's edicts could contradict each other, and how this could cause considerable confusion in the legal system. The main issue at stake here is what happens when the levir is already married and exercising the levirate would result in his having two wives.

A man named Liu San was engaged to be married when his older brother died. He then married his brother's wife in a levirate union but still wanted to go through with the marriage to his original fiancée. Her family sued to prevent the marriage, since she would become the second wife and would no longer be the principal wife. (Her brother's widow brought the case on her behalf.) The suit came before an unnamed circuit in the Central Province. The circuit authorities carefully laid out the problem. First they noted that the levirate marriage took place during the mourning period for the first husband, which would be a reason for the marriage to be annulled. Next they cited Khubilai's edict of 1271, eleventh month (calling it a "statute"), that a man should take his older brother's widow in levirate marriage (see case 18.49), and then quoted verbatim the imperial regulation of earlier that same year that prohibited a man from taking two wives (18.2). Upon review, the Ministry of Revenue cited Khubilai's edict of 1271 on the levirate to rule that the levirate marriage should stand and that Liu San should additionally go ahead and marry his original fiancée. They showed no regard for the problem of having two wives; indeed, Mongol law famously allowed a man to have multiple principal wives. As for the matter of the mourning period, they merely indicated that the circuit should handle the matter "in light of these circumstances." It is not clear what sort of punishment, if any, that would entail, and in point of fact, the issue of marriage during the mourning period was not resolved until some years later. The case has a poignant note, as the cause of death of the older brother is given as suicide.

18.54 *A husband's younger brother takes his sister-in-law in a levirate union and also marries his original fiancée*[49]

In the tenth year of the *zhiyuan* period (1273), a document from the Ministry of Revenue of the Central Secretariat states:
We received your dispatch, as follows:

> Hu A-Guo filed a lawsuit, stating:
>
>> Old Liu in the second month of the seventh year of the *zhiyuan* period (1270) solicited Zhao Er and Ma A-Liu as go-betweens and arranged the engagement of my, A-Guo's, little sister-in-law Hu Chage to marry his younger son Liu San.[50] Last year, in the sixth month, Liu Er hanged himself and died. Within just two weeks, his brother Liu San took Liu Er's wife A-Guo[51] and married her in a levirate union.
>
> We obtained the testimony of all those involved. After careful consideration, we note that, Liu Wen[52] in the seventh year of the *zhiyuan* period (1270) first got engaged to his wife Hu Chage, but as of now, he has not gone and final-

---

49. YDZ 18:24a–b, pp. 703–704.
50. The text reads Liu Er (Liu Two), but it is clear from what follows that this must be Liu San (Liu Three). Later Liu San's name is also given as Liu Wen.
51. Coincidentally, the widowed sister-in-law has the same family name as the plaintiff (or there could be a misprint in the text).
52. That is, Liu San.

ized the marriage by welcoming her into his home. Then, within a year of his older brother's death, on his own initiative[53] he married A-Guo, the wife of his deceased brother, in a levirate union as his principal wife. The wife to whom he was originally engaged, Hu Chage, is twenty years old. She has already reached marriageable age. If we let Liu Wen and his sister-in-law A-Guo get married during the mourning period for A-Guo's husband, according to the law they are liable for prosecution and the marriage should be annulled. At the same time, if we have the man in question finalize his marriage to Hu Chage and welcome her into his home, there has also been a Statute[54] issued, saying:

A husband's younger brother should marry his sister-in-law in a levirate union.

Then if we rule that Liu Wen also take Hu Chage and make her his wife, there has additionally been an Imperial Regulation,[55] humbly received, an item of which reads:

If one who has a wife already marries another wife, even if there has been an amnesty, the marriage is annulled.

We humbly respect the edict. There has been no previous ruling in a case like this to use as a precedent. We humbly request that you pass down a clear decision.

We the Ministry of the Secretariat have investigated and found that, according to the report that we received, on the thirteenth day of the third month[56] of the ninth year of the *zhiyuan* period (1272), Liu Er hanged himself and died. Even though it was during the mourning period for her husband, his wife trusted and followed Liu Cong, the oldest brother of Liu San, and in the end, on the twelfth day of the second month of the tenth year of the *zhiyuan* period (1273) she agreed to marry her younger brother-in-law in a levirate union. The Imperial Edict, humbly received, an item of which reads that the husband's younger

---

53. That is, without consulting Hu Chage's family.

54. This term, *tiaoge* 條格, starts a new line and is elevated one character space, indicated here by capitalization. The quote that follows is a rough paraphrase of Khubilai's edict of 1271 legalizing the levirate for all peoples (see case 18.49).

55. This term, *shengzhi tiaohua* 聖旨條畫, starts a new line and is elevated two character spaces. The quote that follows cites verbatim Item 5 of Khubilai's edict of 1271, second month (see case 18.2).

56. The text above says sixth month.

brother should take his sister-in-law in levirate marriage, is not the same as the regulation about one who has a wife already marrying another wife. The current situation should be allowed to stand. Have the younger brother Liu San take his sister-in-law A-Guo in levirate marriage. Moreover, have him pay the rest of the betrothal gifts and according to the law marry Hu Chage, to whom he was originally engaged. In addition, as for the offense to which Liu Cong[57] and Liu Wen have confessed, the circuit should adjudicate the matter in light of these circumstances. We order you to give this ruling your careful consideration and enforce it as above.

18.55

This case, dated 1318, presents a striking example of how marriage policies could be reversed under Yuan rule in China. It also reinforces that widow chastity could be used to escape a levirate marriage. A widow with four children went home to live with her father, and over the next four years resisted attempts by her mother-in-law to force her into a levirate marriage with one or another of her husband's younger brothers. Finally, according to the widow's testimony, her mother-in-law tricked her into returning to the household, where she was violently raped by one of the brothers with the collusion of the others. The widow, Tian A-Duan, filed a lawsuit to escape the forced remarriage. The circuit in Jiangzhe Branch Secretariat that first ruled on the case, the Ministry of Punishments, and the Central Secretariat all roundly condemned the actions of the brother-in-law. Moreover, the record of the plaint includes a graphic description of the rape, repeated again in the ruling, which further reinforces the air of moral outrage in the language of the document. This sympathy for the widow is in sharp contrast to the ruling in case 18.51, dated 1273, where the circumstances were almost identical. In that earlier case, the Ministry of Revenue cited the fact of the rape and the widow's being thus "sullied" to uphold the levirate remarriage, even under multiple circumstances that violated Chinese marriage law and even though the widow vowed to stay chaste. Here, in 1318, the authorities rejected the levirate marriage, allowed the widow to return home, and severely punished the brother-in-law with a beating of 97 strokes of the heavy stick. The other brothers who had colluded also received some punishment. The only

---

57. Reading *cong* 琮 for *zong* 宗.

acknowledgment of Khubilai's levirate law in the ruling was the provision that if the widow remarried, she would have to marry the brother-in-law who had violated her.

Earlier, in 1309, Emperor Khaishan (Wuzong, r. 1307–1311) had approved a law that required a widow who wished to stay chaste to do so in the home of her in-laws (see case 18.26). This case of 1318 demonstrates the problems that could arise from such a break with traditional Chinese practice. By this time a new emperor was on the throne, Ayurbarwada (Renzong, r. 1311–1320), who was more sympathetic to Chinese Confucian traditions. Under his administration, the ruling here leans toward protecting the sanctity of widow chastity and sexual purity and in so doing returns some modicum of autonomy to the widow by allowing her to return to her father's household to stay chaste. The ruling did not, however, overturn the levirate, which remained legal for Chinese until 1330. The punishment for rape meted out here is much more lenient than sentences prescribed in the Chinese codes before and after the Yuan.[58] This likely reflects both the generally more lenient sentences found in Yuan law compared to formal law codes of other dynasties and the legal operation of the levirate for Chinese, which if enforced as in earlier cases would make the rape legal. The sentence of 97 strokes (lowered by the Central Secretariat from the 107 strokes prescribed by the Ministry of Punishments) for the rape of a widow by her brother-in-law became a precedent and is included in the statutes listed in the "Treatise on Punishments" found in the Yuan dynastic history.[59]

---

58. The Tang code prescribed two years' penal servitude for rape of a woman without a husband and life exile for rape of a relative within the fifth degree of mourning, such as a sister-in-law. See TLSY 26:493–494 (Art. 410, 411); Johnson 1997, 473–475. The Taihe code of the Jin prescribed strangulation for rape of a married woman and one degree less for an unmarried woman (YDZ 45:2b). The Ming code prescribed strangulation for rape of a woman without a husband and decapitation for rape of a relative within the fifth degree of mourning, whether or not the woman was married. See Jiang 2005, 214–216 (Art. 390, 392). It is not clear, however, how often these harsh sentences were actually carried out.

59. YS 104:2654; Ratchnevsky and Aubin 1972–1985, 4:56. For more on the significance of this case and the background of the Confucianization of the law during this period of the Yuan, see Birge 1995; Birge 2002, 269–271. This case is also discussed in Hung 1992, 312–313; Ratchnevsky 1968, 61n21.

18.55 *Tian Changyi forcibly marries his sister-in-law in a levirate union*[60]

In the fifth year of the *yanyou* period (1318), second month, sixth day, the Jiangzhe Branch Secretariat received a communiqué from the Central Secretariat, as follows:

A report from the Ministry of Punishments states:

We respectfully received your Secretarial communication, as follows:

A communiqué from the Liaoyang Branch Secretariat states:

A document from Daning Circuit reads:

According to a dispatch from Li Prefecture,[61] Tian A-Duan filed a written plaint, as follows:

In the tenth month of the second year of the *huangqing* period (1313), my husband Tian Qianyang died, leaving behind me, A-Duan, and four children. I have been observing mourning in the home of my father, Duan Cong. On the twenty-seventh day of the third month of the fourth year of the *yanyou* period (1317), my mother-in-law, A-Ma, led her son Tian Wu'er to our house and said to my father, Duan Cong: "I told Tian Changyi to marry your daughter. But you can't stand that guy because of the bad deeds he's done in the past, so you wouldn't let him marry her. Now, how about if I have Wu'er here marry your daughter instead?" My father, Duan Cong, replied, "My girl is observing mourning and keeping her chastity. And she has four children. How can she remarry?" My mother-in-law, A-Ma, summoned me, A-Duan, to go to her house to cook a meal to eat. In the afternoon, I wanted to go back home. But suddenly without warning, my brother-in-law Tian Changyi took me, A-Duan, and dragged me into the main room of the house where he lived. He closed the door and ordered his brother Tian Lu'er to watch it.

---

60. YDZ 18:24b–25a, pp. 704–705.

61. This prefecture corresponds to modern Harqin (Chinese, Kalaqin) Left Wing Mongolian Autonomous County, under the jurisdiction of Chaoyang City in Liaoning Province. To the north was the seat of Daning Circuit, modern Ningcheng, northeast of Beijing and Chengde, just inside the border of today's Inner Mongolia Autonomous Region. Both were in Liaoyang Branch Secretariat in the Yuan.

Then [his other brother] Tian Wu'er grabbed my two hands, while Tian Changyi took a cudgel and hit me twice on the left shoulder so I couldn't move. Then they tied my, A-Duan's, hair to the window lattice and stripped off my clothes. My brother-in-law Tian Wu'er held my hands down so that his older brother Tian Changyi could consummate the levirate marriage.

We obtained the confession of Tian Changyi. The offense he has committed greatly harms civilized traditions and destroys human moral relations. We rule provisionally that he be punished by 97 strokes of the heavy stick, one degree less than the sentence prescribed by the precedent on "Forcible Rape."[62] Nevertheless, we sincerely worry that we may be in error. Since this concerns a universal precedent, we think it would be appropriate to have the relevant Ministry render a decision.

This was sent to us at the Ministry of Punishments. We deliberated and conclude: Tian A-Duan's husband died, and she kept her chastity for six years.[63] Then her brother-in-law Tian Changyi tricked her into going to his house. First he ordered his younger brother Tian Lu'er to watch the door. Then he told Tian Wu'er to grab the woman's two hands, while he himself beat her with a cudgel. He tied her down by her hair and stripped off her clothes. Then he violently raped her. The offense he has committed corrupts principles, destroys moral customs, and greatly harms civilized traditions. We rule that Tian Changyi should be punished by 107 strokes of the heavy stick, by analogy to the precedent on "Forcible Rape of a Woman without a Husband." His younger brother Tian Wu'er and the others should be sentenced accordingly, in light of the circumstances. Tian A-Duan is allowed to return to her natal family and keep her chastity. If she seeks to remarry, she will be liable for prosecution according to the statutes, and the eligible

62. In 1265 the Ministry of Punishments prescribed a beating of 107 strokes of the heavy stick for "Forcible Rape of a Woman without a Husband." In 1273 they established that this applied to women and girls older than ten *sui*. The precedent was cited again in a ruling of 1312. See YDZ 45:2a–3b. Rulings in 1307 and 1315 by the Ministry of Punishments prescribed death for the rape of a girl under ten *sui* (YDZ 45:2b–3a, 3b–4a).

63. This is by Chinese counting from the year 1313 to 1318, counting both the first and last year during which she was widowed.

levir, herein convicted, is allowed to marry her in a levirate union.[64] If our report receives your approval, and you promulgate this ruling widely, it will serve to encourage the improvement of debauched customs. We present this report for your thorough consideration.

Report received. We the Metropolitan Secretariat deliberated and conclude: the crime to which Tian Changyi has confessed should be punished by 97 strokes of the heavy stick, one degree less than the sentence for "Forcible Rape of a Woman without a Husband." As for the rest, we approve the ruling of the Ministry. We send you [the Branch Secretariat] this communiqué for your careful consideration and request that you enforce it as above.

Section 8: No Levirate Marriage

18.56

This case, dated seventh month of 1270, shows that even at this early date, before Khubilai made the levirate legal for all peoples in 1271, Chinese in the north were beginning to practice the steppe custom of the levirate and were appealing to what they understood to be Mongol (or Jurchen) law to justify their actions. In this case, a man tried to force the widow of his father's younger brother to marry him with the blessing of his father, who claimed that such levirate unions were legal at the time. The widow sued. The Ministry of Revenue decided in her favor, citing the provision in the Taihe code of the Jin that such aunt-nephew marriages violated laws that prohibited marriages across generational lines and between relatives within certain degrees of mourning. Upon review, the Central Secretariat further cited the provision in the Taihe code, then in effect in north China, that people of different ethnic groups should follow their own laws and could not appeal to the law of another group. They moreover declared that the widow, though already married at this point, could return to her natal home to remain chaste or to remarry as she wished. With this ruling, the Central Secretariat was upholding traditional Chinese marriage law that granted widows considerable autonomy. As the cases presented earlier show, this was to change later in the Yuan. This case points to the difficulties of maintaining separate laws for different people in one geographic

---

64. Reading *xu* 續 for *shu* 贖.

area, and this may help explain Khubilai's decision to unify marriage law the following year. But note that Khubilai legalized the levirate only for unions with a man's sister-in-law or father's secondary wives (case 18.49), not between nephew and aunt, as in this case.[65]

At the time of this lawsuit, seventh month of 1270, the Secretariat for State Affairs was in existence as an additional level of bureaucracy between the Central Secretariat and the Six Ministries. But we find here that they defer to the Central Secretariat for a decision, merely passing the case along from the Ministry of Revenue without an opinion.

18.56 *A nephew may not marry his aunt in a levirate union*[66]

In the seventh year of the *zhiyuan* period (1270), seventh month, a document from the Ministry of Revenue of the Secretariat for State Affairs states:
A dispatch from Hejian Circuit[67] reads:

Sun Wage, the wife of the younger brother of Fu Bochuan, testified as follows:

My father- and mother-in-law and my husband Fu San all died at the same time, and I have been observing mourning in accordance with the law. Then, just before the fourth watch at night, on the thirtieth day of the tenth month of the sixth year of the *zhiyuan* period (1269), my nephew Fu Tianshou grabbed me, Wage, under my clothes and tried to rape me but didn't succeed. When it got light, I went to the home of my nephew Zhang Lü to live there. My husband's older brother Fu Da claims that according to the current regulations, a nephew should marry his aunt in a levirate union.

We humbly request that you pass down a clear decision.
This Ministry has investigated and found an earlier dispatch from Hejian Circuit, which reads:

Wang Hei'er paid betrothal gifts and married his aunt Xu Liunu in a levirate union.

---

65. The prohibition on aunt-nephew levirate for Chinese was reinforced in a ruling of 1304 (see TZTG 3:152 [Art. 58]).

66. YDZ 18:26a, p. 707.

67. In modern Hebei Province. During the Yuan, Hejian Circuit was within the Central Province, so its dispatch goes directly to the Ministry of Revenue.

The Old Regulations state, "For a nephew to marry his aunt constitutes marrying within the mourning circle and across generations, which is equivalent to an illegal sexual relationship."[68] According to the law, the marriage must be annulled. Wang Hei'er is from a Han Chinese lineage.[69] We submitted this report to the Secretariat for State Affairs, and respectfully received a superior communication in reply, as follows:

We sent this to the Central Secretariat and received their communiqué in reply, as follows:

We deliberated and determined that, the Old Regulations state: "When people of the same ethnic group offend against each other, they should be adjudicated according to their own customary laws."[70] Han Chinese and others may not appeal to the laws of other groups. We approve the ruling of the Ministry to be in effect until a decision is issued to serve as a universal precedent: the levirate marriage is not allowed. If the woman in question after the mourning period is over wishes to keep her chastity or wishes to return home and remarry, she is allowed to do so. Even though Xu Liunu is already married, the marriage should be annulled.

We [the Secretariat for State Affairs] order you to distribute this to all subordinate offices and correct the situation according to the law.

18.57

In a case very similar to case 18.56 just above and dated one month later in 1270, the Central Secretariat rejected the practice of levirate marriage in all forms by Han Chinese living in the north and ruled that the widow in question could return to her natal family to stay chaste or remarry as she wished. As in the earlier decision, they cited the Taihe code of the Jin, then in effect in north China, which stated that people of different ethnic groups should follow their own laws. The Central Secretariat reiterated that Chinese could not appeal to the law of other groups, though using the same wording as above, they acknowl-

68. Reading qi 期 for qi 欺. For the equivalent law in the Tang code, see TLSY 14: 264 (Art. 183); Johnson 1997, 162–163.

69. The term "Han'er ren" (漢兒人) can refer to residents of north China in general, including Jurchens, Tanguts, Uighurs, and so forth, but here it clearly means only Han Chinese in contrast to other peoples, such as Jurchens or Khitans, who practiced the levirate. This usage is the most common in these cases, thus my translation "Han Chinese." See discussion in Liu Xiao 2013.

70. The Central Secretariat is quoting the Taihe code of the Jin. The nearly identical line appears in the Tang code (TLSY 6:133 [Art. 48]; Johnson 1979, 252).

edged that their ruling was only provisional until a formal ruling was handed down on the matter, as happened the next year, when Khubilai legalized the levirate for all peoples.

The lawsuit being adjudicated was brought by the older brother of a widow who claimed that, after she had observed mourning for her husband, her father-in-law was preventing her from returning to her natal family, wanting her instead to marry a relative of her late husband. The Ministry of Revenue cited a similar case involving a military household from a different circuit, which also came before them, and sent the matter to its Law Office for an opinion. The Law Office cited the Taihe code to say that Han Chinese were not permitted to practice the levirate, implying both military and civilian households. As seen in the previous document, the Ministry of Revenue passed up the case to the Secretariat for State Affairs, who deferred to the Central Secretariat for a final decision.

18.57 *Han Chinese may not practice the levirate*[71]

In the seventh year of the *zhiyuan* period (1270), eighth month, a document from the Secretariat for State Affairs states:

A report from the Ministry of Revenue reads as follows:

A document from Nanjing Circuit states:

A dispatch from Xi Prefecture reads:[72]

Ding Song of a civilian household filed a plaint, stating:

In the first year of the *zhongtong* era (1260), together with my mother as marriage sponsor, I arranged the engagement of my younger sister Dingnu to marry Dai'er, the oldest son of Shi Xiaoliu of this prefecture. In the second year of the *zhiyuan* period (1265), my sister's husband died, and my sister Dingnu observed mourning for four years. [Afterwards,] her father-in-law would not let her return home but instead ordered his son Liang'er or his nephew Yaolü to marry her in a levirate union. Dingnu refused to comply.

[This Ministry has investigated and found] an earlier dispatch from Hejian Circuit, which reads:

A-Liu, the wife of Zhao Yi of a military household [filed a plaint, stating]:

---

71. YDZ 18:26a–b, pp. 707–708.

72. Xi Prefecture is modern Xi County in Henan Province. The seat of Nanjing Circuit is modern Kaifeng, about 320 kilometers (200 miles) to the north.

> My daughter Qing'er observed mourning for her deceased husband, Cui Jian'er. When her mourning was completed, her husband's older brother Cui Da ordered his younger brother Lüju to marry her in a levirate union, and he wouldn't let her return home.

We sent this to the Law Office, which investigated thoroughly and found that the Old Regulations state: "Han Chinese and Bohai people are not included among those who may inherit a wife from male relatives within the mourning circle."

We [the Secretariat for State Affairs] sent this to the Central Secretariat and received their communiqué in reply, as follows:

> We deliberated and determined that, the Old Regulations state: "When people of the same ethnic group offend against each other, they should be adjudicated according to their own customary laws." Han Chinese may not appeal to the laws of other groups. Until a decision is issued to serve as a universal precedent, levirate marriage is not allowed. If the woman in question after the mourning period is over wishes to keep her chastity or wishes to return home and remarry, she is allowed to do so. We send you this communiqué and request that you give it your careful consideration.

We the Secretariat Office have already sent a superior communication to the Ministry of Revenue to be distributed widely to the various circuits, who will post official notices to proclaim this publicly. In addition, we order you to enforce this as above.

18.58

We saw in the previous section that, after Khubilai's decree of 1271, twelfth month, legalizing the levirate for all peoples under Yuan jurisdiction, the central government initially enforced the levirate harshly, even when it contradicted long-established Chinese marriage law. This case is the first of several in this section that reveal that, by 1273 judges were beginning to allow all sorts of exceptions to forced levirate marriages, under various circumstances.

This decision, dated sixth month of 1273, addresses the issue of levirate marriage when the two parties lived in separate households. A man sued to force his fifty-year-old widowed sister-in-law into a levirate union, "in accordance with the regulations," but she refused and countersued, saying that she wished to stay chaste. Note that the woman was widowed in the fourth month of 1270, before Khubilai's decree. Her brother-in-law likely attempted to marry her after he learned of the decree.

The case was adjudicated at three different administrative levels, and all three rejected the levirate. The local court emphasized the advanced age of the widow, her wish to stay chaste, and the fact that she had an adult son. (Explicit reference to this court is missing, but the decision can be inferred from the wording of the document.) On review, the circuit authorities further emphasized that the widow and her brother-in-law resided in two separate taxpaying households, and they stated the age of the widow, "fifty," and that of her son, "thirty-six." They issued a provisional decision to reject the levirate marriage but appealed to the Ministry of Revenue for a precedent-setting decision. The Ministry of Revenue upheld the verdict of the circuit, again noting the age of the widow and the fact that she had an adult son to care for her, and explicitly emphasizing the issue of two taxable households.

The title attached to this case by the editors of the *Yuan dianzhang* highlights the issue of the two separate households—indeed, the problem of maintaining households on the tax registers was paramount during the Yuan. In this case, the levirate would have reduced the two taxable households to one. In later cases, widows in similar circumstances successfully resisted levirate marriages.[73] The issues of a widow's age and a vow of chastity reappear in other verdicts as criteria for rejecting levirate marriages and restoring some autonomy to once-married women.[74]

18.58 *One may not marry in a levirate union across two separate households*[75]

In the tenth year of the *zhiyuan* period (1273), sixth month, a document from the Ministry of Revenue of the Secretariat for State Affairs states:
We received your dispatch, as follows:
[A document from the prefecture states:][76]
Liu Gui filed a plaint, stating:

---

73. Conversely, in case 18.60 the levirate is upheld on the basis that the younger brother will take over the taxes and corvée of the household.
74. See, for instance, case 18.46, also dated 1273.
75. YDZ 18:26b, p. 708.
76. We can infer this missing sentence, or one like it, from the rest of the case.

> In the fourth month of the seventh year of *zhiyuan* (1270), my own older brother Liu Guoyü passed away from an illness. He left behind my sister-in-law, Madam Ma, and in accordance with the regulations, I married her in a levirate union.
>
> This widow is advanced in age and has a son who is already grown to adulthood. She is keeping her chastity and will not remarry.[77]

Document received. We the circuit authorities deliberated and conclude: at the time that Liu Gui filed the plaint about taking his sister-in-law in a levirate union, Liu Gui and his sister-in-law Liu A-Ma lived in two separate households each liable for taxes and corvée. A-Ma was fifty years old and wished to keep her chastity and not remarry. Moreover, she had a son, Liu Bing, who was thirty-six. We cannot approve the levirate marriage. Since this ruling will stand as a precedent for a long time, we humbly request that you consider this matter thoroughly.

This Ministry deliberated over the matter. It is the case that Liu A-Ma filed a written plaint stating that she wished to keep her chastity. Moreover, she already has an adult son to care for her. In addition, the two households are separately liable for taxes and corvée. We approve the decision [of the circuit authorities]. The levirate marriage is not allowed. Have this enforced.

18.59A

In Mongol customary law, the levirate operated only when a younger relative inherited an older relative's wife, and Khubilai explicitly legalized inheritance of an older brother's or father's widow. This meant that the wife was often older than the levir whom she was forced to marry. This custom ran contrary to Chinese law and practice, where men often married women much younger than themselves, or obtained young concubines. The idea that a man could inherit a wife only from an older relative was not well understood by the Chinese, as demonstrated in this and the case that follows. In this first case, a Chinese of relatively high office, the Director-General of Nanjing Circuit (modern Kaifeng) married the widow of his younger brother in a levirate union. The matter was discovered by the Regional Surveillance Office under the Censorate, which

---

77. In my reading of this case, this is the local office speaking. Note that the wording strongly suggests that they do not favor the levirate marriage.

passed it up to the Central Secretariat for a verdict. On the Central Secretariat's behalf, the Ministry of Punishments issued the harsh verdict of 87 strokes and dismissal from office. His sister-in-law was similarly punished with 57 strokes.[78] Noteworthy is the strong Neo-Confucian language condemning the levirate marriage, even though the prohibition on older-brother levirs was a thoroughly Mongol concept, quite alien to the Chinese.

18.59A *An older brother takes his younger brother's widow in a levirate union, and the marriage is annulled*[79]

In the twelfth year of the *zhiyuan* period (1275), fourth month, a document from the Central Secretariat states:

A report from the office of the Censorate reads:

> The Regional Surveillance Office of Shaanxi Sichuan Region[80] investigated and discovered that, Tian Dacheng, the former Director-General of Nanjing Circuit,[81] married his younger brother's wife, A-Zhao, in a levirate union. We have obtained his confession. We [the Censorate] humbly request that you render a clear decision.

We sent this to the Ministry of [Punishments],[82] which rendered a decision as follows:

> Tian Dacheng wantonly married his younger brother's wife in an illegal levirate union. Such action destroys human moral relations and truly damages civilized traditions. In light of the circumstances, we sentence him to

---

78. This case appears in the basic annals of Khubilai Khan in the Yuan dynastic history. See YS 8:161–162. There it is recorded that Khubilai ordered that the official be beaten 80 strokes and barred from office for three years. But the man had died by the time of the verdict, and his wife was publicly beaten 80 strokes instead. Two years later, in 1277, the punishments were standardized at a more severe level (see next case, 18.59B).

79. YDZ 18:26b, p. 708.

80. This region and its surveillance office existed between 1271 and 1279, with its administrative offices at Jingzhao 京兆 (modern Xian).

81. Modern Kaifeng, in Henan Province. Tian Dacheng was the son of a regional military commander in north China who early on joined the Mongol forces and thereby received various offices and awards, including the posthumous title of Prince (*wang* 王). See YS 151:3579–3580; *Yu'an ji*, 6:37–38; *Quan Yuanwen* 2:168–170.

82. The text reads "Ministry of War" (*bing bu*), but I accept the suggestion of Professor Chen Gaohua that this is probably a mistake for the Ministry of Punishments. The Ministry of War makes no sense here, and the Ministry of Punishments adjudicated the similar case in 1277 that is recorded as part of this same document in the *Yuan dianzhang* (case 18.59B just below).

a beating of 87 strokes and dismissal from office. We sentence A-Zhao to 57 strokes, and annul her marriage to Dacheng.

18.59B

The previous case of 1275 raised the issue of an older brother inheriting a younger brother's widow. In this case two years later, labeled merely "case continued" (*you* 又), the Ministry of Punishments issued a set of harsh penalties for all those involved in the marriage. These became standardized and are included in the "Treatise on Punishments" in the Yuan dynastic history.[83] The sentence for the levir himself, a beating of 107 strokes of the heavy stick, is two degrees harsher than that for the official Tian Dacheng above (case 18.59A). Tian may have received a lighter punishment as an office holder. In any event, rather than acknowledging Chinese sensibilities, which bent toward older men marrying younger women, the Mongol-Yuan regime doubled down on their condemnation of this form of the levirate. Even the wife, who may not have entered the marriage voluntarily, was punished with a potentially fatal beating of 97 strokes. It is noteworthy that the plaint here was filed by someone with the wife's surname of Duan, presumably a male relative of the wife, which further suggests that the wife and her family were trying to resist the levirate marriage in this case.

18.59B *Case continued*[84]

In the fourteenth year of the *zhiyuan* period (1277), eighth month,[85] the Ministry of Punishments of the Central Secretariat received a memo from the Ministry of Rites, as follows:

> A dispatch from Pingyang Circuit reads:
>
> > Duan Jixiu of a military household in Gaoping County[86] filed a plaint, stating: "Zhang Yi married his younger brother's wife in a levirate union." We obtained confessions from those involved.

---

83. YS 103:2643; Ratchnevsky and Aubin 1972–1985, 2:130–131 (Art. 401). As discussed in Chapter 2, "Treatise on Punishments" (*Xingfazhi*) was copied from the Yuan legal compilation *Jingshi dadian* (Liu Xiao 2004), which dates the standardization to no later than 1332.

84. YDZ 18:26b–27a, pp. 708–709.

85. This case is cited as a precedent in a decision dated 1321. This later record adds "twenty-first day" to the date. See YDZXJ *Hunyin*:4a.

86. In Pingyang Circuit (later renamed Jinning Circuit), just north of modern Luoyang. Since Pingyang Circuit in the Yuan was within the Central Province, their dispatch could go directly to one of the Six Ministries.

We submit this memo and request that you give it your careful consideration.

Memo received. We the Ministry of the Secretariat[87] deliberated and conclude: Even though Zhang Yi in his testimony has said that his mother, A-Wang, approved of his taking his younger brother's wife in a levirate union, in the end it is still unlawful. We sentence him to a beating of 107 strokes. A-Duan [his wife] is sentenced to 97 strokes, and the marriage is annulled. As for his mother, A-Wang, who sponsored the marriage, if we do not punish her as a warning, it will sully the rites and damage propriety. If she has not passed the age of exemption, we sentence her to 57 strokes.[88] The matchmaker, Li Kexiao, is sentenced to 37 strokes.

We submitted this report and respectfully received a Secretarial decree from the Central Hall, which reads:

We approve the report. Have this enforced.

18.60

The following is one of the most historically significant cases in the entire *Yuan dianzhang*. The Ministry of Revenue in this ruling established that a woman could evade a levirate union by remaining celibate and not remarrying at all. This set the stage for a series of legal privileges given to chaste widows in the following years, and it opened up new avenues for female agency that came to be very significant in later centuries. The case also demonstrates the complicated legal atmosphere of the Yuan dynasty. In this text, dated 1276, the Ministry of Revenue cites as a precedent its own earlier ruling made at the request of the Central Secretariat. In that earlier decision, the Ministry carefully reconciles two conflicting edicts issued by Khubilai. It cites Khubilai's regulations of 1271, second month, that said a widow who wished to stay chaste should be allowed to do so and could not be forced into a remarriage (case 18.2). It then cites Khubilai's edict of 1271, twelfth month, that said a man could force a sister-in-law or a father's secondary wife to marry him in a levirate union (case 18.49). In a

---

87. That is, the Ministry of Punishments.

88. In traditional Chinese law, people over seventy or under fifteen were allowed to escape corporal punishment with a payment of cash. The provision is found in the Tang code and the "Treatise on Punishments" in the Yuan dynastic history (TLSY [Art. 30] 4:80–81; Johnson 1979, 169; YS 102:2609).

ruling that represented a clever hybrid of Chinese traditional marriage law and Mongol customary law, the Ministry then ruled that if the woman in question (in this case, a Muslim woman who filed the suit) wished to remain chaste and not remarry, she could not be forced into a levirate marriage. The Ministry then issued a general ruling based on this precedent, stating that a woman who kept her chastity and remained unmarried could not be forced into a levirate union, but it added the proviso that if she remarried, both she and her new partner would be liable for punishment and she could be forced to marry the potential levir.[89]

In this document we catch a glimpse of two legally savvy females, who were both able to sway the court in their favor. In the earlier precedent quoted here, the Muslim woman Fatima filed a lawsuit against her brother-in-law and won her case to be allowed to remain unmarried to him. In the main ruling, the widow A-Zhuang bravely declares that if her determination to keep her chastity is "contrary to principle" (*feili* 非理) she will accept a punishment of 107 strokes, the most severe punishment applied to marriage cases in the Yuan. Her appeal to the concept of *li,* meaning both legal and moral principles, is especially noteworthy, and she, too, wins her case and is allowed to remain unmarried.

In the lawsuit of widow A-Zhuang, both sides show familiarity with details of the law and appeal to what they understand the law to contain. From this we can discern a general increase in legal knowledge on the part of commoners, undoubtedly helped by the growing number of legal advisors operating at this time. Another point of note is that the local ruling went against widow A-Zhuang on the basis that since her brother-in-law had inherited his deceased older brother's tax and corvée obligations, he should be allowed to inherit his widow. (In the case of Fatima, the Muslim widow, she declared that she would continue to be liable for the household taxes and corvée.) The Ministry of Revenue rejected this proposition and ruled in support of widow chastity. (The text does not make clear whether widow A-Zhuang would also continue to pay

---

89. This final ruling is also found in TZTG 3:148 (Art. 48) in a truncated version of this case. For further discussion of the historical significance of this decision, see Birge 2002, 245–247; Birge 1995, 125–126.

the household tax assessments, an issue of major concern to the Ministry of Revenue.)

18.60 *A woman who stays chaste may not be taken in a levirate union*[90]

In the thirteenth year of the *zhiyuan* period (1276), third month, a certified document from the Ministry of Revenue of the Central Secretariat states:
A dispatch from Zilai Circuit reads:[91]

[A dispatch from] Putai County states:[92]

Han Jin filed a plaint as follows:

My older brother Han Da passed away, leaving behind my sister-in-law A-Zhuang. I wish to marry her in a levirate union in accordance with the regulations.

We questioned A-Zhuang and obtained her deposition, as follows:

Han Da has died, and on my own volition I wish to stay chaste. I will not get remarried to anyone, and I will not become the wife of my husband's younger brother Han Jin. If there is anything about my actions that is contrary to principle, I am willing to submit to a beating of 107 strokes.

This county considered the matter carefully. Han Jin inherited his older brother Han Da's taxes and corvée obligations. According to legal principles he should be allowed to marry his sister-in-law in a levirate union.

We [Zilai Circuit] humbly request that you pass down a clear decision.[93]

This Ministry investigated and found a recent juridical communication that we respectfully received from the Central Secretariat, which [starting with an original report] states:

---

90. YDZ 18:27a, p. 709.

91. Zilai Circuit was located in north-central Shandong, just east of modern-day Jinan City, and was within the Central Province; thus, as seen in the text, it sends its dispatch directly to the Ministry of Revenue without passing through the Central Secretariat. In 1287 its name was changed to Banyang 般陽 Circuit.

92. Putai County was within Zilai Circuit, to the northeast of its administrative seat. We can infer from what follows that the document they are quoting is the content of a dispatch from the county.

93. This is Zilai Circuit passing the case up to the Ministry of Revenue for a decision.

[We received your dispatch, as follows:][94]

Fatima of Cao Prefecture[95] filed a plaint, stating:

> Hasan, the younger brother of my deceased husband, wants to take
> me, Fatima, in a levirate union. I will not remarry but wish to stay chaste.
> I will live with my son and be liable for taxes and corvée.

We submitted this report[96] and respectfully received a Secretarial decree
from the Central Hall, which reads:

> We sent this to the Ministry of Revenue, which investigated the matter
> and issued a ruling, as follows:
>
>> In the eighth year of the *zhiyuan* period (1271), second month, we
>> humbly received Imperial Regulations, one item of which reads in part
>> as follows:
>>
>>> If a woman whose husband has died wishes to stay chaste after the
>>> mourning period is over, she should be allowed to do so. Her father-
>>> and mother-in-law may not on their own initiative arrange a remar-
>>> riage for her.[97]
>>
>> Also, in the eighth year of the *zhiyuan* period (1271), twelfth month,
>> fourteenth day, we humbly received an Imperial Edict, which reads in
>> part as follows:
>>
>>> One should take a father's secondary wife or one's sister-in-law in
>>> levirate marriage.[98]
>>
>> We humbly respect the Imperial Edicts. This Ministry has deliberated
>> and concludes: it being the case that the woman in question wishes to stay
>> chaste and not remarry, we rule that she be allowed to stay chaste. We
>> submitted this report and respectfully received a Secretarial decree from
>> the Central Hall, stating:
>>
>>> We approve the ruling.

94. This line is inferred by what follows. Moreover, in order for the following text to make
sense, this dispatch must be going to a ministry other than the Ministry of Revenue.

95. Cao Prefecture was in southwest Shandong, northeast of modern-day Kaifeng. It was
administered directly by the Central Secretariat, which explains why the case went directly to
one of the Six Ministries without going to any circuit in between. From the names Fatima and
Hasan, we can infer that the protagonists in this case are Muslim.

96. Reading *cheng* 呈 for *ci* 此.

97. This is the regulation found in Khubilai's edict of 1271, second month (see case 18.2,
Item 6), with one phrase cut out. The complete version is also found in case 18.26.

98. This is the seminal case found in 18.49.

Now, regarding the dispatch currently before us, this Ministry has further deliberated over the matter and has decided that, from now on, if a woman is staying chaste in this way, a potential levir may not harass or disturb her. She is to be allowed to stay chaste. Nevertheless, if she seeks to remarry, both she and her new partner will be liable for punishment and the eligible levir will be allowed to marry her. Have this promulgated widely in the hope that it will eliminate lawsuits. We submitted this report and respectfully received a Secretarial decree from the Central Hall, stating:

We approve the report. Have it enforced.

18.61

This case follows the trend in the late 1270s for the Yuan government to back away from the harsh imposition of the levirate seen in the early 1270s after Khubilai's decree, and instead to allow various exceptions to the levirate. In this case, a father brings his widowed daughter back home, but her father-in-law sues for her to marry her young brother-in-law, whom she helped raise. In its verdict, dated 1277, the Ministry of Revenue sides with the widow and her father against her father-in-law and rejects a levirate union. The Ministry cites three reasons for its ruling: (1) the widow raised her young brother-in-law from when he was young, (2) the levir is a whole generation younger than his widowed sister-in-law, and (3) her father has no other children to care for him and thus needs his daughter at home. It is noteworthy that a daughter is allowed to return to her natal family to be the caregiver of an aging parent. This represents the older Chinese practice of a widow returning to her natal family in contradiction to Neo-Confucian ideas of a wife's primary duty being to live with and care for her in-laws even after being widowed. At the same time, the repeated references to the mourning period show a resurgence of Confucian-oriented concerns over keeping the mourning period and not remarrying during it, even in a levirate union. Also noteworthy is the Jurchen name of the plaintiff (Wanyan Sizheng), who is identified as a Confucian. Jurchens, like Mongols, traditionally practiced the levirate, so the rejection of the levirate here signals that the Ministry of Revenue is applying unified laws across all ethnic groups, a practice ushered in by Khubilai's decree of 1271. The text includes some corruptions, but the meaning is clear.

18.61 *A woman who raised her brother-in-law may not be taken by him in levirate marriage*[99]

In the fourteenth year of the *zhiyuan* period (1277), first month, ninth day, Shuntian Circuit[100] respectfully received a certified document from the Ministry of Revenue of the Secretariat for State Affairs,[101] as follows:

[We received your dispatch, which reads:][102]

> [A document from] the Municipal Affairs Office states:
>
>> Wanyan Sizheng, a lay Confucian,[103] filed a plaint, stating:
>>
>>> My in-law Xu Wang called back my son's widow, Chouchou, to live in his home, and he won't let her come back. But since the mourning period is over, he should let my younger son, Zouyu, marry her in a levirate union.
>>
>> Document received. We obtained the testimony of all those involved. We humbly request that you consider this matter.

We the Ministry of the Secretariat deliberated over the matter. It is the case that A-Xu, widow of the plaintiff's deceased son, has already completed the mourning period for her husband. Also, she raised her husband's younger brother, Zouyu, from when he was little. Moreover, the difference in age between them is a whole generation, and she is not willing to marry him in a levirate union. In addition, Xu Wang is old and alone and has no other son or daughter to care for him. We cannot approve the levirate marriage. We order that you investigate this matter further. If there is no discrepancy, then allow Xu Chou[chou] to take care of her father, Xu Wang, in his home, in accordance with the law. Be sure there is no error.

---

99. YDZ 18:27a–b, pp. 709–710.

100. This is modern Baoding in Hebei Province, part of the Central Province during the Yuan. There is a mistake here, for the name of this circuit changed from Shuntian to Baoding in 1275, two years before this decision. Possibly the case was sent up by Shuntian Circuit two years earlier, before the name change, and the response came back with the old name attached.

101. This should read "Central Secretariat," since the Secretariat for State Affairs did not exist at this time. Furthermore, the space that is supposed to precede the name of this office in the text is placed in the wrong position, before "respectfully received."

102. This line is inferred by what follows.

103. This term suggests he is registered in an officially designated Confucian household, one of the many hereditary occupational categories defined by the Yuan government. The word "lay" is odd, but might indicate merely that he is not a member of any clergy or holds no formal position, say in a Confucian school.

18.62

In this ruling, dated 1281, the Ministry of Rites follows up on the decision of the Ministry of Revenue of 1277 in the previous case (18.61) and issues a general ruling to serve as a precedent outlawing levirate marriages when the age difference between the widow and the levir was too great. The Ministry of Rites cites an earlier decision of its own, rendered in 1279, to make its case. The Ministry did not provide a definite cutoff point, but in one of these examples the widow was eighteen and the levir nine, and in the other the widow was twenty-eight and the levir twelve. In all these cases, the Ministry of Rites allowed the widows to remarry an outsider, upholding the autonomy of widows found in traditional Chinese law before the Yuan.

18.62 *When the age difference between a widow and her brother-in-law is too great, there is no levirate marriage*[104]

In the eighteenth year of the *zhiyuan* period (1281), fourth month, a document from the Ministry of Rites of the Central Secretariat states:
We received your dispatch, as follows:[105]

> A dispatch from Quzhou County reads: "Xu A-Zhao of a military household and Bu Da are disputing a marriage."

Dispatch received. [This Ministry] has investigated and found an earlier dispatch from Pingyang Circuit, which reads:[106]

> Lu Xian of a military household filed a plaint, stating:
>
>> I hired a go-between and paid betrothal gifts to conclude the engagement of Sheng'er, the daughter of Cui Hui, to marry my son Lu Zhongxing. Zhongxing passed away from an illness, and I want to have my younger son

---

104. YDZ 18:27b, p. 710.

105. This dispatch is coming from Guangping Circuit, in modern Hebei Province, about 120 kilometers (75 miles) north of Kaifeng. In the Yuan it was part of Central Province and included Quzhou County, mentioned in the next line, whose dispatch it is passing along to the Ministry of Rites. Quzhou County was located just northeast of the circuit capital and has the same name today.

106. This earlier case is found in TZTG 3:150 (Art. 54), from which we know that it dates to 1279, twelfth month. The TZTG record gives the basis of the ruling as the fact that the wife was only engaged when the husband died, not that the age difference between her and the levir was too great. Pingyang Circuit was just west of Guangping, also in Central Province.

Si'er marry Sheng'er in a levirate union. But my in-law Cui Hui has taken
Sheng'er and betrothed her to marry Li Sun'er.

We the Ministry of the Secretariat deliberated and conclude: Cui Sheng'er is
eighteen years old; Lu Si'er is only nine years old. Their difference in age is too
great. We cannot allow the levirate marriage. We rule that the betrothal gifts
and money that Lu Xian originally paid should be retrieved from Cui Hui and
returned. Lu Xian should wait until Lu Si'er has grown to adulthood and then
obtain another wife for him. Cui Sheng'er is allowed to get remarried and become the wife of Li Sun'er, to whom she is already engaged. This seems appropriate. We submitted this report and respectfully received a Secretarial decree
from the Central Hall, stating: "We sent this to the Ministry of Rites.[107] We
approve the report. Have it enforced." Secretarial decree respectfully received.
We already sent this down and notified the circuit in question.

Now, regarding the matter in the dispatch that is currently before us, we the
Ministry of the Secretariat deliberated over the matter. Bu Chunlian'er is twenty-
eight years old. Her younger brother-in-law Xu Guanglü is twelve years old.
Their difference in age is too great. In addition, Bu Chun[lian]'er has already
remarried and become the wife of Liu Si. We order that you adjudicate this according to the above precedent.

18.63

The ruling recorded in this case, dated 1289, outlaws levirate marriage where
the levir is the husband's cousin of a different surname. The matter begins with
a lawsuit by a widow of some means who sues in the circuit court to prevent her
husband's cousin from forcing her into a levirate union and to recover her property, seized by her late husband's older brother. The circuit sides with her but
passes the case up for review. The Ministry of Rites rules in favor of the widow,
and the Central Secretariat concurs, with the implication that the ruling will
stand as a precedent in future cases.

The widow wins her case to get back the property that originally belonged
to her husband (including slaves and bondservants), and she is allowed to stay
chaste and reside with her adult son, to whom, significantly, the property is returned. She is ordered to continue to provide subsidies for the military service

107. This phrase would seem to be superfluous, since the case has already been adjudicated
by the Ministry of Rites.

of her husband's older brother, which her household had been doing previously. This identifies hers as an "auxiliary military household," which helped equip the actual soldier from a different household. Her role as head of a functioning military household no doubt weighed in her favor, and the Central Secretariat expresses its concern for maintaining the military subsidy. But the wording of the case suggests that the ruling prohibiting cousin levirate was a general one, applying to all households, military and civilian, and indeed this ruling is included in the "Treatise on Punishments" in the Yuan dynastic history, applied to everyone.[108]

18.63 *The son of the husband's aunt and uncle may not marry the widow in a levirate union*[109]

In the twenty-sixth year of the *zhiyuan* period (1289), sixth month, twenty-seventh day, the Ministry of Rites of the Central Secretariat respectfully received a juridical communication from the Central Secretariat, as follows:
The [original] report from your Ministry states:
A dispatch from Pingluan Circuit reads:
Xie A-Song of a military household filed a plaint, stating:
My husband, Xie Hei'er, passed away, and Fu Xing, the son of his aunt and uncle, took me, A-Song, in a levirate marriage. Moreover, his older brother Xie Chang seized my late husband's original share of property.
This is a case of one household with two surnames and cousins of different surnames getting married. But there has not been a ruling in such a case to use as a precedent.
This Ministry deliberated and concludes: even though Xie Chang, Xie Hei'er, and Fu Xing are registered as one household, heretofore they resided separately. After Xie Hei'er died, Xie A-Song resided with her son Sengjia'er and helped subsidize the military service of her husband's older brother [Xie Chang]. Moreover Fu Xing is Xie Hei'er's first cousin of a different surname. We do not find any regulation allowing the son of a husband's aunt and uncle, a cousin of a different surname, to marry the widow in a levirate union. Even if Fu Xing took A-Song in levirate marriage by mutual agreement, in the end it would still be unlawful. We rule that the

108. YS 102:2644.
109. YDZ 18:27b–28a, pp. 710–711.

marriage be annulled. Furthermore, the property that Xie Chang seized from his younger brother Hei'er should be returned to the possession of Sengjia'er. We order that Xie A-Song reside with her son and subsidize Xie Chang's military service.

We of the Central Hall have deliberated and conclude: heretofore there has been no regulation allowing the son of the husband's aunt and uncle, a cousin of a different surname, to marry the widow in a levirate union. We order the circuit in question to adjudicate the case of Xie Chang, Fu Xing, and the others and annul the marriage. Moreover, the personnel and property that Xie Chang seized from Xie Hei'er must be returned to the possession of Xie Hei'er's son Sengjia'er. He is to reside with A-Song, who will stay chaste and subsidize the military service. Have this sent to the Ministry to be enforced as above.

18.64

This case illustrates efforts on the part of a local office of the Censorate to address problems of famine, wife-selling, and the breakup of families in the Jiangnan region. It also reveals the divided responsibilities of different branches of the Yuan government and the limits of authority of the feared Censorate. It confirms the problems of famine and impoverishment found in parts of the lower Yangzi area during the Yuan, and reveals that the levirate was practiced in the south as well as the north.

The document does not originate from a lawsuit but rather from the Regional Investigation Office of Zhedong, located in Wuzhou Circuit (modern Jinhua in Zhejiang Province), which is seeking a ruling from above to protect women whose husbands, driven by hunger and poverty, have sold them into a second marriage. It wants to prohibit a younger brother of the first husband from suing for a levirate union with his former sister-in-law after the first husband has died and the former sister-in-law has borne children to her second husband.

The Regional Investigation Office sends its request to the Jiangnan Branch Censorate, which forwards it to the main Censorate in the capital, Dadu, which, significantly, cannot issue such a ruling itself. Instead it must pass the request to the Central Secretariat, which sends it to the Ministry of Rites, which in turn issues the general prohibition as requested. The Ministry of Rites, like the local Regional Investigation Office, shows surprising compassion for the plight

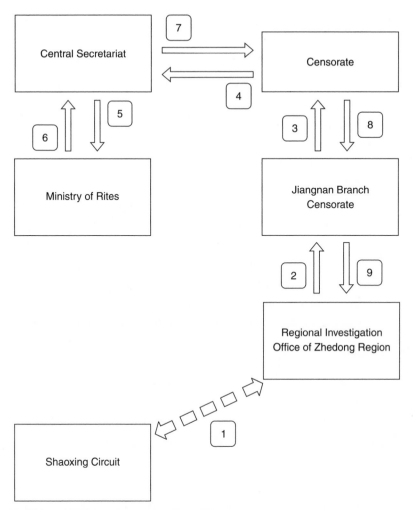

Chart 6. Case 18.64, document flow demonstrating Censorate's appeal to the executive administration for a ruling.

of husbands selling their wives, in seeming contradiction to their other rulings found in the *Yuan dianzhang* strictly outlawing this practice

Chart 6 illustrates how the request comes up through the Censorate administration, crosses over to the executive branch, then goes back over to the Censorate branch and down to the locale.

18.64 *When the older brother has died and his wife has remarried, the younger brother-in-law may not take the wife in a levirate union*[110]

In the second year of the *yanyou* period (1315), fifth month, a superior communication from the Branch Censorate[111] reads:

We received a communiqué from the main Censorate, as follows:

We received your communiqué, which reads:[112]

A dispatch from the Regional Investigation Office of Zhedong Region states:[113]

In Shaoxing Circuit[114] and other places, because of famine conditions, people are selling their wives. There are cases where, after the first husband has already died and the wife has remarried, and after children are born to the new couple, the younger brother of the first husband tries to seize upon the law and take back the wife in a levirate union. This is not the same as the well-established precedent of the younger brother marrying his sister-in-law in a levirate union. We ought to approve what has been suggested and prohibit this practice.

It would be appropriate to have the relevant Ministry render a decision.[115]

We send you this communiqué and request that you give it your thorough consideration.

Communiqué received. We submitted a report to the Central Secretariat and respectfully received a superior communication, which reads in part as follows:

---

110. YDZ 18:28a, p. 711. The table of contents of the *Yuan dianzhang* gives this case the slightly more descriptive title "The younger brother of a woman's previous husband may not take her in a levirate union." See YDZ *mulu*:15a.

111. We see from what follows that this is the Jiangnan Branch Censorate (full name, Branch Censorate for the Several Jiangnan Regions), whose administrative headquarters was in Jiankang, modern Nanjing. See Farquhar 1990, 242–243.

112. This is the original communiqué from the Jiangnan Branch Censorate to the main Censorate, which the main Censorate is quoting in its response.

113. The Zhedong Region was one of ten regions within the Jiangnan Branch Censorate. Its administrative seat was in Wuzhou Circuit, modern Jinhua City in Zhejiang Province.

114. Modern Shaoxing City, southeast of Hangzhou. Shaoxing was the circuit neighboring Wuzhou to the northeast, where the Regional Investigation Office was located.

115. This is the branch censorate talking to the main Censorate. Note that the Censorate cannot itself issue a legal decision. It must seek such a ruling from one of the Six Ministries via the Central Secretariat, as happens here.

We sent this to the Ministry of Rites, which deliberated and concluded:

In every locale there are impoverished commoners who encounter famine conditions such that the husband and wife can no longer protect each other, and the husband sells the wife into another marriage. The circumstances leave no alternative. Then when the first husband has already died, and the wife has already borne children by her second husband, the first husband's younger brother sues to marry the wife in a levirate union, appealing to the regulation allowing a younger brother to take his sister-in-law in levirate marriage. We rule that these practices should all be prohibited. If you deign to approve this report, we recommend that it be distributed widely to the subordinate offices. This would be appropriate. We submit this report for your thorough consideration.

Report received. We the Metropolitan Secretariat order you to enforce this as above.

CHAPTER EIGHT

Sections 9–12

Secondary Wives; Marriage between Slaves and Commoners; Marriage of Entertainers; Marriage during the Mourning Period

Section 9: Secondary Wives

18.65

This case, dated 1273, first month, again addresses conflicts between Mongol customary law and pre-Yuan Chinese codified law, in this instance the issue of a man having two principal wives. Having multiple principal wives was widely practiced among Mongols but was prohibited by traditional Chinese law, which allowed for only one principal wife but any number of concubines. Khubilai addressed this issue in his edict of 1271, second month (case 18.2), in which he kept Mongol and Chinese law separate by prohibiting multiple wives but exempting Mongols from the prohibition. The document here suggests that Chinese men in the north were adopting Mongol customs and marrying more than one principal wife. We learn from the *Tongzhi tiaoge,* which also records this decision, that the Regional Surveillance Office of Shaanxi Region sent up a dispatch to the main Censorate stating that men who had reached the age of forty with no children were obtaining second wives to produce heirs. They recommended that such marriages not be annulled but that, if the second wife was willing, her status be changed to that of a concubine (thus complying with Chinese law and Khubilai's 1271 edict).[1] We can surmise that the main Censorate sent this request to the Central Secretariat, which passed it along to the Min-

---

1. TZTG 4:163 (Art. 69). On the servile status of concubines found in Song evidence, see Ebrey 1986. On the growing presence of concubines in elite discourses in the Song and Yuan, and the complicated issue of their status, see Bossler 2013.

istry of Revenue. The Ministry agreed with the original suggestion, and herein issued a general ruling, which the Central Secretariat approved and passed back to the main Censorate, as seen in this document.

Of interest is the start time for the regulation. The Ministry declares that second marriages contracted before the twenty-fifth day of the first month of 1271 may stand. Only for marriages after that time does the second wife have to be demoted to concubine status. This same start date is given for Item 4 in Khubilai's decree of 1271, second month (case 18.2), the prohibition on same-surname marriage. No definitive law operated in north China during the early Yuan, and the Ministry evidently felt it could not punish infractions committed before the law was fixed by Khubilai's decree of 1271, second month.[2] This ruling was clearly meant to settle the matter of multiple wives, but just a few months later, in 1273, the Ministry of Revenue partially reversed itself (case 18.54) when it allowed a levir to take as wives both his sister-in-law and original fiancée, giving precedence to Khubilai's edict of 1271, twelfth month, legalizing the levirate for all peoples (case 18.49). The Ministry of Rites, however, subsequently relaxed this harsh enforcement of levirate law by the Ministry of Revenue, when in three rulings (two dated 1279 and one, 1300) it prohibited levirate marriages when the levir was already married or engaged, for both patrilocal and uxorilocal marriages.[3]

Also of note is that the punishment for marrying twice recorded in this document is merely that the marriage be annulled. The Tang and Song codes prescribed one year of penal servitude for having more than one principal wife, and the Ming code meted out a beating of 90 strokes.[4] The Yuan administration by 1332 had specified the punishment as a beating of 47 strokes in addition to the marriage being annulled,[5] still a relatively light sentence com-

2. On this issue and the problem of adjudication in the absence of a law code, see Birge 2010.

3. See TZTG 3:149 (Art. 50); TZTG 3:149–150 (Art. 53); TZTG 3:150 (Art. 55).

4. TLSY 13:255 (Art. 177); Johnson 1997, 154–155; SXT 13:214; Jiang 2005, 84 (Art. 109). The Tang and Ming codes forbid making a wife into a concubine. Interestingly, the Ming code also forbids a man from taking a concubine unless he is forty years of age or older and has no sons, the same circumstance cited by the Shaanxi Regional Surveillance Office that was the background for this ruling in the Yuan.

5. YS 102:2643. It is possible that a beating was already prescribed by the Ministry of Punishments in 1273 at the time of this *Yuan dianzhang* case but was just not included in this record in the *Yuan dianzhang*.

pared to that prescribed by legal codes of Chinese dynasties before and after the Yuan.

18.65 *Regulation that one who has a wife already may marry a concubine*[6]

In the tenth year of the *zhiyuan* period (1273),[7] the main Censorate respectfully received a superior communication from the Central Secretariat, as follows:

[A report] from the Ministry of Revenue reads:

> We have rendered a decision, as follows: When one who has a wife already marries another wife, if the second marriage took place before the eighth year of the *zhiyuan* period (1271), first month, twenty-fifth day, it is allowed to stand. If the second marriage took place after that date, as long as the second wife is truly willing, it is permitted to change her status to that of a concubine. From now on, according to the Regulations previously issued, one who has a wife already may not seek to marry a second principal wife. Moreover, if one seeks to marry a concubine, one must establish a clear marriage contract to marry her.

We the Metropolitan Secretariat approve the report. We order you to enforce it as above.

18.66

This short document, dated 1276, provides an intriguing follow-up to 18.65 just above. Once again, the Central Secretariat is issuing a ruling in response to a case from the main Censorate regarding second wives. But this time, three years later, they seem to allow for a second wife who is not actually a concubine. We can surmise that the local office of the Censorate has annulled the second marriage in this case and confiscated the betrothal gifts paid. But the Central Secretariat reverses this decision and allows the second marriage to stand. It labels the new wife a "secondary wife" (*ci qi* 次妻) and proclaims that this is not the same as a "principal wife" (*zheng qi* 正妻). This ruling suggests that at this time the Central Secretariat recognized three types of wives: principal, secondary, and concubine. It also fits with Mongol customary law, where a man could have multiple "wives,"

---

6. YDZ 18:29a, p. 713.
7. From the TZTG (4:163 [Art.69]), we know this ruling was in the first month.

but the first wife was of higher status in the household than subsequent wives, though these latter were not of servile status as a Chinese concubine would be. In this light, we can interpret this ruling as an attempt by the Central Secretariat to reconcile steppe practices with Chinese custom to generate a body of unified law that could be applied to all peoples in the realm.

18.66 *One who has a wife already may marry a secondary wife*[8]

In the thirteenth year of the *zhiyuan* period (1276), the main Censorate submitted a report to the Central Secretariat, stating:

> Meng Kui had a wife already when he additionally married Wang Xiu'er to be his secondary wife.

In response [the main Censorate] respectfully received a superior communication, as follows:

> We deliberated and conclude that, Meng Kui has already married Wang Xiu'er to be his secondary wife. She is not his principal wife. The marriage should stand, and the betrothal gifts that were previously confiscated should be returned.

Section 10: Marriage between Slaves and Commoners

18.67

The following four cases address the intriguing issue of intermarriage between slaves and free commoners, and they demonstrate the sometimes contradictory efforts by the Yuan state to prevent people from crossing status boundaries. In the first case, dated 1269, the Ministry of Revenue ostensibly outlaws marriage between free commoners and slaves. But within the same verdict the Ministry contradicts itself by proclaiming that if the two parties are "truly willing," then the marriage can go forward, provided, as in all legally sanctioned marriages, that the parties establish a proper marriage contract. The Ministry of Revenue, moreover, allows marriages contracted previous to their ruling to stand, reflecting the lack of any officially sanctioned code in effect at this time.[9] Slaves

---

8. YDZ 18:29a, p. 713.
9. But note the very next case (18.68) where the Ministry in 1271 cites the Jin code ("Old Regulations") outlawing slave-commoner marriages to annul such a marriage that took place in 1268.

and commoners had evidently been intermarrying up to this time in the absence of any formal legal prohibition, and even this attempt to outlaw the practice reveals a distinctly ambivalent attitude and lack of conviction. The Ministry does not specify any punishment other than annulling the marriage. By contrast, the Tang and Ming codes outlawed any intermarriage between free commoners and people of servile status and imposed harsh punishments.

This ruling does not clarify the status of the spouses after the marriage or that of their children. But these questions are addressed in subsequent rulings that follow. In this case of 1269, the plaintiff claims that the slave husband misrepresented his status, and this complaint is often repeated.

These cases reflect the proliferation of slavery during the Yuan dynasty and the complicated status relations that this generated. Slaves existed in much greater numbers under the Mongols than in the preceding Song dynasty, partly because of the large number of war captives who were sold into slavery. A special market for selling humans existed in the capital, Dadu. At the same time, the highly developed economy of Song and Jin China and fluid social relations made fixed status boundaries hard to maintain. These cases provide a glimpse into this contentious and contradictory world.

18.67 *Male and female slaves may not marry free commoners*[10]

In the sixth year of the *zhiyuan* period (1269), second month, a document from the Ministry of Revenue of the Central Secretariat states:

A dispatch from En Prefecture[11] reads in part as follows:

Li Shen filed a written plaint, stating:

In the third year of the *zhongtong* era (1262), Yang Niu'er, the slave of Director-General Zhai, pretended to be a free commoner and married my daughter Mainu.[12]

We apprehended the go-between, the sponsor, and all those involved, and obtained testimony from each of them. This indicated that the plaintiff in

---

10. YDZ 18:30a, p. 715.

11. In the western part of Shandong Province, just northwest of the modern city of Jinan. En Prefecture was within the Central Province of the Yuan, so its dispatch goes directly to the Ministry of Revenue.

12. The meaning of these names, like many in the Yuan, warrants noting. The male slave's name, Niu'er, means "Ox" (with the "er" ending used commonly in animal names), and the free commoner bride's name, Mainu, means "Buy a Slave" or "Purchased Slave."

fact knew that Yang Niu'er was a slave, yet he accepted betrothal gifts and completed the engagement. By now, seven years have passed. We have obtained the written testimony of the plaintiff, but there has been no previous ruling in a case like this to use as a precedent. We submit this dispatch and humbly request that you pass down a clear decision.

Dispatch received. We the Ministry of the Secretariat deliberated together and determine: with regard to male and female slaves getting married to free commoners, those who were married or engaged in a previous year or whose cases were already adjudicated by the authorities may abide by these earlier rulings.[13] They are not included in this decision, and they may remain married as before.[14] For all others, we rule that, after the first day of the first month of the sixth year of the *zhiyuan* period (1269), male and female slaves may not marry free commoners or invite them in as uxorilocal husbands. If there are those who are truly willing, and they each establish a written marriage contract, they are permitted to marry. We submitted this report and respectfully received a Secretarial decree from the Central Hall, stating:

Send this to the Ministry of Revenue. We approve the decision. Have it enforced.

18.68

This document of 1271, seventh month, addresses more directly the issue of escaped slaves pretending to be free commoners in order to get married. Unlike case 18.67, this time the Ministry of Revenue accepts that fraud was committed and that the commoner entered the marriage unknowingly. (Note the stronger language of the document to emphasize this point.) They stipulate that the marriage be annulled in such cases, and that the children go with the mother and become free commoners.

The document starts with the case of an escaped male slave from the area of the capital (modern Beijing), with the Jurchen name Wangna Boshu, who married a commoner bride in 1268. In responding to the circuit's request for a verdict, the Ministry cites an earlier, undated, decision sent down to the same circuit, where an escaped male slave named Geng Ji became the invited-in husband of a free commoner woman. In this earlier case, the bride's mother filed

---

13. Reading *bing* 并 for *jing* 井.
14. Reading *zhu* 住 for *wang* 往.

the plaint, and she wins her suit. The Ministry annuls the marriage and orders the slave to return the betrothal gifts that he had received.[15] The Ministry cites the Jin code ("Old Regulations") as the basis for their decision, but they enforce it much more leniently by merely annulling the marriage rather than punishing the slave with two years' penal servitude, as in the Jin code, or even any beating.[16] Returning to the case of the Jurchen slave Wangna Boshu, the Ministry applies its precedent and again annuls the marriage. This time the slave-husband paid the betrothal gifts, and they are not returned, but he is able to recover the funds he paid to the go-betweens who arranged the fraudulent marriage. The Ministry also orders that the children born to the couple go with the mother and become free commoners. The Ministry cites an amnesty's having occurred to avoid further punishment of the parties.

This marriage took place in 1268, before the Ministry of Revenue's general prohibition of slave-commoner marriages took effect, in 1269, but presumably it is ruled illegal because of the slave's fraudulently representing himself as a commoner. Another interesting twist in the case is that the bride is a widow, and her deceased first husband's younger brother extorts "betrothal gift" money from the slave by threatening to file a lawsuit forcing the widow to marry him in a levirate union. It is noteworthy that even low-level commoners seem to have had enough knowledge of the law and access to the courts to use the levirate law for extortion and blackmail in this way.

18.68 *An escaped slave fraudulently pretends to be a free commoner in order to get married*[17]

In the eighth year of the *zhiyuan* period (1271), seventh month, a document from the Ministry of Revenue of the Secretariat for State Affairs states:
A dispatch that we received from Zhongdu Circuit[18] reads:

---

15. Note that since this is an uxorilocal marriage, the betrothal gifts are paid by the bride's side to the groom.

16. It is possible that the slave received some additional punishment such as a beating that is not recorded here.

17. YDZ 18:30a–b, pp. 715–716. Reading *wang* 妄 for *qie* 妾.

18. This was the circuit that included the capital Dadu (modern Beijing). In 1273 its name was changed to Dadu Circuit.

We interrogated the escaped slave Wangna Danshu and obtained his confession to a crime, as follows:

> In the year of *renzi* (1252) I was registered as a slave in the household of my master Wangli Boshu.[19] In the second year of the *zhiyuan* period (1265), I turned against my master and escaped. In the fifth year of the *zhiyuan* period (1268), I got married to Yang Fen'er, the younger sister of the deceased commoner Yang Wei, of Xianghe County.[20]

The testimony of Yang Fen'er did not differ from this. Depositions from the go-between Liu Bin and from A-Li, the wife of Yang Wei, the deceased sponsor of the marriage, also agreed with this. But in addition, they testified that Zhang Yuan, the younger brother of Yang Fen'er's deceased first husband Zhang Ze, filed a lawsuit accusing Yang Wei of illegally taking his [Zhang Yuan's] sister-in-law and arranging a remarriage to someone else without consulting him, and therefore they paid Zhang Yuan goods worth two ingots of paper money as betrothal gifts to buy out the levirate marriage.[21] We obtained the confession of Zhang Yuan, stating, "Seeing that they did indeed arrange a proper marriage with a go-between after the mourning period was over, I should not have exacted money from them."

> We will separately adjudicate the crime of the slave Wangna Danshu escaping his master. But regarding the matter of slaves getting married to free commoners and the matter of Zhang Yuan having received money [to buy out the levirate union], we humbly request that you pass down a clear decision.

In regard to this matter, we investigated and found the case of Zhai A-Zhang of this same circuit, who filed a written plaint, stating:

---

19. In this year, 1252, a general registration of the population was carried out.

20. Reading *he* 河 for *a* 阿. This county was directly administered by Zhongdu Circuit at this time. It has the same name today and is about 40 kilometers (25 miles) southeast of modern Beijing.

21. In other words, Yang Fen'er is a widow, and the younger brother of her deceased husband is trying to use his right to a levirate union to extort "betrothal gift" money from the go-betweens. Later in the document the circuit asks the Ministry of Revenue if such action can be legal.

Geng Ji, the escaped slave of Yeli Buhua,[22] fraudulently pretended [to be a free commoner] and became the permanent invited-in husband of my daughter Liunu.

According to the Old Regulations:[23]

When one fraudulently pretends that a male or female slave is a free commoner and arranges for him or her to become the husband or wife of a free commoner, the punishment is two years of penal servitude. When the male or female slave arranges the marriage him- or herself, the punishment is the same. Each party returns to his or her correct status.

Geng Ji is indeed the escaped slave of Yeli Buhua, so according to the Old Regulations his marriage to Zhai Liunu should be annulled. This is a case of the male side committing fraud, so the betrothal gifts that Zhai A-Zhang originally paid should be returned to her possession. We already sent this down to the circuit in question to notify them of this decision.

Now, with regard to the dispatch currently before us, the situation is analogous. We the Ministry of the Secretariat deliberated over the matter. If it is the case that Wangna Danshu truly is the escaped slave of Wangli Boshu, and that in the second year of the *zhiyuan* period (1265)[24] he pretended to be a free commoner and married Yang Fen'er, then this is a case of the male side committing fraud, and according to the regulations the marriage should be annulled and the wife should return to her family. The betrothal gifts are not returned. The children born to the marriage should go with the mother and become free commoners. In addition, the goods and money worth fifteen *liang* of paper currency that Liu Bin [the go-between] obtained in payment should be returned to Wangna Danshu. Regarding the matter of the older brother Yang Wei and the others who arranged the remarriage of Yang Fen'er without consulting Zhang Yuan, and who in order to avoid a plaint paid two ingots of paper currency exacted by Zhang Yuan, plus the matter of Wangna Danshu's crime [of pretending to be a commoner], since these were before the Amnesty,[25] they need not be further prosecuted.

22. This name is Mongolian. It is probably Er-Bukha ("manly bull") but could also be El-Bukha ("state bull").

23. The following quote from the Taihe code of the Jin is found verbatim in the Tang code (TLSY 14:270 [Art. 191]; Johnson 1997, 171).

24. The text earlier gives the year of the marriage as the fifth year of *zhiyuan* (1268).

25. This character starts a new line and is raised one space to show respect for the emperor's amnesty, which I have indicated by capitalization.

18.69

This document records a memorial to the throne addressing the problem of men from north China going to the south and tricking women by pretending to marry them, then selling these women off as slaves. The Central Secretariat gets approval from Khubilai Khan to outlaw this practice, and it sends out a general proclamation to that effect.

Human trafficking was common during the Yuan, of which this case represents just one aspect. We learn from other sources that around the time of this case in particular, during and after the invasions of the south, but in later years as well, large numbers of commoners from the south, usually male or female children, were kidnapped and brought north where they were sold in the large slave markets of Dadu and Shangdu. The government made attempts to stop the practice, as in this document, but it is not clear how successful these were.[26]

The memorial here from the Central Secretariat, Khubilai's response, and the subsequent proclamation are all in Sino-Mongolian, giving the language of the case an informal, immediate feel. This case is also found in the *Tongzhi tiaoge*, which combines it with another ruling that forbids male slaves to marry free commoner women.[27] The title here in the *Yuan dianzhang* seems to come from that ruling. A more apt title here might read something like "One may not marry a free commoner woman, then sell her off as a slave." The final ruling is included in the "Treatise on Punishments" in the Yuan dynastic history.[28]

18.69 *A male slave may not marry a free commoner woman*[29]

In the thirteenth year of the *zhiyuan* period (1276), eleventh month, second day, a document from the Central Secretariat states:

We submitted a memorial to the throne, an item of which reads:

Officials, itinerant traders, soldiers, and people of all professions come to the Jiangnan region and take as wives the daughters of Jiangnan com-

---

26. On this trafficking, see Ebisawa 1983.

27. TZTG 3:158–159 (Art. 65). The TZTG version is slightly expanded and gives the year as 1277 (*zhiyuan* 14), rather than 1276.

28. YS 103:2644.

29. YDZ 18:30b, p. 716.

moners or already married women who have no sons. But they deceive the women and sell them off as slaves to other people. This situation is thoroughly unbeneficial. We all deliberated and conclude: people must not be allowed to marry commoners and then surreptitiously sell them off as slaves.

When we thus submitted the memorial to the throne, in response we respectfully received an Imperial Edict, stating:

Do it like that!

We humbly respect the Imperial Edict. We order you to give this your careful consideration and proclaim it widely. From now on, when people go to the south and seek wives to marry, they must engage a go-between and establish a marriage contract, according to the regulations. They may not marry deceitfully. If there are those who marry a woman, then sell her off as a slave, the situation must be rectified immediately. The money received in the sale will be confiscated by the government, and both the buyer and seller will be liable for punishment.

18.70

This document, dated 1288, from the Secretariat for State Affairs is a follow-up and in many respects a reversal of the decision by the Ministry of Revenue in 1271, seen in 18.68, that allowed women married to slaves to have their marriages annulled and to take their children with them into free status.[30] Here, the Secretariat for State Affairs steps in and argues in a memorial to the throne that by allowing commoner wives of male slaves routinely to annul their marriages and claim free status for themselves and their children, the law is encouraging slaves to escape and set up free-status families. They question how a commoner family could arrange the marriage of a daughter without carefully questioning the groom about his status. Khubilai agrees and proclaims that commoners should not marry their daughters to slaves, but that if they do, the daughters (and thus their children) should become slaves. The proliferation of war captives sold off as slaves in Yuan society may have made these situations more common than in other dynasties.

---

30. In 1271, the Secretariat for State Affairs was in existence, but there is no mention of it in the document of case 18.68.

The image portrayed by the Central Secretariat is again one where even low-level commoners or slaves have a good understanding of the law and can argue in court to their advantage. At the same time, during an era of increasing mobility and socioeconomic changes, Khubilai and his advisors are seen to be fighting a losing battle to maintain status boundaries and keep slaves as slaves generation after generation.

This case is found in the *Tongzhi tiaoge* with some slight differences in wording.[31] Khubilai's final ruling, that any commoner woman who marries a slave will became a slave herself, is found in the Yuan dynastic history.[32] The entire document is in Sino-Mongolian.

18.70 *A free commoner may not marry a male or female slave*[33]

In the twenty-fifth year of the *zhiyuan* period (1288), tenth month, sixteenth day, a document from the Secretariat for State Affairs states:[34]

We submitted a memorial to the throne, an item of which reads:

Common people are taking their daughters and marrying them to other people's slaves. When the husband dies, they say, "The wife and children should be free commoners, according to the law." Before the marriage, they should ask, "What status person are you?" Why would they marry off their daughters without asking this? If they married off their daughter clearly knowing that the husband was someone's slave, then after the marriage if they try to say "This is the daughter of a free commoner family, so by law she should be a free commoner," this is not right. If this is allowed, there will be many slaves escaping from their masters.

Thus said the memorial. In response, we received an Imperial Edict, stating:

If people clearly know that one has said, "I am someone's slave," then they should not marry their daughters to him. But if they do marry their daughter to a slave, then by law she should become a slave.

Thus said the Imperial Edict. We humbly respect it.

---

31. TZTG 3:159–160 (Art. 66). I have punctuated the text differently from this in several places.

32. YS 103:2644.

33. YDZ 18:31a, p. 717. The table of contents of the *Yuan dianzhang* has the more accurate title of "Regulations on female commoners marrying slaves" (良人嫁驅體例) (YDZ *Mulu*:15a).

34. The TZTG (3:159 [Art. 66]) gives the date as thirteenth day.

Section 11: Marriage of Entertainers

18.71A

The following two cases deal once again with what the Yuan government perceived to be the problem of people crossing status boundaries. The Mongols tried to maintain a system of fixed status and occupational groups, which were key to the smooth functioning of their administration. Marriage created a bridge by which to cross such status boundaries. Cases 18.71A and 18.71B nicely illustrate this dilemma with the case of female entertainers. The powerful Bureau of Imperial Household Provisions maintained a register of such entertainers through its Musicians and Entertainers Office.[35] These women were required to render service to the court on a rotation basis. In these documents the Musicians and Entertainers Office complains that local officials and powerful gentry are forcing these talented women into fraudulent marriages, thus removing them from the service rolls. They request that marriages between female entertainers and non-entertainers be outlawed. Khubilai agrees and furthermore orders local officials and members of powerful families to stop forcing female entertainers to marry them. The Central Secretariat then promulgates the order through the Ministry of Punishments. A truncated version of this case is found in the *Tongzhi tiaoge*.[36]

---

35. The Bureau of Imperial Household Provisions (Xuanhui yuan 宣徽院) had a multitude of functions and was close to the emperor, with a rank that varied from 3A to 1B. It supplied the court with both goods and services, mostly obtained through tribute exacted from households registered in fixed occupational groups. It also provisioned imperial princes at the capital and chose members of the keshig, the imperial guard. In addition, the bureau controlled vast agricultural colonies and was responsible for recovering runaway slaves and livestock (YS 87:2200; Farquhar 1990, 73; Ratchnevsky and Aubin 1972–1985, 1:143–146).

The Musicians and Entertainers Office (Jiaofang si 教坊司) was responsible for supplying musicians and other entertainers to the imperial court, which it did by exacting periodic service from members of hereditary households registered in this occupational group. From 1268 to 1279 the office came under the supervision of the Bureau of Imperial Household Provisions, as it is here. After various iterations, in 1320 it came under the direct control of the Ministry of Rites (YS 85:2139; Farquhar 1990, 195). At times it did not exist as a separate office, but its duties, including maintaining the registers of entertainer households, were then handled by another entity. Female entertainers included courtesans. For a reference to women on these service rolls in Yuan drama, see Hayden 1978, 121.

36. TZTG 3:155–156 (Art. 62).

18.71A *Regulations on female entertainers getting married: 2 Items*[37]

In the fifteenth year of the *zhiyuan* period (1278), the Ministry of Punishments of the Central Secretariat respectfully received a superior communication from the Central Secretariat, as follows:

A report from the Bureau of Imperial Household Provisions states:

A dispatch from the Musicians and Entertainers Office reads:

Entertainers in households registered with our office all wander from circuit to circuit like clouds. Nowadays, consequently, certain officials from these circuits and rich and powerful families who have money to throw away purchase unwilling entertainers. Or they forcibly seize young women who are liable for service to the court, those who have made a name for themselves, who are good at singing and dancing, or who are talented at makeup and adornment, and using fraudulent go-betweens they secretly marry them as wives and concubines. We worry that this will interfere with the service rotation of those liable for service to the court.[38] We humbly request that these marriages be prohibited.

Dispatch received. In the seventh month on the eighteenth day, we sent a memorial to the throne, and respectfully received an Imperial Edict, stating:

As for these entertainers who are liable for service to the court, ordinary commoners must stop getting married to them. Entertainers must be betrothed to people within their group. Those others, officials and rich households, must stop forcibly marrying them. This must be prohibited.

We humbly respect the Imperial Edict. We already sent this down to the Office of Musicians and Entertainers to notify them of this decision. In addition, we submit this report and humbly request that you issue a prohibition.

We the Metropolitan Secretariat order you [the Ministry of Punishments] humbly to respect the edict and enforce this prohibition.

---

37. YDZ 18:32a, p. 719.

38. In other words, the office worries that too few women will be left on the registers to fulfill the entertainment duties required by the court.

18.71B

Fifteen years after Khubilai's edict forbidding female entertainers from marrying regular commoners, in 1293, the staff of the Musicians and Entertainers Office requested that the emperor reissue the prohibition. (We can conclude that the first order was not sufficiently effective.) They sent their request to the Central Secretariat, which obtained the desired edict. This document, as it states, is a direct translation from Mongolian of the request from the Office (whose staff, listed here, all have non-Chinese names), and a record of the response in Mongolian from Khubilai, in the year before his death. The colloquial tone of the Sino-Mongolian in which his speech is recorded leaves a strong impression of the casual and impatient tone in which the aging Khubilai utters his commands. And in an amusing twist, Khubilai tacks on to his edict an order for his provincial officials to look out for good-looking girls to send up to him.[39]

18.71B *[Item 2]*[40]

In the thirtieth year of the *zhiyuan* period (1293) the Branch Secretariat received[41] a communiqué from the Central Secretariat, as follows:

We have received a document in Mongolian from Mubarak-Shah, which in translation reads in part:

> We officials of the Musicians and Entertainers Office,[42] Mubarak-Shah, Temür-Bukha, Ali, Chakir, and others, send this message to you, the officials of the Central Secretariat:

---

39. See Marco Polo's comments on Khubilai staffing his harem in this way (Latham 1958, 122–123; Komroff 1930, 124–127).

40. YDZ 18:32a, p. 719. The *Yuan dianzhang* provides no new title for this case, although the table of contents has "Another regulation" (YDZ *Mulu*:15a, p. 47).

41. The text does not state which branch secretariat is receiving this communiqué, but we learn from the content that it was sent from the Central Secretariat to all the branch secretariats.

42. Following the *Yuanshi*, Farquhar (1990, 195) writes that the office did not exist at this time and that its duties were handled by the Office for the Imperial Ceremonial Guards, but this document demonstrates that that is incorrect and the office continued to exist as a separate bureau.

> Previously there was an Imperial Edict issued, which stated, "Girls who are entertainers must stop getting married to commoners." At this time, how about submitting a memorial to the Emperor requesting that this be publicized to them again?

We submitted a memorial and received a reply, as follows:

> Yes, do it like that. Tell the officials of the provinces that entertainers must stop getting married to common people. They must marry among themselves. And if there are any good-looking girls out there, send them up for me to see!

Thus said the edict. We humbly respect it.

18.72

This document records an order from the newly installed emperor, Renzong (Ayurbarwada, r. 1311–1320), once again outlawing marriage between female entertainers and men from families outside this occupational group. The emperor's words, recorded in Sino-Mongolian, ring with a personal tone as he recounts how a trusted advisor came to grief because of his marriage to an entertainer. The edict goes on specifically to name in the prohibition members of the emperor's personal bodyguard, the keshig, and officials in the bureaucracy, as well as commoner men in general. And Emperor Renzong tries to put more teeth into the order by threatening punishment—not just annulment of the marriage—although the punishment is not specified here.[43] This edict suggests that the emperor's concern has shifted to the moral decline and personal ruin of his chief officers rather than ensuring an adequate supply of women and diversion for himself and his court, as we saw in Khubilai's edicts in the previous cases. This fits with Emperor Ayurbarwada's general tilt toward Confucian ethics, seen in other policies during his reign. This case appears almost verbatim in the *Tongzhi tiaoge*.[44]

---

43. The "Treatise on Punishments" in the Yuan dynastic history records a punishment of 57 strokes and dismissal from office for officials who took a courtesan (*chang* 娼) as a wife or concubine (YS 103:2643). The Ming code uses language that matches this case in outlawing marriages of officials to entertainers, punished similarly by a beating of 60 strokes; *Da Ming lü* 6:698; Jiang 2005, 87 (Art. 119).

44. TZTG 3:156–157 (Art. 63).

18.72　*It is forbidden to take an entertainer as one's wife*[45]

A communiqué from the Central Secretariat reads:

In the fourth year of the *zhida* era (1311), eighth month, eighteenth day, Privy Councilor Li[46] respectfully received a special Imperial Edict, stating:

> Simkha-Sidi[47] took a female entertainer as his wife, and as a result he lost his life. From now on, entertainers must only marry other entertainers. If those among our personal keshig guard,[48] or officials in the bureaucracy, or other people take a female entertainer as a wife, they will be liable for committing a crime and the marriage must be annulled.

Thus said the Imperial Edict. We humbly respect it.

Section 12: Marriage during the Mourning Period

18.73

Marriage during the mourning period for a parent or husband was harshly punished in the Tang code: three years of penal servitude for the principals and 100 strokes for those who facilitated the marriage. With the Mongol takeover of north China in the thirteenth century, however, there was no clear law in effect governing such marriages; and as recorded in this document, dated 1270, people in north China frequently married during the mourning period. Nevertheless, Confucian ethics prescribed strict periods of mourning for the death of a relative, and the reference in this case to lawsuits over marriages during mourning suggests that many people still understood this custom to be supported by law.

---

45. YDZ 18:32a–b, pp. 719–720.

46. This official can be identified as Li Meng 李孟 (1255–1321), the famous Confucian scholar who was the tutor and mentor of Ayurbarwada, the emperor Renzong (YS 175:4084–4090; Hsiao 1994, 513–515). Just after ascending the throne in 1311, Ayurbarwada appointed Li Meng to be a Privy Councilor, a position Li held from the second to the twelfth month (YS 112:2817).

47. The *Tongzhi tiaoge* has *si* 思 for *en* 恩, in this name (Chinese, Xinhasidi) which I am following here (TZTG 3:156). This name appears to be Mongolian, but the person cannot otherwise be identified.

48. Literally "those people who are close to us," meaning the emperor's bodyguards, called the keshig. See TZGT 3:157n2. Note that the emperor refers to himself in the plural, an example in Sino-Mongolian of the royal "we."

Here, the Ministry of Revenue makes a recommendation to prohibit marriage during the mourning period. Its main argument is to fix the law to give judges the means to resolve lawsuits over marriage during mourning. In flowery Confucian language, the Ministry also argues that such a law governing marriage can help improve "public morals." The Ministry cites an "Old Regulation," here understood to be the Taihe code of the Jin dynasty, which repeats the Tang code prohibition and the prescribed punishment of three years' penal servitude. The Ministry of Revenue here merely specifies that the marriage be annulled.

Note that the prohibition has a start date, the first day of the next year, before which marriages contracted during the mourning period may stand. Also, the new prohibition does not apply to Mongols or Inner Asians. It is aimed only at "Bohai and Han Chinese (Han'erren)," those residents of north China who are understood to practice traditional Chinese marriage customs. At this date, 1270, the Mongol regime was still trying to apply different laws to different ethnic groups, a policy that changed soon after in the twelfth month of 1271, when Khubilai abrogated the Taihe code and attempted to issue laws that applied to all people in the Yuan empire. This case is repeated verbatim in the "Ministry of Punishments" section of the *Yuan dianzhang*.[49]

18.73 *Getting married during the mourning period*[50]

In the seventh year of the *zhiyuan* period (1270), twelfth month, a document from the Ministry of Revenue of the Secretariat for State Affairs states:
We have investigated and note that, the death of a parent brings grieving until the end of one's life. The husband is Heaven to the wife, and once she has married, she does not marry again.[51] Nowadays, we receive dispatches one after the other from every locality reporting that people are often getting married during the mourning period for parents or husbands, causing a proliferation of troublesome lawsuits. Since there is no fixed regulation governing this matter, it is difficult to adjudicate these cases. We have investigated and ascertained that the Old Regulations state:

49. YDZ 41:17a. It has the alternate title here "Those who get married while in mourning are to be punished."
50. YDZ 18:33a, p. 721.
51. This is a quote from the Tang code. See TLSY 13:257 (Art. 179); cf. Johnson 1997, 157. The same sentiment is found in case 18.11, where the author also quotes the Confucian classic *Yijing* (Book of Changes), to which the code alludes.

One who gets married during mourning for a parent or a husband is punished by three years of penal servitude and the marriage is annulled. One
who knows of the mourning but helps facilitate the marriage is punished
three degrees less.[52]

We the Ministry of the Secretariat have deliberated and conclude: if we do not
promulgate a clear prohibition, there will be lawsuits without end. This will truly
damage customs and undermine government. In light of this we have carefully
examined the matter and recommend the establishment of the following restrictions, to be in effect until a decision is issued to serve as a universal precedent.
The start date will be the first day of the first month of the eighth year of the
zhiyuan period (1271). Those Bohai, Han Chinese, and others who have gotten
married during mourning for a parent or a husband before this date may remain married. Those who marry after this date will be liable for a crime according to the law, and their marriages will be annulled.[53] In this way lawsuits
can be avoided, and we hope that public morals will gradually improve. We submitted this report and respectfully received a reply from the Secretariat for
State Affairs, stating:

We sent this to the Central Secretariat and received their communiqué in
reply, as follows:

We approve the report. Have it enforced.

18.74

This case documents attempts by Confucian officials to use the law to impose
a particular vision of Confucian ethics on the populace of south China. At issue
is respect for the mourning period and limits on remarriage of widows; the document is dated 1278, soon after the Mongol conquest of the south. One or
more lower officials in what we can infer to be the Huguang Branch Secretariat
(modern Hunan, Guangxi, western Guangdong, and most of Guizhou) take
issue with a widow, Du A-Chen, for cremating her deceased husband and
throwing his ashes in the river, then remarrying, all within a few days of her

52. This same line appears verbatim in the Tang code, except that the reduction in punishment for the facilitator of the marriage is five degrees in the Tang code instead of three
degrees. This may indicate the generally harsh punishments found in the Jin code, or it could
be a mere copying error (TLSY 13:257 [Art. 179]).

53. Reading *fan* 犯 for *ge* 格, as found later in the *Yuan dianzhang,* in the Ministry of Punishments version of this case (YDZ 41:17a).

husband's death. In tones reminiscent of Neo-Confucian proselytizers, they argue that such actions must be punished to prevent the collapse of social ethics. Their superiors in the branch secretariat agree, and they mete out beatings of 37 to 77 strokes to those involved and annul the marriage. Then they issue a general prohibition on remarriage during the mourning period for one's husband. The title of the case indicates that this ruling was understood to apply broadly as a judicial precedent.

This entire case is repeated verbatim, including the title, in the "Ministry of Punishments" section of the *Yuan dianzhang*. In fact, the last line of the case appears only in the Ministry of Punishments version.[54]

18.74 *Precedent-setting decision regarding a wife who cremated her husband and remarried*[55]

In the fifteenth year of the *zhiyuan* period (1278), a document from the Branch Secretariat states:

A document from Tanzhou Circuit reads:[56]

A document from the Municipal Affairs Office states:

Qin A-Chen, from an ordinary household, filed a plaint, stating:

My maternal cousin Du Qing got sick and died. His widow A-Wu took his bones and scattered them in the river, then she got remarried to be the wife of Peng Qianyi.

We obtained the confession of the offender Du A-Wu to her crime, as follows:

On the twelfth day of the first month of this year, my husband Du Qing died of an illness. On the eighteenth day, I cremated him and then had my husband's maternal cousin Tang Xing give the bones to Zhao Baisan to scatter in the river. On the twenty-eighth day, with the help of the go-between First Sister Chen, I received paper money, silver jewelry, and other items [as betrothal gifts] and got remarried to be the wife of Peng Qianyi. I should not have done any of this.

---

54. YDZ 41:17a–b, pp. 1539–1540.

55. YDZ 18:33a, p. 721.

56. Modern Changsha in Hunan Province. Tanzhou was the administrative seat of the Huguang Branch Secretariat at this time (Farquhar 1990, 381–382).

The confessions of First Sister Chen, Zhao Baisan, and Tang Xing agreed with this account.

We in the Secretariat Office have carefully considered this matter and humbly note that, the foundation of human moral relations is the principle that the husband is Heaven to the wife, and once she has married, she does not marry again.[57] The crime that A-Wu has committed corrupts morals and damages customs. If we do not strictly outlaw this behavior, we sincerely worry that the newly incorporated territories of the south[58] will gradually decline, and public morals will degenerate.

[Recommendation approved.][59] We [the superiors of the branch secretariat] have already sent down a verdict to Tanzhou Circuit to punish A-Wu with a beating of 77 strokes of the heavy stick and the annulment of her marriage. She should live with her daughter Zhenniang and observe mourning, in order to fulfill her moral duty as a wife. Moreover, the betrothal gifts she received should be turned over to the Branch Secretariat. As to the matter of Peng Qianyi illegally getting married, in accordance with his confession, he should be punished with a beating of 47 strokes. The go-between, First Sister Chen, and the person who scattered the remains, Zhao Baisan, should each be punished with 47 strokes.[60] Tang Xing should be given a beating of 37 strokes with the heavy stick. In addition, we order that this be distributed to all subordinate offices and a strict prohibition be enforced.

18.75

This document addresses two examples, dated 1288 and 1298, of men getting married during the wake of a close family member. In the first, a military officer named Wang Jizu brings his new wife into his home and kneels before the coffin of his just-deceased father to complete his marriage. In the second, a man whose son has just died quickly adopts his nephew and marries him to his deceased son's wife, all in the presence of the son's coffin. Both cases are decided by the Ministry of Rites, which uses the earlier case as a precedent when adjudicating

---

57. Again quoting the Tang code (TLSY 13:257 [Art. 179]).
58. Jiangnan, "south of the river," meaning south of the Yangzi, that is, south China.
59. Some statement such as this is missing in the document but can be inferred.
60. The text after this point is taken from YDZ 41:17b.

the later one. The Ministry of Rites condemns both marriages and orders them annulled. The military officer Wang Jizu is additionally dismissed from office.

We find here a mismatch between local practices and Confucian ideals, the latter as understood by the Ministry of Rites. In both cases, the protagonists quite intentionally delayed the burial and hurried to contract the marriage in the presence of the deceased. Indeed, in the years after 1271, the Ministry of Revenue, which handled marriage cases at that time, did not systematically enforce the mourning period, and these examples suggest that many people, even officials, did not consider it unethical, and certainly not illegal, to contract a marriage during mourning or during the wake, as here.[61] But by 1288 the Ministry of Rites had taken over most marriage cases, and as seen here they were more intent on imposing Confucian values on the population. Interestingly, both cases involved hereditary military households. The earlier case, dated 1288, involved a military household from the area of modern Datong, in Shanxi in the north, and was passed up to the central government from a Pacification Office of a region. The later case, dated 1298, involved a military officer, and it went to the Bureau of Military Affairs rather than up the civilian bureaucracy. This office passed it along to the Central Secretariat, which sent it to the Ministry of Rites for the ruling.

This record does not give any punishment beyond the annulment of the marriages, in one case after a son is born. But the "Treatise on Punishments" of the Yuan dynastic history, using language similar to this case, prescribes for marriage during the wake of a parent a beating of 87 strokes of the heavy stick, annulment of the marriage, and confiscation of the betrothal gifts. If the protagonist is an official, he is dismissed from office. The wife was not punished.[62] This case can

61. The behavior of Wang Jizu kneeling before his father's coffin is suggestive of announcing the marriage to ancestors, found in traditional Chinese wedding rituals. In 1271, the Ministry of Rites adopted the text of the *Family Rituals* by the Southern Song Neo-Confucian Zhu Xi (1130–1200), with some modifications for people of modest means, as official wedding procedure for all peoples (YDZ 30:1a–2a; TZTG 3:138–143). It prescribes reporting the engagement to ancestral spirits, in an offering hall or in front of spirit tablets (Ebrey 1991a, 51, 192). Ebrey (1991a, 51n11) notes that a Ming revision prescribes reporting "only to the deceased father." See also Ebrey 1991b, 202, for discussions of changes in rituals. On the vicissitudes of Yuan policy toward the mourning period, see the commentary to cases 18.2, 18.5, and 18.15.

62. YS 103:2643; Ratchnevsky and Aubin 1972–1985, 2:130–131 (Art. 389). The next line of the *Yuanshi* text (Art. 390) specifies that one who gets engaged during the mourning period for a parent is punished two degrees less than the punishment for completing the marriage (YS 103:2643).

also be found in the "Ministry of Punishments" section of the *Yuan dianzhang*, the source of several corrections in this text.[63]

18.75 *A marriage contracted during a wake must be annulled*[64]

In the second year of the *dade* period (1298), the Branch Secretariat received a communiqué from the Central Secretariat, as follows:

A report from the Bureau of Military Affairs states:

> Zhang Deqing filed a plaint, stating:
>
>> Wang Jizu, a chiliarch within this jurisdiction,[65] got married when in mourning for his father, while the body still lay out for the wake.
>
> We obtained the written confession of Wang Jizu, as follows:
>
>> It is a fact that on the twentieth day of the sixth month of the first year of the *yuanzhen* period (1295), my father, Wang Xi, passed away. I brought my fiancée, Ma Dajie, into my home. Kneeling before the coffin, we paid obeisance to my father's spirit and completed the marriage. On the twenty-third day, I buried my father Wang Xi.
>
> We present this report for your thorough consideration.

Report received. We sent this to the Ministry of Rites, which investigated the matter and issued a ruling, as follows:

> In the twenty-fifth year of the *zhiyuan* period (1288),[66] during the tenth month, we respectfully received a superior communication from the Secretariat for State Affairs, as follows:
>
>> The report from you, the Ministry of Rites, states:
>>
>>> A memo from the Pacification Office of Hedong Shanxi Region reads:[67]
>>>
>>>> Wang Zhuseng, the son of Wang Zhonglu[68] of a military household in Lin Prefecture of Taiyuan Circuit,[69] on the thirtieth day of the

---

63. YDZ 41:2a. It has the title here of "Wang Jizu contracts a marriage during the wake" and is the first case under the heading "Unfilial."

64. YDZ 18:33b, p. 723.

65. A chiliarch (*qianhu*) was the leader of a chiliarchy, one of the decimal military units founded by the Mongols, consisting nominally of one thousand households.

66. Reading "twenty-fifth" for "fifteenth," following the text of this case found in the "Ministry of Punishments" section (YDZ 41:2a).

67. This region covered the area of modern Shanxi Province and part of Inner Mongolia. The administrative seat—that is, the Pacification Office—was at modern Datong. It belonged to the Central Province, so its memo went directly to the Ministry.

68. Reading *zhong* 仲 for *shen* 伸, following the text below and YDZ 41:2a.

69. Reading *tai* 太 for *fang* 方, following YDZ 41:2a.

twelfth month of the twenty-first year of the *zhiyuan* period (1284) got married to He Zhenzhen. During the first month of the twenty-third year of the *zhiyuan* period (1286), Wang Zhuseng died. While the body still lay out in the home for the wake, Wang Zhonglu arranged the adoption of Wang Tang'er, the son of Wang Zhongfu, to be his son.[70] He had Wang Tang'er and He Zhenzhen kneel before the coffin and pay obeisance to the spirit of Wang Zhuseng, then get married in a levirate union. On the second day of the second month, he finally completed the burial of Wang Zhuseng. Since the levirate marriage, a son has already been born to the couple.

This Ministry has investigated and found that among the Imperial decrees issued there is a regulation allowing one to marry one's sister-in-law in a levirate union and another regulation allowing a widow to stay chaste after the mourning period for her husband. Wang Tang'er did not even wait to bury his older brother, but on the night of the wake he kneeled before the body to pay obeisance and married his sister-in-law He Zhenzhen. He has greatly harmed civilized traditions. If we decide this according to earlier rulings, it would be appropriate for the marriage to be annulled.

We the Metropolitan Secretariat[71] approve the decision. We order that the marriage of Wang Tang'er and He Zhenzhen be annulled.

This Ministry deliberated and concludes: when his father had died and the body still lay out for the wake, Wang Jizu forgot his grief and contracted a marriage. Nothing corrupts principles and damages moral customs as seriously as this. We examined this matter thoroughly. We recommend that, following the decision of the Metropolitan Secretariat, you send a superior communication to the Bureau of Military Affairs and have them adjudicate an annulment of the marriage. As for Wang Jizu, we rule that he should be dismissed from office. This would be appropriate. We hereby present this report.

We the Metropolitan Secretariat[72] approve the report. Enforce it as above.

70. This is likely Wang Zhonglu's brother, or possibly an agnatic cousin.
71. That is, the Secretariat for State Affairs.
72. Here this is the Central Secretariat.

Translation of Title Page of the *Yuan dianzhang*[1]

In the seventh year of the *dade* period (1303), a communication from the Central Secretariat reads in part as follows:

> We received a report from the Specially Appointed Control Officers of Jiangxi as follows:[2]
>
>> We humbly request that statutes and precedents that have been issued from the *zhongtong* era (1260) to the present be collected and made into a book, to be distributed throughout the land.
>
> We note that we previously received a [report] from the Censorate, as follows:

1. This text of a communication from the Central Secretariat, dated 1303, appears on the first page of the *Yuan dianzhang*. See figure 3.2. It conveys the impression that the work enjoyed official endorsement from the government.

2. The Specially Appointed Control Officers (*fengshi xuanfu* 奉使宣撫) appear as special imperial envoys to regions (*dao* 道) during the *dade* period (1297–1308), as here, and then again at the end of the dynasty. Two people were assigned to this post in the third month of 1303, the Chinese official Chen Ying 陳英 (b. 1247) and an Inner Asian named Mubarak (Mubala 木八剌), who could be one of several people. See YS 21:449; Wang Deyi, Li Rongcun, and Pan Bocheng 1979–1982, 2:1277–1278, 4:2475–2476. The office became more regularized under Emperor Shundi (r. 1333–1368), who appointed trusted officials temporarily to regions, largely as an end-run around the bureaucracy, in an attempt to curb rampant malfeasance by officials and ostensibly to relieve the suffering of the people. These were given broad powers, even to carry out executions in some instances. As unrest broke out toward the end of the dynasty, these officials were additionally called on to reward successful military leaders. See YS 92:2342–2343. The regions headed by these officers were different from the two more regular units of that name under the executive and Censorate bureaucracies, headed by Pacification Commissioners (*xuanwei shi* 宣慰使) and Investigation Commissioners (*lianfang shi* 廉訪使) respectively.

Until the Dynasty has established fixed laws, all the high offices of the Dynastic Court under the leadership of the Central Secretariat should each gather and arrange by subject Imperial Regulations and statutes and precedents issued by the court from the beginning of the *zhong-tong* era (1260) to today, then copy them into a book for reference. Furthermore, the Investigating Censors and the Regional Surveillance Offices of each region should be ordered to scrutinize them to check if they are complete or not. Then officials will have something to follow and government orders will not be disregarded.

We [the Central Secretariat] have already distributed this to all subordinate offices to be enforced according to the above. Now regarding the report that is currently before us, we order you to give it your careful consideration and enforce it accordingly.

Marriage Cases from Chapter 18 of the *Yuan dianzhang* in Chronological Order

Case Number	Year of Case and Month (if known)	Case Number	Year of Case and Month (if known)
18.4	1268.10	18.49	1271.12
18.5	1268.10	18.39	1272
18.43	1268.10	18.41	1272
18.48	1269	18.45	1272.6
18.67	1269.2	18.50	1272.10
18.1	1269.3	18.46	1273
18.44	1269.3	18.51	1273
18.6	1269.5	18.54	1273
18.27	1269.10	18.65	1273
18.73	1270.12	18.52	1273.3
18.7	1270.4	18.8	1273.4
18.56	1270.7	18.53	1273.5
18.57	1270.8	18.9	1273.6
18.28	1270.11	18.34	1273.6
18.2	1271.2	18.58	1273.6
18.38	1271.5	18.10	1273.12
18.3	1271.7	18.42	1275
18.68	1271.7	18.11	1275.3
18.20	1271.8	18.59A	1275.4
18.24	1271.11	18.12	1275.11

Case Number	Year of Case and Month (if known)	Case Number	Year of Case and Month (if known)
18.66	1276	18.21	1297.7
18.60	1276.3	18.75	1298
18.69	1276.11	18.22	1298.8
18.61	1277.1	18.30	1299.11
18.59B	1277.8	18.16	1300.4
18.71A	1278	18.40	1301.8
18.74	1278	18.17	1302.4
18.62	1281.4	18.47	1303
18.29	1282.1	18.31	1304.3
18.35	1285	18.26	1309.9
18.13	1286.8	18.23	1310.11
18.14	1288.10	18.32	1311.8
18.70	1288.10	18.72	1311.8
18.36	1289.4	18.33	1312.4
18.63	1289.6	18.18	1313.5
18.15	1291.6	18.64	1315.5
18.71B	1293	18.55	1318.2
18.25	1293.9	18.19	1319.4
18.37	1296		

Marriage Cases from Chapter 18 of the *Yuan dianzhang* with Dates

Case Number	Year of Case and Month (if known)	Case Number	Year of Case and Month (if known)
18.1	1269.3	18.21	1297.7
18.2	1271.2	18.22	1298.8
18.3	1271.7	18.23	1310.11
18.4	1268.10	18.24	1271.11
18.5	1268.10	18.25	1293.9
18.6	1269.5	18.26	1309.9
18.7	1270.4	18.27	1269.10
18.8	1273.4	18.28	1270.11
18.9	1273.6	18.29	1282.1
18.10	1273.12	18.30	1299.11
18.11	1275.3	18.31	1304.3
18.12	1275.11	18.32	1311.8
18.13	1286.8	18.33	1312.4
18.14	1288.10	18.34	1273.6
18.15	1291.6	18.35	1285
18.16	1300.4	18.36	1289.4
18.17	1302.4	18.37	1296
18.18	1313.5	18.38	1271.5
18.19	1319.4	18.39	1272
18.20	1271.8	18.40	1301.8

Case Number	Year of Case and Month (if known)	Case Number	Year of Case and Month (if known)
18.41	1272	18.60	1276.3
18.42	1275	18.61	1277.1
18.43	1268.10	18.62	1281.4
18.44	1269.3	18.63	1289.6
18.45	1272.6	18.64	1315.5
18.46	1273	18.65	1273
18.47	1303	18.66	1276
18.48	1269	18.67	1269.2
18.49	1271.12	18.68	1271.7
18.50	1272.10	18.69	1276.11
18.51	1273	18.70	1288.10
18.52	1273.3	18.71A	1278
18.53	1273.5	18.71B	1293
18.54	1273	18.72	1311.8
18.55	1318.2	18.73	1270.12
18.56	1270.7	18.74	1278
18.57	1270.8	18.75	1298
18.58	1273.6		
18.59A	1275.4		
18.59B	1277.8		

Bibliography

Primary sources are listed by short title, as in the footnotes, followed by full title if different and publication information. Secondary sources are listed by author or editor.

Primary Sources

Da Ming ling 大明令 [The Great Ming commandment]. Orig. 1368. In *Huang Ming zhishu* 皇明制書, 6 vols. edited and compiled by Zhang Lu 張鹵 (1523–98). Taibei: Chengwen chuban she, 1969.

Da Ming lü. Da Ming lü jijie fuli 大明律集解附例 [The Great Ming code with collected commentaries and appended sub-statutes], 30 *juan*. 1610 edition. Taibei: Taiwan xuesheng shuju, 1970.

Da Yuan shengzheng guochao dianzhang 大元聖政國朝典章. See *Yuan dianzhang*.

Dao yuan leigao 道園類稿 [Classified writings from the garden of the Way], 50 *juan*. Yu Ji 虞集 (1272–1348). *Yuan ren wenji zhenben congkan* 元人文集珍本叢刊 [Rare editions of Yuan collected works], vols. 5–6. Taibei: Xinwenfeng chuban gongsi, 1985.

Chijŏng chogyŏk. See *Zhizheng tiaoge.*

Guochao wenlei 國朝文類 [Writings of the dynastic state]. Su Tianjue 蘇天爵 (1294–1352). Orig. 1336. SBCK chubian suoben, vol. 107. Taibei: Taiwan shangwu yinshuguan, 1967.

Guochao wenlei 國朝文類 [Writings of the dynastic state]. Su Tianjue 蘇天爵 (1294–1352). Orig. 1336. *Riben gong nei ting shu ling bu cang Song Yuan ban Han ji xuankan* 日本宮內廳書陵部藏宋元版漢籍選刊 [Selected Song and Yuan editions of Chinese writings held in the Japanese imperial palace], vols. 167–170. Shanghai: Shanghai guji chubanshe, 2012.

Hanmo quanshu. Xinbian shiwen leiju hanmo quanshu 新編事文類聚翰墨全書 [Newly compiled complete guide to letter writing with brush and ink arranged topically],

134 *juan*. Liu Yingli 劉應李 (d. 1311). Orig. 1307. *Siku quanshu zunmu congshu* ed.; Guangdong: Jilü shushe chuban, 1995.

Heicheng chutu wenshu. *Heicheng chutu wenshu: Hanwen wenshujuan* 黑城出土文書: 漢文文書卷. [Documents excavated at Khara Khoto: Documents in Chinese]. Edited by Li Yiyou 李逸友. Beijing: Kexue chubanshe, 1991.

Jinhua ji. *Jinhua Huang xiansheng wenji* 金華黃先生文集 [Collected works of Huang Jin of Jinhua], 43 *juan*. Huang Jin 黃溍 (1277–1357). SBCK chubian suoben, vol. 77. Taibei: Taiwan shangwu yinshuguan, 1967.

Jinshi 金史 [Dynastic history of the Jin]. Tuo Tuo 脫脫 (1314–1355) et al. Beijing: Zhonghua shuju, 1975.

Liaoshi 遼史 [Dynastic history of the Liao]. Tuo Tuo 脫脫(1314–1355) et al. Beijng: Zhonghua shuju, 1974.

Liwen jilan 吏文輯覽. [Collected writings for clerks to peruse]. Anon. Korean text of early Ming. Reprinted as appendix to: Maema Kyōsaku 前間恭作 and Suematsu Yasukazu 末松保和, *Kundoku Ribun: Ribun shūran fu* 訓讀吏文: 吏文輯覽附, 317–378. Tokyo: Kokusho Kankōkai, 1975.

Lixue zhinan 吏學指南 [Guidebook for clerks]. Xu Yuanrui 徐元瑞 [active 14th century]. Taibei: Wenhai chubanshe, 1979.

Lixue zhinan wai san zhong 吏學指南 外三種 [Guidebook for clerks, with three other titles]. Xu Yuanrui 徐元瑞 [active 14th century]. Punctuated and collated by Yang Ne 楊訥. [Hangzhou]: Zhejiang guji, 1988.

Luting shishi 虜廷事實 [Factual information from the land of the caitiffs]. Anon. In *Shuofu sanzhong* 說郛三種 [Three books of *Shuofu*]. Tao Zongyi 陶宗儀. (fl. 1360s) et al. Shanghai: Guji chuban she, 1988.

Ma Shitian wenji 馬石田文集 [Collected works of Ma Zuchang], 15 + 1 *juan*. Ma Zuchang 馬祖常 (1279–1338). *Yuan ren wenji zhenben congkan* 元人文集珍本叢刊 [Rare editions of Yuan collected works], vol. 6. Taibei: Xinwenfeng chuban gongsi, 1985.

Menggu mishi jiaokan ben 蒙古秘史校勘本 [The Secret History of the Mongols: collated and corrected edition]. Huhehaote: Nei Menggu renmin chubanshe, 1980.

Mengwu'er shiji 蒙兀兒史記 [Historical records of the Mongols]. Tu Ji 屠寄 (1856–1921). In *Yuanshi erzhong* 元史二種 [Yuan history, two titles]. Shanghai: Guji chubanshe, 1989.

Miaoxue dianli wai er zhong 廟學典禮外二種 [Regulations and rituals of Confucian schools with two other titles]. Edited and punctuated by Wang Ting 王頲. Yuandai shiliao congkan. [Hangzhou]: Zhejiang guji, 1992.

Ming Rongyu tang ke Shuihu zhuan tu 明容與堂刻水滸傳圖 [Illustrations from the Ming Rongyu hall edition of the *Shuihu zhuan*]. Orig. late Ming. Beijing: Zhonghua shu ju, 1965.

Minggong shupan qingmingji. See *Qingmingji*.

Mu'an ji 牧庵集 [Collected works of Yao Sui], 36 *juan*. Yao Sui (1238–1313). SBCK ji bu, vols. 1427–1434. Shanghai: Shangwu yinshuguan, 1929.

Qian yantang wenji 潛研堂文集 [Collected works of Qian Daxin], 50 + 10 + 10 *juan*. Qian Daxin 錢大昕 (1738–1804). SBCK ji bu, vols. 1850–1865. Shanghai: Shangwu yinshuguan, 1929.

Qingmingji (QMJ). *Minggong shupan qingmingji* 名公書判清明集 [Collection of decisions by famous judges to clarify and enlighten]. Anon. Orig. 1261. Rpt. of 1569 edition. Beijing: Zhonghua shuju, 1987.

Qingya ji 青崖集, 5 *juan*. Wei Chu 魏初 (1226–1286). Wenyuan ge SKQS, vol. 1198. Taibei: Taiwan shangwu yinshuguan, 1983.

Qiujian wenji. *Qiujian xiansheng daquan wenji* 秋澗先生大全文集 [Complete collected works of Wang Yun], 100 *juan*. Wang Yun 王惲 (1227–1304). SBCK chu bian ji bu; suoben vol. 74. Shanghai: Shanghai shangwu yinshuguan, 1965.

QMJ. See *Qingmingji*.

Quan Yuanwen 全元文 [Complete writings of the Yuan] 60 vols. Chief editor Li Xiusheng 李修生. Nanjing: Jiangsu guji chubanshe, 1999; reprint, Nanjing: Fenghuang chubanshe, 2004.

Sanchao beimeng huibian 三朝北盟會編 [Collection of documents relating to treaties with the north during three reigns]. Xu Mengxin 徐夢莘 (1126–1207). Taibei: Wenhai chuban she, 1962.

Shilin guangji (1988). *Shilin guangji* 事林廣記 [Expanded compilation of myriad matters]. Attr. to Chen Yuanjing 陳元靚 (ca. 1200–1266), with later anon. additions. Photoreproduction of Yuan, *zhishun* (1330–1333) edition. Kyoto: Chūbun shuppansha, 1988.

Shilin guangji (1999). *Shilin guangji* 事林廣記 [Expanded compilation of myriad matters]. Attr. to Chen Yuanjing 陳元靚 (ca. 1200–1266), with later anon. additions. Photoreproduction of 1340 edition. Beijing: Zhonghua shuju, 1999.

Shuofu 說郛 [Writings on matters near and far]. Tao Zongyi 陶宗儀 (fl. 1360s) et al. In *Shuofu sanzhong* 說郛三種 [Three books of *Shuofu*]. Shanghai: Guji chuban she, 1988.

Siku quanshu zongmu 四庫全書總目 [Catalog of the Complete library of the four treasuries]. Yong Rong 永瑢 et al. Orig. 1782. Beijing: Zhonghua shuju, 1987.

Sitanyin disanci zhongya kaogu. *Sitanyin disanci zhongya kaogu suohuo hanwen wenshu* (fei Fojing bufen) 斯坦因第三次中亞考古所獲漢文文書 (非佛經部分) [Chinese documents found by Aurel Stein during his third Central Asian archaeological trip (non-Buddhist texts)]. Edited by Zhi Sha and Frances Wood. Shanghai: Shanghai cishu chubanshe, 2005.

Song xingtong 宋刑統 (SXT) [Collected penal laws of the Song]. Dou Yi 竇儀 (914–966) et al. Beijing: Zhonghua shuju, 1984.

Tanglü shuyi 唐律疏議 (TLSY). Orig. 737. Zhangsun Wuji 長孫無忌 (d. 659) et al. Punctuated by Liu Junwen 劉俊文. Beijing: Zhonghua shuju, 1983.

TLSY. See *Tanglü shuyi*.

Tongzhi tiaoge jiaozhu 通制條格校注 (TZTG) [Statutes from the *Comprehensive Regulations*]. Orig. 1322. Punctuated and annotated by Fang Linggui 方齡貴. Beijing: Zhonghua shuju, 2001.

TZTG. See *Tongzhi tiaoge jiaozhu.*

Wu Wenzheng gong ji 吳文正公集 [Collected works of Wu Cheng], 49 *juan.* Wu Cheng 吳澄 (1249–1333). *Yuanren wenji zhenben congkan,* vols. 3–4. Taibei: Xinwenfeng chubanshe, 1985.

Xin Yuanshi 新元史. [New history of the Yuan], 257 *juan.* Ke Shaomin 柯劭忞 (1850–1933). In *Yuanshi erzhong* 元史二種 [Two books of Yuan history]. Shanghai: Guji chubanshe, 1989.

Xingtong fushu 刑統賦疏 [Commentary on the *Xingtong fu* (Ode to the Song code)]. Shen Zhongwei 沈仲緯 (14th cent.). Rpt. in Huang Shijian 黃時鑑 ed. *Yuandai falü ziliao jicun* 元代法律資料輯存, 164–213. Hangzhou: Zhejiang guji chuban she, 1988.

YDZ. See *Yuan dianzhang.*

YDZXJ. See *Yuan dianzhang xinji.*

YS. See *Yuanshi.*

Yu'an ji 寓庵集 [Collected works of Li Ting], 8 *juan.* Li Ting 李庭 (1194–1277). CSJC xubian, vol. 134. Shanghai: Shanghai shudian, [1994].

Yuan dianzhang (YDZ). *Dayuan shengzheng guochao dianzhang* 大元聖政國朝典章 [Statutes and precedents of the sacred administration of the great Yuan dynastic state]. 3 vols. Orig. 1322. Photoreproduction of Yuan dynasty edition: Taibei: Guoli gugong bowuyuan, 1976. [Cited in text as YDZ. All references in the text and footnotes are to this edition unless otherwise noted.]

Yuan dianzhang (1964). *Dayuan shengzheng guochao dianzhang* 大元聖政國朝典章 [Statutes and precedents of the sacred administration of the great Yuan dynastic state]. 2 vols. Orig. 1908, with postface by Shen Jiaben 沈家本 (Shen edition), based on Qing-era ms. Taibei: Wenhai chubanshe, 1964; reprinted 1974.

Yuan dianzhang (1972). *Dayuan shengzheng guochao dianzhang* 大元聖政國朝典章 [Statutes and precedents of the sacred administration of the great Yuan dynastic state], 16 fascicules, 4 boxes. Orig. 1322. Photoreproduction of Yuan dynasty edition: Taibei: Guoli gugong bowuyuan, 1972.

Yuan dianzhang (1976). See *Yuan dianzhang* (YDZ).

Yuan dianzhang (1990). *Yuan dianzhang* 元典章 [Statutes and precedents of the Yuan]. Haiwang cun guji congkan. Beijing: Zhongguo shudian, 1990.

Yuan dianzhang (1998). *Dayuan shengzheng guochao dianzhang* 大元聖政國朝典章 [Statutes and precedents of the sacred administration of the great Yuan dynastic state]. 3 vols. Orig. 1322. Reprint of Taibei: Guoli gugong bowuyuan, 1976, edition (with cumulative page numbers); Beijing: Zhongguo guangbo dianshi chubanshe, 1998.

Yuan dianzhang (2002). *Dayuan shengzheng guochao dianzhang; Xinji zhizhi tiaoli* 大元聖政國朝典章; 新集至治條例 [Statutes and precedents of the sacred administration of the great Yuan dynastic state; together with the New collection of statutes and precedents from the *zhizhi* period (1321–1323)]. In *Xuxiu Siku quanshu,* vol. 787. Shanghai: Guji chubanshe, 2002.

Yuan dianzhang (2011). See Chen Gaohua et al. 2011.

Yuan dianzhang (2016). See Hung Chin-fu 2016.

Yuan dianzhang xinji (YDZXJ). *Dayuan shengzheng dianzhang xinji zhizhi tiaoli* 大元聖政典章新集至治條例 [New collection of statutes and precedents of the Yuan from the *zhizhi* period (1321–1323)]. Supplement to *Dayuan shengzheng guochao dianzhang* (YDZ) 大元聖政國朝典章 [Statutes and precedents of the sacred administration of the great Yuan dynastic state]. Orig. 1322. Photoreproduction of Yuan edition: Taibei: Guoli gugong bowuyuan, 1976.

Yuan hunli gongju kao 元婚禮貢舉考. [Yuan wedding rituals and imperial examinations]. In *Miaoxue dianli wai san zhong* 廟學典禮外三種. Edited and punctuated by Wang Ting 王頲. [Hangzhou]: Zhejiang guji, 1992.

Yuandai falü. Yuandai falü ziliao jicun 元代法律資料輯存 [Collection of Yuan legal materials]. Edited and punctuated by Huang Shijian 黃時鑑. Hangzhou: Zhejiang guji chubanshe, 1988.

Yuandai zouyi jilu 元代奏議集錄. [Collection of memorials from the Yuan period]. Edited and punctuated by Chen Dezhi 陳得芝, Qiu Shusen 邱樹森, He Zhaoji 何兆吉. Hangzhou: Zhejiang guji chubanshe, 1998.

Yuanshi (YS) 元史 [Yuan dynastic history]. Song Lian 宋濂 (1310–1381) et al. Beijing: Zhonghua shuju, 1976, rpt. 1992.

Zazhu 雜著 [Various writings]. Hu Zhiyu 胡祇遹 (1227–1295). Rpt. of *juan* 21–23, in *Lixue zhinan wai san zhong* 吏學指南外三種 [Guidebook for clerks, with three other titles], punctuated and collated by Yang Ne 楊訥, 195–264. [Hangzhou]: Zhejiang guji, 1988.

Zhizheng Jinling xinzhi 至正金陵新志 [New gazetteer of Jinling from the *zhizheng* era (1341–1368)], 15 *juan*. Zhang Xuan 張鉉 (fl. 14th century). Orig. 1344. Taibei: Chengwen chubanshe, 1983.

Zhizheng tiaoge 至正條格 (ZZTG) [*Chijŏng chogyŏk*] [Statutes of the *zhizheng* era (1341–1367)]. 2 vols. Orig. 1348. Han'gukhak Chungang Yŏn'guwŏn 韓國學中央研究院 [Academy of Korean Studies]. Seoul: Hyumŏnisŭt'ŭ [Humanist Press], 2007.

Zhongguo cang Heishuicheng. Zhongguo cang Heishuicheng Hanwen wenxian 中國藏黑水城漢文文獻. [Documents in Chinese from Khara Khoto held in China]. 10 vols. Edited by Ta La 塔拉, Du Jianlu 杜建錄, Gao Guoxiang 高國祥. Nei Menggu wenwu kaogu yanjiu suo 內蒙古自治區文物考古研究所. Beijing: Guojia tushuguan chubanshe, 2008.

Zishan daquanji 紫山大全集 [Complete collected works of Hu Zhiyu], 26 *juan*. Hu Zhiyu 胡祇遹 (1227–1295). Wenyuan ge SKQS, vol. 1196. Taibei: Taiwan shangwu yinshuguan, 1983.

ZZTG. See *Zhizheng tiaoge*.

Secondary Sources

Abe Takeo 安部健夫. 1972. *Gendaishi no kenkyū* 元代史の研究 [Studies of Yuan history]. Tokyo: Sōbunsha.

Abu-Lughod, Janet L. 1989. *Before European Hegemony: The World System A.D. 1250–1350.* New York: Oxford University Press.

Ahmed, Salahuddin. 1999. *A Dictionary of Muslim Names.* New York: New York University Press.

Allsen, Thomas. 1994. "The Rise of Mongolian Empire and Mongolian Rule in North China." In *Cambridge History of China, Vol. 6, Alien Regimes and Border States,* edited by Herbert Franke and Denis Twitchett. Cambridge: Cambridge University Press.

———. 2006. *The Royal Hunt in Eurasian History.* Philadelphia: University of Pennsylvania Press.

Atwood, Christopher Pratt. 2004. *Encyclopedia of Mongolia and the Mongol Empire.* Facts on File library of world history. New York: Facts On File.

Aubin, Francoise. 2004. "Some Characteristics of Penal Legislation among the Mongols (13th–21st Centuries)." In *Central Asian Law: A Historical Overview: A Festschrift for the Ninetieth Birthday of Herbert Franke,* edited by Wallace Johnson and Irina Popova, 119–151. Lawrence, Kans.: Society for Asian Legal History.

Barbieri-Low, Anthony J., and Robin D. S. Yates. 2015. *Law, State, and Society in Early Imperial China: A Study with Critical Edition and Translation of the Legal Texts from Zhangjiashan Tomb no. 247.* 2 vols. Leiden: Brill.

Birge, Bettine. 1989. "Chu Hsi and Women's Education." In *Neo-Confucian Education: The Formative Stage,* edited by Wm. Theodore de Bary and John Chaffee, 325–367. Berkeley: University of California Press.

———. 1995. "Levirate Marriage and the Revival of Widow Chastity in Yüan China." *Asia Major* 8 (2): 107–146.

———. 2002. *Women, Property, and Confucian Reaction in Sung and Yüan China (960–1368).* Cambridge: Cambridge University Press.

———. 2003. "Women and Confucianism from Song to Ming: The Institutionalization of Patrilineality." In *The Song-Yuan-Ming Transition in Chinese History,* edited by Richard von Glahn and Paul Smith, 212–240. Cambridge, Mass.: Harvard University Press.

———. 2008. "Law of the Liao, Chin, and Yuan and Its Impact on the Chinese Legal Tradition." In *Zhongguoshi xinlun, falüshi fence: Zhongguo chuantong falü wenhua zhi xingcheng yu zhuanbian* 中國史新論－ 法律史分冊： 中國傳統法律文化之形成與轉變 [New perspectives on Chinese history, legal history: the formation and transformation of traditional Chinese legal culture], edited by Liu Liyan 柳立言, 443–503. Taibei: Zhongyang yanjiu yuan, Lianjing.

———. 2009. "Sexual Misconduct in Mongol-Yuan Law, with Some Observations on Chinggis Khan's Jasagh." Proceedings of the Ninth International Congress of Mongolists, Ulaanbaatar, Aug. 2006. *Mongolica: An International Annual of Mongol Studies* 23 (44).

———. 2010. "Sources of Law in Mongol-Yuan China (1260–1368): Adjudication in the Absence of a Legal Code." In *Miscellanea Asiatica: mélanges en l'honneur de Françoise Aubin* [Festschrift in honour of Françoise Aubin], edited by

Denise Aigle et al., 387–406. Sankt Augustin, Germany: Institut Monumenta Serica.

———. 2011. "The Influence of Gender on the Adjudication of Yuan Marriage Disputes." Paper presented at Symposium on the Effects of Gender, Religion, Race, and Status on Adjudication in Traditional China, Institute for History and Philology, Academia Sinica, Taipei, Taiwan, Nov. 4.

———. 2017. "How the Mongols Mattered: A Perspective from Law." In *New Interpretations of Mongolian and Inner Asian History*, edited by Morris Rossabi. Leiden: Brill.

Birge, Bettine, and Anne Broadbridge. Forthcoming. "Women and Gender under Mongol Rule." In the *Cambridge History of the Mongol Empire,* edited by Michal Biran and Hodong Kim. Cambridge: Cambridge University Press.

Bodde, Derk, and Clarence Morris. 1967. *Law in Imperial China: Exemplified by 190 Ch'ing Dynasty Cases (Translated from the Hsing-an hui-lan), with Historical, Social, and Juridical Commentaries.* Cambridge, Mass.: Harvard University Press.

Bol, Peter K. 1987. "Seeking Common Ground: Han Literati under Jurchen Rule." *Harvard Journal of Asiatic Studies* 47 (2): 461–538.

———. 1992. *"This Culture of Ours": Intellectual Transitions in T'ang and Sung China.* Stanford, Calif.: Stanford University Press.

———. 2008. *Neo-Confucianism in History.* Harvard East Asian Monographs 307. Cambridge, Mass.: Harvard University Press.

Bossler, Beverly. 2013. *Courtesans, Concubines, and the Cult of Female Fidelity: Gender and Social Change in China, 1000–1400.* Harvard-Yenching Institute Monograph Series 83. Cambridge, Mass.: Harvard University Press.

Bourgon, Jerome, and Pierre-Emmanuel Roux. 2016. "The Chosŏn Law Codes in an East Asian Perspective." In *The Spirit of Korean Law: Korean Legal History in Context,* edited by Marie Seong-Hak Kim, 19–51. Brill's Asian Law series, vol. 3. Leiden: Brill.

Boyle, John A., trans. 1971. *The Successors of Genghis Khan.* Translated from the Persian of Rashīd al-Dīn. New York and London: Columbia University Press.

Brose, Michael C. 2002. "Central Asians in Mongol China: Experience of 'Other' from Two Perspectives." *Medieval History Journal* 5 (2): 267–289.

———. 2005. "Uyghur Technologists of Writing and Literacy in Mongol China." *T'oung Pao* 91 (4–5): 396–435.

———. 2007. *Subjects and Masters: Uyghurs in the Mongol Empire.* Bellingham, Wash.: Center for East Asian Studies, Western Washington University.

———. 2008. "People in the Middle: Uyghurs in the Northwest Frontier Zone." In *Battlefronts Real and Imagined: War, Border, and Identity in the Chinese Middle Period,* edited by Don J. Wyatt, 253–289. New York: Palgrave Macmillan.

Cai Meibiao 蔡美彪. 1955. *Yuandai baihua bei jilu* 元代白話碑集錄 [Collected steles in colloquial language from the Yuan period]. Beijing: Kexue chubanshe.

Chaffee, John. 2006. "Diasporic Identities in the Historical Development of the Maritime Muslim Communities of Song-Yuan China." *Journal of the Economic and Social History of the Orient* 49 (4): 395–420.

———. 2008. "At the Intersection of Empire and World Trade: The Chinese Port City of Quanzhou (Zaitun), Eleventh-Fifteenth Centuries." In *Secondary Cities and Urban Networking in the Indian Ocean Realm, c. 1400–1800*, edited by Kenneth R. Hall, 99–122. Lanham, MD: Rowman & Littlefield Publishers.

———. 2009. "Muslim Merchants and Quanzhou in the Late Yuan-Early Ming: Conjectures on the Ending of the Medieval Muslim Trade Diaspora." In *The East Asian Mediterranean—Maritime Crossroads of Culture, Commerce, and Human Migration*, edited by Angela Schottenhammer, 115–132. Wiesbaden: Harrassowitz Verlag.

Chan, Hok-lam. 1990. "The Yüan Currency System." Appendix 3. In *The Government of China under Mongolian Rule: A Reference Guide*, edited by David Farquhar, 445–460. Stuttgart: Franz Steiner.

Chan, Hok-lam and Wm. T. de Bary, eds. 1982. *Yüan Thought: Chinese Thought and Religion under the Mongols*. New York: Columbia University Press.

Chan, Wing-tsit. 1982. "Chu Hsi and Yüan Neo-Confucianism." In *Yüan Thought: Chinese Thought and Religion under the Mongols*, edited by Hok-lam Chan and Wm. Theodore de Bary, 197–231. New York: Columbia University Press.

Chang Bide 昌彼得. 1972. "Ba Yuanfang kanben *Da Yuan shengzheng guochao dianzhang*" 跋元坊刊本大元聖政國朝典章 [Postface to the Yuan edition of the *Statutes and precedents of the sacred administration of the great Yuan dynastic state*]. Postface in *Dayuan shengzheng guochao dianzhang* 大元聖政國朝典章, 1–10. Taibei: Gugong bowuyuan.

Chen Gaohua 陳高華. 1982. "Lun Yuandai de junhu" 論元代的軍戶 [Military households of the Yuan]. *Yuanshi luncong* 元史論叢 1: 72–90.

———. 2000. "Lun Yuandai de chengwei xisu" 論元代的稱謂習俗 [On naming practices in the Yuan period]. *Zhejiang xuekan* 5: 123–130.

———. (2000) 2005. "Yuandai de shenpan jigou he shenpan chengxu" 元代的審判稱機構和審判程序 [Judicial organization and judicial procedure in the Yuan period]. In *Chen Gaohua wenji* 陳高華文集 [Collected works of Chen Gaohua], 108–167. Shanghai: Shanghai cishu chubanshe.

———. 2015. *The Capital of the Yuan Dynasty*. Honolulu: Silk Road Press.

Chen Gaohua 陳高華 and Shi Weimin 史衛民. 2000. *Zhongguo jingji tongshi: Yuandai jingji juan* 中國經濟通史: 元代經濟卷 [The economic history of China: the economy of the Yuan period]. Beijing: Jingji ribao chubanshe.

———. 2010. *Yuandai Dadu Shangdu yanjiu* 元代大都上都研究 [Studies of the capitals Dadu and Shangdu in the Yuan period]. Beijing: Zhongguo renmin daxue chubanshe.

Chen Gaohua 陳高華, Zhang Fan 張帆, and Liu Xiao 劉曉. 2004. "'Yuan dianzhang, Hubu, Lulin' jiaoshi" 《元典章•戶部•祿廩》校释 [*Yuan dianzhang*, Hubu section, Lulin chapter, punctuated and annotated]. *Zhongguo shehui kexueyuan lishi yanjiusuo xuekan* 中國社會科學院歷史研究所學刊 3: 329–367.

———. 2005. "'*Yuan dianzhang,* Hubu, Huji' jiaoshi" 《元典章•戶部••戶計》校釋 [*Yuan dianzhang,* Hubu section, Huji chapter, punctuated and annotated). *Jinan shixu* 暨南史学 4: 153–196.

———. 2007. "'*Yuan dianzhang,* Hubu, Fenli' jiaoshi" 《元典章•戶部•分例》校釋 [*Yuan dianzhang,* Hubu section, Fenli chapter, punctuated and annotated]. *Zhongguo shehui kexueyuan lishi yanjiusuo xuekan* 中國社會科學院歷史研究所學刊 4: 439–485.

———. 2008a. "'*Yuan dianzhang,* Hubu, Hunyin' jiaoshi" 《元典章•戶部•婚姻》校釋 [*Yuan dianzhang,* Hubu section, Hunyin chapter, punctuated and annotated]. *Zhongguo shehui kexueyuan lishi yanjiusuo xuekan* 中國社會科學院歷史研究所學刊 5: 243–336.

———. 2008b. "'*Yuan dianzhang,* Hubu, Tianzhai' jiaoshi" 《元典章•戶部•田宅》校釋 [*Yuan dianzhang,* Hubu section, Tianzhai chapter, punctuated and annotated). *Yanjing xuebao* 燕京學報 24: 27–114.

———. 2010. "'*Yuan dianzhang,* Hubu, Chaofa' jiaoshi" 《元典章•戶部•鈔法》校釋 [*Yuan dianzhang,* Hubu section, Chaofa chapter, punctuated and annotated]. *Zhongguo shehui kexueyuan lishi yanjiusuo xuekan* 中國社會科學院歷史研究所學刊 6: 239–307.

———. 2012. "'*Yuan dianzhang,* Hubu, Chaifa' jiaoshi" 《元典章•戶部•差發》校釋 [*Yuan dianzhang,* Hubu section, Chaifa chapter, punctuated and annotated]. *Yuandai wenxian yu wenhua yanjiu* 元代文獻與文化研究 1: 18–35.

Chen Gaohua 陳高華, Zhang Fan 張帆, Liu Xiao 劉曉, and Dang Baohai 党寶海, punctuated and annotated. 2011. *Yuan dian zhang: Da Yuan sheng zheng guo chao dian zhang* 元典章 : 大元聖政國朝典章 [Statutes and precedents of the Yuan: Statutes and precedents of the sacred administration of the great Yuan dynastic state]. 4 vols. Beijing: Zhonghua shuju; Tianjin: Tianjin guji chubanshe.

Chen Yuan 陳垣. 1931. *Shenke Yuan dianzhang jiaobu* 沈刻元典章校補 [Corrections to the Shen edition of the *Yuan dianzhang*], 10 *juan*. Beijing: Beijing daxue yanjiusuo guoxue men.

———. 1934. *Yuan dianzhang jiaobu shili* 元典章校補釋例 [Additional explanations and corrections to the (Shen edition of the) *Yuan dianzhang*], 6 *juan*. Beijing: Guoli zhongyang yanjiu yuan lishi yuyan yanjiu suo.

Ch'en, Paul Heng-chao. 1979. *Chinese Legal Tradition under the Mongols: The Code of 1291 as Reconstructed.* Princeton, N.J.: Princeton University Press.

Chia, Lucille. 2002. *Printing for Profit: The Commercial Publishers of Jianyang, Fujian (11th–17th centuries).* Cambridge, Mass.: Published by Harvard University Asia Center for Harvard-Yenching Institute.

Chü, Ch'ing-yüan. (1956) 1966. "Government Artisans of the Yuan Dynasty." In *Chinese Social History: Translations of Selected Studies,* by E-tu Zen Sun and John De Francis, 234–246. New York: Octagon Books.

Ch'ü, T'ung-tsu. 1965. *Law and Society in Traditional China.* Paris: Mouton and Co.

Cleaves, Francis Woodman. 1950. "Sino-Mongolian Inscription of 1335 in Memory of Chang Ying-jui." *Harvard Journal of Asiatic Studies* 13 (1/2): 1–131.

———. 1951. "Sino-Mongolian Inscription of 1338 in Memory of Jigüntei." *Harvard Journal of Asiatic Studies* 14 (1/2): 1–104.

———. 1952. "Sino-Mongolian Inscription of 1346." *Harvard Journal of Asiatic Studies* 15 (1/2): 1–123.

Crossley, Pamela Kyle. 1999. *A Translucent Mirror: History and Identity in Qing Imperial Ideology.* Berkeley: University of California Press.

Crump, J. I. 1980. *Chinese Theater in the Days of Kublai Khan.* Tucson: University of Arizona Press.

Dardess, John W. 1973. *Conquerors and Confucians: Aspects of Political Change in Late Yüan China.* New York: Columbia University Press.

de Bary, Wm. Theodore. 1981. *Neo-Confucian Orthodoxy and the Learning of the Mind and Heart.* New York: Columbia University Press.

de Pee, Christian. 2007. *The Writing of Weddings in Middle-Period China: Text and Ritual Practice in the Eighth Through Fourteenth Centuries.* Albany: State University of New York Press.

de Rachewiltz, Igor. 1967. "Some Remarks on the Language Problem in Yüan China." *Journal of the Oriental Society of Australia* 5 (Dec.): 65–80.

———. 1989. "The Title Cinggis Qan / Qaghan Reexamined." In Walther Heissig and Klaus Sagaster, eds., *Gedanke und Wirkung: Festschrift zum 90. Geburtstag von Nikolaus Poppe.* Wiesbaden: O. Harrassowitz.

———. 1997. "Marco Polo Went to China," *Zentralasiatische Studien* 27: 34–92.

———. 2004. *The Secret History of the Mongols: A Mongolian Epic Chronicle of the Thirteenth Century.* 2 vols. Leiden: Brill.

———. 2006. "Some Remarks on the 'Chih-yüan I-yü 至元譯語' Alias 'Meng-ku I-yü 蒙古譯語', the First Known Sino-Mongol Glossary." *Acta Orientalia Academiae Scientiarum Hungaricae* 59 (1) (March): 11–28.

de Rachewiltz, Igor, Hok-lam Chan, Hsiao Ch'i-ch'ing, and Peter W. Geier, eds. 1993. *In the Service of the Khan: Eminent Personalities of the Early Mongol-Yüan Period (1200–1300).* Asiatische Forschungen, Bd. 121. Wiesbaden: Otto Harrassowitz Verlag.

Dong, Jieyuan. 1994. *Master Tung's Western Chamber Romance (Tung Hsi-hsiang chu-kung-tiao): A Chinese Chantefable,* translated by Li-li Ch'en. New York: Columbia University Press. Originally published: Cambridge: Cambridge University Press, 1976.

Dull, Jack. 1978. "Marriage and Divorce in Han China." In *Chinese Family Law and Social Change,* edited by David Buxbaum, 23–74. Seattle: University of Washington Press.

Dunnell, Ruth W. 1992. "The Hsia Origins of the Yüan Institution of Imperial Preceptor." *Asia Major* (Princeton, NJ) 3rd series, 5 (1): 85–111.

———. 1996. *The Great State of White and High: Buddhism and State Formation in Eleventh-Century Xia.* Honolulu: University of Hawai'i Press.

———. 2010. *Chinggis Khan: World Conquerer.* Boston: Longman.

Ebisawa, Tetsuo. 1983. "Bondservants in the Yüan." *Acta Asiatica* 45: 27–48.

Ebrey, Patricia. 1986. "Concubines in Sung China." *Journal of Family History* 11: 1–24.

———. 1991a. *Chu Hsi's* Family Rituals: *A Twelfth-Century Manual for the Performance of Cappings, Weddings, Funerals, and Ancestral Rites*. Princeton, N.J.: Princeton University Press.

———. 1991b. *Confucianism and Family Rituals in Imperial China: A Social History of Writing about Rites*. Princeton, N.J.: Princeton University Press.

———. 1992. "Property Law and Uxorilocal Marriage in the Sung Period." In *Family Process and Political Process in Modern Chinese History*, 33–66. Taipei: Institute of Modern History, Academia Sinica.

———. 1993. *The Inner Quarters: Marriage and the Lives of Chinese Women in the Sung Period*. Berkeley: University of California Press.

———. 1996. "Surnames and Han Chinese Identity." In *Negotiating Ethnicities in China and Taiwan*, edited by Melissa Brown, 11–36. Berkeley: Institute of East Asian Studies, University of California.

Elliott, Mark. 2001. *The Manchu Way: The Eight Banners and Ethnic Identity in Late Imperial China*. Stanford, Calif.: Stanford University Press.

———. 2012. "Hushuo: The Northern Other and the Naming of the Han Chinese." In *Critical Han Studies: the History, Representation, and Identity of China's Majority*, edited by Thomas Mullaney, 173–190. Berkeley: University of California Press.

Elman, Benjamin A. 2000. *A Cultural History of Civil Examinations in Late Imperial China*. Berkeley: University of California Press.

Endicott-West, Elizabeth. 1986. "Imperial Governance in Yüan Times." *Harvard Journal of Asiatic Studies* 46 (2): 523–549.

———. 1989. *Mongolian Rule in China: Local Administration in the Yuan Dynasty*. Harvard-Yenching Institute Monograph Series 29. Cambridge, Mass.: Council on East Asian Studies, Harvard University.

———. 1991. "Aspects of Khitan Liao and Mongolian Yuan Imperial Rule: A Comparative Perspective." In *Rulers From the Steppe: State Formation on the Eurasian Periphery*, edited by Gary Seaman and Daniel Marks, 199–222. Los Angeles: Ethnographics Press, Center for Visual Anthropology, University of Southern California.

Fang Linggui 方齡貴. 2001. See *Tongzhi tiaoge*, under primary sources.

———. 2004. *Yuanshi congkao* 元史叢考 [Collected evidential studies on Yuan history]. Beijing: Minzu chubanshe.

Farmer, Edward L. 1995. *Zhu Yuanzhang and Early Ming Legislation: The Reordering of Chinese Society Following the Era of Mongol Rule*. Leiden: Brill.

Farquhar, David M. 1981. "Structure and Function in the Yüan Imperial Government." In *China Under Mongol Rule*, edited by John D. Langlois, 25–55. Princeton, N.J.: Princeton University Press.

———. 1990. *The Government of China under Mongol Rule: A Reference Guide*. Stuttgart: Franz Steiner.

Franke, Herbert. 1953. "Could Mongol Emperors Read and Write Chinese?" *Asia Major,* New Series 3 (1): 28–41.

———. 1959. "Some Notes on the Cambridge MS. of Yüan Tien-chang." *Asia Major,* New Series 7 (1): 66–73.

———. 1975. "Chinese Texts on the Jurchen (I): A Translation of the Jurchen Monograph in the San-cha'o Pei-Meng Hui-pien." *Zentralasiatische Studien* 9: 119–186.

———. 1978. "From Tribal Chieftain to Universal Emperor and God: The Legitimation of the Yuan Dynasty." Munich: Verlag der Bayerischen Akademie der Wissenschaften.

———. 1980. "Women under the Dynasties of Conquest." In *La Donna Nella Cina Imperiale e Nella Cina Repubblicana,* edited by Lionello Lanciotti, 23–43. Florence: Leo S. Olschki Editore.

———. 1981. "Jurchen Customary Law and the Chinese Law of the Chin Dynasty." In *State and Law in East Asia: Festschrift Karl Bünger,* edited by Dieter Eikemeier and Herbert Franke, 215–233. Wiesbaden: Otto Harrassowitz.

———. 1987. "The Role of the State as a Structural Element in Polyethnic Societies." In *Foundations and Limits of State Power in China,* edited by S. R. Schram, 87–112. Hong Kong: The Chinese University Press, the Chinese University of Hong Kong.

———. 1989. "The Legal System of the Chin Dynasty." In *Ryū Shiken hakushi shōju kinen Sōshi kenkyū ronshū* 劉子健博士頌寿紀念宋史研究論集 [Collected studies in Sung history dedicated to Professor James T. C. Liu in celebration of his seventieth birthday], edited by Kinugawa Tsuyoshi 衣川強, 387–409. Tokyo: Dōhōsha.

———. 1992. "Chinese Law in a Multinational Society: The Case of the Liao (987–1125)." *Asia Major* 3rd series, 5 (2): 111–127.

———. 1994. "The Chin Dynasty." In *The Cambridge History of China, Vol. 6: Alien Regimes and Border States, 907–1368,* edited by Herbert Franke and Denis Twitchett, 215–320. Cambridge: Cambridge University Press.

———. 2004. "Some Reflections on Multinationality: The Example of Former Empires in East Asia." In *Central Asian Law: An Historical Overview, A Festschrift for the Ninetieth Birthday of Herbert Franke,* edited by Wallace Johnson and Irina Popova, 1–12. Topeka, Kans.: Society for Asian Legal History, Hall Center for the Humanities, University of Kansas.

Franke, Herbert, and Denis Twitchett, eds. 1994. *The Cambridge History of China, Vol. 6, Alien Regimes and Border States, 907–1368.* Cambridge: Cambridge University Press.

Funada Yoshiyuki 舩田善之. 1999. "*'Gen tensho' dokkai no tame ni: kōgusho, kenkyū bunken ichiran wo kanete*" 『元典章』読解のために —工具書・研究文献一覧を兼ねて– [Research notes and bibliography for reading the *Yuan dianzhang*]. *Chūgoku gogaku kenkyū: "Kai pian"* 中國語學研究: 開篇. Vol 18: 113–128.

Gendai no hōsei kenkyū han 元代 の 法制 研究班 [Yuan law research group]. 2007. *"Gen tenshō reibu* kōtei to yakuchū (1)" '元典章 禮部' 校定 と 譯注 (1) [Annotated critical text and a Japanese translation of *Yuan dianzhang,* vol. 28, *Li-bu I*]. *Tōhō gakuhō* 東方學報 81 (Sept.): 137–189.

———. 2008a. *"Gen tenshō reibu* kōtei to yakuchū (2)" '元典章 禮部' 校定 と 譯注 (2) [Annotated critical text and a Japanese translation of *Yuan dianzhang,* vol. 29, *Li-bu II,* being a report of the research project on Legal Institutions in the Yuan Period, organized by Iwai Shigeki]. *Tōhō gakuhō* 東方學報 82 (March): 169–211.

———. 2008b. *"Gen tenshō reibu* kōtei to yakuchū (3)" '元典章 禮部' 校定 と 譯注 (3) [Annotated critical text and a Japanese translation of *Yuan dianzhang,* vol. 30, *Li-bu III,* being a report of the research project on Legal Institutions in the Yuan Period, organized by Iwai Shigeki]. *Tōhō gakuhō* 東方學報 83 (Sept.): 219–294.

Giles, Herbert A. 1898. *A Catalogue of the Wade Collection of Chinese and Manchu Books in the Library of the University of Cambridge.* Cambridge: Cambridge University Press.

Guoli gugong bowuyuan 國立故宮博物院. 1971. *Gugong tushu wenxian xuancui* 故宮圖書文獻選萃 [Select Chinese rare books and historical documents in the National Palace Museum]. Taibei: Guoli gugong bowuyuan, National Palace Museum.

———. 1983. *Guoli gugong bowuyuan shanben jiuji zongmu* 國立故宮博物院善本舊籍總目 [Catalogue of rare books in the National Palace Museum]. 2 vols. Taibei: Guoli gugong bowuyuan.

Guy, R. Kent. 1987. *The Emperor's Four Treasuries: Scholars and the State in the Late Ch'ien-lung Era.* Harvard East Asian Monographs 129. Cambridge, Mass.: Harvard University Press.

Hansen, Valerie. 1995. *Negotiating Daily Life in Traditional China: How Ordinary People Used Contracts, 600–1400.* New Haven: Yale University Press.

Hayden, George A. 1978. *Crime and Punishment in Medieval Chinese Drama: Three Judge Pao Plays.* Cambridge, Mass.: Council on East Asian Studies, Harvard University.

Hegel, Robert E., and Katherine Carlitz. 2007. *Writing and Law in Late Imperial China: Crime, Conflict, and Judgement.* Seattle: University of Washington Press.

Holmgren, Jennifer. 1986. "Observations on Marriage and Inheritance Practices in Early Mongol and Yüan Society, with Particular Reference to the Levirate." *Journal of Asian History* 20 (2): 127–192.

Hong Jinfu 洪金富. See Hung, Chin-fu.

Hsiao, Ch'i-ch'ing [Xiao Qiqing] 蕭啟慶. 1978a. "Yuandai de ruhu: Rushi diwei yanjin shi shang de yizhang" 元代 的儒戶: 儒士地位演進史上的一章 [Confucian households in the Yuan period: One chapter in the historical evolution of the position of Confucian scholars]. *Dongfang wenhua* 東方文化 16: 151–178.

———. 1978b. *The Military Establishment of the Yuan Dynasty.* Harvard East Asian monographs 77. Cambridge, Mass.: Council on East Asian Studies, Harvard University.

———. 1994. "Mid-Yüan Politics." In *Cambridge History of China, Vol. 6: Alien Regimes and Border States,* edited by Herbert Franke and Denis Twitchett, 490–560. Cambridge: Cambridge University Press.

Hu Xingdong 胡興東. 2007. *Yuandai minshi falü zhidu yanjiu* 元代民事法律制度研究 [The system of civil law in the Yuan period]. Beijing: Zhonghua shehui kexue chubanshe.

Huang Qinglian 黃清連. 1977. *Yuandai huji zhidu yanjiu* 元代戶計制度研究. Taibei: Guoli Taiwan daxue wenxue yuan.

Huang Shijian 黃時鑑, edited and punctuated. 1986. *Tongzhi tiaoge* 通制條格 [Statutes from the *Comprehensive Regulations* (of the Yuan)]. Orig. 1323. Hangzhou: Zhejiang guji chubanshe.

———. 1988. See *Yuandai falü*, under primary sources.

Hucker, Charles O. 1985. *A Dictionary of Official Titles in Imperial China.* Stanford, Calif.: Stanford University Press.

Hummel, Arthur W. 1943. *Eminent Chinese of the Ch'ing Period, 1644–1912.* Washington D.C.: U.S. Government Printing Office.

Hung, Chin-fu [Hong Jinfu] 洪金富. 1982. *The Censorial System of Yuan China.* Ph.D. diss., Harvard University.

———. 1987. "Shumuzi renming shuo" 數目字人名說 [On numbers as names]. *Shiyusuo jikan* 58 (2): 281–379.

———. 1988. "'Qinci' zaiyi" "欽此" 再議 [Further discussion of the term "qinzi"]. In *Guoshi shilun: Tao Xisheng xiansheng jiuzhi rongqing zhushou lunwen ji* 國史釋論: 陶希聖先生九秩榮慶祝壽論文集. [Interpretive essays on national history: collected essays in honor of Prof. Tao Xisheng on his ninetieth birthday], edited by Liansheng Yang, vol. 2, 635–656. Taibei: Shihuo chubanshe.

———. 1992. "Yuandai de shouji hun" 元代的收繼婚 [Levirate marriage in the Yuan]. In *Zhongguo jinshi shehui wenhua shi lunwen ji* 中國近世社會文化史論文集 [Papers on Society and Culture of Early Modern China], 279–314. Taipei: Academia Sinica, Institute of History and Philology.

———. 1997a. "Yuandai Hanren yu fei Hanren tong hun wenti chutan 元代漢人與非漢人通婚問題初探 (1) [Preliminary discussion of the question of Han Chinese marrying non-Han people, Pt. 1]" *Shihuo yuekan* 食貨月刊 6.12: 1–19.

———. 1997b. "Yuandai Hanren yu fei Hanren tong hun wenti chutan 元代漢人與非漢人通婚問題初探 (2) [Preliminary discussion of the question of Han Chinese marrying non-Han people, Pt. 2]" *Shihuo yuekan* 食貨月刊 7.1: 11–51.

———. 2003. *Yuandai taixian wenshu huibian* 元代臺憲文書匯編 [Collected Censorial documents of the Yuan]. Taibei: Zhongyang yanjiuyuan lishi yuyan yanjiu suo.

———. 2016. *Yuan dianzhang: Hong Jinfu jiaoding ben* 元典章: 洪金富校定本 [Institutes of the Yüan dynasty: Punctuated and collated by Hung Chin-fu]. 4 vols.

Special Publications No. 110. Taibei: Zhongyang yanjiuyuan lishi yuyan yanjiu suo; Institute of History and Philology, Academia Sinica.

Idema, Wilt L. 2010. *Judge Bao and the Rule of Law: Eight Ballad-Stories from the Period 1250–1450*. Singapore: World Scientific.

Idema, Wilt L., and Stephen H. West. 1982. *Chinese Theater, 1100–1450: A Source Book*. Wiesbaden: Franz Steiner.

Iiyama Tomoyasu 飯山知保. 2011. *KinGen jidai no kahoku shakai to kakyo seido: mō hitotsu no "shijinsō"* 金元時代 の 華北社會 と 科舉制度: もう一つの「士人層」 [Northern Chinese society and the examination system in the Jin and Yuan period]. Waseda University Academic Series, no. 14. Tokyo: Waseda University Press.

———. 2014. "A Career between Two Cultures: Guo Yu, a Chinese Lituratus in the Yuan Bureaucracy." *Journal of Song-Yuan Studies* 44: 471–501.

Iwai Shigeki 岩井茂樹. See Gendai no hōsei kenkyū han.

Iwamura Shinobu 岩村忍 and Tanaka Kenji 田中謙二. 1964. *Kōteibon Gentenshō keibu* 校定本 元典章 刑部 [Punctuated edition of the Ministry of Punishments section of the *Yuan dianzhang*], 2 vols. Kyoto: Kyoto daigaku Jinbun kagaku kenkyūjo.

Jagchid Sechin [Zhaqi Siqin] 札奇斯欽. 1980a. "Shuo jiu *Yuanshi* zhong de 'zhaluhuchi' bingjian lun Yuan chu de Shangshu sheng" 說舊元史中的 '札魯忽赤' 並兼論元初的尚書省 [On the darughachi of the old Yuan history with a discussion of the Secretariat for State Affairs in the early Yuan]. In *Menggushi luncong*, vol. 1, by Jagchid Sechin, 233–363. Taibei: Xuehai chubanshe.

———. 1980b. "Shuo jiu *Yuanshi* zhong de 'daluhuachi'" 說舊元史中的 '達魯花赤'. In *Menggushi luncong*, vol. 1, by Jagchid Sechin, 465–631. Taibei: Xuehai chubanshe. Orig: Wenshizhe xuebao 13 (1964): 293–441.

Jay, Jennifer W. 1991. *A Change in Dynasties: Loyalism in Thirteenth-Century China*. Bellingham, Wash.: Western Washington University.

Jiang, Yonglin, trans. 2005. *The Great Ming Code/Da Ming lü*. Seattle: University of Washington Press.

———. 2011. *The Mandate of Heaven and the* Great Ming Code. Seattle and London: University of Washington Press.

Johnson, Linda Cooke. 2011. *Women of the Conquest Dynasties: Gender and Identity in Liao and Jin China*. Honolulu: University of Hawai'i Press.

Johnson, Wallace, trans. 1979. *The T'ang Code,* vol. 1, *General Principles*. Princeton, N.J.: Princeton University Press.

———. 1997. *The T'ang Code,* vol. 2, *Specific Articles*. Princeton, N.J.: Princeton University Press.

Johnson, Wallace, and Denis Twitchett. 1993. "Criminal Procedure in T'ang China." *Asia Major*, 3rd series, 6 (2): 113–146.

Kane, Daniel. 1989. *The Sino-Jurchen Vocabulary of the Bureau of Interpreters*. Bloomington: Indiana University Press.

Kara, György. 2003. "Mediaeval Mongol Documents from Khara Khoto and East Turkestan in the St. Petersburg Branch of the Institute of Oriental Studies." *Manuscripta Orientalia* 9 (2): 3–40.

———. 2005. *Books of the Mongolian Nomads: More than Eight Centuries of Writing Mongolian,* translated by John Krueger. Indiana University Uralic and Altaic Studies, vol. 171. Bloomington: Indiana University, Research Institute for Inner Asian Studies.

Kim, Marie Seong-Hak, ed. 2016. *The Spirit of Korean Law: Korean Legal History in Context.* Brill's Asian Law series, vol. 3. Leiden: Brill.

Ko, Dorothy. 2005. *Cinderella's Sisters: A Revisionist History of Footbinding.* Berkeley, Calif.: University of California Press.

Kobayashi Takashiro 小林高四郎. 1977. "Gendai hōseishi jō no kyūrei ni tsuite" 元代法制史上の旧例に就いて [Concerning the "Old Regulations" in Yuan legal history]. In *Egami namio kyōju koki kinen ronshū, minzoku bunka hen* 江上波夫教授古稀記念論集. 民族·文化篇 [Collected essays for Professor Egami Namio in commemoration of his 70th birthday: peoples and civilization volume], edited by Egami Namio 江上波夫. Tokyo: Yamakawa shuppansha.

Kobayashi Takashiro 小林高四郎 and Okamoto Keiji 岡本敬二. 1964–1976. *Tsūsei jōkaku no kenkyū yakuchū* 通制條格の研究譯註 [Translation and commentary of the *Tongzhi tiaoge*], 3 vols. Tōkyō: Chūgoku Keihōshi Kenkyūkai.

Komroff, Manuel, ed. 1930. *The Travels of Marco Polo (the Venetian).* Garden City, N.Y.: Garden City Publishing Co.

Lagerwey, John, Pierre Marsone, Vincent Goossaert, and Jan Kiely, eds. 2015. *Modern Chinese Religion.* Leiden: Brill.

Langlois, John D., Jr. 1981. " 'Living Law' in Sung and Yuan Jurisprudence." *Harvard Journal of Asiatic Studies* 41 (1): 165–217.

———. 1982. "Law, Statecraft, and the *Spring and Autumn Annals* in Yüan Political Thought." In *Yüan Thought: Chinese Thought and Religion under the Mongols,* edited by Hok-lam Chan and Wm. Theodore de Bary, 89–152. New York: Columbia University Press.

Latham, Ronald, trans. 1958. *The Travels of Marco Polo.* London: Penguin Books.

Lau Nap-yin [Liu Liyan] 柳立言. 1994. "Songdai tongju zhidu xia de suowei 'gongcai' " 宋代同居制度下的所謂共財 [So-called 'common property' under the co-residence system of the Song]. *Zhongyang yanjiu yuan, lishi yuyan yanjiu suo jikan* 65 (2): 253–305.

———. 2015. "Changes to Women's Legal Rights in the Family from the Song to the Ming." In *Modern Chinese Religion,* edited by John Lagerwey, et al., 643–717. Leiden: Brill.

Lau Nap-yin [Liu Liyan] 柳立言, ed. 2008. *Zhongguoshi xinlun, falüshi fence: Zhongguo chuantong falü wenhua zhi xingcheng yu zhuanbian* 中國史新論－法律史分冊: 中國傳統法律文化之形成與轉變 [New perspectives on Chinese history, legal history: The formation and transformation of traditional Chinese legal culture]. Taipei: Zhongyang yanjiu yuan, Lianjing.

———. 2013. *Xingbie, zongjiao, zhongzu, jieji yu Zhongguo chuantong sifa* 性別, 宗教, 種族, 階級與中國傳統司法 [Gender, religion, race, and class in traditional Chinese judicial practice]. Taipei: Zhongyang yanjiu yuan lishi yuyan yanjiu suo.

Legge, James, trans. (1895) 1960. *The Mencius.* Vol. 2 of *The Chinese Classics with a Translation, Critical and Exegetical Notes, Prolegomena, and Copious Indexes.* Reprint, Hong Kong: Hong Kong University Press.

———. (1899) 1963. *The I Ching.* New York: Dover Publications.

Li Yiyou 李逸友. 1992. "Heicheng chutu de Yuandai hetong hunshu" 黑城出土的元代合同婚書 [A Yuan marriage contract unearthed in Khara Khorum]. *Wenwu tiandi* 2: 30–31.

Li Yiyou 李逸友, ed. 1991. See *Heicheng chutu wenshu*, under primary sources.

Li Zhi'an 李治安. 2003. *Yuandai zhengzhi zhidu yanjiu* 元代政治制度研究 [Research on the administrative system of the Yuan period]. Beijing: Renmin chuban she.

Liu Liyan 柳立言. See Lau Nap-yin.

Liu Pujiang 劉浦江. 1999. "Shuo 'Hanren': LiaoJin shidai minzu ronghe de yi ge cemian" 說 '漢人': 遼金時代民族融合的一個側面 [Speaking of "Hanren": An aspect of ethnic mixing in the Liao and Jin periods]. In *Liao Jin shilun* 遼金史論, 109–127. Shenyang: Liaoning University Press.

Liu Xiao 劉曉. 2004. "Zailun *Yuanshi, Xingfa zhi* de shiyuan: Cong *Jingshi dadian, Xiandian* yipian yiwen tanqi" 再論《元史·刑法志》的史源—從《經世大典·憲典》一篇佚文談起 [More on the origins of the *Yuanshi* "Xingfazhi"—from the perspective of a missing piece of the "Xiandian" section of the *Jingshi dadian*]. *Beida shixue* 北大史學 10 (1): 92–101.

———. 2013. "Yuandai sifa shenpan zhong zhongzu yinsu de yingxiang" 元代司法審判中種族因素的影響 [The influence of ethnicity in Yuan legal trials]. In Xingbie, zongjiao, zhongzu, jieji yu Zhongguo chuantong sifa 性別, 宗教, 種族, 階級與中國傳統司法 [Gender, religion, race, and class in traditional Chinese judicial practice], edited by Liu Liyan 柳立言, 199–227. Taipei: Zhongyang yanjiu yuan lishi yuyan yanjiu suo.

Liu Yingsheng 劉迎勝. 2013. *Meng Yuan diguo yu 13–15 shiji de shijie* 蒙元帝國與13–15 世紀的世界 [The Mongol Yuan empire and the world of the thirteenth to fifteenth centuries]. Beijing: Sanlian shudian.

MacCormack, Geoffrey. 2008. "A Reassessment of the 'Confucianization of the Law' from the Han to the T'ang." In *Zhongguoshi xinlun, falüshi fence: Zhongguo chuantong falü wenhua zhi xingcheng yu zhuanbian* 中國史新論－ 法律史分冊：中國傳統法律文化之形成與轉變 [New Perspectives on Chinese History, Legal History: The Formation and Transformation of Traditional Chinese Legal Culture], edited by Liu Liyan 柳立言. Taipei: Academia Sinica-Lianjing.

———. 2011. "Judicial Reasoning in the Southern Song." *Journal of Song-Yuan Studies* 41: 107–189.

Maema Kyōsaku 前間恭作 and Suematsu Yasukazu 末松保和. 1975. *Kundoku Ribun: Ribun shūran fu* 訓讀吏文：吏文輯覽附. Tokyo: Kokusho Kankōkai.

Matsuda Kōichi 松田孝一. 1990. "Iwayuru Genchō no 'gungo su' ni tsuite" いわゆる元朝の軍戶數について [On the total number of military households in the Yüan dynasty]. In *Higashi Ajia no hō to shakai: Nunome Chōfū Hakushi koki kinen ronshū* 東アジアの法と社会：布目潮渢博士古稀記念論集 [Law and society in East

Asia: collected essays in celebration of the 70th birthday of Dr. Nunome Chōfū], edited by Nunome Chōfū Hakushi Kinen Ronshū Kankōkai 布目潮渢博士記念論集刊行会, 441–462. Tokyo: Kyūko Shoin.

McCausland, Shane. 2011. *Zhao Mengfu: Calligraphy and Painting for Khubilai's China.* Hong Kong: Hong Kong University Press.

McKnight, Brian E. 1972. *Village and Bureaucracy in Southern Sung China.* Chicago: University of Chicago Press.

———. 1996. "Divorce in Sung China." In *Di er jie Songshi xueshu yantao hui lunwen ji* 第二屆宋史學術研討會論文集 [Proceedings of the Second Symposium on Sung History]. Taipei: Zhongguo wenhua daxue shixue yanjiu suo.

McKnight, Brian E., and James T. C. Liu, trans. 1999. *The Enlightened Judgments, Ch'ing-ming Chi: The Sung Dynasty Collection.* Albany: State University of New York Press.

Meng Siming 蒙思明. (1938) 2006. *Yuandai shehui jieji zhidu* 元代社會階級制度 [The class system of the Yuan period]. Beiping: Harvard-Yenching; reprint, Shanghai: Renmin chubanshe.

Miya Noriko 宮紀子. 2001. "Sei Fushin 'Shisho shoto' chuppan shimoku kō—DaiGen urusu chika niokeru Konan bunjin no hoju" 程復心「四書章圖」出版始末考−大元 ウルス 治下における 江南文人の 保舉− [An investigation of the publication of Cheng Fuxin's *Sishu zhangtu*: the advancement of a Jiangnan literatus under the great Yuan ulus]. *Nairiku Ajia gengo no kenkyū* 16: 71–122.

———. 2006. *Mongoru jidai no shuppan bunka* モンゴル時代の出版文化 [Publication culture in the Mongol period]. Nagoya: Nagoya Daigaku Shuppankai.

Miyazaki Ichisada 宮崎市定. (1954) 1975. "SōGen jidai no hōsei to saiban kikō: Gentenshō seiritsu no jidaiteki shakaiteki haikei" 宋元時代の法制と裁判機構—元典章成立の時代的社會的背景 [The structure of law and trial procedure in the Song and Yuan: the historical and social background of the *Yuan dianzhang*]. Orig. *Tōhō gakuhō.* Reprint in *Ajiashi kenkyū* アジア史研究 [Studies in Asian history], vol. 4, 170–305. Kyoto: Dōhōsha.

———. 1980. "The Administration of Justice during the Sung Dynasty." In *Essays on China's Legal Tradition,* edited by Jerome Cohen, Randle Edwards, and Fumei Chang Chen, 56–75. Princeton, N.J.: Princeton University Press.

Morgan, David. 1986. *The Mongols.* Oxford, U.K.: Blackwell.

Morita Kenji 森田憲司, ed. 2004. *Jūsan, jūyon seki Tō Ajia shiryō tsūshin* 13, 14 世紀東アジア史料通信 [Newsletter on historical documents in 13–14th century East Asia], no. 2 (Dec.). Research Project on "Historical Documents in 13–14th Century East Asia," JSPS, Basic Research (B)(1), Japan.

Mote, Frederick. 1994a. "Chinese Society under Mongol Rule, 1215–1368." In *Cambridge History of China,* vol. 6, *Alien Regimes and Border States,* edited by Herbert Franke and Denis Twitchett, 616–664. Cambridge: Cambridge University Press.

———. 1994b. "Bibliographic Essays: A Note on Traditional Sources for Yüan History." In *Cambridge History of China,* vol. 6, *Alien Regimes and Border States,* edited by Herbert Franke and Denis Twitchett, 689–699. Cambridge: Cambridge University Press.

———. 1999. *Imperial China 900–1800*. Cambridge, Mass.: Harvard University Press.

Munkuyev, N. Ts. 1970. "Two Mongolian Printed Fragments from Khara-Khoto." In *Mongolian Studies*, vol. 14, edited by Louis Ligeti, 341–357. Amsterdam: B. R. Grüner.

Murata Jirō 村田治郎 and Fujieda Akira 藤枝晃, eds. 1955–1958. Kyoyōkan 居庸關 [Juyong pass]. 2 vols. Kyōto Daigaku Kōgakubu; Tokyo: Zayūhō Kankōkai.

Niida Noboru 仁井田陞. (1940) 1991. "Gentenshō no seiritzu to Daitokutenshō" 元典章の成立と大德典章 [The *Dade dianzhang* and the origins of the *Yuan dianzhang*]. *Shigaku zasshi* 51: 9. Reprint in *Chūgoku hōseishi kenkyū* 中國法制史研究 [Studies in Chinese legal history], vol. 4: *Hō to kanshū, hō to dōtoku* 法と慣習, 法と道德 [Law and custom; law and morality], 182–199. 1964; reprint, Tokyo: Tōkyō daigaku shuppankai.

———. (1959) 1991. "Kindai keihō kō" 金代刑法考 [An investigation of Jin period penal law]. In *Chūgoku hōseishi kenkyū* 中国法制史研究 [Research on Chinese legal law], vol. 1: *Keihō* 刑法 [Penal Law], 453–524. 1964; reprint, Tokyo: Tōkyō daigaku shuppankai.

———. (1964) 1991a. *Chūgoku hōseishi kenkyū* 中國法制史研究 [Studies in Chinese legal history], vol. 1: *Keihō* 刑法 [Penal Law]. Reprint, Tokyo: Tōkyō daigaku shuppankai.

———. (1964) 1991b. *Chūgoku hōseishi kenkyū* 中國法制史研究 [Studies in Chinese legal history], vol. 4: *Hō to kanshū, hō to dōtoku* 法と慣習, 法と道德 [Law and custom; law and morality]. Reprint, Tokyo: Tōkyō daigaku shuppankai.

Niwa Tomosaburō 丹羽友三郎. 1994. *Chūgoku gendai no kansatsukansei* 中国元代の監察官制 [The surveillance system of the Yuan dynasty in China]. Tokyo: Kōbundō.

Okamoto Keiji 岡本敬二. 1965. "Gendai no shasei to goson" 元代の社制と鄉村 [The village and the commune system in the Yuan]. *Rekishi kyōiku* 歷史教育 13 (9): 15–25.

Okamoto Keiji 岡本敬二, ed. See Kobayashi Takashiro and Okamoto Keiji.

Peng Xinwei 彭信威. 2007. *Zhongguo huobi shi* 中國貨幣史 [A history of Chinese currency]. Shanghai: Renmin chubanshe. Originally published 1954.

Poppe, Nikolas. 1954. Grammar of Written Mongolian. Wiesbaden: Otto Harrassowitz.

Qiu Shusen 邱樹森, ed. 2000. *Yuanshi cidian* 元史辭典 [Dictionary of Yuan history]. Jinan: Shangdong jiaoyu chubanshe.

Rashīd al-Dīn. See Boyle.

Ratchnevsky, Paul. 1968. "The Levirate in the Legislation of the Yuan Dynasty." In *Tamura hakushi shoju tōyōshi ronso* [Asiatic studies in honor of Dr. Tamura Jitsuzō on the occasion of his sixty-fourth birthday], 45–62. Tokyo: Dōhōsha.

————. 1991. *Genghis Khan: His Life and Legacy,* translated and edited by Thomas Nivison Haining. Oxford: Blackwell.

————. 1993. "Jurisdiction, Penal Code, and Cultural Confrontation under Mongol-Yüan Law." *Asia Major,* 3rd series 4 (1): 161–179.

Ratchnevsky, Paul, and Francoise Aubin. 1972–1985. *Un Code des Yüan.* 4 vols. Paris: Collège de France, Institut des Hautes Etudes Chinoises. (Vol. 1 orig. Paris: Ernest Leroux, 1937.)

Robinson, David M. 2009. *Empire's Twilight: Northeast Asia under the Mongols.* Harvard-Yenching Institute Monograph Series 68. Cambridge, Mass.: Harvard University Press.

Rossabi, Morris. 1979. "Khubilai Khan and the Women in His Family." In *Studia Sino-Mongolica: Festschrift für Herbert Franke,* edited by Wolfgang Bauer. Wiesbaden: Franz Steiner Verlag.

————. 1981. "The Muslims in the Early Yuan Dynasty." In *China under Mongol Rule,* edited by John D. Langlois, 257–95. Princeton, N.J.: Princeton University Press.

————. 1988. *Khubilai Khan: His Life and Times.* Berkeley: University of California Press.

————. 2008. "Notes on Khubilai Khan: Religious Toleration or Political Expediency?" In *Intellectual and Cultural Studies in Honor of Isenbike Togan,* edited by Nurten Kilic-Schubel and Ilker Evrim Binbas. Istanbul: Ithaki Publishers.

Rossabi, Morris, ed. 1983. *China among Equals: The Middle Kingdom and Its Neighbors, 10th–14th Centuries.* Berkeley: University of California Press.

Schurmann, Herbert F. 1956. *Economic Structure of the Yüan Dynasty: Translation of Chapters 93 and 94 of the Yüan shih.* Harvard-Yenching Institute Series 16. Cambridge, Mass.: Harvard University Press.

Shi Weimin 史衛民. 1993. "Yuanchao qianqi de xuanfu si yu xuanwei si" 元代前期的宣撫司與宣慰司 [The *xuanfu si* and the *xuanwei si* in the early Yuan]. *Yuanshi luncong* 元史論叢 no. 5. Beijing: Zhongguo shehui kexue chuban she.

Shiga Shūzō 滋賀秀三. 1967. *Chūgoku kazokuhō no genri* 中國家族法の原理 [Principles of the Chinese family system]. Reprint, Tokyo: Sōbunsha, 1981.

Sloane, Jesse. 2014. "Mapping a Stateless Nation: 'Bohai' Identity in the Twelfth to Fourteenth Centuries." *Journal of Song-Yuan Studies* 44: 365–403.

Smith, John. 1970. "Mongol and Nomadic Taxation." *Harvard Journal of Asiatic Studies* 30: 46–86.

Smith, Paul. 1998. "Fear of Gynarchy in an Age of Chaos: Kong Qi's Reflections on Life in South China under Mongol Rule." *Journal of the Economic and Social History of the Orient* 41 (1): 1–95.

Smith, Paul J., and Richard von Glahn, eds. 2003. *The Song-Yuan-Ming Transition in Chinese History.* Harvard East Asian Monographs 221. Cambridge, Mass.: Harvard University Asia Center.

Sommer, Matthew H. 2000. *Sex, Law, and Society in Late Imperial China.* Stanford, Calif.: Stanford University Press.

———. 2015. *Polyandry and Wife-Selling in Qing Dynasty China: Survival Strategies and Judicial Interventions*. Oakland, Calif.: University of California Press.

Standen, Naomi. 2003. "Raiding and Frontier Society in the Five Dynasties." In *Political Frontiers, Ethnic Boundaries, and Human Geographies in Chinese History*, edited by Nicola Di Cosmo and Don Wyatt. London: Routledge Curzon.

———. 2007. *Unbounded Loyalty: Frontier Crossings in Liao China*. Honolulu: University of Hawai'i Press.

Steinhardt, Nancy Shatzman. 1983. "The Plan of Khubilai Khan's Imperial City." *Artibus Asiae* 44: 137–158.

———. 2007. "Yuan Dynasty Tombs and Their Inscriptions: Changing Identity for the Chinese Afterlife." *Ars Orientalis* 37: 138–172.

Sugiyama Masaaki 杉山正明. 1997. *Yūbokumin kara mita sekaishi: minzoku mo kokkyō mo koete* 遊牧民から見た世界史：民族も国境もこえて [World history from the perspective of nomadic peoples: Beyond ethnic groups and national borders]. Tokyo: Nihon keizai shinbunsha.

———. 1998. "Chūō Yūrashia no rekishiteki kōzu" 中央ユーラシアの歴史的構図 [An historical outline of Central Eurasia]. In *Iwanami kōza sekai rekishi* 岩波講座世界歴史 [Iwanami courses in world history], 11, edited by Kabayama Kōichi. Tokyo: Iwanami Shoten.

———. 2004. *Mongoru teikoku to Dai Gen urusu* モンゴル帝国と大元ウルス [The Mongol empire and the great Yuan *ulus*]. Kyoto: Kyōto daigaku gakujutsu shuppankai.

Sun, E-Tu Zen, and John De Francis. (1956) 1966. *Chinese Social History: Translations of Selected Studies*. New York: Octagon Books.

Takahashi, Hirōmi 高橋弘臣. 2000. *Genchō kahei seisaku seiritsu katei no kenkyū* 元朝貨幣政策成立過程の研究 [Research on the establishment of Yuan dynasty policies on currency]. Tokyo: Tōyō Shoin.

Tanaka Kenji 田中謙二. 1964. "Gentenshō ni okeru Mōbun chokuyakutai no bunshō" 元典章における蒙文直譯體の文章 [Direct translation from Mongolian in the *Yuan dianzhang*]. In *Gentenshō no buntai* 元典章の文體 [The language of the *Yuan dianzhang*], by Yoshikawa Kōjirō and Tanaka Kenji, 47–161. Kyoto: Kyōto daigaku jinbun kagaku kenkyūjo.

———. 1965. "Gentenshō bunsho no kōsei" 元典章文書の構成 [The composition of the documents in the *Yuan dianzhang*]. *Tōyōshi kenkyū* 23 (4): 92–117.

———. 2000. "Gentenshō bunsho no kenkyū" 元典章文章の研究 [Studies of the *Yuan dianzhang* documents]. In *Tanaka Kenji chosakushū* 田中謙二著作集 [Collected works of Tanaka Kenji], vol. 2, 275–458. Tokyo: Kyūko Shoin.

Tao, Jing-shen. 1988. *Two Sons of Heaven: Studies in Sung-Liao Relations*. Tucson: University of Arizona.

Theiss, Janet M. 2004. *Disgraceful Matters: The Politics of Chastity in Eighteenth-Century China*. Berkeley: University of California Press.

Tian Jianping 田建平. 2003. *Yuandai chuban shi* 元代出版史 [A history of publishing in the Yuan]. Shijiazhuang: Hebei renmin chuban she.

Tillman, Hoyt Cleveland. 1992. *Confucian Discourse and Chu Hsi's Ascendancy.* Honolulu: University of Hawai'i Press.

———. 1995. "Confucianism under the Chin and the Impact of Sung Confucian Tao-hsüeh." In *China under Jurchen Rule: Essays on Chin Intellectual and Cultural History,* edited by Hoyt Cleveland Tillman and Stephen H. West, 71–114. Albany: State University of New York Press.

Tillman, Hoyt Cleveland, and Stephen H. West, eds. 1995. *China under Jurchen Rule: Essays on Chin Intellectual and Cultural History.* Albany: State University of New York Press.

Uematsu Tadashi 植松正. 1972. "Ishū *Shigen shinkaku* narabini kaisetsu" 彙集『至元新格』並びに解説 [A reconstruction of the *Zhiyuan xinge* with commentary]. *Tōyōshi kenkyū* 東洋史研究 30 (4): 1–29.

———. 1980. *Gen tenshō nendai sakuin* 元典章年代索引 [Chronological index to the *Yuan dianzhang*]. Tokyo: Dōhōsha.

———. 1992. "Institutions of the Yüan Dynasty and Yüan Society." *Gest Library Journal* 5 (1): 57–69.

———. 2004. "*Gentensho* bunsho bunseki hō" 元典章文書分析法 [How to analyze documents in the *Yuan dianzhang*]. In *Jūsan, jūyon seki Tō Ajia shiryō tsūshin* 13, 14 世紀東アジア史料通信 [Newsletter on historical documents in 13–14th century East Asia], no. 2 (Dec.), edited by Morita Kenji 森田憲司. Research Project on "Historical Documents in 13–14th Century East Asia," JSPS, Basic Research (B)(1), Japan.

Von Glahn, Richard. 1996. *Fountain of Fortune Money and Monetary Policy in China, 1000–1700.* Berkeley: University of California Press.

Wang, Chelsea Zi. 2017. "Dilemmas of Empire: Movement, Communication, and Information Management in Ming China, 1368–1644." Ph.D. dissertation, Columbia University.

Wang Deyi 王德毅, Li Rongcun 李榮村, and Pan Bocheng 潘柏澄. 1979–1982. *Yuanren zhuanji ziliao suoyin* 元人傳記資料索引 [Index to biographical materials of Yuan figures]. Taibei: Xinwen feng.

Wang Gungwu. 1983. "The Rhetoric of a Lesser Empire: Early Sung Relations with Its Neighbors." In *China Among Equals,* edited by Morris Rossabi, 47–65. Berkeley: University of California Press.

Watson, Rubie. 1986. "The Named and the Nameless: Gender and Person in Chinese Society." *American Ethnologist* 13 (4): 619–631.

West, Andrew. 2011. "Cloud Platform at Juyongguan." *Diary of a Rambling Antiquarian.* Accessed August 29, 2016. http://babeldiary.blogspot.com/2011/08/cloud-platform-at-juyongguan.html.

West, Stephen H., and W. L. Idema. 1995. *The Story of the Western Wing.* Berkeley: University of California Press.

———. 2010. *Monks, Bandits, Lovers, and Immortals: Eleven Early Chinese Plays.* Indianapolis: Hackett Pub. Co.

Wilkinson, Endymion. 2015. *Chinese History: A New Manual.* 4th ed. Harvard-Yenching Monograph Series 100. Cambridge, Mass.: Harvard University Press.

Wittfogel, Karl, and Feng Chia-sheng. 1949. *History of Chinese Society: Liao.* Philadelphia: American Philosophical Society.

Wolf, Arthur. 1981. "Women, Widowhood, and Fertility in Pre-modern China." In *Marriage and Remarriage in Populations of the Past,* edited by Jacques Dupâquier et al. London and New York: Academic Press.

Wolf, Arthur P., and Chieh-shan Huang. 1980. *Marriage and Adoption in China, 1845–1945.* Stanford, Calif.: Stanford University Press.

Wolf, Margery. 1968. *The House of Lim: A Study of a Chinese Farm Family.* Englewood Cliffs, N.J.: Prentice-Hall.

———. 1972. *Women and the Family in Rural Taiwan.* Stanford, Calif.: Stanford University Press.

Wu Han 吳晗. 1959. "Song Yuan yilai lao baixing de chenghu" 宋元以來老百姓的稱呼 [Appellations of common people from the Song and Yuan on]. *Remin ribao* 2: 27. Also available in *Wu Han wenji* 吳晗文集 (Collected works of Wu Han), vol. 4, 170–173. Beijing: 1988.

Xiao Qiqing. See Hsiao, Ch'i-ch'ing.

Yang Ne 楊訥. 1975. "Yuandai nongcun shezhi yanjiu" 元代農村社制研究 [Research on rural villages and the commune system in the Yuan]. In *Yuandai shehui jingji shi lun ji* 元代社會經濟史論集 [Essays on social and economic history of the Yuan], edited by Zhou Kangxie 周康燮, 1–18. Hong Kong: Chongwen shudian. Original 1965, Lishi yanjiu 歷史研究, no. 4.

Yang Xiaochun 楊曉春. 2012. *Yuan Ming shiqi Hanwen Yisilan jiao wenxian yanjiu* 元明時期漢文伊斯蘭教文獻研究 [Studies on Muslim documents in Chinese during the Yuan and Ming]. Beijing: Zhonghua shuju.

Yang Zhijiu 楊志玖. 1985. "Yuandai de jige Dashiman" 元代的幾個答失蠻 [Some people named Dashman in the Yuan]. In *Yuanshi sanlun* 元史三論 [Three studies on Yuan history], by Yang Zhijiu, 211–225. Beijing: Renmin chubanshe.

Yao Dali 姚大力. 1982. "Yuanchao keju zhidu de xingfei ji qi shehui beijing" 元朝科舉制度的行廢及其社會背景 [The operation of the Yuan examination system and its social context]. *Yuanshi ji beifang minzu shi yanjiu jikan* no. 6: 26–59.

———. 1983. "Jinmo Yuanchu lixue zai beifang de chuanbo" 金末元初理學在北方的傳播 [The dissemination of Neo-Confucianism in north China during the late Jin and early Yuan dynasties]. *Yuanshi luncong* 2: 217–224.

———. 1986. "Lun Yuanchao xingfa tixi de xingcheng" 論元朝刑法體系的形成 [The system of penal law in the Yuan]. *Yuanshi luncong* 元史論叢 3: 105–129.

Ye Qianzhao 葉潛昭. 1972. *Jinlü zhi yanjiu* 金律之研究 [Research on the Jin code]. Taibei: Shangwu yinshuguan.

Yilinzhen 亦鄰真. 1982. *Yuandai yingyi gongdu wenti* 元代硬譯公牘文體 [The language of directly translated official documents of the Yuan]. *Yuanshi luncong* 元史論叢 1: 164–178.

Yoshikawa Kōjirō 吉川幸次郎 and Tanaka Kenji 田中謙二. 1964. *Gentenshō no buntai* 元典章の文體 [The language of the *Yuan dianzhang*]. Supplement to *Gentenshō keibu dai issatsu* 校定本 元典章 刑部 第一册 [Punctuated edition of the Ministry of Punishments section of the *Yuan dianzhang*, vol. 1], edited by Iwamura Shinobu and Tanaka Kenji. Kyoto: Kyōto daigaku Jinbun kagaku kenkyūsho.

Yuan law research group. See Gendai no hōsei kenkyū han.

Zeng Daiwei 曾代偉. 1995. *Jinlü yanjiu* 金律研究 [Research on Jin law codes]. Taipei: Wunan tushu chuban gongsi.

Zhang Chongyan 張重艷 and Yang Shuhong 楊淑紅. 2015. *Zhongguo cang Heishuicheng suo chu Yuandai lüling yu cisong wenshu zhengli yu yanjiu* 中國藏黑水城所出 元代律令與詞訟文書整理與研究 [Collation of and research on Yuan legal documents from Khara Khoto held in China]. Beijing : Zhishi chanquan chubanshe.

Zhang Fan 張帆. 1997. *Yuandai zaixiang zhidu yanjiu* 元代宰相制度研究 [The grand councillor system in the Yuan]. Beijing: Beijing daxue chubanshe.

———. 2007. "Du *Zhizheng tiaoge* 'Duanli' hunyin tiaowen zhaji: yu *Yuan dianzhang Hubu Hunhin* guanxi tiaowen de bijiao" 讀《至正條格 斷例》婚姻案文札 記—與《元典章 戶部 婚姻》相關條文的比較 [Notes on reading marriage cases from the "Duanli" section of the *Zhizheng tiaoge*, with a comparison to related cases in the Marriage chapter, Hubu Section, of the *Yuan dianzhang*]. In *Jinian Xu Daling jiaoshou danchen bashiwu zhounian xueshu lunwenji* 紀念許大齡教授 誕辰八十五週年學術論文集 [Collected essays in commemoration of the 85th birthday of Prof. Xu Daling], edited by Wang Tianyou and Xu Kai, 56–71. Beijing: Beijing daxue chuban she.

Zhaqi Siqin 札奇斯欽. See Jagchid Sechin.

Zhou Qingshu 周清澍. 2001. "Yuanchao dui Tangnuwuliang hai ji qi zhouwei diqu de tongzhi" 元朝對唐努烏梁海及其周圍地區的統治 [Yuan rule over Tannu Uriankhai and its surrounding areas]. In *Yuanmeng shizha* 元蒙史劄 [Notes on Yuan and Mongol History], 290–313. Hohhot: Neimenggudaxue chubanshe.

Zu Shengli 祖生利 and Li Chongxing 李崇興, punct. 2004. *Dayuan shengzheng guochao dianzhang: Xingbu* 大元聖政國朝典章 [Statutes and precedents of the sacred administration of the great Yuan dynastic state: Ministry of Punishments section]. Taiyuan, China: Shanxi guji chubanshe.

Acknowledgments

This book would not have been possible without the generous help and support of many colleagues, mentors, and friends. I have been fortunate to be able to confer about the *Yuan dianzhang* with scholars from China, Taiwan, and Japan for many hours over many years. In particular, I had the honor and the privilege of working with the Yuan History Research Group at the Chinese Academy of Social Sciences in Beijing in 2003–2004, during the initial stages of the translation. I am grateful to the director of this group, Chen Gaohua, for inviting me to participate in the group and for his continued support of my work since then. My official sponsor during my stay in Beijing was Liu Xiao of the Institute of History, Chinese Academy of Social Sciences, and he could not have done more to facilitate my research work, from answering endless questions about texts to introducing me to sources. My discussions with Liu Xiao continued during his subsequent sojourn in Los Angeles as a visiting scholar and my ensuing visits to Beijing. Zhang Fan of Peking University similarly gave generously of his time and erudition during my initial year in Beijing and in numerous later meetings. My deepest gratitude goes to them both for their endless patience and generous sharing of their learning.

I first began work on the *Yuan dianzhang* in 1994 while a visiting scholar in Taipei, Taiwan, where Hung Chin-fu of the Academia Sinica kindly invited me to attend his seminar at National Tsing Hua University, which was reading the text. Thereafter, Hung Chin-fu has magnanimously continued to share his deep knowledge in correspondence and meetings, and to answer my questions throughout the process of preparing this book for publication. Lau Nap-yin of the Institute of History and Philology at the Academia Sinica has been instrumental to my research in countless ways, from his original sponsorship of my affiliation with the Academia Sinica to steering me to resources and sending me books. I am deeply indebted to them both. I benefited greatly from early meetings in the United States and Asia conferring about passages in the *Yuan dianzhang* with Sugiyama Masaaki of Kyoto University and Yao Dali of Fudan University in Shanghai. I thank them for their precious time. Iwai Shigeki of the Kyoto University Jinbun kagaku kenkyūsho kindly shared with me work of the Yuan Law Research Group, which he directs. I've also profited greatly from discussions of the text with Yang Xiaochun of Nanjing University, who has also given me indispensable help finding materials.

My work has been aided immeasurably by colleagues in Japan who have variously sent me books, hosted my visits, and engaged in discussions of Yuan history and the *Yuan dianzhang*. Special thanks go to Morita Kenji, Matsuda Kōichi, Iiyama Tomoyasu, Funada Yoshiyuki, Ihara Hiroshi, Sue Takeshi, Kojima Tsuyoshi, and Fuma Susumu. My former teachers in Japan have similarly supported my work unstintingly with great generosity: Chikusa Masaaki, Kinugawa Tsuyoshi, Tonami Mamoru, Shiba Yoshinobu, and the late Yanagida Setsuko. I have been deeply moved by their kindness, and I am deeply grateful to each of them.

My colleague Deng Xiaonan in Beijing has acted as my host in China and has been unfailing in her kindness and support. I am greatly indebted to Luo Xin for including me in his Mongolia project, which first took me to the Mongolian steppe. I have also benefited from the help and encouragement of colleagues and friends in China and Taiwan, including Liu Yingsheng, Huang K'uan-ch'ung, Dang Baohai, Zhang Pingfeng, Kang Peng, Gu Xiulin, Zhang Nan, and Zang Jian. I also thank Zhang Xiqing, Li Xiaocong, Wang Xiaofu, and Wuyun Gaowa.

I wish to express special appreciation to my wonderful Mongolian-language teachers, György Kara, Tserenchunt Legden, and Brian Baumann, who taught me with unflagging patience. I also convey my deep appreciation to my Mongolian colleagues who led expeditions to the Mongolian countryside in which I participated and who introduced me to the material culture of Inner Asia: A. Ochir, Kh. Lkhagvasuren, and the late Ts. Ganbaatar.

This project would not have come to fruition without the help and support of colleagues and friends in the United States and beyond, who shared their knowledge and offered friendship and encouragement at every stage. My deepest appreciation goes to John Chaffee and Morris Rossabi, and also to Christopher Atwood, Peter Bol, Michael Brose, Ruth Dunnell, Patricia Ebrey, Mark Elliott, Charlotte Furth, Brian McKnight, Frieda Murck, Joan Piggott, Brett Sheehan, Paul Smith, Nancy Steinhardt, Richard von Glahn, and Stephen West. Christopher Atwood in addition gave me invaluable help with Mongolian names and other linguistic issues. My heartfelt thanks go to Robert Hymes, who has generously imparted his wisdom and supported my endeavors throughout my career. Françoise Aubin has been a font of courage, inspiration, and joy, for which I am profoundly grateful. I wish also to pay tribute to my formative teachers who taught me the love of classical texts and an appreciation of historical method, especially Denis Twitchett, Frederick Mote, James T. C. Liu, and Charles Parkin. Denis Twitchett and Frederick Mote in particular urged me to work on translating the *Yuan dianzhang*. I especially thank those who read all or part of the manuscript and who offered valuable suggestions and comments: Endymion Wilkinson, Haiwei Liu, Brett Sheehan, John Chaffee, and two anonymous readers for Harvard University Press. I received invaluable research assistance at various stages of the project from Jingyu Xue, Haiwei Liu, Song Gang, and Jillian Barndt. I have also benefited from comments at talks and lectures related to the project, and I thank my students, both graduate and undergraduate, for their insights. Special thanks go to my editor at Harvard University Press, Kathleen Mc-Dermott, for her expert advice and for making this publication possible, and to Angela Piliouras, of Westchester Publishing Services, for guiding the book through production with great care and patience.

I owe much gratitude to the very helpful staff at libraries around the world. Thanks go especially to Kenneth Klein, Lillian Yang, and other staff at the East Asian Library at the University of Southern California; the staff of the University of Southern California Law Library, and those at Doheny and Leavey Libraries; Hong Cheng, Tomoko Bialock, David Poepoe, and other staff at the East Asian Library and the Young Research Library of the University of California, Los Angeles; Jianye He of the C. V. Starr East Asian Library at the University of California, Berkeley; Kenneth Harlin of the C. V. Starr East Asian Library at Columbia University; Charles Aylmer of the Cambridge University Library; and the staff of the library in the Institute of History, Chinese Academy of Social Sciences, Beijing. I thank Wang Yueh-Ching of the National Palace Museum, Yang Xiaochun, and Lau Nap-yin for help in obtaining the graphics, and Isabelle Lewis for drawing the maps.

The main work of translation was undertaken in Beijing on a Fulbright Research Fellowship from the U.S. Department of State. I was able to study the Mongolian language with the support of a New Directions Fellowship from the Andrew W. Mellon Foundation. The write-up of the project was funded by a Scholar Grant from the Chiang Ching-kuo Foundation for International Scholarly Exchange and a Fellowship for University Teachers from the National Endowment for the Humanities. I received additional indispensable funding from a University of Southern California Office of the Provost grant for Advancing Scholarship in the Humanities and Social Sciences, the University of Southern California James H. Zumberge Research and Innovation Fund, and the Office of the Dean of the Dana and David Dornsife College of Letters, Arts and Sciences at the University of Southern California.

I have benefited from the camaraderie and encouragement of wonderful friends. I am especially grateful to Constance Orliski, Suzanne Ahmed Leonora, Mary Phillips, and Beatrice and Paul Germain. I also thank my siblings, in-laws, and other members of my family for their encouragement and generosity over these years, especially Margit, Norman, Pia, Valery, and Kay. Most of all my deepest gratitude goes to my husband, Peter R. Lee, and my son, Henry Birge-Lee, for their unconditional support and encouragement at every stage of this project. Peter was always ready to help with the project and support me in every way possible as this book took shape over the years. And Henry, in addition to being my computer guru and providing sage advice at key moments, served as a constant inspiration and reminder of what is most important in life. To them this book is lovingly dedicated.

In the end, I am solely responsible for the content of this book and the errors and shortcomings that remain.

Index

Figures and charts indicated by page numbers in italics